THE AMERICAN ⸻

A Concise Restatement
of
THE LAW GOVERNING LAWYERS

Compiled

by

VINCENT R. JOHNSON
Professor of Law
St. Mary's University School of Law

and

SUSAN SAAB FORTNEY
George Mahon Professor
Texas Tech University School of Law

ST. PAUL, MN
AMERICAN LAW INSTITUTE PUBLISHERS
2007

Mat #40661125

ISBN 978-0-314-97820-2

FOREWORD

The American Law Institute's work on The Law Governing Lawyers had its genesis in 1985 when Professor Geoffrey C. Hazard, Jr., then ALI's Director, recommended that the Institute consider a "mini-Restatement" dealing with lawyer-client confidentiality. Fifteen years later, that suggestion had grown into an important work of legal scholarship that owed much to the devoted effort and commitment of Reporter Charles W. Wolfram of Cornell and Associate Reporters John Leubsdorf of Rutgers and Thomas D. Morgan of George Washington University. The Restatement is unique in the history of ALI projects because of its focus on a single profession.

The Restatement of The Law Governing Lawyers is broader in scope than state and federal ethics codes based on the ABA Model Rules of Professional Conduct or its predecessor, the Model Code of Professional Responsibility. It deals with issues that the codes generally do not address, such as the formation of the client-lawyer relationship, legal malpractice (as opposed to the codes' emphasis on professional discipline), and the potential liability of lawyers to third-party nonclients. Like other Restatements, it draws heavily on decisional law, while the ethics codes have the form and force of statutes or administrative regulations. Based in part on those earlier code formulations, the Restatement in its turn has influenced the ABA's most recent updates of the Model Rules in 2002 and 2003.

The original two-volume Restatement of The Law Governing Lawyers contained almost 1300 pages of text. This Concise Restatement of The Law Governing Lawyers, at roughly one-quarter that size, joins the Institute's previously published Concise Restatements of Property and Torts and like them is intended primarily for use by the law-school community. It was assembled by Vincent R. Johnson, Professor of Law at St. Mary's University School of Law in San Antonio, and Susan Saab Fortney, George H. Mahon Professor of Law at Texas Tech University School of Law. They have compiled this volume for use in both basic and advanced American law-school courses devoted to professional responsibility, legal ethics, or legal malpractice, either in lieu of a textbook or as supplementary reading. Despite its more compact format, this volume reproduces all black-letter sections of the Restatement in full, and each section is accompanied by relevant commentary. None of the Restatement's original language has been changed; it appears here as it has been quoted and relied upon by the courts. In order to

FOREWORD

reduce the volume to a reasonable size, all Reporter's Notes as well as most comments dealing with scope and cross-references, have been omitted. Where necessary, comment headings appear in brackets to connect paragraphs or illustrations to particular comments. All text omissions are indicated by asterisks so that readers seeking further guidance can easily find the omitted material in the unabridged Restatement, which is available in most law-school libraries and online. Also available in print and online are the annual Pocket Parts and Interim Case Citations pamphlets reporting cases that have cited particular provisions of the Restatement.

The Institute is grateful to Professors Johnson and Fortney for assembling this compilation and hope that it will help introduce new generations of lawyers to the study, essential for our profession, of the law governing lawyers.

LANCE LIEBMAN
DIRECTOR
THE AMERICAN LAW INSTITUTE

September 2006

THE AMERICAN LAW INSTITUTE

The American Law Institute was created in 1923 as a private organization of judges, lawyers, and legal scholars seeking to respond to "general dissatisfaction with the administration of justice" by working for improvement of the law. The Institute's primary goal, as stated in its charter, was to "promote the clarification and simplification of the law and its better adaptation to social needs." The incorporators included William Howard Taft and Charles Evans Hughes; Benjamin Cardozo and Learned Hand were among the early leaders.

From the beginning, the ALI worked on "Restatements" of the common law with the goal of helping the systematic development of the law and the pursuit of consistent legal doctrine among the states. The first Restatements were on the subjects of Agency, Conflict of Laws, Contracts, Judgments, Property, Restitution, Security, Torts, and Trusts. Subsequent Restatement projects have included The Foreign Relations Law of the United States, Unfair Competition, and The Law Governing Lawyers. Other major ALI projects have included the Uniform Commercial Code (for which the ALI has a partner, the National Conference of Commissioners on Uniform State Laws), the Model Penal Code, Principles of Corporate Governance, and Principles of the Law of Family Dissolution.

The ALI's working method is to choose for each project one or more experts, usually law professors, as "Reporters" and to subject each of their successive drafts to detailed review by "Advisers" consisting of judges, lawyers, and academics and by a special consultative group of interested Institute members. After appropriate revision, a draft is next submitted for review to the Institute's Council, a governing body of some 60 members drawn widely from the various branches of the legal profession, and then, as a "Tentative Draft," to the membership as a whole at the Institute's Annual Meeting, during which time it is also made generally available for public comment and review. When the project in its entirety has been approved by both the Council and the membership, a process that can take many years, the final, official text is prepared for publication.

The Institute's membership includes judges, practitioners, and law teachers from all areas of the United States as well as many foreign countries, selected on the basis of professional achievement and demonstrated interest in the improvement of the law. Ex officio

NOTE

members include the Chief Justice and Associate Justices of the Supreme Court of the United States, the Chief Judges of the federal courts of appeals and the highest courts of the states, law school Deans, and the Presidents of the American Bar Association, state bar associations, and other prominent legal organizations.

TABLE OF CONTENTS

———

TABLE OF CONTENTS

Section **Page**

TABLE OF CONTENTS

ix

TABLE OF CONTENTS

TABLE OF CONTENTS

TABLE OF CONTENTS

TOPIC 4. CONFLICTS OF INTEREST WITH A FORMER CLIENT

TOPIC 5. CONFLICTS OF INTEREST DUE TO A LAWYER'S OBLIGATION TO A THIRD PERSON

RESTATEMENT OF THE LAW THIRD

———

RESTATEMENT OF THE LAW

THE LAW GOVERNING LAWYERS

———

INTRODUCTION

———

Lawyers are regulated by moral, professional, and legal constraints in discharging their several responsibilities as representatives of clients, officers of the legal system, and public citizens having special responsibilities for the quality of justice. This Restatement addresses only those constraints imposed by law—that is, official norms enforceable through a legal remedy administered by a court, disciplinary agency, or similar tribunal. Remedies against lawyers include professional discipline, an award of damages, denial of a fee claim or an order of restitution of fees already paid, disqualification from a representation, and conviction for crime (see Chapter 1, Topics 2–4).

Other constraints, such as ideals and habits of morality, will often guide conduct of a good person who also aspires to serve as an honorable and public-spirited lawyer, and much more powerfully and pervasively than merely legal obligations. A good lawyer is also guided by ideals of professionalism and by an understanding of sound professional practice. Extensive consideration of such nonlegal factors is not undertaken here. However, they have obvious significance in a good lawyer's life and in the self-concept of the legal profession. On occasion reference will be made in this Restatement to such nonlegal factors when relevant in explaining the rationale for a rule of law or in stating, for example, what factors a lawyer may legitimately take into account in deciding whether and how to act (see, e.g., § 32(3)(f) & Comment j

thereto) or what advice a lawyer may provide to a client (see § 94(3) & Comment *h* thereto).

This Restatement undertakes to restate much of the law governing lawyers, but not all of it. Again, the criteria for selecting some topics and excluding others had nothing to do with any weighing of the intrinsic importance of the included and omitted topics. For a variety of other reasons, this Restatement omits extensive consideration of issues relating to lawyer advertising and solicitation, the right to the assistance of counsel, group legal services, and similar practice situations. The Restatement also omits extensive consideration of some issues that are importantly grounded in complex statutory regulations, such as that of court-awarded attorney fees (compare § 38(3)(b) and Comment *f* thereto (allocation of court-awarded fee between client and lawyer); § 125, Comment *f* (conflict-of-interest problems raised by fee-shifting); § 110, Comment *g* (fee-shifting as a procedural sanction)), and the question of the application of provisions of federal securities statutes and regulations to lawyers practicing in that realm (compare § 51, Comment *a* (consideration of federal securities-law issues as beyond the scope of the Restatement's discussion of the duty of care to nonclients) and § 95, Comment *a* (similar exclusion in instance of lawyer opinion letters)). The Restatement also does not deal extensively with areas in which governing law is, many purposes, applied to lawyers no differently than to others, such as is true of regulation of a law partnership or professional corporation under partnership and corporate law (compare § 9, Comment *b* (law applicable to questions of internal structure, management, and operation of various forms of law firms)).

CHAPTER 1

REGULATION OF THE LEGAL PROFESSION

TOPIC 1. REGULATION OF LAWYERS—IN GENERAL

§ 1. Regulation of Lawyers—In General

Upon admission to the bar of any jurisdiction, a person becomes a lawyer and is subject to applicable law governing such matters as professional discipline, procedure and evidence, civil remedies, and criminal sanctions.

Comment:

* * *

b. Lawyer codes and background law. Today, as for the last quarter-century, professional discipline of a lawyer in the United States is conducted pursuant to regulations contained in regulatory codes that have been approved in most states by the highest court in the jurisdiction in which the lawyer has been admitted. Such codes are referred to in this Restatement as lawyer codes. Those codes are more or less patterned on model codes published by the American Bar Association, but only the version of the code officially adopted and in force in a jurisdiction regulates the activities of lawyers subject to it. While in most jurisdictions the lawyer code is adopted and subject to revision only through action of the highest court in the state (see Comment *c* hereto), in all jurisdictions at least some legislation is applicable to lawyers and law practice. See, e.g., § 56, Comments *i* and *j* (federal legislation and state consumer-protection laws applicable to lawyers); § 58(3) and Comment *b* thereto (statutes authorizing lawyers to practice in the form of limited-liability partnerships and similar types of law firms); § 68 and following (attorney-client privilege). Federal district courts generally have adopted the lawyer code of the jurisdiction in which the court sits, and all federal courts exercise the power to regulate lawyers appearing before them. Some administrative agencies, primarily within the federal government, have also regulated lawyers practicing before the agency, sometimes through lawyer codes adopted by the agency and specifically applicable to those practitioners. Although uniformity is desirable for many purposes, lawyer codes in fact differ markedly in certain respects from one jurisdiction to another, and no state follows any nationally promulgated bar-association model in all respects.

* * *

c. The inherent powers of courts. The highest courts in most states have ruled as a matter of state constitutional law that their power to regulate lawyers is inherent in the judicial function. Thus, the grant of judicial power in a state constitution devolves upon the courts the concomitant regulatory power. The power is said to derive both from the historical role of courts in the United States in regulating lawyers through admission and disbarment and from the traditional practice of courts in England. Admitting lawyers to practice (see § 2), formulating and amending lawyer codes (see Comment *b*), and regulating the system of lawyer discipline (see § 5, Comment *b*) are functions reserved in most states to the highest court of the state. Nonetheless, other tribunals, such as hearing bodies in administrative agencies, perform the important role of implementing the lawyer codes in adjudicating disputes when and to the extent their provisions are relevant (see Comment *b* hereto & Topic 3, Introductory Note).

* * *

[*d.* *The role of bar associations.*]

* * *

In a number of states, membership in the state's bar association is compulsory, in the sense that a lawyer otherwise appropriately admitted to practice must maintain active membership in the bar association as a condition of retention of a valid license to practice law within the jurisdiction. (Such mandatory bars are sometimes called "integrated" bars.) Decisions of the United States Supreme Court have limited the extent to which a member of such a mandatory bar association can be required to pay any portion of dues that supports activities not germane to the organization's functions in providing self-regulation. Those generally include activities of a political or ideological nature not directly connected to the regulation of lawyers and maintenance of the system of justice. Under those decisions, the bar must maintain a system for allocating dues payments for permissible and noncovered purposes and a process to permit lawyers to regain the portion of dues collected for noncovered purposes.

* * *

TOPIC 2. PROCESS OF PROFESSIONAL REGULATION

* * *

TITLE A. ADMISSION TO PRACTICE LAW

Introductory Note

* * *

In most states, initial admission to practice as a lawyer results from successful completion of a process of college and legal education, bar examination, submission of a bar application with supporting indications of compliance with the state's requirements, including good moral character, and scrutiny by a committee on admission. Formal admission to practice customarily takes the form in most states of a swearing-in ceremony before the state's highest court.

* * *

§ 2. Admission to Practice Law

In order to become a lawyer and qualify to practice law in a jurisdiction of admission, a prospective lawyer must comply with requirements of the jurisdiction relating to such matters as education, other demonstration of competence such as success in a bar examination, and character.

Comment:

* * *

b. Admission to practice in general. Admission to practice and maintenance of a license to practice law in a condition of good standing authorizes a lawyer to perform all functions of other lawyers so admitted, both in the law office and in all of the courts of the state (see § 3). Each state administers a separate system for admission of applicants to the state's bar. There is theoretically no limit on the number of jurisdictions in which a lawyer may be admitted to practice, although the difficulty and expense of complying with multiple-admission and good-standing requirements impose practical limits.

Beyond matter-by-matter admission through pro hac vice arrangements (see § 3, Comment *e*), approximately half of the states permit a lawyer in good standing in the bar of another state to gain permanent admission (admission "on motion") without the need for any, or at least for a full, bar examination. Some states condition on-motion eligibility on comity—requiring that a state in which the lawyer is currently admitted accord a substantially similar privilege to lawyers from the on-motion state. After compliance with applicable requirements, those states accord the admitted lawyer the full powers of a lawyer regularly admitted.

Each federal district court, court of appeals, specialized federal court, and the Supreme Court presently maintains a separate bar. While separate admission and maintenance of membership is required as a condition to practice in each of those courts, that is readily accomplished on application, except in those courts that impose an additional requirement of admission to the local bar. In each, admission to the bar of a state is necessary and suffices for most purposes. In addition, as in most state courts, admission to the bar of a federal

6

court pro hac vice (see § 3, Comment *e*) is available to a lawyer in good standing in another bar. Some federal administrative agencies maintain their own bars, but by statute admission to the bar of a state suffices as qualification to practice before almost all federal agencies.

* * *

d. Character requirements. A license to practice law confers great power on lawyers to do good or wrong. Lawyers practice an occupation that is complex and often, particularly to nonlawyers, mysterious. Clients and others are vulnerable to wrongdoing by corrupt lawyers. Hence, as far back as the first bars in medieval England efforts have been made to screen candidates for the bar with respect to their character. The process has occasionally been controversial because of the difficulty of defining the standards of character thought to be minimal, the difficulty of ensuring fair application of any standards that may be agreed upon, the risk of either invasive inquiry or invidious application of standards under the claim of rigorous examination, and the overriding difficulty of predicting future professional conduct from a necessarily abbreviated personal history and the committee's access to such past activities as are sufficiently public to be checked. The standard stated in the Section of moral character appropriate for a lawyer reflects the basis on which most states pursue inquiry into the present character of an applicant. The central inquiry concerns the present ability and disposition of the applicant to practice law competently and honestly.

* * *

f. Residence requirements. Under federal constitutional decisions, local residence may not be required as a condition of admission or continued membership; similarly, United States citizenship may not be required as a condition of admission to or membership in a state's bar. In contrast, some courts have upheld the requirement of maintenance of an in-state office.

* * *

TITLE B. AUTHORIZED AND UNAUTHORIZED PRACTICE

* * *

§ 3. Jurisdictional Scope of the Practice of Law by a Lawyer

A lawyer currently admitted to practice in a jurisdiction may provide legal services to a client:

    (1) at any place within the admitting jurisdiction;

    (2) before a tribunal or administrative agency of another jurisdiction or the federal government in

compliance with requirements for temporary or regular admission to practice before that tribunal or agency; and

(3) at a place within a jurisdiction in which the lawyer is not admitted to the extent that the lawyer's activities arise out of or are otherwise reasonably related to the lawyer's practice under Subsection (1) or (2).

Comment:

* * *

c. Required maintenance of a lawyer's admitted status. In general, only a lawyer who is in current compliance with applicable legal requirements in the admitting jurisdiction (see § 2) for maintaining the lawyer's law license in a currently effective status is qualified to practice law there. Those conditions vary by jurisdiction and can be technical in nature. In some few jurisdictions, for example, maintenance of a valid license is conditioned on maintaining an office within the jurisdiction for the practice of law (see § 2, Comment *f*). Many jurisdictions now require a minimum number of hours per year of qualifying continuing legal education.

A lawyer who was once admitted to practice in a state violates the prohibition against unauthorized practice by continuing to practice law in the state notwithstanding disbarment or suspension, lapse of the lawyer's license to practice in the state (for example, for failure to pay mandatory bar dues or, as indicated above, to comply with applicable continuing-legal-education requirements), resignation, or assumption of nonactive status (as when the lawyer retires or moves to another state). Lapse can occur for failure to file an annual renewal application with self-certification of compliance with the indicated requirements. Any such unauthorized practice by a lawyer is a violation of the state's lawyer code and thus subjects the lawyer to discipline. It may also violate a statutory prohibition in the state against unauthorized practice of law. Such impermissible practice by a lawyer may also lead, among other remedies, to forfeiture of an otherwise valid claim for legal fees (see § 37). When lapse of license for such reasons is not directly related to continuing competence to practice, it does not by itself indicate either legal malpractice or incompetent representation in a criminal-defense representation.

* * *

[*e.   Extra-jurisdictional law practice by a lawyer.*]

* * *

The rules governing interstate practice by nonlocal lawyers were formed at a time when lawyers conducted very little practice of that nature. Thus, the limitation on legal services threatened by such rules imposed little actual inconvenience. However, as interstate and international commerce, transportation, and communications have expanded, clients have increasingly required a truly interstate and international range of practice by their lawyers. (To a limited extent, many states recognize such needs in the international realm by providing for limited practice in the state by foreign legal consultants. See § 2, Comment *g.*) Applied literally, the old restrictions on practice of law in a state by a lawyer admitted elsewhere could seriously inconvenience clients who have need of such services within the state. Retaining locally admitted counsel would often cause serious delay and expense and could require the client to deal with unfamiliar counsel. Modern communications, including ready electronic connection to much of the law of every state, makes concern about a competent analysis of a distant state's law unfounded. Accordingly, there is much to be said for a rule permitting a lawyer to practice in any state, except for litigation matters or for the purpose of establishing a permanent in-state branch office. Results approaching that rule may arguably be required under the federal interstate commerce clause and the privileges and immunities clause. The approach of the Section is more guarded. However, its primary focus is appropriately on the needs of clients.

The extent to which a lawyer may practice beyond the borders of the lawyer's home state depends on the circumstances in which the lawyer acts in both the lawyer's home state and the other state. At one extreme, it is clear that a lawyer's admission to practice in one jurisdiction does not authorize the lawyer to practice generally in another jurisdiction as if the lawyer were also fully admitted there. Thus, a lawyer admitted in State A may not open an office in State B for the general practice of law there or otherwise engage in the continuous, regular, or repeated representation of clients within the other state.

Certainty is provided in litigated matters by procedures for securing the right to practice elsewhere, although the arrangement is limited to appearances as counsel in individual litigated matters. Apparently all states provide such a procedure for temporary admission of an unadmitted lawyer, usually termed admission pro hac vice. (Compare admission on-motion to the right to practice generally within a jurisdiction as described in § 2, Comment *b.*) Although the decision is sometimes described as discretionary, a court will grant

9

admission pro hac vice if the lawyer applying for admission is in good standing in the bar of another jurisdiction and has complied with applicable requirements (sometimes requiring the association of local counsel), and if no reason is shown why the lawyer cannot be relied upon to provide competent representation to the lawyer's client in conformance with the local lawyer code. Such temporary admission is recognized in Subsection (2). Courts are particularly apt to grant such applications in criminal-defense representations. Some jurisdictions impose limitations, such as a maximum number of such admissions in a specified period. Admission pro hac vice normally permits the lawyer to engage within the jurisdiction in all customary and appropriate activities in conducting the litigation, including appropriate office practice. Activities in contemplation of such admission are also authorized, such as investigating facts or consulting with the client within the jurisdiction prior to drafting a complaint and filing the action.

A lawyer who is properly admitted to practice in a state with respect to litigation pending there, either generally or pro hac vice, may need to conduct proceedings and activities ancillary to the litigation in other states, such as counseling clients, dealing with co-counsel or opposing counsel, conducting depositions, examining documents, interviewing witnesses, negotiating settlements, and the like. Such activities incidental to permissible practice are appropriate and permissible.

Transactional and similar out-of-court representation of clients may raise similar issues, yet there is no equivalent of temporary admission pro hac vice for such representation, as there is in litigation. Even activities that bear close resemblance to in-court litigation, such as representation of clients in arbitration or in administrative hearings, may not include measures for pro hac vice appearance. Some activities are clearly permissible. Thus, a lawyer conducting activities in the lawyer's home state may advise a client about the law of another state, a proceeding in another state, or a transaction there, including conducting research in the law of the other state, advising the client about the application of that law, and drafting legal documents intended to have legal effect there. There is no per se bar against such a lawyer giving a formal opinion based in whole or in part on the law of another jurisdiction, but a lawyer should do so only if the lawyer has adequate familiarity with the relevant law. It is also clearly permissible for a lawyer from a home-state office to direct communications to persons and organizations in other states (in which the lawyer is not separately admitted), by letter, telephone, telecopier, or other forms of electronic communication. On the other hand, as with litigation, it would be impermissible for a lawyer to set up an office for the general practice of nonlitigation law in a jurisdiction in which the lawyer is not admitted as described in § 2.

When other activities of a lawyer in a non-home state are challenged as impermissible for lack of admission to the state's bar, the context in which and purposes for which the lawyer acts should be carefully assessed. Beyond home-state activities, proper representation of clients often requires a lawyer to conduct activities while physically present in one or more other states. Such practice is customary in many areas of legal representation. As stated in Subsection (3), such activities should be recognized as permissible so long as they arise out of or otherwise reasonably relate to the lawyer's practice in a state of admission. In determining that issue, several factors are relevant, including the following: whether the lawyer's client is a regular client of the lawyer or, if a new client, is from the lawyer's home state, has extensive contacts with that state, or contacted the lawyer there; whether a multistate transaction has other significant connections with the lawyer's home state; whether significant aspects of the lawyer's activities are conducted in the lawyer's home state; whether a significant aspect of the matter involves the law of the lawyer's home state; and whether either the activities of the client involve multiple jurisdictions or the legal issues involved are primarily either multistate or federal in nature. Because lawyers in a firm often practice collectively, the activities of all lawyers in the representation of a client are relevant. The customary practices of lawyers who engage in interstate law practice is one appropriate measure of the reasonableness of a lawyer's activities out of state. Association with local counsel may permit a lawyer to conduct in-state activities not otherwise permissible, but such association is not required in most instances of in-state practice. Among other things, the additional expense for the lawyer's client of retaining additional counsel and educating that lawyer about the client's affairs would make such required retention unduly burdensome.

* * *

§ 4. Unauthorized Practice by a Nonlawyer

A person not admitted to practice as a lawyer (see § 2) may not engage in the unauthorized practice of law, and a lawyer may not assist a person to do so.

11

Comment:

[*a. Scope and cross-references.*]

* * *

A nonlawyer who impermissibly engages in the practice of law may be subject to several sanctions, including injunction, contempt, and conviction for crime.

* * *

c. Delineation of unauthorized practice. The definitions and tests employed by courts to delineate unauthorized practice by nonlawyers have been vague or conclusory, while jurisdictions have differed significantly in describing what constitutes unauthorized practice in particular areas.

Certain activities, such as the representation of another person in litigation, are generally proscribed. Even in that area, many jurisdictions recognize exceptions for such matters as small-claims and landlord-tenant tribunals and certain proceedings in administrative agencies. Moreover, many jurisdictions have authorized law students and others not admitted in the state to represent indigent persons or others as part of clinical legal-education programs.

Controversy has surrounded many out-of-court activities such as advising on estate planning by bank trust officers, advising on estate planning by insurance agents, stock brokers, or benefit-plan and similar consultants, filling out or providing guidance on forms for property transactions by real-estate agents, title companies, and closing-service companies, and selling books or individual forms containing instructions on self-help legal services or accompanied by personal, nonlawyer assistance on filling them out in connection with legal procedures such as obtaining a marriage dissolution. The position of bar associations has traditionally been that nonlawyer provision of such services denies the person served the benefit of such legal measures as the attorney-client privilege, the benefits of such extraordinary duties as that of confidentiality of client information and the protection against conflicts of interest, and the protection of such measures as those regulating lawyer trust accounts and requiring lawyers to supervise nonlawyer personnel. Several jurisdictions recognize that many such services can be provided by nonlawyers without significant risk of incompetent service, that actual experience in several states with extensive nonlawyer provision of traditional legal services indicates no significant risk of harm to consumers of such services, that persons in need of legal services may be significantly aided in obtaining assistance at a much lower price than would be entailed by segregating out a portion of a transaction to be handled by a lawyer for a fee, and that many persons can ill afford, and most persons are at least inconvenienced by, the typically higher cost of lawyer services. In addition, traditional common-law and statutory consumer-protection measures offer significant protection to consumers of such nonlawyer services.

    d. Pro se appearance. Every jurisdiction recognizes the right of an individual to proceed "pro se" by providing his or her own representation in any matter, whether or not the person is a lawyer. Because the appearance is personal only, it does not involve an issue of unauthorized practice. The right extends to self-preparation of legal documents and other kinds of out-of-court legal work as well as to in-court representation. In some jurisdictions, tribunals have inaugurated programs to assist persons without counsel in filing necessary papers, with appropriate cautions that court personnel assisting the person do not thereby undertake to provide legal assistance. The United States Supreme Court has held that a person accused of crime in a federal or state prosecution has, as an aspect of the right to the assistance of counsel, the constitutional right to waive counsel and to proceed pro se. In general, however, a person appearing pro se cannot represent any other person or entity, no matter how close the degree of kinship, ownership, or other relationship.

* * *

TITLE C. PROFESSIONAL DISCIPLINE

Introductory Note

* * *

    In most states and the District of Columbia, lawyer disciplinary proceedings are similar to and must comply with due-process standards applicable to administrative-enforcement proceedings. Many states have followed all or most of the recommended procedures and institutional arrangements specified in the ABA's Model Rules for Lawyer Disciplinary Enforcement, which were devised in light of applicable due process and similar constraints. Thereunder, a professional, independent disciplinary counsel is charged with responsibility to prosecute offenses, often following review by a screening body to determine whether probable cause exists warranting formal charges. Formal charges are heard by a neutral panel, composed primarily of lawyers but often having significant nonlawyer membership, appointed by the court and often without involvement of any bar association. Written charges make known to the lawyer the nature of the offense and its circumstances. Rules governing depositions in civil actions are applied; other discovery is conducted informally, subject to superintendence by the hearing panel. Beyond discovery, proceedings are governed by the rules of procedure and evidence applied in civil litigation. Some jurisdictions open the record of proceedings, including the

13

hearing, once a determination of probable cause is made. The standard of proof in most jurisdictions is clear and convincing evidence, that is, evidence establishing the truth of the charged offense beyond a mere preponderance of the evidence but not necessarily beyond a reasonable doubt. Matters on which a responding lawyer bears the burden of persuasion must be proved by a preponderance of the evidence (on readmission, see below). Review is typically available in the highest court of the jurisdiction, which exercises independent judgment with respect to both findings of fact and conclusions of law on all issues, including the sanction imposed.

The sanctions imposed in lawyer-discipline proceedings seek to protect clients and the public, to deter wrongful conduct by other lawyers, and specifically to deter future wrongful conduct seemingly threatened by the lawyer found to have violated mandatory rules. Many disciplinary tribunals, either by decision or rule, look to the ABA Standards for Imposing Lawyer Sanctions for guidance in structuring appropriate sanctions. Traditional sanctions create a present or prospective impediment to the lawyer's right to practice, ranging in ascending severity from informal or formal admonition to suspension or, in most jurisdictions, permanent disbarment. Other sanctions may be available either in general, such as a requirement to pay costs, or in specific instances apparently warranting them, such as ordering restitution or suspending sanctions during a period of probation during which the lawyer will submit to guidance of a lawyer mentor or other monitoring of the lawyer's practice. Interim suspension may be available when the charge is shown to be supported by probable cause and the acts charged indicate clearly that the lawyer would present a danger to clients or others if permitted to continue practicing pending final outcome.

A lawyer suspended in a disciplinary proceeding for a limited period (60 days under the ABA Model Standards for Disciplinary Enforcement) is typically reinstated automatically on expiration of the stated time. A lawyer suspended for a longer period or who has been disbarred must apply for readmission to the bar and bears the burden of demonstrating rehabilitation. Given the adjudicated basis for interrupting the lawyer's practice, readmission requires a higher showing of ability to practice law and to comply with professional standards than in the case of a recent law-school graduate applying for initial admission. The lawyer must show specific facts indicating that the lawyer is rehabilitated and currently able and willing to practice law in compliance with professional responsibilities. Testimonials from lawyers are relevant only if they demonstrate thorough familiarity both with the conduct causing suspension and with specific steps the lawyer has taken to achieve rehabilitation. Voluntary testimonials from judges would violate the judicial code of most jurisdictions and should not be accepted.

Lawyers incapacitated due to impairments such as those caused by substance abuse may pose particular risk of harm to clients, the public, and legal institutions. Many bar associations maintain programs of intervention and support for lawyers who are afflicted with substance abuse but are able to continue practice. When a lawyer's work is seriously affected by disability rather than by a state of mind warranting a finding of a disciplinary violation (see § 5, Comment *d*), most jurisdictions provide for lawyer disability proceedings. Procedures generally follow those in lawyer disciplinary actions (see id., Comment *i*), with interim suspension, procedures for psychiatric or other appropriate evaluation, and diversion into rehabilitation programs. A finding of disability results in suspension from practice until the lawyer can demonstrate rehabilitation from the impairing condition.

* * *

§ 5. Professional Discipline

(1) **A lawyer is subject to professional discipline for violating any provision of an applicable lawyer code.**

(2) **A lawyer is also subject to professional discipline under Subsection (1) for attempting to commit a violation, knowingly assisting or inducing another to do so, or knowingly doing so through the acts of another.**

(3) **A lawyer who knows of another lawyer's violation of applicable rules of professional conduct raising a substantial question of the lawyer's honesty or trustworthiness or the lawyer's fitness as a lawyer in some other respect must report that information to appropriate disciplinary authorities.**

Comment:

* * *

b. Grounds for lawyer discipline—in general. In all jurisdictions, the process of professional regulation has generally been closely connected to courts, the bodies that traditionally, and now, also control admission to practice (see § 1, Comments *a* & *d*). The traditional standard for measuring the propriety of the lawyer's conduct was that of "conduct unbecoming a lawyer" as elaborated in decisions ruling on such disciplinary proceedings. In the decades after adoption by the ABA of its 1908 Canons of Ethics, some jurisdictions began to rely on provisions of the Canons as stating grounds for discipline. In 1969 and 1983, the ABA adopted explicitly regulatory approaches to stating the grounds for lawyer discipline (see § 1, Comment *b*). Today, every state has adopted a lawyer code defining sanctionable offenses, and in general discipline is administered only for a violation so defined. States also maintain relatively formal codes of procedure for adjudicating a charge of a disciplinary violation, most of which are modeled on the ABA Model Rules for Lawyer Disciplinary Enforcement (as amended 1996) and similar predecessor compilations. Those procedures are subject to constitutional and statutory constraints under both federal and state law. In selecting among available disciplinary sanctions, many states are also guided by the ABA Standards for Imposing Lawyer Sanctions (adopted 1986, as amended 1992).

* * *

Professional duties defined in lawyer codes are mainly concerned with lawyer functions performed by a lawyer in the course of representing a client and causing harm to the client, to a legal institution such as a court, or to a third person. Those duties extend further, however, and include some lawyer acts that, even if not directly involving the practice of law, draw into question the ability or willingness of the lawyer to abide by professional responsibilities. Every jurisdiction, for example, reserves the power to subject a lawyer to professional discipline following conviction of a serious crime (see Comment *g*), regardless of whether the underlying acts occurred in the course of law practice. Such acts are a proper basis for discipline regardless of where they occur.

For the most part, lawyer codes prohibit stated offenses by individual lawyers. Law firms as such are not subject to professional discipline, although at least two states now impose the obligations of their lawyer codes on law firms as well as on individual lawyers.

    c. General provisions of lawyer codes. Modern lawyer codes contain one or more provisions (sometimes referred to as "catch-all" provisions) stating general grounds for discipline, such as engaging "in conduct involving dishonesty, fraud, deceit or misrepresentation" (ABA Model Rules of Professional Conduct, Rule 8.4(c) (1983)) or "in conduct that is prejudicial to the administration of justice" (id. Rule 8.4(d)). Such provisions are written broadly both to cover a wide array of offensive lawyer conduct and to prevent attempted technical manipulation of a rule stated more narrowly. On the other hand, the breadth of such provisions creates the risk that a charge using only such language would fail to give fair warning of the nature of the charges to a lawyer respondent (see Comment *h*) and that subjective and idiosyncratic considerations could influence a hearing panel or reviewing

16

court in resolving a charge based only on it. That is particularly true of the "appearance of impropriety" principle (stated generally as a canon in the 1969 ABA Model Code of Professional Responsibility but purposefully omitted as a standard for discipline from the 1983 ABA Model Rules of Professional Conduct). Tribunals accordingly should be circumspect in avoiding overbroad readings or resorting to standards other than those fairly encompassed within an applicable lawyer code.

* * *

e. Attempts to commit disciplinary violations. As stated in Subsection (2), a lawyer's attempt to violate a specific rule of a lawyer code constitutes a sanctionable offense. A charge of attempt is independently significant only when some essential element of a completed offense is not present. As with the charge of attempt in criminal law, disciplinary bodies must determine that the proof presented sufficiently demonstrates that the lawyer had the requisite intent (see Comment *d*), that the lawyer took a substantial step in a course of conduct planned to culminate in the lawyer's commission of the offense, and that evidence concerning that step is as a whole strongly corroborative of the lawyer's purpose. Compare Model Penal Code § 5.01 (1985) (defining offense of criminal attempt).

* * *

g. Lawyer criminal conduct as a basis for discipline. Criminal law applies in most respects to acts of lawyers, either in representing clients or in other capacities and activities (see § 8). An act constituting a violation of criminal law is also a disciplinary offense when the act either violates a specific prohibition in an applicable lawyer code or reflects adversely on the lawyer's honesty, trustworthiness, or fitness as a lawyer. Those formulations have replaced in most jurisdictions a formerly employed standard stated in terms of criminal acts constituting "moral turpitude," a phrase that, while meaningful to individuals, is vague and may lead to discriminatory or otherwise inappropriate applications. Whether a criminal act reflects adversely on a lawyer's fitness depends on the nature of the act and the circumstances of its commission. The standard is applicable to criminal acts wherever they may occur, so long as they are also treated as criminal at the place of occurrence.

* * *

i. Reporting misconduct of a lawyer or judge. Subsection (3) states the rule found in the lawyer code of most jurisdictions. The rule is applicable to violations by lawyers whether or not in the same firm. In the case of a junior lawyer in a firm who knows of misconduct by a senior lawyer, including a supervisory lawyer (see § 11), reporting the

17

violation to the firm's managing body or another senior lawyer does not satisfy the requirement (unless the junior lawyer reasonably assumes in the circumstances that those informed will report the offense), but may impose a similar requirement on other lawyers thus informed. By its terms, the rule is inapplicable to a lawyer's own violation.

The duty to disclose wrongdoing by another lawyer typically does not require disclosure of confidential client information protected as stated in § 60. If disclosure of such information is subject to an exception, for example because a client has consented to its disclosure for that purpose (see § 62), the duty to disclose applies. With respect to timing of a report of wrongdoing, the requirement is commonly interpreted not to require a lawyer involved in litigation or negotiations to make a report until the conclusion of the matter in order to minimize harm to the reporting lawyer's client. Lawyer codes also commonly provide an exception for information learned in counseling another lawyer in a substance-abuse or similar program.

* * *

The requirement applies when a lawyer has knowledge, which may be inferred from the circumstances (see Comment *d*). Knowledge is assessed on an objective standard. It includes more than a suspicion that misconduct has occurred, and mere suspicion does not impose a duty of inquiry. Compare § 11 (duties of supervision). Knowledge exists in an instance in which a reasonable lawyer in the circumstances would have a firm opinion that the conduct in question more likely than not occurred.

As an officer of the court, a lawyer must report to appropriate disciplinary authorities a known violation by a judge of an applicable rule of judicial conduct that raises a substantial question of the judge's fitness for judicial office. In jurisdictions where judges remain subject to discipline as lawyers, a report to an appropriate lawyer disciplinary agency may also be independently required by terms of the rule applicable to reporting lawyer violations.

* * *

TOPIC 3.   CIVIL JUDICIAL REMEDIES IN GENERAL

* * *

§ 6.   Judicial Remedies Available to a Client or Nonclient for Lawyer Wrongs

For a lawyer's breach of a duty owed to the lawyer's client or to a nonclient, judicial remedies may be available through judgment or order entered in accordance with the standards applicable to the remedy awarded, including standards concerning limitation of remedies. Judicial remedies include the following:

(1) awarding a sum of money as damages;

(2) providing injunctive relief, including requiring specific performance of a contract or enjoining its nonperformance;

(3) requiring restoration of a specific thing or awarding a sum of money to prevent unjust enrichment;

(4) ordering cancellation or reformation of a contract, deed, or similar instrument;

(5) declaring the rights of the parties, such as determining that an obligation claimed by the lawyer to be owed to the lawyer is not enforceable;

(6) punishing the lawyer for contempt;

(7) enforcing an arbitration award;

(8) disqualifying a lawyer from a representation;

(9) forfeiting a lawyer's fee (see § 37);

(10) denying the admission of evidence wrongfully obtained;

(11) dismissing the claim or defense of a litigant represented by the lawyer;

(12) granting a new trial; and

(13) entering a procedural or other sanction.

Comment:

[*a. Scope and cross-references.*]

* * *

Availability of a particular remedy is subject to customary rules applicable to the remedy, including the general principle that duplicative remedies not be awarded. With respect to limitation of remedies, see Comment *n*.

* * *

b. Damages. The most common kind of case in which damages are allowed is a claim of malpractice by a client against a lawyer. See generally Chapter 4. On the extent of damage remedies available to a nonclient against a lawyer, see generally §§ 51 and 56.

* * *

d. Preventing unjust enrichment. A court in a civil action may order a lawyer to return specific property, such as client property wrongfully retained by a lawyer (see § 45). See also § 60(2) (accounting for profits from improper use of confidential information). Disciplinary authorities are also sometimes empowered to order restitution as a disciplinary sanction (see § 5, Comment *j*). On forfeiture of a lawyer's fees, see § 37.

e. Rescission or reformation of a transaction. Cancellation of an instrument with otherwise legal effect would be appropriate when, for example, a lawyer obtains a deed to a client's property through undue influence in violation of limitations on business dealings with a client (see § 126) or on client gifts to lawyers (see § 127) or when the instrument was prepared by a lawyer representing clients with substantial conflicts of interests (see § 130). The remedy implements substantive standards applicable to lawyers as an expression of the strong public policy of the jurisdiction.

* * *

i. Disqualification from a representation. Disqualification of a lawyer and those affiliated with the lawyer from further participation in a pending matter has become the most common remedy for conflicts of interest in litigation (see Chapter 8). Disqualification draws on the inherent power of courts to regulate the conduct of lawyers (see § 1, Comment *c*) as well as the related inherent power of judges to regulate the course of proceedings before them and to issue injunctive and similar directive orders (see Comment *c* hereto). Disqualification, where appropriate, ensures that the case is well presented in court, that confidential information of present or former clients is not misused, and that a client's substantial interest in a lawyer's loyalty is protected. In most instances, determining whether a lawyer should be disqualified involves a balancing of several interests and is appropriate only when less-intrusive remedies are not reasonably available.

The costs imposed on a client deprived of a lawyer's services by disqualification can be substantial. At a minimum, the client is forced to incur the cost of finding a new lawyer not burdened by conflict in whom the client has confidence and educating that lawyer about the facts and issues. The costs of delay in the proceeding are borne by that client in part, but also by the tribunal and society. Disqualification is often the most effective sanction for a conflict of interest and will likely continue to be vigorously applied where necessary to protect the integrity of a proceeding or an important interest of the moving party. In applying it, however, tribunals should be vigilant to prevent its use as a tactic by which one party may impose unwarranted delay, costs, and other burdens on another. In an appropriate case, additional or other remedies may be appropriate, such as professional discipline (see § 5), legal-malpractice recovery (see Chapter 4), fee forfeiture (see § 37 & Comment *d* hereto), rescission or reformation of an instrument (see Comment *d* hereto), various procedural remedies (see Comments *j-m* hereto), or possible criminal sanctions (see § 8). Injunctive relief (see Comment *c* hereto) may be appropriate in a matter not before a tribunal, so that disqualification in a proceeding already underway cannot be sought.

The costs associated with disqualification require that standing to seek disqualification ordinarily be limited to present or former clients who would be adversely affected by the continuing representation, whether or not they are parties to the present litigation. Tribunals should not ordinarily permit parties who are not directly affected to invoke the putative interests of an absent client with whom they are not in privity. However, concerns about the fairness of the processes of tribunals may require that tribunals in some cases raise conflicts issues on their own motion or permit a party who otherwise lacks standing to raise the issue. Particularly in criminal prosecutions (see § 129, Comment *c*), a court may intervene where necessary to protect a defendant against the ineffective assistance of counsel that may result from a conflict of interest.

* * *

A file of the work done on a matter before disqualification by a disqualified lawyer may be provided to a successor lawyer in circumstances in which doing so does not threaten confidential information (see generally § 59) of the successful moving client. The party seeking to justify such a transfer may be required to show both that no impermissible confidential client information is contained in the material transferred, and that the former and new lawyers exchange none in the process of transferring responsibilities for the matter.

Illustration:

1. Lawyer was retained by Defendant to defend a claim for breach of warranty. Lawyer prepared a memorandum of legal research on the question of proper venue and made notes of interviews with three of Defendant's employees who had substantial knowledge of the processes used in manufacture of the product. Shortly thereafter, Lawyer's firm hired New Lawyer,

who had been actively working on the case on behalf of Plaintiff at a former firm. Even if Lawyer would be disqualified from continuing to represent Defendant in the case (compare §§ 123–124), the interview notes and memorandum of law could be made available to successor counsel for Defendant because Defendant can show that they were not enhanced or otherwise based on confidential information of Plaintiff revealed by New Lawyer to Lawyer.

* * *

j. Denying the admissibility of evidence. If the admission of evidence on behalf of a party would violate the obligation owed by a lawyer to a client or former client (see generally § 60) or was obtained by a lawyer in violation of the lawyer's obligation not to mislead a nonclient (see § 98), the tribunal may exercise discretion to exclude the evidence, even if the evidence is not otherwise subject to exclusion because of the attorney-client privilege (see § 68 and following) or the work-product immunity (see § 87 and following). Exclusion is proper where it would place the parties in the position they would have occupied if the lawyer had not obtained the confidential information in the first place.

k. Dismissing a claim or defense. When a litigant bases an essential element of a claim or defense entirely on confidential client information improperly disclosed by a lawyer (see generally § 60), the tribunal may exercise discretion to dismiss the claim or defense. Such extreme relief is appropriate when no less drastic relief would adequately remedy the disclosure. If, on the other hand, the tribunal finds that the claim or defense would have been made notwithstanding the disclosure, a more appropriate remedy may be disqualification of the revealing lawyer if the lawyer presently represents the responding party and suppression of only such evidence (see Comment *j*) as would not be properly discoverable.

* * *

m. Procedural or other sanctions. Most tribunals possess the power to provide sanctions against participants in litigation, including lawyers, who engage in seriously harassing or other sanctionable activities. See generally § 1; see also § 110. Such sanctions include an award of attorney fees to a party injured by the lawyer's conduct, a fine, or a reprimand. In appropriate circumstances, the court may determine that the client was blameless and the lawyer fully blameworthy and accordingly direct that the full weight of a sanction entered against a party be borne only by the lawyer and not by the lawyer's client (see § 110, Comment *g*). Rarely will such relief entail an award from the offending lawyer to that lawyer's own client.

However, such an order may be appropriate, for example, when, due to the lawyer's offensive activities, the lawyer's client has retained another lawyer and the court retains jurisdiction to award such a sanction against the predecessor lawyer.

* * *

§ 7.   Judicial Remedies Available to a Lawyer for Client Wrongs

A lawyer may obtain a remedy based on a present or former client's breach of a duty to the lawyer if the remedy:

(1) is appropriate under applicable law governing the remedy; and

(2) does not put the lawyer in a position prohibited by an applicable lawyer code.

Comment:

* * *

[b.   *Rationale.*]

* * *

Illustrations:

1. In a written contract by which Client retained Lawyer to provide legal services in a personal-injury case, Client agreed to give Lawyer at least 30 days' notice of discharge. Client was a person not experienced in dealings with lawyers, and the representation was a routine personal-injury action. Client later discharged Lawyer without giving prior notice. Lawyer filed suit against Client, seeking damages for Client's violation of the 30-day-notice agreement. Due to Client's right to discharge Lawyer at any time (see § 32), the tribunal should refuse to enforce the 30-day limitation restricting that right.

2. Same facts as in Illustration 1, except that Client is a large organization represented in the negotiations with Lawyer by inside legal counsel. The matter involves an unusual time and capital commitment by Lawyer, necessitating that Lawyer hire additional professional and clerical assistance, terminate representation of other clients, and train office staff to deal with a complex set of technical issues entailed in representing Client. In the circumstances, the 30-day-notice requirement is not unreasonable, as it protects clear and legitimate interests of Lawyer and does

not in the circumstances unduly burden Client's right of discharge.

* * *

TOPIC 4. LAWYER CRIMINAL OFFENSES

* * *

§ 8. Lawyer Criminal Offenses

The traditional and appropriate activities of a lawyer in representing a client in accordance with the requirements of the applicable lawyer code are relevant factors for the tribunal in assessing the propriety of the lawyer's conduct under the criminal law. In other respects, a lawyer is guilty of an offense for an act committed in the course of representing a client to the same extent and on the same basis as would a nonlawyer acting similarly.

Comment:

[*a. Scope and cross-references.*]

* * *

On counseling a client about activity of doubtful legality, see § 94(2) and Comment *c* thereof. On limits on a lawyer's civil liability to others based on the lawyer's advising and assisting acts of clients, see § 56, Comments *b* and *c*.

b. Rationale. Lawyers play an important public role by informing clients about law and the operation of the legal system and providing other assistance to clients. In counseling clients a lawyer may appropriately advise them about the legality of contemplated activities (see § 94, Comment *c*). A lawyer is, of course, not generally liable under the law of crimes for a client's criminal acts solely because the lawyer advised or otherwise assisted the client in the underlying activities that constituted the offense, such as when a lawyer did not know of the client's intended use of the advice or where the lawyer attempted to dissuade the client from committing the offense. A lawyer may, however, cross the divide between appropriate counseling and criminal activity. As with persons in other occupations and professions, lawyers functioning on behalf of a client remain subject to the requirements of criminal law. The Section and Comments indicate in general how criminal law may apply to a lawyer's activities.

* * *

[d.   *Responsibility as a principal.*]

* * *

Illustration:

1. Knowing that Client would submit a document to a government agency in compliance with a reporting requirement, Lawyer knowingly prepares the document with materially false statements. Client, relying on Lawyer's representations, believes the statements to be true and submits the false document. Client, lacking knowledge, is guilty of no offense. Lawyer, who acted with knowledge and with intent that Client submit a false document, is guilty as a principal for the offense of submitting a false document to a government agency.

* * *

TOPIC 5.   LAW–FIRM STRUCTURE AND OPERATION

* * *

TITLE A.   ASSOCIATION OF LAWYERS IN LAW ORGANIZATIONS

* * *

§ 9.   Law–Practice Organizations—In General

(1) A lawyer may practice as a solo practitioner, as an employee of another lawyer or law firm, or as a member of a law firm constituted as a partnership, professional corporation, or similar entity.

(2) A lawyer employed by an entity described in Subsection (1) is subject to applicable law governing the creation, operation, management, and dissolution of the entity.

(3) Absent an agreement with the firm providing a more permissive rule, a lawyer leaving a law firm may solicit firm clients:

(a) prior to leaving the firm:

(i) only with respect to firm clients on whose matters the lawyer is actively and substantially working; and

(ii) only after the lawyer has adequately and timely informed the firm of the lawyer's intent to contact firm clients for that purpose; and

(b) after ceasing employment in the firm, to the same extent as any other nonfirm lawyer.

Comment:

* * *

b. Forms of private law-practice organizations and the law regulating them. A law firm established as a partnership is generally subject to partnership law with respect to questions concerning creation, operation, management, and dissolution of the firm. Originally in order to achieve certain tax savings, law firms were permitted in most states to constitute themselves as professional corporations. Most such laws permitted that form to be elected even by solo practitioners or by one or more lawyers who, through their professional corporation, became partners in a law partnership. Pursuant to amendments to the partnership law in many states in the early 1990s, associated lawyers may elect to constitute the organization as a limited-liability partnership, with significant limitations on the personal liability of firm partners for liability for acts for which they are not personally responsible (see Comment *c*). Correspondingly, some states permit lawyers to form limited-liability companies. Lawyers who are members of professional corporations or limited-liability companies are subject to statutory and court rules applicable to such organizations set up to practice law.

* * *

f. Of-counsel relationships to law firms. Traditionally, some lawyers have maintained "of counsel" relationships with a private-practice law firm. By customary usage, the term suggests that the lawyer is associated with the firm on a substantial, although part-time, basis because semi-retired or because of extensive duties in another organization not involved in the practice of law (such as a corporation or law school). The term "of counsel" may also refer to lawyers newly arrived at the firm, as on a trial basis. Other firms employ other terminology, such as "special counsel," to refer to one of the foregoing. Such relationships are significant primarily to reflect firm culture and practices, for purposes of advertising and to determine the imputation of conflicts of interest. In some jurisdictions, holding oneself out as of counsel requires that the lawyer maintain a continuous and substantial relationship with the law firm (although likely with reduced duties). For purposes other than advertising, the legal significance of the relationship can vary depending on the purpose for which the question is posed. On whether an of-counsel lawyer is subject to or causes imputed disqualification, see § 123, Comment *c(ii)*.

g. Temporary, contract, or consulting lawyers. A lawyer, law firm, or law department of an organization may contract to obtain the services of a temporary lawyer, either for a particular project or for a relatively short period. The nature of the association in all events is such that the lawyer has no assured expectation of long-term employment with the firm. The lawyer's employment rights and obligations are determined by the terms of the lawyer's contract with the hiring firm. Whether the lawyer is considered an employee of the law firm or an independent contractor is determined under the law generally applicable to employment.

* * *

h. Associated lawyers. Lawyers in separate law firms or practicing solo may collaborate on a single matter or series of matters for the purpose of representing a single client or a series of clients with related matters. Their powers, rights, and obligations with respect to each other (including their respective rights to receive fees earned in the matter, to withdraw from the matter, and to insist that other lawyers with whom they are associated share in the work or fees) are determined under the express or implied terms of their particular agreement of association and the law applicable to the form of association that they thus elect. That form may be, for example, a joint venture, a principal-agent relationship, or a common-law partnership. On fee-splitting, see § 47.

i. Departure of a firm lawyer to compete. A lawyer's departure from a law firm with firm clients, lawyers, or employees, unless done pursuant to agreement, can raise difficult legal issues. Departing a firm or planning to do so consistently with valid provisions of the firm agreement is not itself a breach of duty to remaining firm members. Thus, a lawyer planning a departure to set up a competing law practice may make such predeparture arrangements as leasing space, printing a new letterhead, and obtaining financing. It is also not a breach of duty to a former firm for a lawyer who has departed the firm to continue to represent former firm clients who choose such representation, so long as the lawyer has complied with the rules of Subsection (3). Delineating what other steps may permissibly be taken consistent with such duties requires consideration of the nature of the duties of the departing lawyer to the firm, the duty of the firm to the departing lawyer such as under the firm agreement, as well as the interests of clients in continued competent representation, in freely choosing counsel, and in receiving accurate and fair information from both the departing lawyer and the firm on which to base such a choice. On a client's choice whether to remain with the firm or to follow the departing lawyer, see § 13, Comment *b*; § 31, Comment *f*; § 32, Comment *i*; § 33, Comment *b*; compare § 32(1) (client's right to discharge lawyer at any time). As a matter of the law of advertising and solicitation, under most lawyer codes in-person or telephonic contact with persons whom the lawyer has been or was formerly actively representing is not impermissible. Under decisions of the United States Supreme Court, direct-mail solicitation is constitutionally protected against an attempt by the state generally to outlaw it.

However, as a matter of the departing lawyer's duties to the law firm, the client is considered to be a client of the firm (see § 14, Comment *h*). The departing lawyer generally may not employ firm resources to solicit the client, may not employ nonpublic confidential information of the firm against the interests of the firm in seeking to be retained by a firm client (when not privileged to do so, for example to protect the interests of the client), must provide accurate and reasonably complete information to the client, and must provide the client with a choice of counsel. As stated in Subsection (3), a departing lawyer accordingly may not solicit clients with whom the lawyer actually worked until the lawyer has either left the firm (Subsection (3)(b)) or adequately informed the firm of the lawyer's intent to contact firm clients for that purpose (Subsection (3)(a)). Such notice must give the firm a reasonable opportunity to make its own fair and accurate presentation to relevant clients. In either event, the lawyer and the firm are in positions to communicate their interest in providing representation to the client on fair and equal terms. If a lawyer and firm agree that the lawyer is free to solicit existing firm clients more extensively than as provided in Subsection (3), their relationship is controlled by such agreement. For example, it might be agreed that a departing lawyer may seek to represent some clients as an individual practitioner or as a member of another firm. On limitations on agreements that have the effect of restricting a departing lawyer's law practice, and hence the ability of clients to obtain counsel, see § 13.

With respect to other firm lawyers and employees, a lawyer may plan mutual or serial departures from their law firm with such persons, so long as the lawyers and personnel do nothing prohibited to either of them (including impermissibly soliciting clients, as above) and so long as they do not misuse firm resources (such as copying files or client lists without permission or unlawfully removing firm property from its premises) or take other action detrimental to the interests of the firm or of clients, aside from whatever detriment may befall the firm due to their departure.

* * *

TITLE B. LIMITATIONS ON NONLAWYER INVOLVEMENT IN A LAW FIRM

* * *

§ **10.** **Limitations on Nonlawyer Involvement in a Law Firm**

(1) A nonlawyer may not own any interest in a law firm, and a nonlawyer may not be empowered to or actually direct or control the professional activities of a lawyer in the firm.

(2) A lawyer may not form a partnership or other business enterprise with a nonlawyer if any of the activities of the enterprise consist of the practice of law.

(3) A lawyer or law firm may not share legal fees with a person not admitted to practice as a lawyer, except that:

(a) an agreement by a lawyer with the lawyer's firm or another lawyer in the firm may provide for payment, over a reasonable period of time after the lawyer's death, to the lawyer's estate or to one or more specified persons;

(b) a lawyer who undertakes to complete unfinished legal business of a deceased lawyer may pay to the estate of the deceased lawyer a portion of the total compensation that fairly represents services rendered by the deceased lawyer; and

(c) a lawyer or law firm may include nonlawyer employees in a compensation or retirement plan, even though the plan is based in whole or in part on a profit-sharing arrangement.

Comment:

* * *

b. Rationale. This Section is based on lawyer-code limitations on law-firm structure and practices. Those limitations are prophylactic and are designed to safeguard the professional independence of lawyers. A person entitled to share a lawyer's fees is likely to attempt to influence the lawyer's activities so as to maximize those fees. That could lead to inadequate legal services. The Section should be construed so as to prevent nonlawyer control over lawyers' services, not to implement other goals such as preventing new and useful ways of providing legal services or making sure that nonlawyers do not profit indirectly from legal services in circumstances and under arrangements presenting no significant risk of harm to clients or third persons.

* * *

d. *Referral arrangements.* Under the rule of Subsection (3), a lawyer may not pay or agree to pay a nonlawyer for referring a client to the lawyer. Such arrangements would give the nonlawyer an incentive to refer to lawyers who will pay the highest referral fee, rather than to lawyers who can provide the most effective services. They also would give the nonlawyer referring person the power and an incentive to influence the lawyer's representation by an explicit or implicit threat to refer no additional clients or by appealing to the lawyer's sense of gratitude for the referral already made. That incentive is not present when the referral comes from a nonprofit referral service. Moreover, a lawyer may pay an advertising, marketing, or similar service for providing professional services in connection with the lawyer's own permissible efforts to advertise for clients. Fee-splitting with a lawyer admitted only in another jurisdiction is subject to § 47 but not to Subsection (3) hereof.

e. *Compensation of nonlawyer employees.* This Section, of course, does not prohibit a lawyer from providing compensation to secretaries, nonlawyer professionals, and other permanent or temporary employees. That is so even though their compensation indirectly comes from the lawyer's fees and the employees hence have some interest in maximizing the lawyer's fee income. Compare § 47, Comment b; on the duty to supervise all such nonlawyer personnel, see § 11. Such compensation may be a percentage of or otherwise contingent on the lawyer's income, so long as the compensation is not contingent on the lawyer's revenue in an individual matter. Thus, under Subsection (3)(c), nonlawyer employees may join in a profit-sharing plan for compensation or retirement. Under tax regulations certain kinds of retirement and similar plans must often be made available to all employees on specified terms of equality.

* * *

f. *Nontraditional forms of law practice.* The rule against splitting fees with nonlawyers has been one ground for the prohibition of partnerships between lawyers and nonlawyers when the practice of law is an activity of the partnership and for the prohibition of profit-making professional law corporations with stock owned by nonlawyers. This Section does not prohibit a law firm from cooperating with a legally separate partnership or other organization of nonlawyers in providing multi-disciplinary services to clients. The Section allows a lawyer employed and compensated by a nonprofit public-interest organization or a union to remit court-awarded fees to the employing organization, provided that the organization uses the funds only for legal services.

  g. *Lawyer involvement in ancillary business activities.* Ancillary business activities of lawyers can be conducted consistent with the Section and with other applicable requirements. A lawyer may, for example, operate a real-estate agency, insurance agency, title-insurance company, consulting enterprise, or similar business, along with a law practice. So long as each enterprise bills separately and so long as the ancillary enterprise does not engage in the practice of law, involvement of both the lawyer's law practice and the lawyer's ancillary business enterprise in the same matter does not constitute impermissible fee-splitting with a nonlawyer, even if nonlawyers have ownership interests or exercise management powers in the ancillary enterprise.

  However, a lawyer's dual practice of law and the ancillary enterprise must be conducted in accordance with applicable legal restrictions, including those of the lawyer codes. Among other things, the lawyer's self-interest in promoting the enterprise must not distort the lawyer's judgment in the provision of legal services to a client, including in making recommendations of the lawyer's own ancillary service. To avoid misleading the client, a lawyer must reveal the lawyer's interest in the ancillary enterprise when it should be reasonably apparent that the client would wish to or should assess that information in determining whether to engage the services of the other business. The lawyer must also, of course, avoid representing a client (or do so only with informed client consent) in a matter in which the ancillary enterprise has an adverse interest of such a kind that it would materially and adversely affect the lawyer's representation of the client (see § 125). The lawyer must also disclose to the client, unless the client is already sufficiently aware, that the client will not have a client-lawyer relationship with the ancillary business and the significance of that fact. Other disclosures may be required in the course of the matter. For example, when circumstances indicate the need to do so to protect an important interest of the client, the lawyer must disclose to the client that the client's communications with personnel of the ancillary enterprise—unlike communications with personnel in the lawyer's law office (see § 70, Comment *g*)—are not protected under the attorney-client privilege. If relevant, the lawyer should also disclose to the client that the ancillary business is not subject to conflict-of-interest rules (see generally Chapter 8) similar to those applicable to law practice.

A lawyer's provision of services to a client through an ancillary business may in some circumstances constitute the rendition of legal services under an applicable lawyer code. As a consequence, the possibly more stringent requirements of the code may control the provision of the ancillary services, such as with respect to the reasonableness of fee charges (§ 34) or confidentiality obligations (§ 60 and following). When those services are distinct and the client understands the significance of the distinction, the ancillary service should not be considered as the rendition of legal services. When those conditions are not met, the lawyer is subject to the lawyer code with respect to all services provided. Whether the services are distinct depends on the client's reasonably apparent understanding concerning such considerations as the nature of the respective ancillary-business and legal services, the physical location at which the services are provided, and the identities and affiliations of lawyer and nonlawyer personnel working on the matter.

* * *

TITLE C. SUPERVISION OF LAWYERS AND NONLAWYERS WITHIN AN ORGANIZATION

* * *

§ 11. A Lawyer's Duty of Supervision

(1) A lawyer who is a partner in a law-firm partnership or a principal in a law firm organized as a corporation or similar entity is subject to professional discipline for failing to make reasonable efforts to ensure that the firm has in effect measures giving reasonable assurance that all lawyers in the firm conform to applicable lawyer-code requirements.

(2) A lawyer who has direct supervisory authority over another lawyer is subject to professional discipline for failing to make reasonable efforts to ensure that the other lawyer conforms to applicable lawyer-code requirements.

(3) A lawyer is subject to professional discipline for another lawyer's violation of the rules of professional conduct if:

(a) the lawyer orders or, with knowledge of the specific conduct, ratifies the conduct involved; or

(b) the lawyer is a partner or principal in the law firm, or has direct supervisory authority over the other lawyer, and knows of the conduct at a time when its consequences can be avoided or mitigated but fails to take reasonable remedial measures.

(4) With respect to a nonlawyer employee of a law firm, the lawyer is subject to professional discipline if either:

(a) the lawyer fails to make reasonable efforts to ensure:

(i) that the firm in which the lawyer practices has in effect measures giving reasonable assurance that the nonlawyer's conduct is compatible with the professional obligations of the lawyer; and

(ii) that conduct of a nonlawyer over whom the lawyer has direct supervisory authority is compatible with the professional obligations of the lawyer; or

(b) the nonlawyer's conduct would be a violation of the applicable lawyer code if engaged in by a lawyer, and

(i) the lawyer orders or, with knowledge of the specific conduct, ratifies the conduct; or

(ii) the lawyer is a partner or principal in the law firm, or has direct supervisory authority over the nonlawyer, and knows of the conduct at a time when its consequences can be avoided or mitigated but fails to take reasonable remedial measures.

Comment:

* * *

b. Rationale. Supervision is a general responsibility of a principal (see Restatement Second, Agency § 503, Comment *f,* & id. §§ 507 & 510). A partner in a law firm or a lawyer with authority to direct the activities of another lawyer or nonlawyer employee of the firm is such a principal. Appropriate exercise of responsibility over those carrying out the tasks of law practice is particularly important given the duties of lawyers to protect the interests of clients (see § 16) and in view of the privileged powers conferred on lawyers by law (see § 1, Comment *b*). Moreover, the requirement of supervision recognizes the reality that lawyers of greater experience and skill will often be able to identify areas of professional concern not apparent either to less-experienced lawyers or to nonlawyers. The supervisory duty, in effect, requires that such additional experience and skill be deployed in reasonably diligent fashion.

c. Exercising supervisory authority. Lack of awareness of misconduct by another person, either lawyer or nonlawyer, under a lawyer's supervision does not excuse a violation of this Section. To ensure that supervised persons comply with professional standards, a supervisory lawyer is required to take reasonable measures, given the level and extent of responsibility that the lawyer possesses. Those measures, such as an informal program of instructing or monitoring another person, must often assume the likelihood that a particular lawyer or nonlawyer employee may not yet have received adequate preparation for carrying out that person's own responsibilities.

d. Delegating supervisory duties. A lawyer may delegate responsibility to supervise another lawyer or a nonlawyer to a person whom the lawyer reasonably believes to have appropriate capacity to exercise such responsibility under this Section. If information indicates to the lawyer that the delegated person is not appropriately providing supervision, the lawyer must take reasonable remedial measures.

Similarly, a partner in a law firm may reasonably delegate responsibility under § 11(1) to a management committee or similar body of appropriate capacity to put in place and implement particular firm measures. Such a partner remains responsible to take corrective steps if the lawyer reasonably should know that the delegated body or person is not providing or implementing measures as described in the Section.

e. Responsibility for directly supervised lawyers; for other lawyers. A lawyer has at least one and, in the case of partners, two general areas of supervisory responsibility with respect to other firm lawyers. Under Subsection (2), a supervising lawyer must actively ensure that a directly supervised lawyer conforms to rules of an applicable lawyer code. That responsibility is borne by all lawyers, whatever their rank otherwise in the firm hierarchy, but only applies with respect to other lawyers over whom they have direct supervisory authority. More broadly, a lawyer who is a partner in a law firm (including an owner of an interest in a professional corporation or similar organization) has a further responsibility under Subsection (3)(b). The partner must take reasonable remedial measures if the partner knows of another firm lawyer's violation of rules of the lawyer code. Such an obligation attaches even if the partner has no direct supervisory authority over the other lawyer. The obligation is not only to prevent such violations (although it includes that), but extends to taking reasonable steps to remedy or mitigate the consequences of the violation. While such a response might include a report of wrongdoing under § 5(3), the requirement of taking reasonable remedial action extends to all known violations and not only those covered by an applicable reporting obligation and in any event may not be sufficiently satisfied through reporting if other reasonably available measures (such as informing a client that a supervised lawyer has wrongfully taken the client's funds) exist.

The Section also contains in Subsection (3)(a) a kind of accessorial liability. No firm lawyer may order or, with knowledge of the specific conduct, ratify a violation of the lawyer code on the part of any other firm lawyer.

f. Responsibility for nonlawyers in a law firm. Duties corresponding to those of a lawyer with respect to other firm lawyers exist with respect to supervising nonlawyers in a law firm. On vicarious liability for acts of such nonlawyers, see § 58, Comments *c* and *e*. Supervision of a nonlawyer must often be more extensive and detailed than of a supervised lawyer because of the presumed lack of training of many nonlawyers on legal matters generally and on such important duties as those on dealing properly with confidential client information (see § 60, Comment *d*) and with client funds and other property (see § 44), which may be different from duties generally imposed in non-law practices and businesses. A lawyer's nonlawyer employees and agents must be properly supervised by the lawyer with respect to such activities as interviewing clients to assure that any advice given is appropriate. If done under appropriate supervision to assure that any inappropriate advice is detected and corrected, such nonlawyer dealings with clients are permissible.

* * *

g. Responsibility for law-firm policies and practices. A lawyer affiliated for the purpose of law practice with other lawyers in a law firm is not privileged to attend only to his or her own activities and those of lawyers (see Comment *d*) and nonlawyers (see Comment *e*) directly under the lawyer's supervision, while ignoring the activities of others within the firm. To the contrary, such a lawyer, if a partner in the firm, has a duty stated in Subsection (1) to ensure that the firm has in place measures giving reasonable assurance that all lawyers in the firm conform to the applicable lawyer code. A similar general supervisory duty of partners exists under Subsection (4)(a)(i) with respect to nonlawyer employees. The extent of that duty corresponds to the lawyer's practical ability to know matters and effect appropriate changes within the firm. A partner with full voting power properly has a more extensive duty than an associate or a lawyer associated only of counsel. On delegation of supervisory duties, see Comment *d*.

For the purposes of the Section, the responsibility of a lawyer extends to the work of the law-practice organization with which the lawyer practices, including a law firm in private practice (whether structured as a sole proprietorship or as a partnership, professional corporation, limited-liability partnership, or similar entity), an office of inside legal counsel in a corporation or similar enterprise, and a legal office of a government agency or an independent government legal agency such as a prosecutor's office or office of an attorney general. Appropriate measures for a particular firm must take account of the particular firm's size, structure, nature of practice, and legal constraints, as well as the foreseeability of particular kinds of supervisory issues arising. Policies and practices of a solo practitioner with a single experienced nonlawyer assistant may be entirely informal, but the policies and practices for a much larger firm with many lawyer and nonlawyer employees must be correspondingly more encompassing. In carrying out those responsibilities, many law firms' policies provide for continuing professional education for both lawyers and nonlawyers.

Either as a matter of firm-wide policy or as matter of effective delegation, a firm must have in place reasonable measures to ensure that lawyer and nonlawyer personnel are reasonably competent for their intended responsibilities and thereafter receive appropriate training, supervision, and support allowing them to recognize and carry out their responsibilities. Reasonable measures must also be taken to ensure that such persons operate under appropriate procedures to avoid conflicts of interest and to prevent conversion or other inappropriate dealing with client funds, fraudulent or otherwise improper billing to clients, and neglect of deadlines important in representing clients.

* * *

§ 12. Duty of a Lawyer Subject to Supervision

(1) For purposes of professional discipline, a lawyer must conform to the requirements of an applicable lawyer code even if the lawyer acted at the direction of another lawyer or other person.

(2) For purposes of professional discipline, a lawyer under the direct supervisory authority of another lawyer does not violate an applicable lawyer code by acting in accordance with the supervisory lawyer's direction based on a reasonable resolution of an arguable question of professional duty.

Comment:

* * *

b.   Responsibility of a supervised lawyer. As indicated in Subsection (1), a lawyer under the direct supervisory authority of another lawyer does not by the fact of supervision become absolved from violations of an applicable lawyer code. Thus, a junior law-firm associate working under the supervision of a senior partner is nonetheless personally responsible to know and apply relevant lawyer-code and other legal requirements in the course of the associate's work. Even a direct instruction from the senior lawyer does not protect the supervised lawyer except to the limited extent provided in Subsection (2) (see Comment *c*). Similarly, attempted instructions or announcements of binding firm policy by a nonlawyer manager, such as the firm's business manager, for example on the manner in which clients are to be charged fees, do not bind even the most junior lawyer in the firm if following such an instruction would violate the lawyer's duty under an applicable lawyer code.

* * *

TITLE D.   RESTRICTIONS ON THE RIGHT TO PRACTICE LAW

* * *

§ 13.   Restrictions on the Right to Practice Law

(1) A lawyer may not offer or enter into a law-firm agreement that restricts the right of the lawyer to practice law after terminating the relationship, except for a restriction incident to the lawyer's retirement from the practice of law.

(2) In settling a client claim, a lawyer may not offer or enter into an agreement that restricts the right of the lawyer to practice law, including the right to represent or take particular action on behalf of other clients.

Comment:

* * *

b.   Law-firm restrictive covenants and a client's choice of counsel. As stated in Subsection (1), a lawyer may not offer or enter into a restrictive covenant with the lawyer's law firm or other employer if the substantial effect of the covenant would be to restrict the right of the lawyer to practice law after termination of the lawyer's relationship with the law firm. The rationale for the rule is to prevent undue restrictions on the ability of present and future clients of the lawyer to make a free choice of counsel. The rule applies to all lawyers in a firm and prohibits both making and accepting such a restriction.

Beyond professional discipline, such rules preclude enforcement of a provision of a firm agreement under which a departing lawyer is denied otherwise-accrued financial benefits on entering into competitive law practice, unless the denial applies to all departing firm lawyers, whether entering into competitive practice or not (including, for example, lawyers who become judges, government counsel, or inside legal counsel for a firm client or who change careers, such as by entering teaching). See § 9, Comment *i*.

An exception recognized in all the lawyer codes is for restriction of a lawyer's right to practice law that is to be enforced upon a lawyer's retirement. The restriction is supportable because it only minimally interferes with the ability of clients to choose counsel freely, given the lawyer's intent to retire from practice.

* * *

c. Restrictive agreements in settling claims. Subsection (2) states the prohibition against restrictive agreements made in settling a client's claim. For example, a defendant as a condition of settlement may insist that the lawyer representing the plaintiff agree not to take action on behalf of other clients, such as filing similar claims, against the defendant. Proposing such an agreement would tend to create conflicts of interest between the lawyer, who would normally be expected to oppose such a limitation, and the lawyer's present client, who may wish to achieve a favorable settlement at the terms offered. The agreement would also obviously restrict the freedom of future clients to choose counsel skilled in a particular area of practice. To prevent such effects, such agreements are void and unenforceable.

* * *

CHAPTER 2

THE CLIENT–LAWYER RELATIONSHIP

TOPIC 1. CREATING A CLIENT–LAWYER RELATIONSHIP

TOPIC 2. SUMMARY OF THE DUTIES UNDER A CLIENT–LAWYER RELATIONSHIP

TOPIC 3. AUTHORITY TO MAKE DECISIONS

TOPIC 4. A LAWYER'S AUTHORITY TO ACT FOR A CLIENT

TOPIC 5. ENDING A CLIENT–LAWYER RELATIONSHIP

* * *

TOPIC 1.   CREATING A CLIENT–LAWYER RELATIONSHIP

Introductory Note: This Topic addresses creation of a relationship of lawyer and client (§ 14) and the duties a lawyer owes to a prospective client (see § 15). A fundamental distinction is involved between clients, to whom lawyers owe many duties, and nonclients, to whom lawyers owe few duties. It therefore may be vital to know when someone is a client and when not. Prospective and former clients receive certain protections, but not all those due to clients.

§ 14.   Formation of a Client–Lawyer Relationship

A relationship of client and lawyer arises when:

(1) a person manifests to a lawyer the person's intent that the lawyer provide legal services for the person; and either

> **(a) the lawyer manifests to the person consent to do so; or**

> **(b) the lawyer fails to manifest lack of consent to do so, and the lawyer knows or reasonably should know that the person reasonably relies on the lawyer to provide the services; or**

(2) a tribunal with power to do so appoints the lawyer to provide the services.

Comment:

    a. Scope and cross-references. This Section sets forth a standard for determining when a client-lawyer relationship begins. Nonetheless, the various duties of lawyers and clients do not always arise simultaneously. Even if no relationship ensues, a lawyer may owe a prospective client certain duties (see § 15; § 60 & Comment *d* thereto). A lawyer representing a client may perform services also benefiting another person, for example arguing a motion for two litigants, without owing the nonclient litigant all the duties ordinarily owed to a client (see § 19(1)). Even if a relationship ensues, the client may not owe the lawyer a fee (see § 17 & Comment *b* thereto; § 38 & Comment *c* thereto; Restatement Second, Agency § 16). When a fee is due, the person owing it is not necessarily a client (see § 134). Moreover, a client-lawyer relationship may be more readily found in some situations (for example, when a person has a reasonable belief that a lawyer was protecting that person's interests; see Comment *d* hereto) than in others (for example, when a person seeks to compel a lawyer to provide onerous services). In some situations—for example, when a lawyer agrees to represent a defendant without knowing that the lawyer's partner represents the plaintiff—a lawyer is forbidden to perform some duties for the client (continuing the representation) while nevertheless remaining subject to other duties (keeping the client's confidential information secret from others, including from the lawyer's own partner).

* * *

b. *Rationale.* The client-lawyer relationship ordinarily is a consensual one (see Restatement Second, Agency § 15). A client ordinarily should not be forced to put important legal matters into the hands of another or to accept unwanted legal services. The consent requirement, however, is not symmetrical. The client may at any time end the relationship by withdrawing consent (see §§ 31, 32, & 40), while the lawyer may properly withdraw only under specified conditions (see §§ 31 & 32). A lawyer may be held to responsibility of representation when the client reasonably relies on the existence of the relationship (see Comment *e*), and a court may direct the lawyer to represent the client by appointment (see Comment *g*). Lawyers generally are as free as other persons to decide with whom to deal, subject to generally applicable statutes such as those prohibiting certain kinds of discrimination. A lawyer, for example, may decline to undertake a representation that the lawyer finds inconvenient or repugnant. Agreement between client and lawyer likewise defines the scope of the representation, for example, determining whether it encompasses a single matter or is continuing (see § 19(1); § 31(2)(e) & Comment *h*). Even when a representation is continuing, the lawyer is ordinarily free to reject new matters.

c. *The client's intent.* A client's manifestation of intent that a lawyer provide legal services to the client may be explicit, as when the client requests the lawyer to write a will. The client's intent may be manifest from surrounding facts and circumstances, as when the client discusses the possibility of representation with the lawyer and then sends the lawyer relevant papers or a retainer requested by the lawyer. The client may hire the lawyer to work in its legal department. The client may demonstrate intent by ratifying the lawyer's acts, for example when a friend asks a lawyer to represent an imprisoned person who later manifests acceptance of the lawyer's services. The client's intent may be communicated by someone acting for the client, such as a relative or secretary. (The power of such a representative to act on behalf of the client is determined by the law of agency.) No written contract is required in order to establish the relationship, although a writing may be required by disciplinary or procedural standards (see § 38, Comment *b*). The client need not necessarily pay or agree to pay the lawyer; and paying a lawyer does not by itself create a client-lawyer relationship with the payor if the circumstances indicate that the lawyer was to represent someone else, for example, when an insurance company designates a lawyer to represent an insured (see § 134).

The client-lawyer relationship contemplates legal services from the lawyer, not, for example, real-estate-brokerage services or expert-witness services. A client-lawyer relationship results when legal services are provided even if the client also intends to receive other services. A client-lawyer relationship is not created, however, by the fact of receiving some benefit of the lawyer's service, for example when the lawyer represents a co-party. Finally, a lawyer may answer a general question about the law, for instance in a purely social setting, without a client-lawyer relationship arising.

* * *

e. The lawyer's consent or failure to object. Like a client, a lawyer may manifest consent to creating a client-lawyer relationship in many ways. The lawyer may explicitly agree to represent the client or may indicate consent by action, for example by performing services requested by the client. An agent for the lawyer may communicate consent, for example, a secretary or paralegal with express, implied, or apparent authority to act for the lawyer in undertaking a representation.

A lawyer's consent may be conditioned on the successful completion of a conflict-of-interest check or on the negotiation of a fee arrangement. The lawyer's consent may sometimes precede the client's manifestation of intent, for example when an insurer designates a lawyer to represent an insured (see § 134, Comment *f*) who then accepts the representation. Although this Section treats separately the required communications of the client and the lawyer, the acts of each often illuminate those of the other.

Illustrations:

1. Client telephones Lawyer, who has previously represented Client, stating that Client wishes Lawyer to handle a pending antitrust investigation and asking Lawyer to come to Client's headquarters to explore the appropriate strategy for Client to follow. Lawyer comes to the headquarters and spends a day discussing strategy, without stating then or promptly thereafter that Lawyer has not yet decided whether to represent Client. Lawyer has communicated willingness to represent Client by so doing. Had Client simply asked Lawyer to discuss the possibility of representing Client, no client-lawyer relationship would result.

2. As part of a bar-association peer-support program, lawyer A consults lawyer B in confidence about an issue relating to lawyer A's representation of a client. This does not create a client-lawyer relationship between A's client and B. Whether a client-lawyer relationship exists between A and B depends on the foregoing and additional circumstances, including the nature of the program, the subject matter of the consultation, and the nature of prior dealings, if any, between them.

Even when a lawyer has not communicated willingness to represent a person, a client-lawyer relationship arises when the person reasonably relies on the lawyer to provide services, and the lawyer, who reasonably should know of this reliance, does not inform the person that the lawyer will not do so (see § 14(1)(b); see also § 51(2)). In many such instances, the lawyer's conduct constitutes implied assent. In others, the lawyer's duty arises from the principle of promissory estoppel, under which promises inducing reasonable reliance may be enforced to avoid injustice (see Restatement Second, Contracts § 90). In appraising whether the person's reliance was reasonable, courts consider that lawyers ordinarily have superior knowledge of what representation entails and that lawyers often encourage clients and potential clients to rely on them. The rules governing when a lawyer may withdraw from a representation (see § 32) apply to representations arising from implied assent or promissory estoppel.

Illustrations:

3. Claimant writes to Lawyer, describing a medical-malpractice suit that Claimant wishes to bring and asking Lawyer to represent Claimant. Lawyer does not answer the letter. A year later, the statute of limitations applicable to the suit expires. Claimant then sues Lawyer for legal malpractice for not having filed the suit on time. Under this Section no client-lawyer relationship was created (see § 50, Comment c). Lawyer did not communicate willingness to represent Claimant, and Claimant could not reasonably have relied on Lawyer to do so. On a lawyer's duty to a prospective client, see § 15.

4. Defendant telephones Lawyer's office and tells Lawyer's Secretary that Defendant would like Lawyer to represent Defendant in an automobile-violation proceeding set for hearing in 10 days, this being a type of proceeding that Defendant knows Lawyer regularly handles. Secretary tells Defendant to send in

the papers concerning the proceeding, not telling Defendant that Lawyer would then decide whether to take the case, and Defendant delivers the papers the next day. Lawyer does not communicate with Defendant until the day before the hearing, when Lawyer tells Defendant that Lawyer does not wish to take the case. A trier of fact could find that a client-lawyer relationship came into existence when Lawyer failed to communicate that Lawyer was not representing Defendant. Defendant relied on Lawyer by not seeking other counsel when that was still practicable. Defendant's reliance was reasonable because Lawyer regularly handled Defendant's type of case, because Lawyer's agent had responded to Defendant's request for help by asking Defendant to transfer papers needed for the proceeding, and because the imminence of the hearing made it appropriate for Lawyer to inform Defendant and return the papers promptly if Lawyer decided not to take the case.

* * *

f. Organizational, fiduciary, and class-action clients. When the client is a corporation or other organization, the organization's structure and organic law determine whether a particular agent has authority to retain and direct the lawyer. Whether the lawyer is to represent the organization, a person or entity associated with it, or more than one such persons and entities is a question of fact to be determined based on reasonable expectations in the circumstances (see Subsection (1)). Where appropriate, due consideration should be given to the unreasonableness of a claimed expectation of entering into a co-client status when a significant and readily apparent conflict of interest exists between the organization or other client and the associated person or entity claimed to be a co-client (see § 131).

Under Subsection (1)(b), a lawyer's failure to clarify whom the lawyer represents in circumstances calling for such a result might lead a lawyer to have entered into client-lawyer representations not intended by the lawyer. Hence, the lawyer must clarify whom the lawyer intends to represent when the lawyer knows or reasonably should know that, contrary to the lawyer's own intention, a person, individually, or agents of an entity, on behalf of the entity, reasonably rely on the lawyer to provide legal services to that person or entity (see Subsection (1)(b); see also § 103, Comment *b* (extent of a lawyer's duty to warn an unrepresented person that the lawyer represents a client with conflicting interests)). Such clarification may be required, for example, with respect to an officer of an entity client such as a corporation, with respect to one or more partners in a client partnership or in the case of affiliated organizations such as a parent, subsidiary, or similar organization related to a client person or client entity. An implication that such a relationship exists is more likely to be found when the lawyer performs personal legal services for an individual as well or where the organization is small and characterized by extensive common ownership and management. But the lawyer does not enter into a client-lawyer relationship with a person associated with an organizational client solely because the person communicates with the lawyer on matters relevant to the organization that are also relevant to the personal situation of the person. In all events, the question is one of fact based on the reasonable and apparent expectations of the person or entity whose status as client is in question.

In trusts and estates practice a lawyer may have to clarify with those involved whether a trust, a trustee, its beneficiaries or groupings of some or all of them are clients and similarly whether the client is an executor, an estate, or its beneficiaries. In the absence of clarification the inference to be drawn may depend on the circumstances and on the law of the jurisdiction. Similar issues may arise when a lawyer represents other fiduciaries with respect to their fiduciary responsibilities, for example a pension-fund trustee or another lawyer.

Class actions may pose difficult questions of client identification. For many purposes, the named class representatives are the clients of the lawyer for the class. On conflict-of-interest issues, see § 125, Comment *f.* Yet class members who are not named representatives also have some characteristics of clients. For example, their confidential communications directly to the class lawyer may be privileged (compare § 70, Comment *c),* and opposing counsel may not be free to communicate with them directly (see § 99, Comment *l).*

* * *

h.   Client-lawyer relationships with law firms. Many lawyers practice as partners, members, or associates of law firms (see § 9(1)). When a client retains a lawyer with such an affiliation, the lawyer's firm assumes the authority and responsibility of representing that client, unless the circumstances indicate otherwise. For example, the lawyer ordinarily may share the client's work and confidences with other lawyers in the firm (see § 61, Comment *d),* and the firm is liable to the client for the lawyer's negligence (see § 58). Should the lawyer leave the firm, the client may choose to be represented by the departing lawyer, the lawyer's former firm, neither, or both (see §§ 31 & 32; see also § 9(3)). On the other hand, a client's retention of a lawyer or firm ordinarily does not permit the lawyer or firm, without further authorization from the client, to retain a lawyer outside the firm at the client's expense to represent the client (see Restatement

Second, Agency § 18). On imputation of conflicts of interest within a law office, see § 123.

* * *

§ 15. A Lawyer's Duties to a Prospective Client

(1) When a person discusses with a lawyer the possibility of their forming a client-lawyer relationship for a matter and no such relationship ensues, the lawyer must:

(a) not subsequently use or disclose confidential information learned in the consultation, except to the extent permitted with respect to confidential information of a client or former client as stated in §§ 61–67;

(b) protect the person's property in the lawyer's custody as stated in §§ 44–46; and

(c) use reasonable care to the extent the lawyer provides the person legal services.

(2) A lawyer subject to Subsection (1) may not represent a client whose interests are materially adverse to those of a former prospective client in the same or a substantially related matter when the lawyer or another lawyer whose disqualification is imputed to the lawyer under §§ 123 and 124 has received from the prospective client confidential information that could be significantly harmful to the prospective client in the matter, except that such a representation is permissible if:

(a) (i) any personally prohibited lawyer takes reasonable steps to avoid exposure to confidential information other than information appropriate to determine whether to represent the prospective client, and (ii) such lawyer is screened as stated in § 124(2)(b) and (c); or

(b) both the affected client and the prospective client give informed consent to the representation under the limitations and conditions provided in § 122.

Comment:

* * *

b. *Rationale.* Prospective clients are like clients in that they often disclose confidential information to a lawyer, place documents or other property in the lawyer's custody, and rely on the lawyer's advice. But a lawyer's discussions with a prospective client often are limited in time and depth of exploration, do not reflect full consideration of the prospective client's problems, and leave both prospective client and lawyer free (and sometimes required) to proceed no further. Hence, prospective clients should receive some but not all of the protection afforded clients, as indicated in the Section and following Comments.

c. *Confidential information of a prospective client.* It is often necessary for a prospective client to reveal and for the lawyer to learn confidential information (see § 59) during an initial consultation prior to their decision about formation of a client-lawyer relationship. For that reason, the attorney-client privilege attaches to communications of a prospective client (see § 70, Comment *c*). The lawyer must often learn such information to determine whether a conflict of interest exists with an existing client of the lawyer or the lawyer's firm and whether the matter is one that the lawyer is willing to undertake. In all instances, the lawyer must treat that information as confidential in the interest of the prospective client, even if the client or lawyer decides not to proceed with the representation (see Subsection (1)(a); see also § 60(2)). The duty exists regardless of how brief the initial conference may be and regardless of whether screening is instituted under Subsection (2)(a)(ii). The exceptions to the principles of confidentiality and privilege apply to such communications (see §§ 61–67).

Subsection (2) states rules parallel to those governing former-client conflicts under § 132, but it relaxes two analogous former-client rules. First, personal disqualification of a lawyer who deals with a prospective client occurs only when the subsequent matter presents the opportunity to use information obtained from the former prospective client that would be "significantly harmful." In contrast, § 132 applies whenever there is a "substantial risk" of adverse use of the former client's confidential information, regardless of the degree of threatened harm. Second, screening is permitted under Subsection (2)(a) so long as the lawyer takes reasonable steps to limit his or her exposure to confidential information during the initial consultation. In contrast, screening under § 124(2)(a) is permissible only when information obtained in the earlier representation would not likely be of significance in the subsequent representation.

In order to avoid acquiring disqualifying information, a lawyer considering whether or not to undertake a new matter may limit the initial interview to such confidential information as reasonably appears necessary for that purpose. Where that information indicates that a conflict of interest or other reasons for nonrepresentation exists, the lawyer should so inform the prospective client or simply decline the representation. If the prospective client still wishes to retain the lawyer, and if consent is possible under § 122(1), consent from any other affected present or former client should be obtained before further confidential information is elicited. The lawyer may also condition conversations with the prospective client on the person's consent to the lawyer's representation of other clients (see § 122, Comment *d*) or on the prospective client's agreement that any information disclosed during the consultation is not to be treated as confidential (see § 62). The prospective client's informed consent to such an agreement frees the lawyer to represent a client in a matter and to use in that matter, but only if the agreement so provides, confidential information received from the prospective client. A prospective client may also consent to a representation in other ways applicable to a client under § 122.

* * *

When a tribunal is asked to disqualify a lawyer based on prior dealings with a former prospective client, that person bears the burden of persuading the tribunal that the lawyer received such information. The prohibition is imputed to other lawyers as provided in § 123, but may be avoided if all personally prohibited lawyers are screened as stated in § 124(2)(b) and (2)(c) (see Subsection (2)(a)). In that situation, screening avoids imputation even when the requirements of § 124(2)(a) have not been met. In deciding whether to exercise discretion to require disqualification, a tribunal may consider whether the prospective client disclosed confidential information to the lawyer for the purpose of preventing the lawyer or the lawyer's firm from representing an adverse party rather than in a good-faith endeavor to determine whether to retain the lawyer. The tribunal may also consider whether the disclosure of significantly harmful confidential information resulted from the failure of the lawyer or the prospective client to take precautions reasonable in the circumstances. In addition to screening, Subsection (2)(b) permits representation if both the former prospective client and any affected present client consent.

Illustrations:

   1. Person makes an appointment with Lawyer to discuss obtaining a divorce from Person's Spouse. During the initial consultation, Lawyer makes no effort to limit the conversation or obtain any agreement on Person's part to nonconfidentiality. During the course of the one-hour discussion, Person discusses his reasons for seeking a divorce and the nature and extent of his and Spouse's property interests. Because Person considers Lawyer's suggested fee too high, Person retains other counsel. Thereafter,

Spouse seeks Lawyer's assistance in defending against Person's divorce action. Lawyer may not accept the representation of Spouse. If Lawyer is screened as provided in § 124(2)(b) and (c), Lawyer's disqualification is not imputed to other members of Lawyer's firm (see Subsection (2)(a)).

2.   The President of Company A makes an appointment with Lawyer, who had not formerly had dealings with Company A. At the outset of the meeting, Lawyer informs President that it will first be necessary to obtain information about Company A and its affiliates and about the general nature of the legal matter to perform a conflicts check pursuant to procedures followed in Lawyer's firm. President supplies that information in a 15–minute meeting, including the information that the matter involves a contract dispute with Company B. The ensuing conflicts check reveals a conflict of interest with another Client of the firm (other than Company B), and Lawyer accordingly declines the representation. Lawyer and the other firm lawyers may continue representing Client (see Subsection (2)(a)).

3.   Same facts as Illustration 2, except that Lawyer is later approached by Company B to represent it in its contract dispute with Company A. Both Lawyer and other firm lawyers may accept the representation unless Company A had disclosed to Lawyer confidential information that could be significantly harmful to Company A in the contract dispute. Even if such a disclosure had been made, if Lawyer is screened as provided in § 124(2)(b) and (c), Lawyer's disqualification is not imputed to other members of Lawyer's firm (see Subsection (2)(a)).

4.   Same facts as Illustration 2, except that President wishes their first meeting both to discuss conflicts facts and to review Lawyer's preliminary thoughts on the merits of the contract dispute. Lawyer states willingness to do so only if Company A agrees that Lawyer would not be required to keep confidential information revealed during the preliminary discussion. President agrees, and the preliminary discussion ranges over several aspects of the dispute. Lawyer later declines the representation because of a conflict involving another firm client. Thereafter, Lawyer is approached by Company B to represent it in its contract dispute with Company A. Lawyer may accept the representation. Because of President's agreement, Lawyer is not required to keep confidential from Company B information learned during the initial consultation.

* * *

e. A lawyer's duty of reasonable care to a prospective client. When a prospective client and a lawyer discuss the possibility of representation, the lawyer might comment on such matters as whether the person has a promising claim or defense, whether the lawyer is appropriate for the matter in question, whether conflicts of interest exist and if so how they might be dealt with, the time within which action must be taken and, if the representation does not proceed, what other lawyer might represent the prospective client. Prospective clients might rely on such advice, and lawyers therefore must use reasonable care in rendering it. The lawyer must also not harm a prospective client through unreasonable delay after indicating that the lawyer might undertake the representation. What care is reasonable depends on the circumstances, including the lawyer's expertise and the time available for consideration (see § 52).

If a lawyer provides advice that is intended to be only tentative or preliminary, the lawyer should so inform the prospective client. Depending on the circumstances, the burden of removing ambiguities rests with the lawyer, particularly as to disclaiming conclusions that the client reasonably assumed from their discussion, for example whether the client has a good claim.

* * *

TOPIC 2. SUMMARY OF THE DUTIES UNDER A CLIENT–LAWYER RELATIONSHIP

* * *

§ 16. A Lawyer's Duties to a Client—In General

To the extent consistent with the lawyer's other legal duties and subject to the other provisions of this Restatement, a lawyer must, in matters within the scope of the representation:

(1) proceed in a manner reasonably calculated to advance a client's lawful objectives, as defined by the client after consultation;

(2) act with reasonable competence and diligence;

(3) comply with obligations concerning the client's confidences and property, avoid impermissible conflicting interests, deal honestly with the client, and not employ advantages arising from the client-

lawyer relationship in a manner adverse to the client; and

　　(4) fulfill valid contractual obligations to the client.

Comment:

* * *

[*c.   Goals of a representation.*]

* * *

The lawyer's duties are ordinarily limited to matters covered by the representation. A lawyer who has agreed to write a contract is not required to litigate its validity, even though the client's general objectives may ultimately be aided by resort to litigation (see §§ 14 & 19). Ordinarily the lawyer may not act beyond the scope of contemplated representation without additional authorization from the client (see § 27, Comment *e*). Nevertheless, some of the lawyer's duties survive termination of the representation (see § 33).

The lawyer's legal duties to other persons also limit duties to the client. On the rules governing conflicts of interest, see Chapter 8. A lawyer owes duties to the court or legal system and to an opposing party in litigation (see Chapters 6 & 7) and may owe duties to certain nonclients who might be injured by the lawyer's acts (see § 51). Sometimes a client's duties to other persons, for example as a trustee or class representative, may impose on the lawyer similar consequential duties (see § 14, Comment *f*). A lawyer may not do or assist an unlawful act on behalf of a client (see §§ 23, 32, & 94). Circumstances also exist in which a lawyer may refrain from pursuing the client's goals through means that the lawyer considers lawful but repugnant (see § 23, Comment *c*; § 32).

* * *

f.   Duties defined by contract. Contracts generally create or define the duties the lawyer owes the client (see Restatement Second, Agency § 376). One or more contracts between client and lawyer may specify the services the lawyer is being retained to provide, the services the lawyer is not obliged to provide, and the goals of the representation. They may address such matters as which lawyers in a law firm will provide the services; what reports are to be provided to the client; whether the lawyer will present a detailed budget for the representation; what arrangements will be made for billing statements for legal services and disbursements; what decisions will be made by the lawyer and what matters decided by the client; and what alternative-dispute-resolution methods the lawyer will explore. Such matters may also be handled by client instructions during the representation (see Topic 3). Various requirements govern client-lawyer contracts (e.g., §§ 18, 19, 22–23, 34–46, 121, & 126–127). A lawyer's intentional failure to fulfill a valid contract may in appropriate circumstances subject the lawyer to professional discipline as well as to contractual remedies.

* * *

§ 17. A Client's Duties to a Lawyer

Subject to the other provisions of this Restatement, in matters covered by the representation a client must:

(1) compensate a lawyer for services and expenses as stated in Chapter 3;

(2) indemnify the lawyer for liability to which the client has exposed the lawyer without the lawyer's fault; and

(3) fulfill any valid contractual obligations to the lawyer.

Comment:

[*a.   Scope and cross-references.*]

* * *

The duties of clients to lawyers are less extensive than those of lawyers to clients. Lawyers owe special duties because clients entrust them with important and sensitive matters, and because the legal system requires diligent and devoted performance of that trust (see § 16, Comment *b*).

* * *

§ 18. Client–Lawyer Contracts

(1) A contract between a lawyer and client concerning the client-lawyer relationship, including a contract modifying an existing contract, may be enforced by either party if the contract meets other applicable requirements, except that:

(a) if the contract or modification is made beyond a reasonable time after the lawyer has begun to represent the client in the matter (see § 38(1)), the client may avoid it unless the lawyer shows that the

contract and the circumstances of its formation were fair and reasonable to the client; and

(b) if the contract is made after the lawyer has finished providing services, the client may avoid it if the client was not informed of facts needed to evaluate the appropriateness of the lawyer's compensation or other benefits conferred on the lawyer by the contract.

(2) A tribunal should construe a contract between client and lawyer as a reasonable person in the circumstances of the client would have construed it.

Comment:

* * *

e. Contracts entered into during a representation. Client-lawyer fee contracts entered into after the matter in question is under way are subject to special scrutiny (cf. Restatement Second, Contracts § 89(a) (promise modifying contractual duty is binding if fair and equitable in view of circumstances unanticipated when contract was made)). A client might accept such a contract because it is burdensome to change lawyers during a representation. A client might hesitate to resist or even to suggest changes in new terms proposed by the lawyer, fearing the lawyer's resentment or believing that the proposals are meant to promote the client's good. A lawyer, on the other hand, usually has no justification for failing to reach a contract at the inception of the relationship or pressing need to modify an existing contract during it. The lawyer often has both the opportunity and the sophistication to propose appropriate terms before accepting a matter. A lawyer is also required to give the client at least minimal information about the fee at the outset (see § 38(1)).

The client's option under this Section to avoid the contract may be exercised during or after the representation. In particular it may be exercised during litigation about the lawyer's fee, because that is when the former client is most likely to seek new counsel and learn the facts relating to the fairness of the contract. The client may exercise the option informally, for example, by protesting against the lawyer's request for payment under the contract. A client who avoids the contract as stated here cannot then enforce its favorable terms against the lawyer, and the client is liable to the lawyer for the fair value of the lawyer's services (see § 39). A client may lose the right to avoid a contract by knowingly reaffirming it when not subject to pressure, for example after the representation concludes. If the client does not choose to avoid the contract, it remains in effect for both parties.

The lawyer may enforce the contract by persuading the tribunal that the contract was fair and reasonable to the client under the circumstances in which it was entered. The showing of fairness and reasonableness must encompass two elements. First, the lawyer must show that the client was adequately aware of the effects and any material disadvantages of the proposed contract, including, if applicable, circumstances concerning the need for modification. The more experienced the client is in such dealings with lawyers, the less the lawyer need inform the client. Likewise, less disclosure is required when an independent lawyer is advising the client about the proposed contract. It will also be relevant to sustaining the contract if the client initiated the request for the modification, such as when a client who is facing unexpected financial difficulty requests that the lawyer change an hourly fee contract to one involving a contingent fee.

Second, the lawyer must show that the client was not pressured to accede in order to avoid the problems of changing counsel, alienating the lawyer, missing a deadline or losing a significant opportunity in the matter, or because a new lawyer would have to repeat significant work for which the client owed or had paid the first lawyer. A test sometimes used has been that an agreement is voidable only if reached after the lawyer has started to perform the services. However, a contract made after the lawyer has been retained but has performed no services could be unfair because of the difficulty of obtaining other counsel in the circumstances. In general, the lawyer must show that a reasonable client might have chosen to accept the late contract, typically because it benefited the client in some substantial way (other than by relieving the client from having to find a new lawyer). Although fairness and reasonableness to the client is the issue, the strength and legitimacy of the lawyer's need for the terms of the late contract are relevant to that issue.

If the client and lawyer made an initial contract and the postinception contract in question is a modification of that contract, the client may avoid the contract unless the lawyer makes the showings indicated in Subsection (1)(a). Postinception modification beneficial to a lawyer, although justifiable in some instances, raises questions why the original contract was not itself sufficiently fair and reasonable. Yet, the scope of the representation and the relationship between client and lawyer cannot always be foreseen at the time of an initial contract. Both client and lawyer might sometimes benefit from adjusting their terms of dealing. Sometimes, indeed, a new contract may be unavoidable, as when a client asks a lawyer to expand the scope of the representation.

Illustration:

2. Client retains Lawyer to conduct a business litigation, agreeing to pay a specified hourly fee, due when the suit is over. After the suit has been brought, the defendant unexpectedly impleads a third party, and the proceedings threaten to require much more of Lawyer's time than the parties had originally expected. Lawyer and Client agree to shift to a contingent-fee arrangement, after Lawyer explains to Client that Lawyer is willing to continue on an hourly fee and points out in reasonable detail the payments by the client and incentives for the lawyer that each arrangement would give rise to in different circumstances. Soon after the contract, the defendant unexpectedly makes and Client accepts a large settlement offer. Lawyer is entitled to recover a contingent fee under the contract, even though hindsight shows that Client would have paid much less under the original hourly fee arrangement.

f. Contracts after a representation ends. Once a lawyer has finished performing legal services, the lawyer's proposal of a fee due is less coercive, although the client may remain influenced by trust that the lawyer will be fair. Such a contract will be enforced if the requirements of Subsection (1)(b) are satisfied, subject to the limits on fees discussed in Comments *a* and *d* hereto and to restrictions on abusive fee collection (see § 41; see also § 54 (limitations on contracts concerning a lawyer's liability for malpractice)).

* * *

Assuming adequate disclosure has been made, the client may accept the validity of a final bill or other postrepresentation fee proposal by paying or agreeing to pay it. If the disclosure requirements of Subsection (1)(b) have been met, the client may not argue that the fee would not have been awarded under § 39 had there been no valid contract. If the requirements of this Section have not been met, the client is not precluded by payment of a final bill from contending that the fee was unreasonably large (see § 34) or otherwise unlawful, although the client's acceptance of the bill may be admissible as evidence to controvert such a challenge (see § 42). The lawyer in such a case may still recover whatever fee is due under a valid previous contract or on the basis of quantum meruit (see § 39).

Illustration:

3. Lawyer and Client validly agree that Client will pay Lawyer $100 per hour. When the matter is resolved, Lawyer

sends a bill for $1,800 which Client pays. Later, Client learns that six of the 18 hours for which Lawyer charged were devoted to writing a memo that Lawyer wrote both for Client's matter and for another matter for another client (who was also charged for the six hours). Although the contract contains a provision that might be read to allow such double charging, the contract might also reasonably be construed to provide that Client should pay for only half of the six hours (see also § 38, Comment *d*). Client's acceptance and payment of the bill does not bar Client from challenging the amount of Lawyer's bill.

* * *

h. Construction of client-lawyer contracts. Under this Section, contracts between clients and lawyers are to be construed from the standpoint of a reasonable person in the client's circumstances. The lawyer thus bears the burden of ensuring that the contract states any terms diverging from a reasonable client's expectations. The principle applies to fee terms (see § 38) as well as other terms. It requires, for example, that a lawyer's contract to represent a client in "your suit" be construed to include representation in appropriate appeals if the lawyer had not stated that appeals were excluded.

Three reasons support this rule. First, lawyers almost always write such contracts (or state them, in the case of oral contracts) and a contract traditionally is interpreted against its author (see Restatement Second, Contracts § 206). Second, lawyers are more able than most clients to detect and repair omissions in client-lawyer contracts. Third, many lawyers consider it important to inform clients about the risks to the client that might arise from the representation, including risks unresolved by a client-lawyer contract.

Many tribunals have expressed the principle as a rule that ambiguities in client-lawyer contracts should be resolved against lawyers. That formulation can be taken to mean that the principle comes into play only when other means of interpreting the contract have been unsuccessful. Under this Section, the principle that the contract is construed as a reasonable client would understand it governs the construction of the contract in the first instance. However, this Section does not preclude reliance on the usual resources of contractual interpretation such as the language of the contract, the circumstances in which it was made, and the client's sophistication and experience in retaining and compensating lawyers or lack thereof. The contract is to be construed in light of the circumstances in which it was made, the parties' past practice and contracts, and whether it was truly negotiated. When the reasons supporting the principle are inapplicable—for

56

example, because the client had the help of its own inside legal counsel or another lawyer in drafting the contract—the principle should be correspondingly relaxed.

* * *

§ 19. Agreements Limiting Client or Lawyer Duties

(1) Subject to other requirements stated in this Restatement, a client and lawyer may agree to limit a duty that a lawyer would otherwise owe to the client if:

(a) the client is adequately informed and consents; and

(b) the terms of the limitation are reasonable in the circumstances.

(2) A lawyer may agree to waive a client's duty to pay or other duty owed to the lawyer.

Comment:

* * *

c. Limiting a representation. Clients and lawyers may define in reasonable ways the services a lawyer is to provide (see § 16), for example to handle a trial but not any appeal, counsel a client on the tax aspects of a transaction but not other aspects, or advise a client about a representation in which the primary role has been entrusted to another lawyer. Such arrangements are not waivers of a client's right to more extensive services but a definition of the services to be performed. They are therefore treated separately under many lawyer codes as contracts limiting the objectives of the representation. Clients ordinarily understand the implications and possible costs of such arrangements. The scope of many such representations requires no explanation or disclaimer of broader involvement.

Some contracts limiting the scope or objectives of a representation may harm the client, for example if a lawyer insists on agreement that a proposed suit will not include a substantial claim that reasonably should be joined. Section 19(1) hence qualifies the power of client and lawyer to limit the representation. Taken together with requirements stated in other Sections, five safeguards apply.

First, a client must be informed of any significant problems a limitation might entail, and the client must consent (see § 19(1)(a)). For example, if the lawyer is to provide only tax advice, the client must be aware that the transaction may pose non-tax issues as well as being informed of any disadvantages involved in dividing the representation among several lawyers (see also §§ 15 & 20).

Second, any contract limiting the representation is construed from the standpoint of a reasonable client (see § 18(2)).

Third, the fee charged by the lawyer must remain reasonable in view of the limited representation (see § 34).

Fourth, any change made an unreasonably long time after the representation begins must meet the more stringent tests of § 18(1) for postinception contracts or modifications.

Fifth, the terms of the limitation must in all events be reasonable in the circumstances (§ 19(1)(b)). When the client is sophisticated in such waivers, informed consent ordinarily permits the inference that the waiver is reasonable. For other clients, the requirement is met if, in addition to informed consent, the benefits supposedly obtained by the waiver—typically, a reduced legal fee or the ability to retain a particularly able lawyer—could reasonably be considered to outweigh the potential risk posed by the limitation. It is also relevant whether there were special circumstances warranting the limitation and whether it was the client or the lawyer who sought it. Also relevant is the choice available to clients; for example, if most local lawyers, but not lawyers in other communities, insist on the same limitation, client acceptance of the limitation is subject to special scrutiny.

* * *

Reasonableness also requires that limits on a lawyer's work agreed to by client and lawyer not infringe on legal rights of third persons or legal institutions. Hence, a contract limiting a lawyer's role during trial may require the tribunal's approval.

Illustrations:

* * *

2. A legal clinic offers for a small fee to have one of its lawyers (a tax specialist) conduct a half-hour review of a client's income-tax return, telling the client of the dangers or opportunities that the review reveals. The tax lawyer makes clear at the outset that the review may fail to find important tax matters and that clients can have a more complete consideration of their returns only if they arrange for a second appointment and agree to pay more. The arrangement is reasonable and permissible. The clients' consent is free and adequately informed, and clients gain

the benefit of an inexpensive but expert tax review of a matter that otherwise might well receive no expert review at all.

3.   Lawyer offers to provide tax-law advice for an hourly fee lower than most tax lawyers charge. Lawyer has little knowledge of tax law and asks Lawyer's occasional tax clients to agree to waive the requirement of reasonable competence. Such a waiver is invalid, even if clients benefit to some extent from the low price and consent freely and on the basis of adequate information. Moreover, allowing such general waivers would seriously undermine competence requirements essential for protection of the public, with little compensating gain. On prohibitions against limitations of a lawyer's liability, see § 54.

* * *

e. Contracts to increase a lawyer's duties. The general principles set forth in this Section apply also to contracts calling for more onerous obligations on the lawyer's part. A lawyer or law firm might, for example, properly agree to provide the services of a tax expert, to make an unusually large number of lawyers available for a case, or to take unusual precautions to protect the confidentiality of papers. Such a contract may not infringe the rights of others, for example by binding a lawyer to aid an unlawful act (see § 23) or to use for one client another client's secrets in a manner forbidden by § 62. Nor could the contract contravene public policy, for example by forbidding a lawyer ever to represent a category of plaintiffs even were there no valid conflict-of-interest bar (see § 13) or by forbidding the lawyer to speak on matters of public concern whenever the client disapproves.

* * *

TOPIC 3.   AUTHORITY TO MAKE DECISIONS

* * *

§ 20. A Lawyer's Duty to Inform and Consult with a Client

(1) A lawyer must keep a client reasonably informed about the matter and must consult with a client to a reasonable extent concerning decisions to be made by the lawyer under §§ 21–23.

(2) A lawyer must promptly comply with a client's reasonable requests for information.

(3) A lawyer must notify a client of decisions to be made by the client under §§ 21–23 and must explain a

matter to the extent reasonably necessary to permit the client to make informed decisions regarding the representation.

Comment:

* * *

c.   Informing and consulting with a client. A lawyer must keep a client reasonably informed about the status of a matter entrusted to the lawyer, including the progress, prospects, problems, and costs of the representation (see Restatement Second, Agency § 381). The duty includes both informing the client of important developments in a timely fashion, as well as providing a summary of information to the client at reasonable intervals so the client may be apprised of progress in the matter.

Important events might affect the objectives of the client, such as the assertion or dismissal of claims against or by the client, or they might significantly affect the client-lawyer relationship, for example issues concerning the scope of the representation, the lawyer's change of address, the dissolution of the lawyer's firm, the lawyer's serious illness, or a conflict of interest. If the lawyer's conduct of the matter gives the client a substantial malpractice claim against the lawyer, the lawyer must disclose that to the client. For example, a lawyer who fails to file suit for a client within the limitations period must so inform the client, pointing out the possibility of a malpractice suit and the resulting conflict of interest that may require the lawyer to withdraw.

The lawyer's duty to consult goes beyond dispatching information to the client. The lawyer must, when appropriate, inquire about the client's knowledge, goals, and concerns about the matter, and must be open to discussion of the appropriate course of action. A lawyer should not necessarily assume that a client wishes to press all the client's rights to the limit, regardless of cost or impact on others. The appropriate extent of consultation is itself a proper subject for consultation. The client may ask for certain information (see Comment *d*) or may express the wish not to be consulted about certain decisions. The lawyer should ordinarily honor such wishes. Even if a client fails to request information, a lawyer may be obligated to be forthcoming because the client may be unaware of the limits of the client's knowledge. Similarly, new and unforeseen circumstances may indicate that a lawyer should ask a client to reconsider a request to be left uninformed.

To the extent that the parties have not otherwise agreed, a standard of reasonableness under all the circumstances determines the appropriate measure of consultation. Reasonableness depends upon such factors as the importance of the information or decision, the extent to which disclosure or consultation has already occurred, the client's sophistication and interest, and the time and money that reporting or consulting will consume. So far as consultation about specific decisions is concerned, the lawyer should also consider the room for choice, the ability of the client to shape the decision, and the time available. When disclosure to the client—for example, of a psychiatric report—might harm the client or others, the lawyer may take that into consideration (see Comment *d* hereto; § 24 & § 46, Comment *c*).

* * *

§ 21. Allocating the Authority to Decide Between a Client and a Lawyer

As between client and lawyer:

(1) A client and lawyer may agree which of them will make specified decisions, subject to the requirements stated in §§ 18, 19, 22, 23, and other provisions of this Restatement. The agreement may be superseded by another valid agreement.

(2) A client may instruct a lawyer during the representation, subject to the requirements stated in §§ 22, 23, and other provisions of this Restatement.

(3) Subject to Subsections (1) and (2) a lawyer may take any lawful measure within the scope of representation that is reasonably calculated to advance a client's objectives as defined by the client, consulting with the client as required by § 20.

(4) A client may ratify an act of a lawyer that was not previously authorized.

Comment:

* * *

c. Agreements. This Section recognizes broad freedom of clients and lawyers to work out allocations of authority (see Restatement Second, Agency § 376). Different arrangements may be appropriate depending on the importance of the case, the client's sophistication and wish to be involved, the level of shared understandings between client and lawyer, the significance and technical complexity of the decisions in question, the need for speedy action, and other considerations. The principal limits on this freedom are §§ 22 and 23 (see also § 19).

* * *

[*d. Client instructions.*]

* * *

A lawyer is not required to carry out an instruction that the lawyer reasonably believes to be contrary to professional rules or other law (see § 23(1) & Comment *c* thereto; see also § 32, Comment *d*) or which the lawyer reasonably believes to be unethical or similarly objectionable. A lawyer may advise a client of the advantages and disadvantages of a proposed client decision and seek to dissuade the client from adhering to it (see § 94(3) & Comment *h* thereto). However, a lawyer may not continue a representation while refusing to follow a client's continuing instruction. For example, if a client instruction violates a valid client-lawyer contract (see § 19, Comment *d*), the lawyer must nonetheless follow the instruction or withdraw (see § 32(3)(g)) (see generally Restatement Second, Agency § 385(2)). A lawyer may, after obtaining any required court permission, withdraw from the representation if the instructions are considered repugnant or imprudent (see § 32(3)(f)) or render the representation unreasonably difficult (see § 32(3)(h)) or if other ground for withdrawal exists under § 32.

* * *

A client who has instructed a lawyer to act in a specified way, having received adequate advice about the risks of the proposed course of action (see § 20), cannot recover for malpractice if the lawyer follows the client's instructions and harm results to the client.

* * *

e. A lawyer's authority in the absence of an agreement or instruction. A lawyer has authority to take any lawful measure within the scope of representation (see § 19) that is reasonably calculated to advance a client's objectives as defined by the client (see § 16), unless there is a contrary agreement or instruction and unless a decision is reserved to the client (see § 22). A lawyer, for example, may decide whether to move to dismiss a complaint and what discovery to pursue or resist. Absent a contrary agreement, instruction, or legal obligation (see § 23(2)), a lawyer thus remains free to exercise restraint, to accommodate reasonable requests of opposing counsel, and generally to conduct the representation in the same manner that the lawyer would recommend to other professional colleagues.

Signing a client's name to endorse a settlement check, however, is normally unauthorized and indeed may be a crime. A lawyer's presumptive authority does not extend to retaining another lawyer outside the first lawyer's firm to represent the client (see Restatement Second, Agency § 18), although a lawyer may consult confidentially about a client's case with another lawyer.

* * *

§ 22.   Authority Reserved to a Client

(1) As between client and lawyer, subject to Subsection (2) and § 23, the following and comparable decisions are reserved to the client except when the client has validly authorized the lawyer to make the particular decision: whether and on what terms to settle a claim; how a criminal defendant should plead; whether a criminal defendant should waive jury trial; whether a criminal defendant should testify; and whether to appeal in a civil proceeding or criminal prosecution.

(2) A client may not validly authorize a lawyer to make the decisions described in Subsection (1) when other law (such as criminal-procedure rules governing pleas, jury-trial waiver, and defendant testimony) requires the client's personal participation or approval.

(3) Regardless of any contrary contract with a lawyer, a client may revoke a lawyer's authority to make the decisions described in Subsection (1).

Comment:

* * *

c. *Delegation, authorization, and ratification; settlements.* This Section forbids a lawyer to make a settlement without the client's authorization. A lawyer who does so may be liable to the client or the opposing party (see § 30) and is subject to discipline. In some circumstances, the opposing party may enforce the settlement against the client (see § 27). The Section also prohibits an irrevocable contract that the lawyer will decide on the terms of settlement. A contract that the lawyer as well as the client must approve any settlement is also invalid (but compare § 125, Comment *f* (contract restricting client's right to bargain away attorney-fee award)).

In the absence of a contrary agreement or instruction, a lawyer normally has authority to initiate or engage in settlement discussions, although not to conclude them (see § 21). A client may authorize a lawyer to negotiate a settlement that is subject to the client's approval or to settle a matter on terms indicated by the client. In class actions, special rules apply; a court, after notice and hearing, may approve a settlement negotiated by the lawyer for the class without the approval of named representatives or members of the class (see § 14, Comment *f*).

The Section allows a client to confer settlement authority on a lawyer, provided that the authorization is revocable before a settlement is reached. A client authorization must be expressed by the client or fairly implied from the dealings of lawyer and client. Thus, a client may authorize a lawyer to enter a settlement within a given range. A client is bound by a settlement reached by such a lawyer before revocation.

* * *

[*d. Decisions specified by this Section.*]

* * *

Constitutional criminal law requires decisions about three matters to be made personally by the client: whether to plead guilty, whether to waive jury trial, and whether to testify. Delegation of those decisions to a lawyer, even a revocable delegation, is not permitted. Guilty pleas in criminal prosecutions have drastic effects for the client. The legal system has strong interests in requiring the defendant to participate personally in securing pleas that are not susceptible to later claims of involuntariness. A criminal defendant's decision whether to waive the right to jury trial or to testify also involves surrender of basic constitutional rights and implicates the defendant's autonomy and participation in the trial.

Whether to appeal is an issue much like whether to settle, and that decision is likewise subject only to revocable delegation.

* * *

§ 23. Authority Reserved to a Lawyer

As between client and lawyer, a lawyer retains authority that may not be overridden by a contract with or an instruction from the client:

(1) to refuse to perform, counsel, or assist future or ongoing acts in the representation that the lawyer reasonably believes to be unlawful;

> **(2) to make decisions or take actions in the representation that the lawyer reasonably believes to be required by law or an order of a tribunal.**

Comment:

* * *

b. Rationale. This Section protects certain public interests. Subsection (1) seeks to discourage unlawful acts. Subsection (2) seeks to avoid evasions by lawyers of their professional responsibilities and accommodates the need of the legal system to expedite litigation by authorizing lawyers to make immediate decisions.

[*c. Performing or assisting acts believed to be unlawful.*]

* * *

If a client's proposed course of action is repugnant but not illegal, the lawyer may decline the representation (see § 14, Comment *b*) or, if consistent with adequate representation, may accept it only on condition that the lawyer will not be required to perform or assist such acts (see § 16). Because the lawyer is more familiar with the vicissitudes of representation and with the lawyer's own moral standards, the lawyer bears the burden of seeking such a contract. With respect to taking moral considerations and professional courtesy into account, see § 21, Comment *e*. However, a lawyer has no right to remain in a representation and insist, contrary to a client's instruction, that the client comply with the lawyer's view of the client's intended and lawful course of action. On a lawyer's right to withdraw based on repugnance or imprudence of a client's intended acts, see § 32(3)(f).

d. Matters entrusted to lawyers by law. The legal system requires counsel to act immediately and definitively in many matters. Trials and hearings cannot be adjourned for client consultation whenever a decision is necessary, nor allowed to proceed subject to reversal if a client claims not to have been consulted or to have given directions that the lawyer disobeyed.

* * *

§ 24. A Client with Diminished Capacity

> **(1) When a client's capacity to make adequately considered decisions in connection with the representation is diminished, whether because of minority, physical illness, mental disability, or other cause, the lawyer must, as far as reasonably possible, maintain a normal client-lawyer**

relationship with the client and act in the best interests of the client as stated in Subsection (2).

(2) A lawyer representing a client with diminished capacity as described in Subsection (1) and for whom no guardian or other representative is available to act, must, with respect to a matter within the scope of the representation, pursue the lawyer's reasonable view of the client's objectives or interests as the client would define them if able to make adequately considered decisions on the matter, even if the client expresses no wishes or gives contrary instructions.

(3) If a client with diminished capacity as described in Subsection (1) has a guardian or other person legally entitled to act for the client, the client's lawyer must treat that person as entitled to act with respect to the client's interests in the matter, unless:

(a) the lawyer represents the client in a matter against the interests of that person; or

(b) that person instructs the lawyer to act in a manner that the lawyer knows will violate the person's legal duties toward the client.

(4) A lawyer representing a client with diminished capacity as described in Subsection (1) may seek the appointment of a guardian or take other protective action within the scope of the representation when doing so is practical and will advance the client's objectives or interests, determined as stated in Subsection (2).

Comment:

* * *

c. Maintaining a normal client-lawyer relationship so far as possible. Disabilities in making decisions vary from mild to totally incapacitating; they may impair a client's ability to decide matters generally or only with respect to some decisions at some times; and they may be caused by childhood, old age, physical illness, retardation, chemical dependency, mental illness, or other factors. Clients should not be unnecessarily deprived of their right to control their own affairs on account of such disabilities. Lawyers, moreover, should be careful not to construe as proof of disability a client's insistence on a view of the client's welfare that a lawyer considers unwise or otherwise at variance with the lawyer's own views.

When a client with diminished capacity is capable of understanding and communicating, the lawyer should maintain the flow of information and consultation as much as circumstances allow (see § 20). The lawyer should take reasonable steps to elicit the client's own views on decisions necessary to the representation. Sometimes the use of a relative, therapist, or other intermediary may facilitate communication (see §§ 70 & 71). Even when the lawyer is empowered to make decisions for the client (see Comment *d*), the lawyer should, if practical, communicate the proposed decision to the client so that the client will have a chance to comment, remonstrate, or seek help elsewhere. A lawyer may properly withhold from a disabled client information that would harm the client, for example when showing a psychiatric report to a mentally-ill client would be likely to cause the client to attempt suicide, harm another person, or otherwise act unlawfully (see § 20, Comment *b*, & § 46, Comment *c*).

A lawyer for a client with diminished capacity may be retained by a parent, spouse, or other relative of the client. Even when that person is not also a co-client, the lawyer may provide confidential client information to the person to the extent appropriate in providing representation to the client (see § 61). If the disclosure is to be made to a nonclient and there is a significant risk that the information may be used adversely to the client, the lawyer should consult with the client concerning such disclosure.

* * *

e. Seeking appointment of a guardian. When a client's diminished capacity is severe and no other practical method of protecting the client's best interests is available, a lawyer may petition an appointment of a guardian or other representative to make decisions for the client. A general or limited power of attorney may sometimes be used to avoid the expense and possible embarrassment of a guardianship.

* * *

[*f. Representing a client for whom a guardian or similar person may act.*]

* * *

When a guardian retains a lawyer to represent the guardian, the guardian is the client.

* * *

67

TOPIC 4. A LAWYER'S AUTHORITY
TO ACT FOR A CLIENT

* * *

§ 25. Appearance Before a Tribunal

A lawyer who enters an appearance before a tribunal on behalf of a person is presumed to represent that person as a client. The presumption may be rebutted.

Comment:

* * *

d. Section inapplicable as between a client and a lawyer. This Section does not apply to proceedings in which the presumption is not necessary to protect the rights of third persons, for example with respect to lawyer-respondents in disciplinary proceedings or in litigation between lawyer and client, where the person seeking relief usually bears the burdens of persuasion and of coming forward with evidence. If, for example, a lawyer brings a suit for fees against a person who denies retaining the lawyer, the lawyer must prove the retainer. If a lawyer is charged with appearing without authority, the person seeking relief must prove the lack of authority.

* * *

§ 26. A Lawyer's Actual Authority

A lawyer's act is considered to be that of a client in proceedings before a tribunal or in dealings with third persons when:

  (1) the client has expressly or impliedly authorized the act;

  (2) authority concerning the act is reserved to the lawyer as stated in § 23; or

  (3) the client ratifies the act.

Comment:

a. Scope, cross-references, and terminology. In general, a client is bound by a lawyer's acts in dealings with third persons discussed in this Section or, under § 27, by giving the lawyer an appearance of authority. For situations in which a client may avoid responsibility for authorized acts because of a lawyer's misconduct, see § 29. The word "act" includes failures to act, for example when a lawyer does not object to something done in court.

* * *

§ 27. A Lawyer's Apparent Authority

A lawyer's act is considered to be that of the client in proceedings before a tribunal or in dealings with a third person if the tribunal or third person reasonably assumes that the lawyer is authorized to do the act on the basis of the client's (and not the lawyer's) manifestations of such authorization.

Comment:

* * *

[*b. Rationale.*]

* * *

Recognizing a lawyer as agent creates a risk that a client will be bound by an act the client never intended to authorize. Several safeguards are therefore included in the apparent-authority principle. First, the client must in fact have retained the lawyer or given the third party reason to believe that the client has done so. Second, the client's own acts (including the act of retaining the lawyer) must have warranted a reasonable observer in believing that the client authorized the lawyer to act. Third, the third person must in fact have such a belief. The test thus includes both an objective and a subjective element (see Restatement Second, Agency § 27). In some circumstances courts will take into account the lawyer's lack of actual authority in deciding whether to vacate a default (see § 29). If the client suffers detriment from a lawyer's act performed with apparent but not actual authority, the client can recover from the lawyer for acting beyond the scope of the lawyer's authority (see Comment *f* hereto & § 30; Restatement Second, Agency § 383).

* * *

d. Lawyer's apparent authority to settle and perform other acts reserved to a client. Generally a client is not bound by a settlement that the client has not authorized a lawyer to make by express, implied, or apparent authority (and that is not validated by later ratification under § 26(3)). Merely retaining a lawyer does not create apparent authority in the lawyer to perform acts governed by § 22. When a lawyer purports to enter a settlement binding on the client but lacks authority to do so, the burden of inconvenience resulting if the

69

client repudiates the settlement is properly left with the opposing party, who should know that settlements are normally subject to approval by the client and who has no manifested contrary indication from the client. The opposing party can protect itself by obtaining clarification of the lawyer's authority. Refusing to uphold a settlement reached without the client's authority means that the case remains open, while upholding such a settlement deprives the client of the right to have the claim resolved on other terms.

* * *

§ 28. A Lawyer's Knowledge; Notification to a Lawyer; and Statements of a Lawyer

(1) Information imparted to a lawyer during and relating to the representation of a client is attributed to the client for the purpose of determining the client's rights and liabilities in matters in which the lawyer represents the client, unless those rights or liabilities require proof of the client's personal knowledge or intentions or the lawyer's legal duties preclude disclosure of the information to the client.

(2) Unless applicable law otherwise provides, a third person may give notification to a client, in a matter in which the client is represented by a lawyer, by giving notification to the client's lawyer, unless the third person knows of circumstances reasonably indicating that the lawyer's authority to receive notification has been abrogated.

(3) A lawyer's unprivileged statement is admissible in evidence against a client as if it were the client's statement if either:

(a) the client authorized the lawyer to make a statement concerning the subject; or

(b) the statement concerns a matter within the scope of the representation and was made by the lawyer during it.

Comment:

* * *

[b.   Attribution of a lawyer's knowledge to a client.]

* * *

A client is not charged with a lawyer's knowledge concerning a transaction in which the lawyer does not represent the client (see Restatement Second, Agency § 272). The knowledge of a lawyer not personally engaged in representing a client but in the same firm is not attributed to the client, unless the lawyer acquiring the knowledge is aware that the information is relevant to his or her firm's representation of the client (see Restatement Second, Agency § 275, Comment *d*). The client might show that the lawyer had forgotten the information or did not perceive its relevance, whenever a client could introduce similar evidence about the client's own state of knowledge. For other limits on attribution, see Restatement Second, Agency §§ 273, 277–280, and 282.

* * *

§ 29.   A Lawyer's Act or Advice as Mitigating or Avoiding a Client's Responsibility

(1) **When a client's intent or mental state is in issue, a tribunal may consider otherwise admissible evidence of a lawyer's advice to the client.**

(2) **In deciding whether to impose a sanction on a person or to relieve a person from a criminal or civil ruling, default, or judgment, a tribunal may consider otherwise admissible evidence to prove or disprove that the lawyer who represented the person did so inadequately or contrary to the client's instructions.**

Comment:

a.   Scope and cross-references. Clients sometimes can defend themselves by blaming their lawyer. Law might permit a client charged with malicious or knowingly unlawful conduct to defend by showing that counsel advised that the conduct was lawful. A client involved in litigation might seek to avoid a sanction on the ground that counsel rather than client has been to blame for a default. In both situations, tribunals are often reluctant to let a client escape responsibility but will nevertheless consider evidence to that effect.

* * *

c.   Advice of counsel. Erroneous legal advice is often no defense, just as ignorance of the law is usually no defense. Nevertheless, in some instances a client can introduce evidence of counsel's advice when the client's knowing violation of law is in dispute, as it often is in criminal cases. The same principle often applies when the client is charged, criminally or civilly, with malice or the like. In actions for malicious prosecution or wrongful use of civil proceedings, for example, if a client relied in good faith on a lawyer's advice that there were good grounds to institute litigation (based on the client's full disclosure), such reliance conclusively establishes probable cause (see Restatement Second, Torts §§ 666 & 675(b)). Usually, however, counsel's advice is merely evidence to be considered in appraising the client's state of mind.

* * *

§ 30. A Lawyer's Liability to a Third Person for Conduct on Behalf of a Client

(1) For improper conduct while representing a client, a lawyer is subject to professional discipline as stated in § 5, to civil liability as stated in Chapter 4, and to prosecution as provided in the criminal law (see § 7).

(2) Unless at the time of contracting the lawyer or third person disclaimed such liability, a lawyer is subject to liability to third persons on contracts the lawyer entered into on behalf of a client if:

(a) the client's existence or identity was not disclosed to the third person; or

(b) the contract is between the lawyer and a third person who provides goods or services used by lawyers and who, as the lawyer knows or reasonably should know, relies on the lawyer's credit.

(3) A lawyer is subject to liability to a third person for damages for loss proximately caused by the lawyer's acting without authority from a client under § 26 if:

(a) the lawyer tortiously misrepresents to the third person that the lawyer has authority to make a contract, conveyance, or affirmation on behalf of the client and the third person reasonably relies on the misrepresentation; or

(b) the lawyer purports to make a contract, conveyance, or affirmation on behalf of the client, unless the lawyer manifests that the lawyer does not warrant that the lawyer is authorized to act or the other party knows that the lawyer is not authorized to act.

Comment:

* * *

[*b. A lawyer's liability on contracts.*]

* * *

Even when the client is a disclosed principal, a lawyer is liable for the compensation of a court reporter, printer, expert, appraiser, surveyor, or other person the lawyer has hired who provides goods or services used by lawyers, and who when doing so reasonably relies on the lawyer's credit as stated in Subsection (2)(b). Liability attaches unless the lawyer disclaims liability or the circumstances show that the third person did not rely on the lawyer's credit, for example if the lawyer was inside legal counsel of the client. Merely disclosing the client's name does not convey that the client rather than the lawyer is to pay. Such persons are likely to rely on the credit of the lawyer because they regularly deal with lawyers, while investigating the reliability of the client might be costly. On a lawyer's right to indemnity from the client, see § 17(2) and § 38, Comment *e*. On a lawyer's advancing litigation expenses, see § 36. The lawyer's liability does not foreclose the supplier from proceeding, additionally or alternatively, against the client in whose behalf the lawyer obtained the goods or services.

* * *

TOPIC 5. ENDING A CLIENT–LAWYER RELATIONSHIP

* * *

§ 31. Termination of a Lawyer's Authority

(1) A lawyer must comply with applicable law requiring notice to or permission of a tribunal when terminating a representation and with an order of a tribunal requiring the representation to continue.

(2) Subject to Subsection (1) and § 33, a lawyer's actual authority to represent a client ends when:

(a) the client discharges the lawyer;

(b) the client dies or, in the case of a corporation or similar organization, loses its capacity to function as such;

(c) the lawyer withdraws;

(d) the lawyer dies or becomes physically or mentally incapable of providing representation, is disbarred or suspended from practicing law, or is ordered by a tribunal to cease representing a client; or

(e) the representation ends as provided by contract or because the lawyer has completed the contemplated services.

(3) A lawyer's apparent authority to act for a client
with respect to another person ends when the other person knows or should know of facts from which it can be
reasonably inferred that the lawyer lacks actual authority, including knowledge of any event described in Subsection (2).

Comment:

* * *

b.   Rationale. Just as mutual consent is usually a prerequisite to
creating the client-lawyer relationship, the end of such consent usually
ends the relationship. Consent might end because client or lawyer
withdraws consent or becomes incapable of giving a valid consent (but
compare Comment *e*). Alternatively, the lawyer might have completed
the representation or have become incapable of providing services to
completion. However, a tribunal might in some circumstances deny a
lawyer leave to withdraw. The rules stated in this Section also protect
third persons who reasonably rely on a lawyer's apparent authority
after the lawyer's actual authority has ended. For the rationale of the
apparent-authority rules, see § 27, Comment *b*.

* * *

e.   A client's death or incompetence. A client's death terminates a
lawyer's actual authority (see Restatement Second, Agency § 120).
The rights of a deceased client pass to other persons—executors, for
example—who can, if they wish, revive the representation. Procedural
rules usually provide for substitution for the deceased client in actions
to which the client was a party. The lawyer for the deceased client
must cooperate in such a transition and seek to protect the deceased
client's property and other rights (see § 33). In extraordinary circumstances, the lawyer may exercise initiative, for example taking an
appeal when the time for doing so would expire before a personal
representative could be appointed (see § 33, Comment *b*).

* * *

[*f.   A lawyer's withdrawal.*]

* * *

When a client retains a lawyer who practices with a firm, the
presumption is that both the lawyer and the firm have been retained

(see § 14, Comment *h*). Hence, when a lawyer involved in a representation leaves the firm, the client can ordinarily choose whether to be represented by that lawyer, by lawyers remaining at the firm, by neither, or by both. In the absence of client direction, whether the departing lawyer continues to have authority to act for the client depends on the circumstances, including whether the client regarded the lawyer to be in charge of the matter, whether other lawyers working on the matter also leave, whether firm lawyers continue to represent the client in other matters, and whether the lawyer had filed an appearance for the client with a tribunal. Similar principles apply when a firm dissolves. When a lawyer leaves a large firm, for example, it can usually be assumed that, absent contrary client instructions or previous contract, the firm continues to represent the client in pending representations and the lawyer does not.

* * *

[*h. Termination by completion of contemplated services.*]

* * *

The course of dealing might not clearly indicate what services were contemplated in the representation or whether the lawyer has a continuing duty to advise the client. Such uncertainty could lead to clients assuming that they were still being represented. Because contracts with a client are to be construed from the client's viewpoint (see § 18), the client's reasonable understanding of the scope of the representation controls. The client's relative sophistication in employing lawyers or lack thereof is relevant.

* * *

§ 32. Discharge by a Client and Withdrawal by a Lawyer

(1) **Subject to Subsection (5), a client may discharge a lawyer at any time.**

(2) **Subject to Subsection (5), a lawyer may not represent a client or, where representation has commenced, must withdraw from the representation of a client if:**

(a) **the representation will result in the lawyer's violating rules of professional conduct or other law;**

(b) **the lawyer's physical or mental condition materially impairs the lawyer's ability to represent the client; or**

(c) **the client discharges the lawyer.**

(3) **Subject to Subsections (4) and (5), a lawyer may withdraw from representing a client if:**

(a) withdrawal can be accomplished without material adverse effect on the interests of the client;

(b) the lawyer reasonably believes withdrawal is required in circumstances stated in Subsection (2);

(c) the client gives informed consent;

(d) the client persists in a course of action involving the lawyer's services that the lawyer reasonably believes is criminal, fraudulent, or in breach of the client's fiduciary duty;

(e) the lawyer reasonably believes the client has used or threatens to use the lawyer's services to perpetrate a crime or fraud;

(f) the client insists on taking action that the lawyer considers repugnant or imprudent;

(g) the client fails to fulfill a substantial financial or other obligation to the lawyer regarding the lawyer's services and the lawyer has given the client reasonable warning that the lawyer will withdraw unless the client fulfills the obligation;

(h) the representation has been rendered unreasonably difficult by the client or by the irreparable breakdown of the client-lawyer relationship; or

(i) other good cause for withdrawal exists.

(4) In the case of permissive withdrawal under Subsections (3)(f)-(i), a lawyer may not withdraw if the harm that withdrawal would cause significantly exceeds the harm to the lawyer or others in not withdrawing.

(5) Notwithstanding Subsections (1)-(4), a lawyer must comply with applicable law requiring notice to or permission of a tribunal when terminating a representation and with a valid order of a tribunal requiring the representation to continue.

Comment:

* * *

b. Discharge by a client. A client may always discharge a lawyer, regardless of cause and regardless of any agreement between them. A client is not forced to entrust matters to an unwanted lawyer. However, a client's discharge of a lawyer is not always without adverse consequence, for example when a tribunal declines to appoint new counsel for an indigent criminal defendant or denies a continuance for the client to seek new counsel.

* * *

d. Approval of a tribunal. Rules of tribunals typically require approval of the tribunal when a lawyer withdraws from a pending matter (see § 31, Comment *c*, & § 105). In applying to a tribunal for approval of withdrawal, a lawyer must observe the requirements of confidentiality (see § 60), unless an exception (see §§ 61–67) applies. In applying to withdraw under Subsection (3)(f), for example, it would not be permissible for the lawyer to state that the client intended to pursue a repugnant objective. A lawyer therefore will often be limited to the statement that professional considerations motivate the application.

* * *

e. A lawyer's reasonable belief. Even if a tribunal concludes that a lawyer was required to withdraw under this Section, the lawyer is not subject to professional discipline or liability to a client if the lawyer reasonably believed, based on adequate investigation and consideration of the relevant facts and law, that withdrawal was not required. Also, a lawyer is not subject to discipline or liability for withdrawing if the lawyer reasonably believed, after similar investigation and consideration, that cause existed. However, when a tribunal is determining whether to compel or allow withdrawal, its concern is not with the lawyer's reasonable belief (except under Subsections (3)(b), (d), & (e) and Subsection (4)) but with whether the requirements stated in the Section have in fact been satisfied.

* * *

h(i). Permissive withdrawal—in general. The rules on lawyer withdrawal are derived primarily from lawyer codes, which list grounds for mandatory and permissive withdrawal. Read literally, those rules might appear to draw a line between permissive and prohibited withdrawal, suggesting that when a stated ground for permissive withdrawal exists, the lawyer may do so regardless of effect on the client. However, given the fiduciary nature of the client-lawyer relationship, in instances of permissive withdrawal under Subsections (3)(f)-(i), the lawyer may not withdraw when the lawyer reasonably holds the stated belief of a significant disproportion between the detrimental effects that would be imposed on the client by the contemplated withdrawal as against detrimental effects that would be imposed on the lawyer or others by continuing the representation. On a lawyer's reasonable belief, see Comment *e* hereto. On withdrawal with client consent, see Comment *i* hereto. On withdrawal for a client's failure to pay the lawyer, see Comment *k* hereto.

Before withdrawing a lawyer must seek to protect the interests of the client by communicating, if feasible, with the client concerning the basis for withdrawal and requesting any corrective action that the client might be able to take (see Comment *n* hereto). For example, before withdrawal for nonpayment of fees (see Comment *k* hereto), the lawyer must request payment and warn that nonfulfillment might lead to withdrawal. The lawyer must also secure the tribunal's approval when applicable law so requires (see Comment *d* hereto) and must protect the client's interests during and after withdrawal (see § 33).

* * *

[*i. Withdrawal with a client's consent.*]

* * *

A lawyer may more readily withdraw when another lawyer is immediately available, for example another lawyer in the same firm. In such a situation, an informed client's consent to the withdrawal ordinarily can be assumed if the client makes no objection. Nevertheless, the client may insist that any lawyer representing the client continue to do so unless the lawyer has cause for withdrawal or can withdraw without material adverse effect on the interests of the client under Subsection (3).

* * *

l. Client obstruction and irreparable breakdown of the relationship. A lawyer may withdraw when a client renders the representation unreasonably difficult, for example, by refusing to communicate with the lawyer or persistently misrepresenting facts to the lawyer. The considerations stated in Comment *h(i)* are relevant in determining whether a client's course of conduct renders the representation unreasonably difficult. Irreparable breakdown of the client-lawyer relationship due to other causes is likewise a ground for withdrawal. However, withdrawal is not warranted simply because a client disagrees with a lawyer, expresses worry or suspicion, or refuses to accept the lawyer's advice about a decision that is to be made by the client (see §§ 21 & 22). Withdrawal is permissible, for example, if the client's refusal to disclose facts to the lawyer threatens to involve the lawyer in fraud or other unlawful acts (compare Comment *f* hereto), compromises the lawyer's professional reputation, or otherwise renders the representation unreasonably difficult.

m. Other good cause for withdrawal. Other grounds for withdrawal might exist, for example inability to work with co-counsel or the lawyer's retirement from law practice or appointment as a judge. In any such instance, the considerations stated in Comment *h(i)* apply.

Continuing to represent a client might impose on a lawyer an unreasonable financial burden unexpected by client and lawyer at the outset of the representation. That is relevant to good cause but not conclusive. Ordinarily, lawyers are better suited than clients to foresee and provide for the burdens of representation. The burdens of uncertainty should therefore ordinarily fall on lawyers rather than on clients unless they are attributable to client misconduct. That a representation will require more work than the lawyer contemplated when the fee was fixed is not ground for withdrawal. However, some jurisdictions regard an unreasonable financial burden as itself good cause for withdrawal.

* * *

§ 33. A Lawyer's Duties When a Representation Terminates

(1) In terminating a representation, a lawyer must take steps to the extent reasonably practicable to protect the client's interests, such as giving notice to the client of the termination, allowing time for employment of other counsel, surrendering papers and property to which the client is entitled, and refunding any advance payment of fee the lawyer has not earned.

(2) Following termination of a representation, a lawyer must:

(a) observe obligations to a former client such as those dealing with client confidences (see Chapter 5), conflicts of interest (see Chapter 8), client property and documents (see §§ 44–46), and fee collection (see § 41);

(b) take no action on behalf of a former client without new authorization and give reasonable notice, to those who might otherwise be misled, that the lawyer lacks authority to act for the client;

(c) take reasonable steps to convey to the former client any material communication the lawyer receives relating to the matter involved in the representation; and

(d) take no unfair advantage of a former client by abusing knowledge or trust acquired by means of the representation.

Comment:

* * *

b. Protecting a client's interests when a representation ends. Ending a representation before a lawyer has completed a matter usually poses special problems for a client. Beyond consultation required before withdrawal (see § 32, Comment *n*), in the process of withdrawal itself a lawyer might be required to consult with the client and engage in other protective measures. New counsel must be found, papers and property retrieved or transferred, imminent deadlines extended, and tribunals and opposing parties notified to deal with new counsel. Lawyers must therefore take reasonably appropriate and practicable measures to protect clients when representation terminates.

* * *

h. Conveying communications to a former client. After termination a lawyer might receive a notice, letter, or other communication intended for a former client. The lawyer must use reasonable efforts to forward the communication. The lawyer ordinarily must also inform the source of the communication that the lawyer no longer represents the former client (see Comment *g* hereto). The lawyer must likewise notify a former client if a third person seeks to obtain material relating to the representation that is still in the lawyer's custody.

A lawyer has no general continuing obligation to pass on to a former client information relating to the former representation. The lawyer might, however, have such an obligation if the lawyer continues to represent the client in other matters or under a continuing relationship. Whether such an obligation exists regarding particular information depends on such factors as the client's reasonable expectations; the scope, magnitude, and duration of the client-lawyer relationship; the evident significance of the information to the client; the burden on the lawyer in making disclosure; and the likelihood that the client will receive the information from another source.

* * *

CHAPTER 3

CLIENT AND LAWYER: THE FINANCIAL AND PROPERTY RELATIONSHIP

TOPIC 1. LEGAL CONTROLS ON ATTORNEY FEES

---

* * *

TOPIC 1. LEGAL CONTROLS ON ATTORNEY FEES

* * *

§ 34. Reasonable and Lawful Fees

A lawyer may not charge a fee larger than is reasonable in the circumstances or that is prohibited by law.

81

Comment:

* * *

[c.   *Unenforceable fee contracts.*]

* * *

The lawyer codes state factors bearing on the reasonableness of fee arrangements. ABA Model Rules of Professional Conduct, Rule 1.5(a) (1983), and ABA Model Code of Professional Responsibility, DR 2–106(B) (1969), enumerate the following factors: "(1) the time and labor required, the novelty and difficulty of the questions involved, and the skill requisite to perform the legal service properly; (2) the likelihood, if apparent to the client, that the acceptance of the particular employment will preclude other employment by the lawyer; (3) the fee customarily charged in the locality for similar legal services; (4) the amount involved and the results obtained; (5) the time limitations imposed by the client or by the circumstances; (6) the nature and length of the professional relationship with the client; (7) the experience, reputation, and ability of the lawyer or lawyers performing the services; and (8) whether the fee is fixed or contingent." Other factors might also be relevant, such as the client's sophistication, the disclosures made to the client, and the client's ability to pay.

Those factors might be viewed as responding to three questions. First, when the contract was made, did the lawyer afford the client a free and informed choice? Relevant circumstances include whether the client was sophisticated in entering into such arrangements, whether the client was a fiduciary whose beneficiary deserves special protection, whether the client had a reasonable opportunity to seek another lawyer, whether the lawyer adequately explained the probable cost and other implications of the proposed fee contract (see § 38), whether the client understood the alternatives available from this lawyer and others, and whether the lawyer explained the benefits and drawbacks of the proposed legal services without misleading intimations. Fees agreed to by clients sophisticated in entering into such arrangements (such as a fee contract made by inside legal counsel in behalf of a corporation) should almost invariably be found reasonable.

Second, does the contract provide for a fee within the range commonly charged by other lawyers in similar representations? To the extent competition for legal services exists among lawyers in the relevant community, a tribunal can assume that the competition has produced an appropriate level of fee charges. A stated hourly rate, for example, should be compared with the hourly rates charged by lawyers of comparable qualifications for comparable services, and the number of hours claimed should be compared with those commonly invested in similar representations. The percentage in a contingent-fee contract should be compared to percentages commonly used in similar representations for similar services (for example, preparing and trying a novel products-liability claim). Whatever the fee basis, it is also relevant whether accepting the case was likely to foreclose other work or to attract it and whether pursuing the matter at the usual fee was reasonable in light of the client's needs and resources. See § 39, Comment *b*, which discusses the fair-value standard applied in quantum meruit cases and possible defects of a market standard.

Third, was there a subsequent change in circumstances that made the fee contract unreasonable? Although reasonableness is usually assessed as of the time the contract was entered into, later events might be relevant. Some fee contracts make the fee turn on later events. Accordingly, the reasonableness of a fee due under an hourly rate contract, for example, depends on whether the number of hours the lawyer worked was reasonable in light of the matter and client. It is also relevant whether the lawyer provided poor service, such as might make unreasonable a fee that would be appropriate for better services, or services that were better or more successful than normally would have been expected (compare §§ 37 & 40 concerning forfeiture of fees). Finally, events not known or contemplated when the contract was made can render the contract unreasonably favorable to the lawyer or, occasionally, to the client. Compare Restatement Second, Contracts §§ 152–154 and 261–265 (doctrines of mistake, supervening impracticality, supervening frustration). To determine what events client and lawyer contemplated, their contract must be construed in light of its goals and circumstances and in light of the possibilities discussed with the client (see id. §§ 294 & 50). A contingent-fee contract, for example, allocates to the lawyer the risk that the case will require much time and produce no recovery and to the client the risk that the case will require little time and produce a substantial fee. Events within that range of risks, such as a high recovery, do not make unreasonable a contract that was reasonable when made.

Illustration:

1. Bank Clerk is charged with criminal embezzlement and retains Lawyer to defend against the charges for a $15,000 flat fee. The next day another employee confesses to having taken the money, and the prosecutor (not knowing of Lawyer's retention by Bank Clerk) immediately drops the charges against Bank Clerk. Lawyer has done nothing on the case beyond speaking with Bank Clerk. In the absence of special circumstances, such as prior discussion of this possibility or the lawyer having rejected another

representation offering a comparable fee in reliance on this engagement, it would be unreasonable for Lawyer to be paid $15,000 for doing so little. Client must pay the fair value of Lawyer's services (see § 39), but more than that is not due and the lawyer must refund the excess if already paid (see § 42). If, however, the prosecutor dropped the charges as the result of a plea bargain negotiated by Lawyer, the rapid disposition would not render unreasonable an otherwise proper $15,000 flat fee. A negotiated disposition without trial is a common event that parties are assumed to contemplate when they agree that the lawyer will receive a flat fee.

* * *

e. *Retainer fees.* The term "retainer" has been employed to describe different fee arrangements. As used in this Restatement, an "engagement retainer fee" is a fee paid, apart from any other compensation, to ensure that a lawyer will be available for the client if required. An engagement retainer must be distinguished from a lump-sum fee constituting the entire payment for a lawyer's service in a matter and from an advance payment from which fees will be subtracted (see § 38, Comment *g*). A fee is an engagement retainer only if the lawyer is to be additionally compensated for actual work, if any, performed. In some jurisdictions, an engagement retainer is referred to as a "general" or "special" retainer. On the effect of premature termination of the representation on an engagement-retainer fee, see § 40.

An engagement-retainer fee satisfies the requirements of this Section if it bears a reasonable relationship to the income the lawyer sacrifices or expense the lawyer incurs by accepting it, including such costs as turning away other clients (for reasons of time or due to conflicts of interest), hiring new associates so as to be able to take the client's matter, keeping up with the relevant field, and the like. When a client experienced in retaining and compensating lawyers agrees to pay an engagement-retainer fee, the fee will almost invariably be found to fall within the range of reasonableness. Engagement-retainer fees agreed to by clients not so experienced should be more closely scrutinized to ensure that they are no greater than is reasonable and that the engagement-retainer fee is not being used to evade the rules requiring a lawyer to return unearned fees (see § 38, Comment *g*, & § 40, Illustrations 2A & 2B). In some circumstances, large engagement-retainer fees constitute unenforceable liquidated-damage clauses (see Restatement Second, Contracts § 356(1)) or are subject to challenge in the client's bankruptcy proceeding.

* * *

g. Unlawful fees. A fee that violates a statute or rule regulating the size of fees is impermissible under this Section. General principles governing the enforceability of contracts that violate legal requirements are set forth in Restatement Second, Contracts §§ 178–185. Statutes or rules in some jurisdictions control the percentage of a contingent fee, generally or in particular categories such as worker-compensation claims or medical-malpractice litigation. Other common legislation limits the fees chargeable in proceedings against the government, forbids contingent fees for legislative lobbying, prohibits public defenders or defense counsel paid by the government from accepting payment from their clients, and prohibits lawyers representing wards of the court from accepting payments not approved by the court. A fee for a service a lawyer may not lawfully perform, such as questioning jurors after a trial where that is forbidden (see § 115), is likewise unlawful regardless of the size of the fee (see Restatement Second, Contracts §§ 192 & 193). A lawyer may not require a client to pay a fee larger than that contracted for, unless the client validly agrees to the increase.

That a fee contract violates some legal requirement does not necessarily render it unenforceable. The requirement might be one not meant to protect clients or one for which refusal to enforce is an inappropriate sanction. For example, when a lawyer violates a lawyer-code requirement that a fee contract be in writing but the client does not dispute the amount owed under it, that violation alone should not make the contract unenforceable. When only certain parts of a contract between client and lawyer contravene the law, moreover, the lawful parts remain enforceable, except where the lawyer should forfeit the whole fee (see § 37).

* * *

§ 35. Contingent–Fee Arrangements

(1) A lawyer may contract with a client for a fee the size or payment of which is contingent on the outcome of a matter, unless the contract violates § 34 or another provision of this Restatement or the size or payment of the fee is:

(a) contingent on success in prosecuting or defending a criminal proceeding; or

(b) contingent on a specified result in a divorce proceeding or a proceeding concerning custody of a child.

(2) Unless the contract construed in the circumstances indicates otherwise, when a lawyer has contracted for a contingent fee, the lawyer is entitled to receive the specified fee only when and to the extent the client receives payment.

Comment:

[a.   Scope and cross-references.]

* * *

A contingent-fee contract is one providing for a fee the size or payment of which is conditioned on some measure of the client's success. Examples include a contract that a lawyer will receive one-third of a client's recovery and a contract that the lawyer will be paid by the hour but receive a bonus should a stated favorable result occur (see § 34, Comment *a*, & § 35).

b.   Rationale. Contingent-fee arrangements perform three valuable functions. First, they enable persons who could not otherwise afford counsel to assert their rights, paying their lawyers only if the assertion succeeds. Second, contingent fees give lawyers an additional incentive to seek their clients' success and to encourage only those clients with claims having a substantial likelihood of succeeding. Third, such fees enable a client to share the risk of losing with a lawyer, who is usually better able to assess the risk and to bear it by undertaking similar arrangements in other cases (cf. Restatement Second, Agency § 445).

Although contingent fees were formerly prohibited in the United States and are still prohibited in many other nations, the prohibition reflects circumstances not present in the contemporary United States. Many other nations routinely award attorney fees to the winning party and often have relatively low, standardized and regulated attorney fees, thus providing an alternative means of access to the legal system, which is not generally available here. Those nations might also regard civil litigation as more of an evil and less of an opportunity for the protection of rights than do lawmakers here. Contingent fees are thus criticized there as stirring up litigation and fostering overzealous advocacy.

* * *

c.   Reasonable contingent fees. A contingent fee may permissibly be greater than what an hourly fee lawyer of similar qualifications would receive for the same representation. A contingent-fee lawyer bears the risk of receiving no pay if the client loses and is entitled to compensation for bearing that risk. Nor is a contingent fee necessarily unreasonable because the lawyer devoted relatively little time to a representation, for the customary terms of such arrangements commit the lawyer to provide necessary effort without extra pay if a relatively large expenditure of the lawyer's time were entailed. However, large fees unearned by either effort or a significant period of risk are unreasonable (see § 34, Comment c, & Illustration 1 thereto).

A tribunal will find a contingent fee unreasonable due to a defect in the calculation of risk in two kinds of cases in particular: those in which there was a high likelihood of substantial recovery by trial or settlement, so that the lawyer bore little risk of nonpayment; and those in which the client's recovery was likely to be so large that the lawyer's fee would clearly exceed the sum appropriate to pay for services performed and risks assumed. A lawyer's failure to disclose to the client the general likelihood of recovery, the approximate probable size of any recovery, or the availability of alternative fee systems can also bear upon whether the fee is reasonable.

Illustration:

1. Client seeks Lawyer's help in collecting life-insurance benefits under a $15,000 policy on Client's spouse and agrees to pay a one-third contingent fee. There is no reasonable ground to contest that the benefits are due, the claim has not been contested by the insurer, and when Lawyer presents it the insurer pays without dispute. The $5,000 fee provided by the client-lawyer contract is not reasonable.

[d. *Reasonable rate and basis of a contingent fee.*]

* * *

The rule stated in Subsection (2) also requires that, unless the contract indicates otherwise, a contingent-fee lawyer is to receive the specified share of the client's actual-damages recovery. For that purpose, recovery includes damages, restitution, back pay, similar equitable payments, and amounts received in settlement. Unless the contract with the client indicates otherwise, the lawyer is not entitled to the specified percentage of items such as costs and attorney fees that are not usually considered damages. In the absence of prior agreement to the contrary, the amount of the client's recovery is computed net of any offset, such as a recovery by an opposing party on a counterclaim.

Illustrations:

2.   Client agrees to pay Lawyer "35 percent of the recovery" in a suit. The court awards Client $20,000 in damages, $500 in costs for disbursements, and $1,000 in attorney fees because of the defendant's discovery abuses. Lawyer is entitled to receive a contingent fee of $7,000 (35% of $20,000), but not 35 percent of the costs' payments. If Lawyer advanced the $500 costs in question, Client must reimburse Lawyer unless their contract validly provides to the contrary (see § 38, Comment *e*). Whether Lawyer is entitled to recover a portion of the $1,000 attorney-fee award requires both interpretation of the fee contract and consideration of the nature of the fee-shifting award (see § 38(3)(b) & Comment *f* thereto).

3.   Same facts as in Illustration 2, except that Lawyer has also expended $1,500 in disbursements not recoverable from the opposing party as costs but recoverable from Client (see § 38(3)(a) & Comment *e* thereto). Unless their contract construed in its circumstances provides otherwise, Lawyer is entitled to reimbursement of the $1,500 out of the $20,000 award and to a contingent fee of $6,475, that is, 35 percent of $18,500, the balance of the award.

e.   Contingent fees in structured settlements. Under "structured settlements" and some legislation, a claimant will receive regular payments over the claimant's lifetime or some other period rather than receiving a lump sum. If so, under the rule of this Section the lawyer is entitled to receive the stated share of each such payment if and when it is made to the client or (when so provided) for the client's benefit, unless the client-lawyer contract provides otherwise. When a contingent-fee contract provides that the fee is to be paid at once if there is a structured settlement and provides no other method of calculation, the fee should be calculated only on the present value of the settlement.

* * *

f(i).   Contingent fees in criminal cases—defense counsel. Contingent fees for defending criminal cases have traditionally been prohibited. The prohibition applies only to representations in a criminal proceeding. It does not forbid a contingent fee for legal work that forestalls a criminal proceeding or work that partly relates to a criminal matter and partly to a noncriminal matter. A lawyer may thus contract for a contingent fee to persuade an administrative agency to terminate an investigation that might have led to civil as well as criminal proceedings or to bring a police-brutality damages suit in which the settlement includes dismissal of criminal charges against the plaintiff.

* * *

g. Contingent fees in divorce or custody cases. Most jurisdictions continue to prohibit fees contingent on securing divorce or child custody. The traditional grounds of the prohibition in divorce cases are that such a fee creates incentives inducing lawyers to discourage reconciliation and encourages bitter and wounding court battles (cf. Restatement Second, Contracts § 190(2)). Since the passage of no-fault divorce legislation, however, public policy does not clearly favor the continuation of a marriage that one spouse wishes to end. Furthermore, in practice, once one spouse retains a lawyer to seek a divorce, a divorce will follow in most cases regardless of the basis of the fee. The principal dispute is likely to be a financial one. The prohibition might hence make it more difficult for the poorer spouse to secure vigorous representation, at least in the relatively rare instances in which law does not provide fee-shifting for the benefit of that client.

The other argument for the prohibition in divorce cases, and the ground for prohibition in custody cases, is that such a fee arrangement is usually unnecessary in order to secure an attorney in a divorce proceeding or custody dispute. The issue usually arises when one or the other spouse has assets, because otherwise there would be no means of paying a contingent fee. If the spouse retaining counsel has assets, no contingent fee is necessary. If it is the other spouse that has assets, the courts will usually require that spouse to pay the first spouse reasonable attorney fees. Again, no contingent fee is necessary.

When either of the two policies supporting the prohibition is inapplicable, the Section should not apply. If, for example, a divorce or custody order has already been finally approved when the fee contract is entered into, there can be little concern that a contingent fee based on the size of the property settlement or child-support payments will discourage reconciliation or custody compromises. (On limitations on post-inception fee contracts, see § 18(1)(a).) In such a situation, the fee is not contingent upon the securing of a divorce or custody order, and this Section does not apply, just as it does not apply to a contingent fee in a property dispute between nondivorcing or already divorced spouses. The prohibition would, however, apply to a contract with a client who is then married that provides for a fee contingent on the amount of the alimony, property disposition, or child-support award but that does not explicitly condition the fee on the grant of a divorce.

* * *

§ 36. Forbidden Client–Lawyer Financial Arrangements

(1) A lawyer may not acquire a proprietary interest in the cause of action or subject matter of litigation that the lawyer is conducting for a client, except that the lawyer may:

(a) acquire a lien as provided by § 43 to secure the lawyer's fee or expenses; and

(b) contract with a client for a contingent fee in a civil case except when prohibited as stated in § 35.

(2) A lawyer may not make or guarantee a loan to a client in connection with pending or contemplated litigation that the lawyer is conducting for the client, except that the lawyer may make or guarantee a loan covering court costs and expenses of litigation, the repayment of which to the lawyer may be contingent on the outcome of the matter.

(3) A lawyer may not, before the lawyer ceases to represent a client, make an agreement giving the lawyer literary or media rights to a portrayal or account based in substantial part on information relating to the representation.

Comment:

* * *

b. Buying legal claims. The rule in § 36(1) prohibiting acquisition of a proprietary interest in a claim the lawyer is litigating developed from restrictions on purchasing claims under the common law of champerty and maintenance. Such purchases were thought to breed needless litigation and to foster the prosecution of claims by powerful and unscrupulous persons. Contingent fees, however, permit lawyers to obtain a substantial economic share of a claim in return for their services (see § 34, Comment *e*, & § 35, Comments *b, c,* & *d*). The economic effect of the rule set forth in this Section is thus limited to prohibiting a lawyer from acquiring too large a share of a claim and from acquiring rights and powers of ownership through an otherwise proper contingent fee. It does not forbid a lawyer from taking an assignment of the whole claim and then pressing it in the lawyer's own behalf, so long as the lawyer has not represented the claim's original owner in asserting the claim. Such a purchase is subject to the requirements of §§ 18 and 126 when the buyer is the seller's lawyer. The arrangement must also be consistent with law concerning the assignment of claims and with champerty prohibitions that still exist in some states.

The justification for the rule in its present form is that a lawyer's ownership gives the lawyer an economic basis for claiming to control the prosecution and settlement of the claim and provides an incentive to the lawyer to relegate the client to a subordinate position (compare §§ 16 & 21–23 (client control over a representation)). The risk in such an arrangement is greater than it would be with a contingent fee; a contingent fee—in addition to being limited in most cases to well less than half of the recovery—is clearly designated as payment for the lawyer's services rendered for the client. The rule also prevents a lawyer from disguising an unreasonably large fee, violative of § 34, by buying part of the claim for a low price.

The Section applies to administrative as well as court litigation but does not reach nonlitigation services such as the incorporation of a business in return for payment in stock (compare § 126 (standard for business transactions with clients)). The Section does not bar a lawyer from owning stock or a similar ownership interest in an enterprise that retains a lawyer to conduct a litigation.

* * *

   c. *Financial assistance to a client.* A lawyer may provide financial assistance to a client as stated in Subsection (2). Lawyer loans to clients are regulated because a loan gives the lawyer the conflicting role of a creditor and could induce the lawyer to conduct the litigation so as to protect the lawyer's interests rather than the client's. This danger does not warrant a rule prohibiting a lawyer from lending a client court costs and litigation expenses such as ordinary- and expert-witness fees, court-reporter fees, and investigator fees, whether the duty to repay is absolute or conditioned on the client's success. Allowing lawyers to advance those expenses is indistinguishable in substance from allowing contingent fees and has similar justifications (see § 35, Comment c), notably enabling poor clients to assert their rights. Requiring the client to refund such expenses regardless of success would have a particularly crippling effect on class actions, where the named plaintiffs often have financial stakes much smaller than the litigation expenses.

* * *

   Loans for purposes other than financing litigation expenses are forbidden in most jurisdictions and under this Section. That prohibition precludes attempts to solicit clients by offering living-expenses loans or similar financial assistance. A few jurisdictions permit such payments, limiting them to basic living and similar expenses and

91

sometimes with the restriction that they not be discussed prior to the lawyer's retention. Such permission is usually based on a policy of enabling clients to avoid being forced to abandon meritorious claims or to agree to inadequate settlements.

d. Publication-rights contracts. Client-lawyer contracts in which the lawyer acquires the right to sell or share in future profits from descriptions of events covered by the representation are likely to harm clients. Such interests could be created directly, such as by assigning the lawyer all or a part interest in such rights, or indirectly, by giving the lawyer a lien on any income received by the client from such a description. Such contracts, however, give the lawyer a financial incentive to conduct the representation so as to increase the entertainment value of the resulting book or show. For example, a criminal-defense lawyer's book about a case might be more valuable if the trial is suspenseful. That might not help the client. Publication also requires the disclosure of information that the lawyer has acquired through the representation, which is prohibited without client consent (see §§ 60(1) & 62). Often, especially in criminal cases, disclosure could harm the client. The client is in a poor position to predict the harm when the publication contract is made at the outset of the case.

* * *

The prohibition does not prevent an informed client from signing a publication contract after the lawyer's services have been performed (see § 31). As a transaction between a former client and lawyer arising out of the representation, such a contract is subject to § 126.

* * *

§ 37. Partial or Complete Forfeiture of a Lawyer's Compensation

A lawyer engaging in clear and serious violation of duty to a client may be required to forfeit some or all of the lawyer's compensation for the matter. Considerations relevant to the question of forfeiture include the gravity and timing of the violation, its willfulness, its effect on the value of the lawyer's work for the client, any other threatened or actual harm to the client, and the adequacy of other remedies.

Comment:

a. Scope and cross-references; relation to other doctrines. Even if a fee is otherwise reasonable (see § 34) and complies with the other requirements of this Chapter, this Section can in some circumstances lead to forfeiture. See also § 41, on abusive fee-collection methods, and § 43, Comments *f* and *g*, discussing the discharge of attorney liens. A client who has already paid a fee subject to forfeiture can sue to recover it (see §§ 33(1) & 42).

* * *

Illustration:

    1. Lawyer has been retained at an hourly rate to negotiate a contract for Client. Lawyer assures the other parties that Client has consented to a given term, knowing this to be incorrect. Lawyer devotes five hours to working out the details of the term. When Client insists that the term be stricken (see § 22), Lawyer devotes four more hours to explaining to the other parties that Lawyer's lack of authority and Client's rejection of the term requires further negotiations. Lawyer is not entitled to compensation for any of those nine hours of time under either § 34 or § 39. The tribunal, moreover, may properly consider the incident if it bears on the value of such of Lawyer's other time as is otherwise reasonably compensable.

* * *

    b. Rationale. The remedy of fee forfeiture presupposes that a lawyer's clear and serious violation of a duty to a client destroys or severely impairs the client-lawyer relationship and thereby the justification of the lawyer's claim to compensation. See Restatement Second, Trusts § 243 (court has discretion to deny or reduce compensation of trustee who commits breach of trust); cf. Restatement Second, Agency § 456(b) (willful and deliberate breach disentitles agent to recover in quantum meruit when agency contract does not apportion compensation). Forfeiture is also a deterrent. The damage that misconduct causes is often difficult to assess. In addition, a tribunal often can determine a forfeiture sanction more easily than a right to compensating damages.

    Forfeiture of fees, however, is not justified in each instance in which a lawyer violates a legal duty, nor is total forfeiture always appropriate. Some violations are inadvertent or do not significantly harm the client. Some can be adequately dealt with by the remedies described in Comment *a* or by a partial forfeiture (see Comment *e*). Denying the lawyer all compensation would sometimes be an excessive sanction, giving a windfall to a client. The remedy of this Section should hence be applied with discretion.

c. *Violation of a duty to a client.* This Section provides for forfeiture when a lawyer engages in a clear and serious violation (see Comment *d* hereto) of a duty to the client. The source of the duty can be civil or criminal law, including, for example, the requirements of an applicable lawyer code or the law of malpractice. The misconduct might have occurred when the lawyer was retained, during the representation, or during attempts to collect a fee (see § 41). On improper withdrawal as a ground for forfeiture, see § 40, Comment *e.*

* * *

d. *A clear and serious violation—relevant factors.* A lawyer's violation of duty to a client warrants fee forfeiture only if the lawyer's violation was clear. A violation is clear if a reasonable lawyer, knowing the relevant facts and law reasonably accessible to the lawyer, would have known that the conduct was wrongful. The sanction of fee forfeiture should not be applied to a lawyer who could not have been expected to know that conduct was forbidden, for example when the lawyer followed one reasonable interpretation of a client-lawyer contract and another interpretation was later held correct.

To warrant fee forfeiture a lawyer's violation must also be serious. Minor violations do not justify leaving the lawyer entirely unpaid for valuable services rendered to a client, although some such violations will reduce the size of the fee or render the lawyer liable to the client for any harm caused (see Comment *a* hereto).

In approaching the ultimate issue of whether violation of duty warrants fee forfeiture, several factors are relevant. The extent of the misconduct is one factor. Normally, forfeiture is more appropriate for repeated or continuing violations than for a single incident. Whether the breach involved knowing violation or conscious disloyalty to a client is also relevant. See Restatement Second, Agency § 469 (forfeiture for willful and deliberate breach). Forfeiture is generally inappropriate when the lawyer has not done anything willfully blameworthy, for example, when a conflict of interest arises during a representation because of the unexpected act of a client or third person.

Forfeiture should be proportionate to the seriousness of the offense. For example, a lawyer's failure to keep a client's funds segregated in a separate account (see § 44) should not result in forfeiture if the funds are preserved undiminished for the client. But forfeiture is justified for a flagrant violation even though no harm can be proved.

The adequacy of other remedies is also relevant. If, for example, a lawyer improperly withdraws from a representation and is consequently limited to a quantum meruit recovery significantly smaller than the fee contract provided (see § 40), it might be unnecessary to forfeit the quantum meruit recovery as well.

* * *

TOPIC 2.   A LAWYER'S CLAIM TO COMPENSATION

* * *

§ 38.   Client–Lawyer Fee Contracts

(1) Before or within a reasonable time after beginning to represent a client in a matter, a lawyer must communicate to the client, in writing when applicable rules so provide, the basis or rate of the fee, unless the communication is unnecessary for the client because the lawyer has previously represented that client on the same basis or at the same rate.

(2) The validity and construction of a contract between a client and a lawyer concerning the lawyer's fees are governed by § 18.

(3) Unless a contract construed in the circumstances indicates otherwise:

(a) a lawyer may not charge separately for the lawyer's general office and overhead expenses;

(b) payments that the law requires an opposing party or that party's lawyer to pay as attorney-fee awards or sanctions are credited to the client, not the client's lawyer, absent a contrary statute or court order; and

(c) when a lawyer requests and receives a fee payment that is not for services already rendered, that payment is to be credited against whatever fee the lawyer is entitled to collect.

Comment:

* * *

[b.   *A lawyer's duty to inform a client.*]

* * *

The lawyer should inform the client early enough so that the client will not be inconvenienced unnecessarily if, upon considering the information, the client decides to seek another lawyer. The basis or rate might be a specified hourly charge, a percentage, or a set of factors on which the fee will be based. If the fee is based on a percentage of recovery (or other base), the client should also be informed if a different percentage applies in the event of settlement, trial, or appeal. For a client sophisticated in retaining lawyers, a statement that "we will charge our usual hourly rates" ordinarily will suffice. The less specific the notice, the less it should control a tribunal passing on the propriety of the fee. Thus, a lawyer's statement "I will charge what I think fair, in light of the hours expended and the results obtained," even if deemed part of a valid contract, does not bind the client or tribunal to accept whatever fee the lawyer thinks fair. The level of information imparted to the client might comply with disciplinary rules but not give rise to an enforceable contract.

* * *

e. Disbursements. Under generally prevailing practice, the actual amount of disbursements to persons outside the office for hired consultants, printers' bills, out-of-town travel, long-distance telephone charges, and the like ordinarily are charges in addition to the lawyer's fee. Reimbursement is limited to the actual amount of disbursements the lawyer was authorized to make under the lawyer's general authority or a more specific delegation or contract (see §§ 21–23). Compare Restatement Second, Agency §§ 438(2)(a) and 439(e) (principal must indemnify agent for payment authorized or necessary in managing principal's affairs or where agent was not officious in making expenditure, principal was benefited, and it would be inequitable not to indemnify). See also § 17 as to a client's duty to indemnify a lawyer for certain expenses. As to whether a nonclient who provides goods and services can hold the client or lawyer liable for them, see §§ 26, 27, and 30.

Court costs and expenses of litigation, such as filing fees, expert-witness fees, and witness expenses, are normally payable by clients. In most states, a lawyer may not advance such expenses unless the client is obligated to repay them out of the client's recovery (see § 36(2) & Comment *c* thereto). Under a contingent-fee contract, however, a client who does not prevail is not liable to the lawyer for court costs and litigation expenses, unless the client agreed to pay them or nonrefundable advances by the lawyer of such costs and expenses are unlawful in the jurisdiction.

Subsection (3)(a) provides that, unless the contract construed in its circumstances provides otherwise, a lawyer may not recover from a client payment in addition to the agreed fee for items of general office and overhead expense such as secretarial costs and word processing. A client lacking knowledge of the lawyer's usual practice cannot be expected to assume that the lawyer will charge extra for such expenses. The lawyer may, however, charge separately for such items if the client was told of the billing practice at the outset of the representation or was familiar with it from past experience with the lawyer or (in the case of a general billing custom in the area) from past experiences with other lawyers.

* * *

g.   An advance payment, engagement-retainer fee, or lump-sum fee. A fee payment that does not cover services already rendered and that is not otherwise identified is presumed to be a deposit against future services. The lawyer's fee for those services will be calculated according to any valid fee contract or, if there is none, under the fair-value standard of § 39. If that fee is less than the deposit, the lawyer must refund the surplus (see § 33(1)). If the fee exceeds the deposit, the client owes the lawyer the difference. The deposit serves as security for the payment of the fee. See also § 43 (considering other security devices); § 44, Comment *f* (considering when lawyer may transfer advance-fee payment to lawyer's personal account).

A client and lawyer might agree that a payment is an engagement-retainer fee (see § 34, Comment *e*) rather than a deposit. Clients who pay a fee without receiving an explanation ordinarily will assume that they are paying for services, not readiness (see § 38(3)(c)). A client and lawyer might also agree that an advance payment is neither a deposit nor an engagement retainer, but a lump-sum fee constituting complete payment for the lawyer's services. Again, the lawyer must adequately explain this to the client. In any event, an engagement-retainer or lump-sum fee must be reasonable (see § 34 & Comment *d* thereto). If the lawyer withdraws or is discharged prematurely or for other misconduct, the contractual fee might be subject to reduction (see § 40, Illustration 3; see also § 37 (fee forfeiture)).

h.   Interest. A client and lawyer may agree for the payment of a reasonable amount in interest on past-due and unpaid charges of the lawyer (see §§ 18 & 34). In the absence of contract, the lawyer's entitlement to interest is determined by other law. Similarly, a lawyer's right to receive interest on cost and similar advances (see § 36(2)) is determined either by contract or other law.

* * *

§ 39. A Lawyer's Fee in the Absence of a Contract

If a client and lawyer have not made a valid contract providing for another measure of compensation, a client owes a lawyer who has performed legal services for the client the fair value of the lawyer's services.

Comment:

* * *

c. Applying the fair-value standard. Assessing the fair value of a lawyer's services might require answers to three questions. What fees are customarily charged by comparable lawyers in the community for similar legal services? What would a fully informed and properly advised client in the client's situation agree to pay for such services? In light of those and other relevant circumstances, what is a fair fee (see Comment *b* hereto)?

In some cases, a standard market rate for a legal service might in fact exist. A lawyer who proves that a standard fee exists in the area should ordinarily be entitled to receive it, unless the client shows that a sophisticated, informed, and properly advised client in the client's situation would have refused to pay the standard fee—for example, because such a client would have decided not to proceed (see Comment *b(ii)* hereto). Similarly, a client should not be required to pay more than the standard fee unless the lawyer shows that, because of the circumstances of the case, a sophisticated, informed, and properly advised client would have agreed to pay a higher fee.

* * *

The standard rate or hourly fee might be modified by other factors bearing on fairness, including success in the representation and whether the lawyer assumed part of the risk of the client's loss, as in a contingent-fee contract (see § 35). Reference can be made to the factors in § 34, Comment *c*. Concerning expenses and disbursements paid by the lawyer and attorney-fee awards and sanctions collected from an opposing party, the principles of § 38(3)(a) and (b) apply.

* * *

§ 40. Fees on Termination

If a client-lawyer relationship ends before the lawyer has completed the services due for a matter and the lawyer's fee has not been forfeited under § 37:

(1) a lawyer who has been discharged or withdraws may recover the lesser of the fair value of the lawyer's services as determined under § 39 and the ratable proportion of the compensation provided by any otherwise enforceable contract between lawyer and client for the services performed; except that

(2) the tribunal may allow such a lawyer to recover the ratable proportion of the compensation provided by such a contract if:

(a) the discharge or withdrawal is not attributable to misconduct of the lawyer;

(b) the lawyer has performed severable services; and

(c) allowing contractual compensation would not burden the client's choice of counsel or the client's ability to replace counsel.

Comment:

* * *

[b. *Measure of compensation when a client discharges a lawyer.*]

* * *

It is an assumption of each of the following Illustrations that the circumstances warrant neither fee forfeiture (see § 37 & Comment *e* hereto) nor contractual recovery (see Comments *c* & *d* hereto).

Illustrations:

1.   Client retained Lawyer to handle Client's divorce. Lawyer requested and Client paid $2,000 in advance, as full payment. After Lawyer had worked eight hours out of the approximately 16 likely to be needed, Client discharged Lawyer in order to hire Client's brother. (a) If the fair value of Lawyer's work is $100 per hour, Lawyer is entitled to $800 for the eight hours actually worked. Lawyer must refund the rest of the $2,000. (b) If the fair value of Lawyer's work is $300 per hour, Lawyer is entitled to that part of the $2,000 applicable to the work performed, that is to $1,000 and not the fair value of $2,400, because $1,000 was the contractual price for the work Lawyer performed, which was approximately half of the work actually contemplated. Lawyer is not entitled to the full $2,000 lump-sum fee because that fee contemplated performance of all work involved in Client's divorce. Accordingly, the $2,000 must be prorated to reflect the extent of Lawyer's actual services.

2.   The same facts as in Illustration 1, except that the $2,000 advance payment is designated in the contract between Client and Lawyer not as full payment for Lawyer's services but as a

nonrefundable engagement retainer (see § 34, Comment *e*). If the fair value of Lawyer's work is $100 per hour, Lawyer is entitled to $800 for the eight hours worked. Because Client and Lawyer had agreed to an engagement retainer to ensure that Lawyer would be compensated for costs incurred in reliance on being retained, Lawyer can also recover for the fair value not exceeding $2,000 (see § 39) of expenses or loss of income Lawyer reasonably incurred by accepting the engagement retainer (see § 34, Comment *e*).

3. The same facts as in Illustration 1, except that the $2,000 payment is designated in the fee contract as a nonrefundable engagement-retainer fee (see § 34, Comment *e*), and the contract between Client and Lawyer further provides that Lawyer is to be compensated at Lawyer's typical hourly rate of $100 per hour. If $100 is the fair value of Lawyer's services, Lawyer is entitled to $800 for the eight hours worked. In addition, if $2,000 is a reasonable amount to charge in the circumstances as an engagement retainer (id.), Lawyer is entitled to retain that $2,000.

* * *

c. Allowing a contractual fee. Allowing a discharged or withdrawing lawyer to recover compensation under a fee contract with the client is sometimes more appropriate than fee forfeiture or recovery of the lesser of fair value and contractual compensation. The most common situation calling for such treatment is where the client discharges a contingent-fee lawyer without cause just before the contingency occurs, perhaps in order to avoid paying the contractual percentage fee. The reasons for the usual restrictions on contractual recovery then do not apply. See Restatement Second, Agency §§ 445 and 454 (recovery of contractual compensation by agent when compensation depends on specified result and principal discharges agent in bad faith).

* * *

Whether the discharge or withdrawal is attributable to the lawyer's misconduct is relevant to whether contractual compensation should be allowed (see Restatement Second, Agency §§ 455 & 456). The claim to contractual compensation of a lawyer discharged without reasonable grounds, or forced to withdraw by a client's misconduct (see § 32), is stronger than that of a lawyer whose acts have provided such grounds, even if not warranting forfeiture of the entire fee (see § 37), or civil liability (see Chapter 4). In the context of Subsection (2), misconduct of the lawyer is not limited to conduct that would warrant professional discipline (see § 5), fee forfeiture (see § 37), or civil liability (see Chapter 4). It also includes other conduct that would cause a reasonable client to discharge the lawyer, for example, a series of errors that reasonably leads the client to doubt the lawyer's competence although they cause no damage and do not constitute incompetence subjecting the lawyer to discipline.

* * *

d.   The measure of compensation when a lawyer withdraws. A lawyer may properly withdraw on various grounds, for example because the client insists that the lawyer perform services in a manner that would violate a lawyer code or refuses to pay the lawyer's proper fees (see § 32). If the requirements of Subsection (2) are not met and there is no forfeiture, the withdrawing lawyer's compensation is limited to the lesser of the contractual fee for the services performed or the fair value of the lawyer's services. Were that not so, lawyers would be encouraged to withdraw before being discharged in order to avoid the rule of Subsection (1).

* * *

[*e.   Forfeiture by a withdrawing or discharged lawyer.*]

* * *

A lawyer who withdraws has the burden of persuading the trier of fact that the withdrawal is not attributable to a clear and serious violation of the lawyer's duty (see § 16) to render loyal and competent service. See Restatement Second, Contracts §§ 237 and 241; compare Restatement Second, Agency § 456 (agent who wrongfully renounces contract or is properly discharged for breach loses all compensation except for services for which contract apportioned compensation, unless agent's breach was not willful and deliberate). For example, a lawyer who knowingly or recklessly undertakes to represent a client in a suit against another client of the lawyer's firm without the consent of both clients in violation of § 128(2) is subject to forfeiture of compensation even though the lawyer's withdrawal is compelled under § 32(2)(a). Withdrawal in violation of § 32 can similarly subject the lawyer to forfeiture.

On the other hand, forfeiture is inappropriate when the lawyer's withdrawal or discharge is not attributable to the lawyer's clear and serious violation of duty to the client. For example, the lawyer might have withdrawn or have been discharged because the client insisted that the lawyer violate professional rules. So also, a merger of a corporate client might have created a conflict of interest, requiring the lawyer to withdraw (see § 121, Comment *e(v)*). Similarly, forfeiture is inappropriate where termination is compelled by events beyond the lawyer's reasonable control, such as the lawyer's death or illness.

* * *

TOPIC 3.   FEE–COLLECTION PROCEDURES

* * *

§ 41.   Fee–Collection Methods

In seeking compensation claimed from a client or former client, a lawyer may not employ collection methods forbidden by law, use confidential information (as defined in Chapter 5) when not permitted under § 65, or harass the client.

Comment:

a. Scope and cross-references. Disciplinary authorities sanction lawyers for abusive fee-collection methods. In appropriate circumstances, violations can give rise to forfeiture of a lawyer's right to compensation (see §§ 37 & 40), to the discharge of a lien (see § 43), or to a claim for damages (see Chapter 4). Courts enforce this Section in fee litigation between lawyers and clients. Lawyers are also subject to the restrictions on debt-collection methods provided by general law (see Comment *b* hereto). Both lawyers, with respect to fee claims in litigation against a client, and clients, with respect to counterclaims for malpractice, are subject to procedural rules requiring a nonfrivolous basis for claims (see § 110). On the requirement that a lawyer refund all unearned fees when a representation ends, see § 33(1). Although fee disputes usually involve past clients, this Section applies also to fee disputes with current clients (see §§ 18, 32, 37, & 40).

* * *

[*c. Limitations on the use or disclosure of confidential client information.*]

* * *

The lawyer may not disclose or threaten to disclose information to nonclients not involved in the suit in order to coerce the client into settling. The lawyer's fee claim must be advanced in good faith and with a reasonable basis. The client information must be relevant to the claim, for example because the client advances defenses that need to be rebutted by disclosure. Even then, the lawyer should not disclose the information until after exploring whether the harm can be limited by partial disclosure, stipulation with the client, or a protective order (see § 64, Comment *e*, & § 65, Comment *d*).

* * *

§ 42. Remedies and the Burden of Persuasion

(1) A fee dispute between a lawyer and a client may be adjudicated in any appropriate proceeding, including a suit by the lawyer to recover an unpaid fee, a suit for a refund by a client, an arbitration to which both parties consent unless applicable law renders the lawyer's consent unnecessary, or in the court's discretion a proceeding ancillary to a pending suit in which the lawyer performed the services in question.

(2) In any such proceeding the lawyer has the burden of persuading the trier of fact, when relevant, of the existence and terms of any fee contract, the making of any disclosures to the client required to render a contract enforceable, and the extent and value of the lawyer's services.

Comment:

* * *

[c. *A lawyer's burden of persuasion.*]

* * *

Illustration:

1. Client and Lawyer agree that Lawyer will represent Client for a fee of $100 per hour and that Client will make a deposit of $5,000. When the representation has been concluded, the parties dispute what fee is due. Client sues to recover $2,000, alleging and introducing evidence tending to show that Lawyer devoted no more than 30 hours to the matter. Lawyer denies this and testifies to devoting 50 hours. If the conflicting evidence leaves the trier of fact in equipoise, it should find for Client.

* * *

§ 43. Lawyer Liens

(1) Except as provided in Subsection (2) or by statute or rule, a lawyer does not acquire a lien entitling the lawyer to retain the client's property in the lawyer's possession in order to secure payment of the lawyer's fees and disbursements. A lawyer may decline to deliver to a client or former client an original or copy of any document prepared by the lawyer or at the lawyer's expense if the client or former client has not paid all fees and disbursements due for the lawyer's work in preparing the document and nondelivery would not unreasonably harm the client or former client.

(2) Unless otherwise provided by statute or rule, client and lawyer may agree that the lawyer shall have a security interest in property of the client recovered for the client through the lawyer's efforts, as follows:

(a) the lawyer may contract in writing with the client for a lien on the proceeds of the representation to secure payment for the lawyer's services and disbursements in that matter;

(b) the lien becomes binding on a third party when the party has notice of the lien;

(c) the lien applies only to the amount of fees and disbursements claimed reasonably and in good faith for the lawyer's services performed in the representation; and

(d) the lawyer may not unreasonably impede the speedy and inexpensive resolution of any dispute concerning those fees and disbursements or the lien.

(3) A tribunal where an action is pending may in its discretion adjudicate any fee or other dispute concerning a lien asserted by a lawyer on property of a party to the action, provide for custody of the property, release all or part of the property to the client or lawyer, and grant such other relief as justice may require.

(4) With respect to property neither in the lawyer's possession nor recovered by the client through the lawyer's efforts, the lawyer may obtain a security interest on property of a client only as provided by other law and consistent with §§ 18 and 126. Acquisition of such a security interest is a business or financial transaction with a client within the meaning of § 126.

Comment:

* * *

b.   Retaining liens on papers and property in a lawyer's posses-sion. A lawyer ordinarily may not retain a client's property or docu-ments against the client's wishes (see §§ 45 & 46). Nevertheless, under the decisional law of all but a few jurisdictions, a lawyer may refuse to return to a client all papers and other property of the client in the lawyer's possession until the lawyer's fee has been paid (see Restatement Second, Agency § 464; Restatement of Security § 62(b)). That law is not followed in the Section; instead it adopts the law in what is currently the minority of jurisdictions.

While a broad retaining lien might protect the lawyer's legitimate interest in receiving compensation, drawbacks outweigh that advan-tage. The lawyer obtains payment by keeping from the client papers and property that the client entrusted to the lawyer in order to gain help. The use of the client's papers against the client is in tension with the fiduciary responsibilities of lawyers. A broad retaining lien could impose pressure on a client disproportionate to the size or validity of the lawyer's fee claim. The lawyer also can arrange other ways of securing the fee, such as payment in advance or a specific contract with the client providing security for the fee under Subsection (4). Because it is normally unpredictable at the start of a representation what client property will be in the lawyer's hands if a fee dispute arises, a retaining lien would give little advance assurance of payment. Thus, recognizing such a lien would not significantly help financially unreliable clients secure counsel. Moreover, the leverage of such a lien exacerbates the difficulties that clients often have in suing over fee charges (see § 41). Efforts in some jurisdictions to prevent abuse of retaining liens demonstrate their undesirability. Some authorities pro-hibit a lien on papers needed to defend against a criminal prosecution, for example. However the very point of a retaining lien, if accepted at all, is to coerce payment by withholding papers the client needs.

Retaining liens are therefore not recognized under this Section except as authorized by statute or rule and to the extent provided under Subsection (4). Under this Section, lawyers may secure fee payment through a consensual charging lien on the proceeds of a representation (Comments *c-f* hereto) and through contractual security interests in other assets of the client (Comment *h*) and other contrac-tual arrangements such as a prepaid deposit. The lawyer may also withhold from the client documents prepared by the lawyer or at the lawyer's expense that have not been paid for (see Comment *c* hereto).

c.   A lawyer's right to retain unpaid-for documents. A client who fails to pay for the lawyer's work in preparing particular documents (or in having them prepared at the lawyer's expense, for example by a retained expert) ordinarily is not entitled to receive those documents. Whether a payment was due and whether it was for such a document depend on the contract between the client and the lawyer, as construed from the standpoint of a reasonable client (see §§ 18 & 38).

Illustrations:

1. Client retains Lawyer to prepare a series of memoranda for an agreed compensation of $100 per hour. Lawyer is to send bills every month. Client pays the first two bills and then stops paying. After five months, Client requests copies of all the memoranda. Lawyer must deliver all memoranda prepared during the first two months, but need not deliver those thereafter prepared until Client makes the payments.

2. The same facts as in Illustration 1, except that Client and Lawyer have agreed that Lawyer is to send bills every six months. After five months, Client requests copies of all the memoranda. Lawyer must deliver them all, because Client has not failed to pay any due bill. Had Client stated in advance that it would not pay the bill, the doctrine of anticipatory breach might allow Lawyer not to deliver. See Restatement Second, Contracts §§ 253, 256, and 257.

* * *

h. A lawyer's duties in enforcing a lien. The fee claim with respect to which a lien is asserted must be advanced in good faith and with a reasonable basis in law and fact. The lawyer must not commingle with the lawyer's own funds any payments subject to the lien (see § 44). The lawyer must not unreasonably delay resolution of disputes concerning the lien and claimed fee.

* * *

i. Other security for attorney fees and disbursements. Under Subsection (4), a lawyer may obtain a consensual security interest in a client's property not otherwise involved in the representation, such as a mortgage on the client's land, a pledge of the client's stocks, or an escrow arrangement. This Section does not prohibit such security arrangements. They are typically created by a writing that informs the client of the obligations secured. Typically they are used when the client's ability or willingness to pay is questionable, and they thus aid such a client (for example, a criminal defendant with nonliquid assets but no money) to obtain counsel.

* * *

TOPIC 4.   PROPERTY AND DOCUMENTS OF CLIENTS AND OTHERS

* * *

§ 44.   Safeguarding and Segregating Property

(1) A lawyer holding funds or other property of a client in connection with a representation, or such funds or other property in which a client claims an interest, must take reasonable steps to safeguard the funds or property. A similar obligation may be imposed by law on funds or other property so held and owned or claimed by a third person. In particular, the lawyer must hold such property separate from the lawyer's property, keep records of it, deposit funds in an account separate from the lawyer's own funds, identify tangible objects, and comply with related requirements imposed by regulatory authorities.

(2) Upon receiving funds or other property in a professional capacity and in which a client or third person owns or claims an interest, a lawyer must promptly notify the client or third person. The lawyer must promptly render a full accounting regarding such property upon request by the client or third person.

Comment:

[*a.   Scope and cross-references.*]

* * *

The requirement of Subsection (1) with respect to property of a third person states the rule of law applicable in proceedings seeking remedies other than professional discipline. In disciplinary proceedings, the lawyer codes typically provide rules for property of third persons as strict as those for clients and which may be more demanding than required for other remedies.

* * *

c.   Regulatory requirements and sanctions. All jurisdictions have rules concerning a lawyer's responsibilities for client property, en-

107

forceable by disciplinary sanctions. Strong sanctions including disbarment have been imposed for converting or even commingling client funds. The rules often specify where the lawyer's bank account must be located, the records the lawyer must keep, and other matters. Many states provide for random audits of lawyer trust accounts, notification of bar authorities by banks when trust accounts are overdrawn, and client security funds to compensate clients injured by misappropriating lawyers.

* * *

d. Safeguarding funds: bank accounts and interest. A lawyer must deposit funds of a client or a third person in an account, usually a trust or client account, separate from the lawyer's own funds, and including those of the lawyer's law practice. The trust account may contain funds of more than one person, but the records must adequately identify the share of each person. The lawyer may not receive interest on such funds. Most states now have arrangements under which certain client funds (usually small amounts) may or must be pooled in accounts, the interest from which is paid to a regulatory authority to fund legal services for the indigent and other similar activities. When trust accounts may bear interest for the benefit of an individual client and the amount and probable duration of the deposit justify the effort and expense involved, the lawyer should arrange for an interest-bearing account, with the interest to be transmitted to the clients. A lawyer holding client funds as a trustee or in other capacities may be required to invest them. See Restatement Third, Trusts (Prudent Investor Rule) §§ 227–229.

e. Scope of the duty to safeguard. This Section applies to all valuable objects including cash, jewelry, and the like, negotiable instruments, deeds, stock certificates, and other papers evidencing title. See also § 46, discussing documents in the lawyer's possession. This Section requires a lawyer to use reasonable measures for safekeeping such objects, for example by placing them in a safe-deposit box or office safe. The reasonableness of measures depends on the circumstances, including the market value of the property, its special value to the client or third person, and special difficulties that would be required to replace it if known to the lawyer, its transferability or convertibility, its susceptibility to loss or other damage, the reasonable customs of lawyers in the community, and the availability and cost of alternative methods of safekeeping.

The terms of an agreement under which the lawyer receives property can modify the obligations imposed by this Section. For example, an escrow contract might require the lawyer serving as escrowee to pay out the escrow funds upon the occurrence of a stated event. A lawyer's obligation to safeguard property may be relaxed by a contract only if any client or third person whose interests are affected gives informed consent, on terms that serve some purpose other than the convenience or profit of the lawyer (see § 19). On business dealing with a client, see § 126.

f. Property belonging to a lawyer. This Section does not apply to property indisputably owned by a lawyer. Thus, when a client does not dispute a lawyer's good-faith claim to a certain amount as a fee then owing, the lawyer may transfer that amount into the lawyer's personal account. See also § 21, Comment *e*, discussing when a lawyer may validly endorse a check on which the client is payee. Similarly, if a payment to a lawyer is a flat fee paid in advance rather than a deposit out of which fees will be paid as they become due, the payment belongs to the lawyer (see § 38, Comment *g*). A lawyer holding client funds as an advance fee payment may withdraw them for fees as earned, so long as there is no existing dispute about the lawyer's right to do so. In such instances, the lawyer acts rightly in retaining the money even though, for example, the client might later claim that the fee was unreasonable (see §§ 34 & 42) or the advance payment becomes unreasonable in light of later developments (see § 38, Comment *g*; § 34, Comment *d*; & § 40).

* * *

g. Claims of third persons against a client or a lawyer. A lawyer might be in possession of property claimed both by the lawyer's client and by a third person, for example a creditor claiming an interest in the client's property, a previous lawyer of the client claiming a lien on the client's recovery (see §§ 40 & 43), or a person claiming that property deposited with the lawyer by the client was taken or withheld unlawfully from that person. In such circumstances, this Section requires the lawyer to safeguard the contested property until the dispute has been resolved (see § 45, Comments *d* & *e*), but does not prescribe the rules for resolving it. Those rules are to be found in other law. Thus, if a third person claims that property stolen from that person has been used by the client to pay the lawyer's fee, the lawyer's right to keep the payment depends on the law generally applicable to transfers of stolen property. The result might turn on whether the lawyer was a bona fide purchaser for value without notice of the theft, on whether the property was negotiable, or on other circumstances. It might also be affected by statutes providing for the forfeiture of property to the government, to the extent that such statutes validly apply to property used to pay lawyer's fees (see § 45, Comment *f*).

[h. A lawyer's duty to notify and account.]

* * *

When the claimant is a third person whose interests conflict with those of the lawyer's client but to whom the lawyer owes a duty of safekeeping or notification, the lawyer must notify that person of the lawyer's receipt of the property. That situation could exist, for example, where the lawyer is an executor and the third person a legatee, where the law designates the lawyer a constructive trustee for the person because the property has been converted (see § 45, Comment *f*), or where other law imposes a duty on the lawyer to turn over property or funds directly to the third person. The lawyer's duties of confidentiality to the client do not bar such notice because the lawyer may not assist the client to conceal the property from the third person to whom the lawyer owes the duty of safekeeping (see § 45). Moreover, the arrangement under which the lawyer receives property of a third person of adverse interest—for example, an escrow arrangement—can imply that the client and third person have agreed that the lawyer is to protect the third person's interests.

* * *

§ 45. Surrendering Possession of Property

(1) Except as provided in Subsection (2), a lawyer must promptly deliver, to the client or nonclient so entitled, funds or other property in the lawyer's possession belonging to a client or nonclient.

(2) A lawyer may retain possession of funds or other property of a client or nonclient if:

(a) the client or nonclient consents;

(b) the lawyer's client is entitled to the property, the lawyer appropriately possesses the property for purposes of the representation, and the client has not asked for delivery of the property;

(c) the lawyer has a valid lien on the property (see § 43);

(d) there are substantial grounds for dispute as to the person entitled to the property; or

(e) delivering the property to the client or nonclient would violate a court order or other legal obligation of the lawyer.

110

Comment:

* * *

[*b.   Prompt delivery.*]

* * *

How soon the delivery must occur depends on the circumstances (see Restatement Second, Agency § 427, Comment *d*). When the owner asks for delivery of the property, the lawyer must comply with the request. If the lawyer knows that the owner has need to possess the property by a given time, the lawyer should if reasonably possible deliver it by that time. The lawyer ordinarily should not delay longer than necessary to record and transmit the funds (see also § 44, Comment *d*). A client entitled to proceeds of a judgment normally should not have to wait more than a few days to receive the property from the client's lawyer. When the representation ends, moreover, any delay in delivering the client's property can hamper the client's affairs (compare § 43, Comment *b*). On the other hand, during the representation a lawyer is not required, in the absence of client request, to deliver items that might turn out to be needed for the representation (see Comment *c* hereto).

* * *

f.   Stolen goods. The lawyer's duties of confidentiality do not prevent a lawyer from complying with the requirement of this Section to return promptly to its owner property that a client has stolen and placed in the lawyer's possession. The client's transfer of the property as such is ordinarily not a communication subject to the attorney-client privilege (see § 69, Comment *d*). Although the lawyer's knowledge that the goods are stolen from a given person will usually derive from confidential client information (see § 60(1)), a lawyer who knowingly retains stolen goods is helping the thief conceal them from their proper owner, which is a crime. The same would be true were the lawyer, once having taken possession of the goods, to return them to the thief. By asking the lawyer to possess stolen goods, moreover, the client has lost the protection of the attorney-client privilege for any accompanying communications (see § 82).

Although the lawyer must return the goods, there is no requirement that the lawyer explain their provenance or name the thief. To do so voluntarily might well violate the lawyer's duties of confidentiality (see § 60(1)), even though a tribunal might be able to require disclosure (see § 69, Comment *g*, & § 82). In representing the client in defending against a charge of crime, the lawyer may retain the goods long enough to test or inspect them in preparation for the client's defense, though this does not authorize keeping them secret until the trial. (On accepting objects belonging to a client but constituting evidence of crime, see § 119.)

* * *

§ 46. Documents Relating to a Representation

(1) **A lawyer must take reasonable steps to safeguard documents in the lawyer's possession relating to the representation of a client or former client.**

(2) **On request, a lawyer must allow a client or former client to inspect and copy any document possessed by the lawyer relating to the representation, unless substantial grounds exist to refuse.**

(3) **Unless a client or former client consents to non-delivery or substantial grounds exist for refusing to make delivery, a lawyer must deliver to the client or former client, at an appropriate time and in any event promptly after the representation ends, such originals and copies of other documents possessed by the lawyer relating to the representation as the client or former client reasonably needs.**

(4) **Notwithstanding Subsections (2) and (3), a lawyer may decline to deliver to a client or former client an original or copy of any document under circumstances permitted by § 43(1).**

Comment:

* * *

[b.   A lawyer's duty to safeguard documents.]

* * *

A lawyer's duty to safeguard client documents does not end with the representation (see § 33). It continues while there is a reasonable likelihood that the client will need the documents, unless the client has adequate copies and originals, declines to receive such copies and originals from the lawyer, or consents to disposal of the documents.

The lawyer need take only reasonable steps to preserve the documents. For example, a law firm is not required to preserve client documents indefinitely and may destroy documents that are outdated or no longer of consequence. Similarly, a lawyer who leaves a firm may leave with that firm the documents of clients the lawyer represented while with the firm, provided that the lawyer reasonably believes that the firm has appropriate safeguarding arrangements. So long as a lawyer has custody of documents, the lawyer must take reasonable steps in arrangements for storing, using, destroying, or transferring them. If the jurisdiction allows a lawyer's practice to be sold to another lawyer, the lawyer must comply with the rules governing the sale. If a firm dissolves, its members must take reasonable steps to safeguard documents continuing to require confidentiality, for example by entrusting them to a person or depository bound by appropriate restrictions.

c.   A client's right to retrieve, inspect, and copy documents. As stated in Subsection (3), a client is entitled to retrieve documents in possession of a lawyer relating to representation of the client. That right extends to documents placed in the lawyer's possession as well as to documents produced by the lawyer, subject to the right to retain property under a valid lien (see § 43) and to other justifiable grounds as discussed hereafter.

A client is ordinarily entitled to inspect and copy at reasonable times any document relating to the representation in the possession of the client's lawyer (see Restatement Second, Trusts § 173; cf. Restatement Second, Agency § 381). A client's failure to assert the right to inspect and copy files during the representation does not bar later enforcement of that right, so long as the lawyer has properly not disposed of the documents (see Comment *b*).

A lawyer may deny a client's request to retrieve, inspect, or copy documents when compliance would violate the lawyer's duty to another (see Restatement Second, Agency § 381). That would occur, for example, if a court's protective order had forbidden copying of a document obtained during discovery from another party, or if the lawyer reasonably believed that the client would use the document to commit a crime (see § 21). Justification would also exist if the document contained confidences of another client that the lawyer was required to protect.

* * *

A lawyer may refuse to disclose to the client certain law-firm documents reasonably intended only for internal review, such as a memorandum discussing which lawyers in the firm should be assigned to a case, whether a lawyer must withdraw because of the client's misconduct, or the firm's possible malpractice liability to the client. The need for lawyers to be able to set down their thoughts privately in order to assure effective and appropriate representation warrants keeping such documents secret from the client involved. Even in such circumstances, however, a tribunal may properly order discovery of the document when discovery rules so provide. The lawyer's duty to inform the client (see § 20) can require the lawyer to disclose matters discussed in a document even when the document itself need not be disclosed.

 d. *Documents that a lawyer must furnish without request.* Even without a client's request or the discovery order of a tribunal, a lawyer must voluntarily furnish originals or copies of such documents as a client reasonably needs in the circumstances. In complying with that standard, the lawyer should consider such matters as the client's expressed concerns, the client's possible needs, customary practice, the number of documents, the client's storage facilities, and whether the documents originally came from the client. The client should have an original of documents such as contracts, while a copy will suffice for such documents as legal memoranda and court opinions. Except under extraordinary circumstances—for example, when a client retained a lawyer to recover and destroy a confidential letter—a lawyer may keep copies of documents when furnished to a client.

 If not made before, delivery must be made promptly after the representation ends. The lawyer may withhold documents to induce the client to pay a bill only as stated in § 43. During the representation, the lawyer should deliver documents when the client needs or requests them. The lawyer need not deliver documents when the client agrees that the lawyer may keep them or where there is a genuine dispute about who is entitled to receive them (see § 45(2)(c) & Comment c hereto).

 e. *Payment for expenses of delivering documents.* Because a lawyer's normal duties include collection and delivery of documents that came from the client or that the client should have, a lawyer paid by the hour should be compensated for time devoted to that task. Copying expenses may be separately billed when allowed under the principles stated in § 38(3)(a) and Comment e thereto. When the client seeks copies that the lawyer was not obliged to furnish in the absence of such a request, the lawyer may require the client to pay the copying costs.

* * *

TOPIC 5. FEE-SPLITTING WITH A LAWYER NOT IN THE SAME FIRM

* * *

§ 47. Fee–Splitting Between Lawyers Not in the Same Firm

 A division of fees between lawyers who are not in the same firm may be made only if:

(1) (a) the division is in proportion to the services performed by each lawyer or (b) by agreement with the client, the lawyers assume joint responsibility for the representation;

(2) the client is informed of and does not object to the fact of division, the terms of the division, and the participation of the lawyers involved; and

(3) the total fee is reasonable (see § 34).

Comment:

* * *

b. Rationale. The traditional prohibition of fee-splitting among lawyers is justified primarily as preventing one lawyer from recommending another to a client on the basis of the referral fee that the recommended lawyer will pay, rather than that lawyer's qualifications. The prohibition has also been defended as preventing overcharging that may otherwise result when a client pays two lawyers and only one performs services. Beyond that, the prohibition reflects a general hostility to commercial methods of obtaining clients.

Those grounds do not warrant a complete ban on fee-splitting between lawyers. It is often desirable for one lawyer to refer a client to another, either because the services of two are appropriate or because the second lawyer is more qualified for the work in question. Allowing the referring lawyer to receive reasonable compensation encourages such desirable referrals. Lawyers are more able than other referral sources to identify other lawyers who will best serve their client. Even if a referring lawyer is compensated for the referral, that lawyer has several reasons to refer the client to a good lawyer rather than a bad one offering more pay. The referring lawyer will wish to satisfy the client, will to an extent remain responsible for the work of the second lawyer (see Subsection (1) & Comment *c* hereto), and, because fee-splitting arrangements most commonly occur in representations in which only a contingent fee is charged, will usually receive no fee at all unless the second lawyer helps the client to prevail. The reasonable-fee requirement of Subsection (3), moreover, reduces the likelihood that fee-splitting will lead to client overcharging. The balance between the dangers and advantages of fee-splitting is sufficiently close that informed clients should be able to agree to it, provided the safeguards specified in this Section are followed.

One corollary of the justification for fee division is that a lawyer who may not represent clients, for example because of disbarment or conflict of interest, also may not receive part of the fee.

115

c. Division proportional to services performed. There are two bases on which fee division is permissible. The division recognized by Subsection (1)(a) requires that each lawyer who participates in the fee have performed services beyond those involved in initially being engaged by the client. The lawyers' own agreed allocation of the fee at the outset of the representation will be upheld if it reasonably forecasts the amount and value of effort that each would expend. If allocation is not made until the end of the representation, it must reasonably correspond to services actually performed.

d. Division pursuant to joint responsibility. The second basis for fee-splitting, under Subsection (1)(b), allows fee-splitting between lawyers in any agreed proportion when each agrees with the client to assume responsibility for the representation. (Some jurisdictions may impose an upper limit on the total fee, absent explicit client consent.) That means that each lawyer can be held liable in a malpractice suit and before disciplinary authorities for the others' acts to the same extent as could partners in the same traditional partnership participating in the representation (see § 58). Such assumption of responsibility discourages lawyers from referring clients to careless lawyers in return for a large share of the fee.

* * *

i. Sanctions; questions of the enforceability of improper agreements. A fee-splitting agreement that violates this Section renders the participating lawyers subject to professional discipline (see § 5). It also cannot be enforced against the client, may lead to partial or total forfeiture of the lawyers' fee claim (see § 37), and may form the basis for a claim by the client of restitution of the portion of the fee paid to the forwarding lawyer (see § 6, Comment *d*). Some urge that lawyers who enter into an improper fee-splitting arrangement should be able to enforce it against each other, reasoning that neither may charge the other with an impropriety to which both agreed, and that the prohibition on fee-splitting protects clients rather than lawyers. Enforcement, however, encourages lawyers to continue entering into improper fee-splitting agreements. Accordingly, a lawyer who has violated a regulatory rule or statute by entering into an improper fee-splitting arrangement should not obtain a tribunal's aid to enforce that arrangement, unless the other lawyer is the one responsible for the impropriety. On the other hand, although most lawyer codes on the subject require that a fee-splitting agreement be in writing (and the absence of a writing is a disciplinary violation), when the fact of such agreement is clearly established, the absence of a writing by itself should not affect the rights of the lawyers between themselves.

* * *

116

CHAPTER 4

LAWYER CIVIL LIABILITY

Introductory Note

Introductory Note

* * *

Actions under this Chapter are ordinarily referred to as based on a lawyer's "malpractice." That term can refer to various specific grounds of liability. As used in this Chapter, "legal malpractice" or "malpractice" of a lawyer refers to theories of both professional negligence (§ 48) and violation of a fiduciary duty (§ 49).

TOPIC 1. LIABILITY FOR PROFESSIONAL NEGLIGENCE AND BREACH OF FIDUCIARY DUTY

* * *

§ 48. Professional Negligence—Elements and Defenses Generally

In addition to the other possible bases of civil liability described in §§ 49, 55, and 56, a lawyer is civilly liable for

117

professional negligence to a person to whom the lawyer
owes a duty of care within the meaning of § 50 or § 51, if
the lawyer fails to exercise care within the meaning of
§ 52 and if that failure is a legal cause of injury within
the meaning of § 53, unless the lawyer has a defense
within the meaning of § 54.

Comment:

* * *

c. Theories of liability: tort and contract. The action for malpractice based on a lawyer's negligence has much in common with a
tort action for negligence. Both require that the plaintiff establish that
the defendant owed a duty to the plaintiff and that there has been a
breach of such a duty, typically by showing that the defendant has
acted without reasonable care; comparable principles of proximate
cause and measure of damages apply; and both are subject to defenses
such as contributory or comparative negligence. On indemnity and
contribution, see § 53, Comment *i.*

* * *

Ordinarily, a plaintiff may cast a legal-malpractice claim in the
mold of tort or contract or both (see § 55, Comment *c*; Restatement
Second, Agency §§ 400 & 401). Whether the claim is considered in tort
or in contract is usually of practical significance when it must be
decided whether it is subject to a tort or a contract statute of
limitations in a jurisdiction having a different limitations period for
each. Classification for this purpose depends on the language, structure, and policies of the jurisdiction's statutes of limitations and is
beyond the scope of this Restatement. Some jurisdictions assign all
legal-malpractice claims to one category, while others treat some
claims as in contract and others as in tort, depending on the facts
alleged or the relief sought. For other statute-of-limitations issues, see
§ 54, Comment *g*. In some jurisdictions, the classification of a malpractice claim as tort or contract also affects other issues such as the
measure of damages.

* * *

d. A lawyer who is liable in another capacity. Lawyers often act
in a capacity such as that of a trustee, executor, escrow agent, broker,
mediator, or expert witness. A lawyer acting in such a capacity is
subject to liabilities that applicable law assigns to the capacity. If the
lawyer is also representing a client or owes duties to a nonclient under
§ 51, the lawyer is also subject in appropriate circumstances to
liability for professional negligence and breach of fiduciary duty. For

118

example, if a lawyer representing a client in a transaction also acts as an escrow agent in the transaction and negligently exposes the property held in escrow to theft, the lawyer is subject to liability to the client both for legal malpractice and for breach of the duties of an escrow agent. On the other hand, if a lawyer joins a business partnership, without representing the partnership or partners as clients, and proceeds through negligence to expose partnership property to theft, the lawyer is subject to liability to the other partners for breach of duties under partnership law but not for legal malpractice. When those acting in a capacity are immune from certain civil liability, as are judges, arbitrators, and other neutrals who help resolve disputes, a lawyer acting in that capacity is likewise immune from malpractice and other liability. See Restatement Second, Torts §§ 585 and 895D(2); § 57, Comment *e* (prosecutors).

e. A nonlawyer or a lawyer not locally admitted. Some persons not authorized to do so purport to practice law. Such a person might be a lawyer admitted to practice in another jurisdiction but not locally in a situation requiring local admission, a lawyer suspended or disbarred by disciplinary authorities, or a nonlawyer pretending to be a lawyer (see § 1, Comment *g*). Such a person is subject to liability for legal malpractice for negligence and breach of fiduciary duty and for that purpose is held to the same duty of care as a person locally admitted or otherwise authorized to practice law. A lawyer from another jurisdiction is held to the duty of care applied to local lawyers with respect to questions of the content and application of local law.

* * *

g. Preventing malpractice. Lawyers and law firms may seek to prevent negligence, breach of fiduciary duty, and other grounds of liability through such measures as continuing legal education, supervision (see § 4), peer review, case-acceptance and conflict-avoidance procedures, calendaring systems, and professional-responsibility partners or committees. Although this Restatement does not offer advice on what precautions are prudent, lawyers may wish to consult materials that do so. In appropriate circumstances, failure of a lawyer or firm to have in place a particular preventive device, such as a conflict-avoidance procedure, may constitute evidence of failure to exercise the competence and diligence normally exercised by lawyers in similar circumstances within the meaning of § 52(1). On the scope of the prohibition against agreements prospectively limiting liability for malpractice, see § 54(2) and Comment *b* thereto. On liability insurance, see § 58, Comment *h*.

* * *

§ 49. Breach of Fiduciary Duty—Generally

In addition to the other possible bases of civil liability described in §§ 48, 55, and 56, a lawyer is civilly liable to a client if the lawyer breaches a fiduciary duty to the client set forth in § 16(3) and if that failure is a legal cause of injury within the meaning of § 53, unless the lawyer has a defense within the meaning of § 54.

Comment:

* * *

b. Rationale. A lawyer owes a client the fiduciary duties specified in § 16(3): safeguarding the client's confidences (as specified in Chapter 5, Topic 1) and property (as specified in §§ 44–46); avoiding impermissible conflicting interests (as specified in Chapter 8); dealing honestly with the client (as specified in § 20); adequately informing the client (see § 20); following instructions of the client (see § 21); and not employing adversely to the client powers arising from the client-lawyer relationship (as specified in § 16, Comment *e*, referring also to §§ 41, 126, & 127). See generally Restatement Second, Agency §§ 381–395; Restatement Second, Torts § 874 (liability for breach of fiduciary duty); § 16.

c. Classification: breach of fiduciary duty and professional negligence. Many claims brought by clients against lawyers can reasonably be classified either as for breach of fiduciary-duty or for negligence without any difference in result. For example, the duty of care enforced in a negligence action is also a fiduciary duty (§ 16(2)); likewise, the specific duties of lawyers help define both their fiduciary obligations and the contents of their duty of care. Most rules applicable to negligence actions also apply to actions for breach of fiduciary duty. Pleaders typically add a fiduciary-duty claim to a negligence count for reasons of rhetoric or completeness. Whether classifying a claim as one for breach of fiduciary duty affects the applicable limitations period depends on the language, structure, and policies of a jurisdiction's statute of limitations and is beyond the scope of this Restatement.

d. Proving breach. The principles governing proof that a lawyer's acts constitute negligence apply generally to proving breach of fiduciary duty. E.g., § 52, Comment *g* (expert witnesses); § 52(2) (violation of rule or statute); § 48, Comment *f* (choice of law). When the fiduciary duty in question is that of competence or diligence or of proceeding in a manner reasonably calculated to advance the client's lawful objectives (§ 16(1, 2)), the standard of § 52(1) and Comments *b* and *c* thereto controls.

120

Breaches of some fiduciary duties, for example the duty not to use client confidences for the lawyer's profit (§§ 16(3), 60(2)), typically involve intentional conduct, in that the lawyer chooses to act knowing facts that make the act improper. However, a lawyer who violates fiduciary duties to a client is subject to liability even if the violation or the resulting harm was not intended. A lawyer who has acted with reasonable care is not liable in damages for breach of fiduciary duty, but other remedies such as disqualification, restitution, and injunctive or declaratory relief may be available. See Restatement Second, Trusts § 201, Comment *a*; §§ 6 and 55.

Illustrations:

1. Lawyer agrees to represent Client but Lawyer's firm does not search for possible conflicts of interest. Lawyer proceeds to file a complaint. Just before moving for a preliminary injunction, Lawyer discovers that one of Lawyer's partners formerly represented the opposing party in a substantially related matter, requiring Lawyer to withdraw from representing Client in the absence of client consents, which are not obtained (see § 132). A competent conflicts search would have revealed the conflict. As a result of Lawyer's withdrawal, the preliminary injunction is not obtained for several weeks, causing Client loss. Lawyer is subject to liability to Client for negligent breach of fiduciary duty.

2. The same facts as in Illustration 1, except that Lawyer performs an adequate search but no conflict is found because, unknown to the firm, the opposing party changed its name after the prior representation. A competently maintained conflicts system would not have revealed the conflict. Lawyer is not liable to Client for negligent or intentional breach of fiduciary duty, although Lawyer may be required to withdraw from the representation.

* * *

§ 50. Duty of Care to a Client

For purposes of liability under § 48, a lawyer owes a client the duty to exercise care within the meaning of § 52 in pursuing the client's lawful objectives in matters covered by the representation.

Comment:

* * *

[c.   Clients and former clients.]

* * *

After a client-lawyer relationship ends (see § 31), a lawyer's duties to the former client drastically decrease (see § 33, Comment *h*). Yet a lawyer still owes certain duties to a former client, for example, to surrender papers and property to which the client is entitled (see § 33(1)), protect client confidences (see § 60), and avoid certain conflicts of interest (see §§ 132–133). Breach of such duties, which are summarized in § 33, may be remedied through a malpractice action in circumstances coming within this Section. Of course, a former client may also bring a malpractice action, subject to the applicable statute of limitations, to recover for a lawyer's breaches of duty during the relationship. On whether a client-lawyer relationship is a continuing one, see § 31, Comment *h*.

* * *

e.   Lawful objectives. A lawyer may not pursue a client objective or take or assist any act when the lawyer knows that the objective or act is prohibited by law, and the lawyer may decline to pursue objectives or to take or assist acts that the lawyer reasonably believes to be so prohibited (see §§ 23(1) & 94). A lawyer is hence not subject to liability to a client for malpractice for failing to pursue objectives or to take or assist acts that the lawyer reasonably believes to be prohibited by law (including professional rules) (see § 54(1)). Similarly, a lawyer is not subject to liability to a client for performing an act the lawyer reasonably believes to be required by law, even though it impedes the client's objectives. For example, if a lawyer has raised all nonfrivolous objections to discovery of a document in the lawyer's custody but the court has ordered discovery, the lawyer is not subject to malpractice liability for complying with the discovery order, even though the client wishes the lawyer to commit contempt of court by violating the order. The same principles also protect a lawyer from liability to nonclients (see § 51).

When a lawyer reasonably believes that an act or objective is immoral or violates professional courtesy, even if not unlawful, the lawyer may assume that the client would not want that act or objective to be pursued. The lawyer may also: urge a client to refrain from pursuing the act or objective (see § 94(3) & Comment *h* thereto); decline to accept the representation unless the client abandons the act or objective or agrees that the lawyer will not be obliged to perform such acts (see § 21); take morality and professional courtesy into account in making decisions reserved to the lawyer (see § 23); refuse to follow the client's instructions in the circumstances stated in § 21, Comment *e*; and withdraw from the representation in the circumstances stated in § 32(3)(e). None of those courses of conduct violates the duties described in this Section. However, a lawyer must, when it is reasonably feasible, give the client notice of the refusal to pursue an act or objective that the client has requested or directed.

* * *

§ 51. Duty of Care to Certain Nonclients

For purposes of liability under § 48, a lawyer owes a duty to use care within the meaning of § 52 in each of the following circumstances:

(1) to a prospective client, as stated in § 15;

(2) to a nonclient when and to the extent that:

(a) the lawyer or (with the lawyer's acquiescence) the lawyer's client invites the nonclient to rely on the lawyer's opinion or provision of other legal services, and the nonclient so relies; and

(b) the nonclient is not, under applicable tort law, too remote from the lawyer to be entitled to protection;

(3) to a nonclient when and to the extent that:

(a) the lawyer knows that a client intends as one of the primary objectives of the representation that the lawyer's services benefit the nonclient;

(b) such a duty would not significantly impair the lawyer's performance of obligations to the client; and

(c) the absence of such a duty would make enforcement of those obligations to the client unlikely; and

(4) to a nonclient when and to the extent that:

(a) the lawyer's client is a trustee, guardian, executor, or fiduciary acting primarily to perform similar functions for the nonclient;

(b) the lawyer knows that appropriate action by the lawyer is necessary with respect to a matter within the scope of the representation to prevent or rectify the breach of a fiduciary duty owed by the client to the nonclient, where (i) the breach is a crime or fraud or (ii) the lawyer has assisted or is assisting the breach;

(c) the nonclient is not reasonably able to protect its rights; and

(d) such a duty would not significantly impair the performance of the lawyer's obligations to the client.

Comment:

* * *

c. Opposing parties. A lawyer representing a party in litigation has no duty of care to the opposing party under this Section, and hence no liability for lack of care, except in unusual situations such as when a litigant is provided an opinion letter from opposing counsel as part of a settlement (see Subsection (2) and Comment *e* hereto). Imposing such a duty could discourage vigorous representation of the lawyer's own client through fear of liability to the opponent. Moreover, the opposing party is protected by the rules and procedures of the adversary system and, usually, by counsel. In some circumstances, a lawyer's negligence will entitle an opposing party to relief other than damages, such as vacating a settlement induced by negligent misrepresentation. For a lawyer's liability to sanctions, which may include payments to an opposing party, based on certain litigation misconduct, see § 110. See also § 56, on liability for intentional torts.

* * *

[*e. Inviting reliance of a nonclient (Subsection (2)).*]

* * *

In some circumstances, reliance by unspecified persons may be expected, as when a lawyer for a borrower writes an opinion letter to the original lender in a bank credit transaction knowing that the letter will be used to solicit other lenders to become participants in syndication of the loan. Whether a subsequent syndication participant can recover for the lawyer's negligence in providing such an opinion letter depends on what, if anything, the letter says about reliance and whether the jurisdiction in question, as a matter of general tort law, adheres to the limitations on duty of Restatement Second, Torts § 552(2) or those of Ultramares Corp. v. Touche, 174 N.E. 441 (N.Y.1931), or has rejected such limitations. To account for such differences in general tort law, Subsection (2) refers to applicable law excluding liability to persons too remote from the lawyer.

* * *

A lawyer may avoid liability to nonclients under Subsection (2) by making clear that an opinion or representation is directed only to a client and should not be relied on by others. Likewise, a lawyer may limit or avoid liability under Subsection (2) by qualifying a representation, for example by making clear through limiting or disclaiming language in an opinion letter that the lawyer is relying on facts provided by the client without independent investigation by the lawyer (assuming that the lawyer does not know the facts provided by the client to be false, in which case the lawyer would be liable for misrepresentation). The effectiveness of a limitation or disclaimer depends on whether it was reasonable in the circumstances to conclude that those provided with the opinion would receive the limitation or disclaimer and understand its import. The relevant circumstances include customary practices known to the recipient concerning the construction of opinions and whether the recipient is represented by counsel or a similarly experienced agent.

When a nonclient is invited to rely on a lawyer's legal services, other than the lawyer's opinion, the analysis is similar. For example, if the seller's lawyer at a real-estate closing offers to record the deed for the buyer, the lawyer is subject to liability to the buyer for negligence in doing so, even if the buyer did not thereby become a client of the lawyer. When a nonclient is invited to rely on a lawyer's nonlegal services, the lawyer's duty of care is determined by the law applicable to providers of the services in question.

* * *

g. *A liability insurer's claim for professional negligence.* Under Subsection (3), a lawyer designated by an insurer to defend an insured owes a duty of care to the insurer with respect to matters as to which the interests of the insurer and insured are not in conflict, whether or not the insurer is held to be a co-client of the lawyer (see § 134, Comment f). For example, if the lawyer negligently fails to oppose a motion for summary judgment against the insured and the insurer must pay the resulting adverse judgment, the insurer has a claim against the lawyer for any proximately caused loss. In such circumstances, the insured and insurer, under the insurance contract, both have a reasonable expectation that the lawyer's services will benefit both insured and insurer. Recognizing that the lawyer owes a duty to the insurer promotes enforcement of the lawyer's obligations to the insured. However, such a duty does not arise when it would significantly impair, in the circumstances of the representation, the lawyer's performance of obligations to the insured. For example, if the lawyer recommends acceptance of a settlement offer just below the policy limits and the insurer accepts the offer, the insurer may not later seek to recover from the lawyer on a claim that a competent lawyer in the circumstances would have advised that the offer be rejected. Allowing recovery in such circumstances would give the lawyer an interest in recommending rejection of a settlement offer beneficial to the insured in order to escape possible liability to the insurer.

* * *

§ 52. The Standard of Care

(1) **For purposes of liability under §§ 48 and 49, a lawyer who owes a duty of care must exercise the competence and diligence normally exercised by lawyers in similar circumstances.**

(2) **Proof of a violation of a rule or statute regulating the conduct of lawyers:**

(a) **does not give rise to an implied cause of action for professional negligence or breach of fiduciary duty;**

(b) **does not preclude other proof concerning the duty of care in Subsection (1) or the fiduciary duty; and**

(c) **may be considered by a trier of fact as an aid in understanding and applying the standard of Subsection (1) or § 49 to the extent that (i) the rule or statute was designed for the protection of persons in the position of the claimant and (ii) proof of the content and construction of such a rule or statute is relevant to the claimant's claim.**

Comment:

* * *

b. Competence. The duty of competence set forth in this Section is that generally applicable to practitioners of a profession, that is, "the skill and knowledge normally possessed by members of that profession or trade in good standing . . . " (Restatement Second, Torts § 299A). Informed clients expect services of this kind; it is practical for lawyers to provide them; and the practice of the profession will most often be evidence of what clients need. As is generally true for professions, the legal duty refers to normal professional practice to define the ordinary standard of care for lawyers, rather than referring to that standard as simply evidence of reasonableness.

The competence duty, like that for diligence, does not make the lawyer a guarantor of a successful outcome in the representation (see § 55(1)). It does not expose the lawyer to liability to a client for acting only within the scope of the representation (see § 19 & § 54, Comment *b*) or following the client's instructions (see § 21(2) & § 54, Comment *h*). It does not require a lawyer, in a situation involving the exercise of professional judgment, to employ the same means or select the same options as would other competent lawyers in the many situations in which competent lawyers reasonably exercise professional judgment in different ways. The duty also does not require "average" performance, which would imply that the less skillful part of the profession would automatically be committing malpractice. The duty is one of reasonableness in the circumstances.

A trier of fact applying the standard may consider such circumstances as time pressures, uncertainty about facts or law, the varying means by which different competent lawyers seek to accomplish the same client goal, and the impossibility that all clients will reach their goals. Such factors are especially prevalent in litigation. They warrant caution in evaluating lawyers' decisions, although they do not warrant the view, still occasionally asserted, that all decisions taken in good faith are exempt from malpractice liability. Expert testimony by those knowledgeable about the legal subject matter in question is relevant in applying the standard (see Comment *g* hereto). In appropriate circumstances, a tribunal passing on a motion for summary judgment or directed verdict may determine whether a lawyer has satisfied the duty.

The professional community whose practices and standards are relevant in applying this duty of competence is ordinarily that of lawyers undertaking similar matters in the relevant jurisdiction (typically, a state). (On conflict-of-laws problems, see § 5, Comment *h* (lawyer discipline); § 48, Comment *f*.) The narrower "locality test," under which the standards of a local community governed, has seldom been recognized for lawyers. Restatement Second, Torts § 299A, Comment *g*. The locality test is now generally rejected for all professions, because all professionals can normally obtain access to standard information and facilities, because clients no longer limit themselves to local professionals, and because of the practicalities of proof in malpractice cases (see Comment *g* hereto). In many fields of legal practice, for example the preparation of securities-registration statements or the representation of clients in federal court in litigation under federal legislation, there exists a national practice with national standards. In applying the competence duty, however, it may be appropriate to consider factors such as the unavailability of particular research sources in the community where a lawyer practices in light of the difficulty and probable value in the circumstances of having done further research.

c. Diligence. A lawyer must devote reasonable diligence to a representation. The lawyer must perform tasks reasonably appropriate to the representation, including, where appropriate, inquiry into facts, analysis of law, exercise of professional judgment, communication with the client, rendering of practical and ethical advice, and drafting of documents. What kind and extent of effort is appropriate depends on factors such as the scope of the representation (see § 19(1)), the client's instructions (see § 21(2)), the importance of the matter to the client (which may be indicated by the client's own assertions as well as by the matter's probable impact on the client's affairs), the cost of the effort, customary practice, and the time available. A lawyer who informs a client that the lawyer will undertake a specifically described activity is required to do so, as is one properly instructed by a client to take a particular step (see § 21(2)). Circumstances might make it necessary to provide more than one lawyer for a client's matter or to provide appropriate supervision of subordinate lawyers (see § 11) or certain corresponding counsel (see § 58, Comment *e*). When paralegals or other nonlawyers are used, they must be properly supervised. See Restatement Second, Torts § 213; § 58 (vicarious liability of firm and partners); § 11(4) (duty to supervise). Even when a lawyer has been inadequately diligent, the lawyer's breach of duty might not be the legal cause of compensable damage (see § 53), for example if without required investigation the lawyer recommended that the client accept a settlement offer that was in fact a good one.

d. Similar circumstances. A lawyer's representations or disclaimers and qualifications may constitute circumstances affecting what a client is entitled to expect from the lawyer. Thus, a lawyer who represents to a client that the lawyer has greater competence or will exercise greater diligence than that normally demonstrated by lawyers in good standing undertaking similar matters is held to that higher standard, on which such a client is entitled to rely. See Restatement Second, Torts § 299A, Comment *d*. Likewise, a lawyer must "exercise any special skill that he has." Restatement Second, Agency § 379(1). A representation may be made directly, for example when a lawyer claims to be an expert or specialist in a given field through an advertisement or listing or by an assertion of specialization on a letterhead. The representation may be on behalf of the lawyer in question or of a law firm in which the lawyer practices. A lawyer's duty to a nonclient under § 51(2) is governed by a duty of greater competence only when the standard is known to the nonclient. Such a representation has no bearing on a lawyer's liability to a nonclient under § 51(4).

A lawyer may disclaim greater than ordinary competence or possession of specialized knowledge or skill. When a matter is of a kind normally undertaken by specialists, a nonspecialist generally must make such a disclaimer to avoid being held to the specialist duty. If a nonspecialist exercising normal competence would not undertake such a representation, a nonspecialist must (except in an emergency) either refer the case to or associate with a specialist or acquire the competence of an ordinary specialist. For those purposes, a specialty is one so recognized by authorities regulating the bar of the jurisdiction or one generally so recognized by lawyers.

[e.   *Suit by a nonclient.*]

* * *

Illustrations:

     1.   Client instructs Lawyer to write a will leaving a bequest in trust to Beneficiary and to do so within one day because Client is gravely ill. Lawyer does so. After Client's death, the bequest is set aside for a defect that a lawyer of ordinary competence in preparing wills could not reasonably have been expected to discover within one day. Beneficiary sues Lawyer for professional negligence. Beneficiary may not recover. Although Lawyer owes a duty of care to Beneficiary under § 51(3), that duty is recognized to enforce Lawyer's duty to Client to implement Client's wishes, which in this instance included acting with great urgency. Lawyer reasonably complied with Client's request that Lawyer complete the will immediately (see § 19). Time constraints reasonably incurred are relevant to what constitutes ordinary competence (see Comment *b*). Beneficiary cannot exact from Lawyer greater care than Lawyer owed Client (see § 51, Comment *f*).

     2.   Client and Buyer agree that, as a condition to closing a sale of Client's personal property to Buyer, Client will provide an opinion letter by Lawyer regarding liens on the property. Lawyer is aware of the agreement. Client privately instructs Lawyer to rely on Client's own factual assertions in preparing the opinion letter, rather than searching relevant public lien records as customary practice would require. Lawyer relies on Client's assertions and as a result Lawyer's opinion letter does not mention a recorded lien that Buyer discovers only after consummating the

purchase. Lawyer is liable to Buyer for lack of diligence. Lawyer's duty of care to Buyer under § 51(2) is based on Buyer's reasonable reliance, invited by Client, on Lawyer's opinion letter. Although Client and Lawyer might agree, as between themselves, that Lawyer would base the opinion only on facts supplied by Client, that private agreement does not excuse Lawyer from conducting the investigation called for by customary practice in rendering such an opinion. Lawyer might have avoided liability to Buyer by declining to provide the opinion or by making clear to Buyer that Lawyer had relied entirely on Client for information about liens (see § 51, Comment *e*). On a lawyer's obligations in furnishing an opinion, see § 95, Comments *f* and *g*.

* * *

g. Expert testimony. The application of this Section's definition of care or of fiduciary duties usually involves situations and requirements of legal practice unknown to most jurors and often not familiar in detail to judges. Accordingly, a plaintiff alleging professional negligence or breach of fiduciary duty ordinarily must introduce expert testimony concerning the care reasonably required in the circumstances of the case and the lawyer's failure to exercise such care. Such expert testimony is unnecessary when it would be plain to a nonlawyer or is established as a matter of law that the lawyer's acts constitute negligence (for example, when a lawyer allegedly let the statute of limitations expire or withdrew without notifying a client) or breach of fiduciary duty. A defending lawyer may also introduce expert evidence on what constitutes care in the circumstances of the case or to support a defense under § 54(1).

An expert opinion on what constitutes proper conduct in the circumstances of the case may be based on the expert's own experience and judgment and on the expert's knowledge of applicable rules and statutes (see Comment *f* hereto), of literature discussing how lawyers do or should behave, and of the conduct and beliefs of lawyers. The party introducing the opinion must comply with the jurisdiction's evidentiary requirements as to qualifying the expert, the form of the testimony, the materials the expert may rely on in forming an opinion, and the like. As permitted by such rules, parties may also introduce expert evidence on such matters as the range of professional opinion on a legal issue resolved by a lawyer, issues of causation, and damages.

* * *

§ 53. Causation and Damages

A lawyer is liable under § 48 or § 49 only if the lawyer's breach of a duty of care or breach of fiduciary duty was a legal cause of injury, as determined under generally applicable principles of causation and damages.

Comment:

* * *

b. Action by a civil litigant: loss of a judgment. In a lawyer-negligence or fiduciary-breach action brought by one who was the plaintiff in a former and unsuccessful civil action, the plaintiff usually seeks to recover as damages the damages that would have been recovered in the previous action or the additional amount that would have been recovered but for the defendant's misconduct. To do so, the plaintiff must prove by a preponderance of the evidence that, but for the defendant lawyer's misconduct, the plaintiff would have obtained a more favorable judgment in the previous action. The plaintiff must thus prevail in a "trial within a trial." All the issues that would have been litigated in the previous action are litigated between the plaintiff and the plaintiff's former lawyer, with the latter taking the place and bearing the burdens that properly would have fallen on the defendant in the original action. Similarly, the plaintiff bears the burden the plaintiff would have borne in the original trial; in considering whether the plaintiff has carried that burden, however, the trier of fact may consider whether the defendant lawyer's misconduct has made it more difficult for the plaintiff to prove what would have been the result in the original trial. (On a lawyer's right to disclose client confidences when reasonably necessary in defending against a claim, see §§ 64 and 80.) Similar principles apply when a former civil defendant contends that, but for the misconduct of the defendant's former lawyer, the defendant would have secured a better result at trial.

* * *

A plaintiff may show that the defendant's negligence or fiduciary breach caused injury other than the loss of a judgment. For example, a plaintiff may contend that, in a previous action, the plaintiff would have obtained a settlement but for the malpractice of the lawyer who then represented the plaintiff. A plaintiff might contend that the defendant in the previous action made a settlement offer, that the plaintiff's then lawyer negligently failed to inform plaintiff of the offer (see § 20(3)), and that, if informed, plaintiff would have accepted the offer. If the plaintiff can prove this, the plaintiff can recover the difference between what the claimant would have received under the settlement offer and the amount, if any, the claimant in fact received through later settlement or judgment. Similarly, in appropriate circumstances, a plaintiff who can establish that the negligence or fiduciary breach of the plaintiff's former lawyer deprived the plaintiff of a substantial chance of prevailing and that, due to that misconduct, the results of a previous trial cannot be reconstructed, may recover for the loss of that chance in jurisdictions recognizing such a theory of recovery in professional-malpractice cases generally.

* * *

Even when a plaintiff would have recovered through trial or settlement in a previous civil action, recovery in the negligence or fiduciary-breach action of what would have been the judgment or settlement in the previous action is precluded in some circumstances. Thus, the lawyer's misconduct will not be the legal cause of loss to the extent that the defendant lawyer can show that the judgment or settlement would have been uncollectible, for example because the previous defendant was insolvent and uninsured. The defendant lawyer bears the burden of coming forward with evidence that this was so. Placement of this burden on the defending lawyer is appropriate because most civil judgments are collectible and because the defendant lawyer was the one who undertook to seek the judgment that the lawyer now calls worthless. The burden of persuading the jury as to collectibility remains upon the plaintiff.

c. *Action by a civil litigant: attorney fees that would have been due.* When it is shown that a plaintiff would have prevailed in the former civil action but for the lawyer's legal fault, it might be thought that—applying strict causation principles—the damages to be recovered in the legal-malpractice action should be reduced by the fee due the lawyer in the former matter. That is, the plaintiff has lost the net amount recovered after paying that attorney fee. Yet if the net amount were all the plaintiff could recover in the malpractice action, the defendant lawyer would in effect be credited with a fee that the lawyer never earned, and the plaintiff would have to pay two lawyers (the defendant lawyer and the plaintiff's lawyer in the malpractice action) to recover one judgment.

Denial of a fee deduction hence may be an appropriate sanction for the defendant lawyer's misconduct: to the extent that the lawyer defendant did not earn a fee due to the lawyer's misconduct, no such fee may be deducted in calculating the recovery in the malpractice action. The same principles apply to a legal-malpractice plaintiff who was a defendant in a previous civil action. The appropriateness and extent of disallowing deduction of the fee are determined under the standards of § 37 governing fee forfeiture. In some circumstances, those standards allow the lawyer to be credited with fees for services that benefited the client. See § 37, Comment *e*.

* * *

d. Action by a criminal defendant. A convicted criminal defendant suing for malpractice must prove both that the lawyer failed to act properly and that, but for that failure, the result would have been different, for example because a double-jeopardy defense would have prevented conviction. Although most jurisdictions addressing the issue have stricter rules, under this Section it is not necessary to prove that the convicted defendant was in fact innocent. As required by most jurisdictions addressing the issue, a convicted defendant seeking damages for malpractice causing a conviction must have had that conviction set aside when process for that relief on the grounds asserted in the malpractice action is available.

A judgment in a postconviction proceeding is binding in the malpractice action to the extent provided by the law of judgments. That law prevents a convicted defendant from relitigating an issue decided in a postconviction proceeding after a full and fair opportunity to litigate, even though the lawyer sued was not a party to that proceeding and is hence not bound by any decision favorable to the defendant. See Restatement Second, Judgments §§ 27–29. Some jurisdictions hold public defenders immune from malpractice suits.

* * *

f. Attorney fees as damages. Like other civil litigants, the winning party in a malpractice action ordinarily cannot recover its attorney fees and other expenses in the malpractice action itself, except to the limited extent that the jurisdiction allows the recovery of court costs. The rule barring fee recovery has exceptions, which may be applicable in a malpractice action in appropriate circumstances. For example, many jurisdictions allow recovery of attorney fees against a plaintiff or defendant that litigates in bad faith (see also § 110, Comment *g* (litigation sanctions)).

* * *

g. Damages for emotional distress. General principles applicable to the recovery of damages for emotional distress apply to legal-malpractice actions. In general, such damages are inappropriate in types of cases in which emotional distress is unforeseeable. Thus, emotional-distress damages are ordinarily not recoverable when a lawyer's misconduct causes the client to lose profits from a commercial transaction, but are ordinarily recoverable when misconduct causes a client's imprisonment. The law in some jurisdictions permits recovery for emotional-distress damages only when the defendant lawyer's conduct was clearly culpable (see also § 56, Comment *g*).

h. Punitive damages. Whether punitive damages are recoverable in a legal-malpractice action depends on the jurisdiction's generally applicable law. Punitive damages are generally permitted only on a showing of intentional or reckless misconduct by a defendant.

A few decisions allow a plaintiff to recover from a lawyer punitive damages that would have been recovered from the defendant in an underlying action but for the lawyer's misconduct. However, such recovery is not required by the punitive and deterrent purposes of punitive damages. Collecting punitive damages from the lawyer will neither punish nor deter the original tortfeasor and calls for a speculative reconstruction of a hypothetical jury's reaction.

* * *

§ 54. Defenses; Prospective Liability Waiver; Settlement with a Client

(1) **Except as otherwise provided in this Section, liability under §§ 48 and 49 is subject to the defenses available under generally applicable principles of law governing respectively actions for professional negligence and breach of fiduciary duty. A lawyer is not liable under § 48 or § 49 for any action or inaction the lawyer reasonably believed to be required by law, including a professional rule.**

(2) **An agreement prospectively limiting a lawyer's liability to a client for malpractice is unenforceable.**

(3) **The client or former client may rescind an agreement settling a claim by the client or former client against the person's lawyer if:**

(a) **the client or former client was subjected to improper pressure by the lawyer in reaching the settlement; or**

(b) **(i) the client or former client was not independently represented in negotiating the settlement, and (ii) the settlement was not fair and reasonable to the client or former client.**

(4) **For purposes of professional discipline, a lawyer may not:**

(a) **make an agreement prospectively limiting the lawyer's liability to a client for malpractice; or**

(b) settle a claim for such liability with an unrepresented client or former client without first advising that person in writing that independent representation is appropriate in connection therewith.

Comment:

* * *

b. Prospectively limiting liability. An agreement prospectively limiting a lawyer's liability to a client under §§ 48–54 is unenforceable and renders the lawyer subject to professional discipline. The rule derives from the lawyer codes, but has broader application. Such an agreement is against public policy because it tends to undermine competent and diligent legal representation. Also, many clients are unable to evaluate the desirability of such an agreement before a dispute has arisen or while they are represented by the lawyer seeking the agreement (see § 19). The same principles apply also to agreements prospectively waiving the liabilities of lawyers to clients set forth in §§ 33(1), 37, 55, and 56.

However, a lawyer and client may properly take certain measures that may have the effect of narrowing or otherwise affecting the lawyer's liability (see generally § 19 & § 52, Comment *d*). A client and lawyer may agree in advance, subject to §§ 18 and 19, to arbitrate claims for legal malpractice, provided that the client receives proper notice of the scope and effect of the agreement and if the relevant jurisdiction's law applicable to providers of professional services renders such agreements enforceable (see also § 6, Comment *h*; compare § 42, Comment *b(iv)* (fee arbitration)). A lawyer may also obtain liability insurance, protecting against the cost of defending and paying claims for legal malpractice, obtain an indemnity arrangement from an employer, or incorporate (see § 58).

* * *

d. Comparative and contributory negligence. In jurisdictions in which comparative negligence is a defense in negligence and fiduciary-breach actions generally, it is generally a defense in legal-malpractice and fiduciary-breach actions based on negligence to the same extent and subject to the same rules. The same is true of contributory negligence and comparative or contributory fault generally. See Restatement Second, Torts §§ 463–496; Restatement Second, Agency § 415. (On intentional torts, see § 56.) In appraising those defenses, regard must be had to the special circumstances of client-lawyer relationships. Under fiduciary principles, clients are entitled to rely on their lawyers to act with competence, diligence, honesty, and loyalty (see § 16), and to fulfill a lawyer's duty to notify a client of substantial malpractice claims (see § 20, Comment c). The difficulty many clients face in monitoring a lawyer's performance is one of the main grounds for imposing a fiduciary duty on lawyers. Except in unusual circumstances, therefore, it is not negligent for a client to fail to investigate, detect, or cure a lawyer's malpractice until the client is aware or should reasonably be aware of facts clearly indicating the basis for the client's claim (see also Comment g hereto). Whether a client should reasonably be so aware may depend, among other factors, on the client's sophistication in relevant legal or factual matters.

* * *

    e. Failure to mitigate damages; assumption of the risk. To the extent that applicable law recognizes them in other negligence actions, the partial defense of failure to mitigate damages and the defense of assumption of the risk apply to legal-malpractice claims. However, their availability is subject to considerations of lawyer fiduciary duties and the characteristics of client-lawyer relationships (see generally Comment d hereto).

    f. In pari delicto. The defense of in pari delicto bars a plaintiff from recovering from a defendant for a wrong in which the plaintiff's conduct was also seriously culpable. To the extent recognized by the jurisdiction for other actions, the defense is available in legal-malpractice actions, subject to consideration of lawyer fiduciary duties and the characteristics of client-lawyer relationships (see generally Comment d hereto). The defense is thus available only in circumstances in which a client may reasonably be expected to know that the activity is a wrong despite the lawyer's implicit endorsement of it, for example when a client claims to have followed the advice of a lawyer to commit perjury.

    g. Statute of limitations. Claims against a lawyer may give rise to issues concerning statutes of limitations, for example, which statute (contract, tort, or other) applies to a legal-malpractice action, what the limitations period is, when it starts to run, and whether various circumstances suspend its running. Such issues are resolved by construing the applicable statute of limitations. Three special principles apply in legal-malpractice actions, although their acceptance and application may vary in light of the particular wording, policies, and construction of applicable statutes.

    First, the statute of limitations ordinarily does not run while the lawyer continuously represents the client in the matter in question or a substantially related matter. Until the representation terminates, the client may assume that the lawyer, as a competent and loyal fiduciary, will deflect or repair whatever harm may be threatened. Cf. §§ 32(2)(a) and 125 (lawyer's duty to withdraw to avoid certain conflicts between lawyer and client interests). That principle does not apply if the client knows or reasonably should know that the lawyer will not be able to repair the harm, or if client and lawyer validly agree (see Subsection (3) hereto) that the lawyer's continuing the representation will not affect the running of the limitations period.

Second, even when the statute of limitations is generally construed to start to run when the harm occurs, the statute does not start to run against a fiduciary such as a lawyer until the fiduciary discloses the arguable malpractice to the client or until facts that the client knows or reasonably should know clearly indicate that malpractice may have occurred. Until then, the client is not obliged to look out for possible defects (see Comment *d* hereto) and may assume that the lawyer is providing competent and loyal service and will notify the client of any substantial claim (see § 20, Comment *c*).

Third, the statute of limitations does not start to run until the lawyer's alleged malpractice has inflicted significant injury. For example, if a lawyer negligently drafts a contract so as to render it arguably unenforceable, the statute of limitations does not start to run until the other contracting party declines to perform or the client suffers comparable injury. Until then, it is unclear whether the lawyer's malpractice will cause harm. Moreover, to require the client to file suit before then might injure both client and lawyer by attracting the attention of the other contracting party to the problem. Whether significant injury has been inflicted by a lawyer's errors at trial when appeal or other possible remedies remain available is debated in judicial decisions. Compliance with decisions holding that injury occurs prior to affirmance on appeal (or similar unsuccessful outcome) may require that a protective malpractice action be filed pending the outcome of the appeal or other remedy.

h. Lawyer action or inaction required by law or client instructions. A lawyer is not liable under § 48 or § 49 for any action or inaction that the lawyer reasonably believed to be required by law, including applicable professional rules and court orders (see § 50, Comment *e*; § 23). When, for example, a jurisdiction's professional rule requires a lawyer to disclose a client's proposed crime when necessary to prevent death or serious bodily harm (compare § 66), a lawyer who reasonably believes that disclosure is required is not liable to a client for disclosing. Similarly, if the rule forbids disclosure of a client's proposed unlawful act not constituting a crime or fraud, a lawyer who reasonably believes that disclosure is forbidden is not liable to a nonclient under § 51. A client may not recover from a lawyer for any action or inaction that the client, after proper advice, instructed the lawyer to take (see § 21(2) & § 52, Comments *c* & *e*). The defense of reasonable belief that a lawyer's acts were required by law does not, however, apply to a claim against a lawyer for restitution under provisions other than §§ 48 and 49, such as § 55, or based on a violation of § 60 or § 121. Whether such a defense applies to such claims depends on the general law governing the claim in question.

When a lawyer relies on a professional rule or other legal requirement as a defense, the trier of fact may be informed, by instruction and through testimony, of its content and construction, and an expert witness may rely on that law in forming an opinion whether the lawyer acted with the care required by § 52(1) (see § 52, Comments *f* & *g*). Whether expert testimony is required for a lawyer to raise such a defense is determined by the principles set forth in § 52, Comment *g*.

Professional rules and other law allow but do not require many acts, either by stating that a lawyer may perform them or by not prohibiting them. Although the permissibility of an act under a professional rule does not constitute a defense to liability under § 48 or § 49, a defending lawyer may, when and to the extent provided by § 52(2) and Comment *f* thereto, use the rule to show the care required in the circumstances.

* * *

TOPIC 2. OTHER CIVIL LIABILITY

* * *

§ 55. Civil Remedies of a Client Other Than for Malpractice

(1) A lawyer is subject to liability to a client for injury caused by breach of contract in the circumstances and to the extent provided by contract law.

(2) A client is entitled to restitutionary, injunctive, or declaratory remedies against a lawyer in the circumstances and to the extent provided by generally applicable law governing such remedies.

Comment:

* * *

c. Contract claims. A client's claims for legal malpractice, as considered in §§ 48–54, can be considered either as tort claims for negligence or breach of fiduciary duty or as contract claims for breach of implied terms in a client-lawyer agreement. Ordinarily, a plaintiff may cast a legal-malpractice claim as a tort claim, a contract claim, or both and often also as a claim for breach of fiduciary duty. The law set forth in §§ 48–54 governs all three kinds of claim. The choice of theory may, however, affect what statute of limitations applies and in some jurisdictions may affect other issues (see § 48, Comment *c*, & § 49, Comments *c*, *d*, & *e*). A client may also assert against a lawyer contractual claims that likewise could be asserted as tort claims or claims of fiduciary breach and are subject to §§ 48–54, such as claims that a lawyer disobeyed the client's valid instruction or an agreement concerning what the lawyer would do (see § 21(1) & (2)).

* * *

A lawyer who warrants to a client that the lawyer will accomplish a specifically described result for the client, knowing that the result has material importance to the client, owes the client a contractual duty to fulfill that warranty. However, a finding of such a warranty may not be based on proof consisting only of general statements of the lawyer expressing an expectation of favorable results. Likewise, such a finding may not be made, absent an unequivocal promise by the lawyer, when it should have been reasonably clear to the client that the result in question depended on factors other than the lawyer's efforts, for example on the actions of another party or a tribunal. Lawyers are thus free to inform clients of the progress and prospects of a representation (see § 20) without incurring the liabilities of a guarantor.

* * *

When a client's contract claim against a lawyer is not subject to §§ 48–54, the law of contracts governs such matters as contract construction (subject to § 18), breach, damages, and defenses (see generally Restatement Second, Contracts). That law is construed in the light of the special circumstances involved in client-lawyer relationships and the policies applicable thereto. On remedies and burdens of persuasion in attorney-fee disputes, see § 42.

* * *

§ 56. Liability to a Client or Nonclient Under General Law

Except as provided in § 57 and in addition to liability under §§ 48–55, a lawyer is subject to liability to a client or nonclient when a nonlawyer would be in similar circumstances.

139

Comment:

* * *

[*c. Advising and assisting acts of clients.*]

* * *

On the other hand, a lawyer is not always free of liability to a nonclient for assisting a client's act solely because the lawyer was acting in the course of a representation (see Comment *b* hereto). Thus, a lawyer who knowingly helps a client deceive a person may be liable for fraud (see Comment *f* hereto). See generally § 94.

In general, a lawyer is not liable for a client's tort unless the lawyer assisted the client through conduct itself tortious or gave substantial assistance to the client knowing the client's conduct to be tortious. See Restatement Second, Torts § 876 (liability of persons acting in concert). Proper advice to a client does not constitute assistance leading to liability. Whether a more onerous standard applies to a lawyer who assists a client's conduct depends on applicable law, which in general requires negligent or intentional misconduct for civil liability to attach to a principal and often requires a higher level of awareness for a lawyer than for a principal.

* * *

§ 57. Nonclient Claims—Certain Defenses and Exceptions to Liability

(1) In addition to other absolute or conditional privileges, a lawyer is absolutely privileged to publish matter concerning a nonclient if:

(a) the publication occurs in communications preliminary to a reasonably anticipated proceeding before a tribunal or in the institution or during the course and as a part of such a proceeding;

(b) the lawyer participates as counsel in that proceeding; and

(c) the matter is published to a person who may be involved in the proceeding, and the publication has some relation to the proceeding.

(2) A lawyer representing a client in a civil proceeding or procuring the institution of criminal proceedings by a client is not liable to a nonclient for wrongful use of civil proceedings or for malicious prosecution if the lawyer has probable cause for acting, or if the lawyer acts primarily to help the client obtain a proper adjudication of the client's claim in that proceeding.

(3) A lawyer who advises or assists a client to make or break a contract, to enter or dissolve a legal relationship, or to enter or not enter a contractual relation, is not liable to a nonclient for interference with contract or with prospective contractual relations or with a legal relationship, if the lawyer acts to advance the client's objectives without using wrongful means.

Comment:

* * *

b.   Rationale. The rules stated in Subsections (1) and (2) protect a lawyer engaging in litigation on behalf of a client from civil actions brought by nonclients. Allowing nonclients to recover for defamation or malicious prosecution or wrongful use of civil proceedings could discourage lawyers from representing clients with proper vigor and thus impede the access of litigants to court. Moreover, the adversary system itself provides some control against improper lawyer conduct in litigation, as does the tribunal's power to govern the conduct of lawyers appearing before it (see § 1, Comment *b*, & § 105, Comment *d*) and the availability of professional discipline (see § 5). This Section thus bars lawyer liability for what would otherwise be defamation in litigation and limits lawyer liability for malicious prosecution and wrongful use of civil proceedings. For the rationale of the privilege set forth by Subsection (3), see Comment *g*.

c.   Defamation privileges. As is true of parties to litigation and other participants such as witnesses, a lawyer is absolutely privileged against defamation liability for publishing a defamatory statement relating to civil or criminal litigation before a tribunal exercising a judicial function, even if the lawyer acts maliciously and knows the statement to be false. See Restatement Second, Torts § 586 (lawyers) and §§ 587–588 (parties and witnesses). "Publication" and "publish" for this purpose has the same meaning as in the law of defamation. Such a tribunal may be a court, administrative tribunal, or arbitrator. The defamatory statement may be made, for example, in a pleading, brief, question to a witness (including a question subject to valid objection), or oral argument. The person allegedly defamed may be a party to the litigation, a witness, or someone else.

Statements made before litigation is instituted are protected if related to a proceeding contemplated in good faith and under serious consideration by a client who is a prospective plaintiff or reasonably anticipated by a client who is a prospective defendant (see id. § 586, Comment *e*). Thus, the privilege covers a statement in a letter to opposing counsel proposing a settlement or in a conversation with a prospective witness even if the contemplated action is never brought or the prospective witness is not called. The privilege is also a defense to other claims where publication or communication is an element of the claim, for example, a claim that a lawyer's statements during a judicial proceeding constituted intentional infliction of emotional distress (see § 56, Comment *g*). (For the different rules applicable to claims of malicious prosecution and the like, see Subsection (2) and Comments *d* and *e* hereto.) The privilege, however, does not protect statements directed to persons not involved in the litigation or statements having no connection with the proceeding (see Restatement Second, Torts § 586, Comment *c*). Thus, a statement to the press is not covered by the privilege, although the distinct privilege for accurate reports of official proceedings covers some such statements (see Restatement Second, Torts § 611). On what constitutes publication of a statement, see Restatement Second, Torts §§ 577–578. On other grounds of liability, see Comments *d* and *f* hereto; § 56, Comment *f* (fraudulent misrepresentation).

* * *

d. Wrongful use of civil proceeding; abuse of process; false arrest. A person who takes an active part in the initiation, continuation, or procurement of civil proceedings is liable in tort to the defendant for wrongful use of civil proceedings if the person acts without probable cause and primarily for a purpose other than securing a proper adjudication of the claim and if (except for ex parte proceedings) the proceedings have terminated in favor of the defendant (see Restatement Second, Torts § 674). In many jurisdictions, only those suffering certain kinds of harm known as special injury may recover. The tort is called malicious prosecution in many jurisdictions.

The effect of the rule stated in this Section is that, in a claim for wrongful use of civil proceedings, the existence of probable cause and of an improper purpose are assessed separately for a lawyer and for the client on whose behalf the civil proceeding was brought. A lawyer is liable only if there was no probable cause for bringing the civil proceeding, the lawyer did not act primarily to aid the client in securing a proper adjudication of the client's claim, and the civil proceeding has terminated in favor of the defending party. Probable cause exists if the lawyer has a reasonable belief that the facts on which the claim is based can be established to the satisfaction of the trier of fact and has a reasonable belief that there is a sound chance that under those facts the claim may be held valid (see Restatement Second, Torts § 675 & Comments *d* & *e* thereto). (On a client's defense of advice of counsel with respect to claims of third persons, see § 29, Comment *c*.) Whether probable cause existed is determined on the basis of the facts known to the lawyer at the time. When there is no dispute as to what facts were so known, the existence of probable cause is an issue of law to be decided by the tribunal, not a jury issue (see Restatement Second, Torts § 681B(1)(c)). A decision by a competent tribunal upholding the client's claim on the merits is ordinarily conclusive evidence of probable cause, even if it is reversed on appeal (see Restatement Second, Torts § 675, Comment *b*).

* * *

g. Advising or assisting a client to break a contract. As with other advisors to a contracting party, lawyers are protected against liability for interfering with contracts or with prospective contractual relations or business relationships. On such liability, see generally Restatement Second, Torts §§ 766–774A. That protection reflects the need of contracting parties for advice and assistance, the difficulty of knowing in advance whether an arguable refusal to perform will be held to constitute an actionable breach of contract, and the view that even an actionable breach may sometimes be defensible. Thus a lawyer may ordinarily, without civil liability, advise a client not to enter a contract or to breach an existing contract. A lawyer may also assist such a breach, for example by sending a letter stating the client's intention not to perform, or by negotiating and drafting a contract, with someone else that is inconsistent with the client's other contractual obligations. The same principles apply to dissolving relationships such as a marriage or business partnership. They likewise apply to advising or assisting a client to interfere with a contract or a prospective contract or business relationship with one party, for example by entering into a contract or relationship with another, or to interfere with a contract or relationship between nonclients.

* * *

TOPIC 3. VICARIOUS LIABILITY

* * *

§ 58. Vicarious Liability

(1) A law firm is subject to civil liability for injury legally caused to a person by any wrongful act or omission of any principal or employee of the firm who was acting in the ordinary course of the firm's business or with actual or apparent authority.

(2) Each of the principals of a law firm organized as a general partnership without limited liability is liable jointly and severally with the firm.

143

(3) A principal of a law firm organized other than as a general partnership without limited liability as authorized by law is vicariously liable for the acts of another principal or employee of the firm to the extent provided by law.

Comment:

* * *

b. Rationale. Vicarious liability of law firms and principals of traditional general partnerships results from the principles of respondeat superior or enterprise liability. See Revised Uniform Partnership Act §§ 305 and 306 (1993); Restatement Second, Agency, Chapter 7; Uniform Partnership Act §§ 13 and 14; § 26, Comment *b*; § 27, Comment *b*; cf. Uniform Partnership Act § 102(f) (partner's knowledge attributed to other partners, unless partner committed or consented to fraud on partnership). Vicarious liability also helps to maintain the quality of legal services, by requiring not only a firm but also its principals to stand behind the performance of other firm personnel. Because many law firms are thinly capitalized, the vicarious liability of principals helps to assure compensation to those who may have claims against principals of a firm.

On the other hand, limited liability is a principle generally accepted for those engaged in gainful occupations, and it may be difficult for a lawyer to monitor effectively the behavior of other lawyers in a firm. For those and other reasons, legislatures have adopted statutes making it possible for lawyers to practice in modified partnerships or other entities in which the principals are not subject to the traditional vicarious liability of general partners. Such entities themselves continue to be vicariously liable for acts of their principals and employees, and their lawyers continue to be liable for their own acts.

c. Firms, principals, and employees. In a law firm organized as a traditional general partnership without limitation of liability, the partners are "principals" within the meaning of this Section, and associates, paraprofessionals, and other employees (including part-time employees while so acting) are "employees." The firm and its principals are ordinarily liable for wrongful acts and omissions of lawyers who have an of-counsel relationship with the firm (see § 123, Comment *c(ii)*), while they are doing firm work. However, the scope of liability for acts of an of-counsel lawyer may be affected by the terms of the of-counsel relationship and the extent of the lawyer's affiliation to the firm apparent to the lawyer's clients. The scope of the of-counsel lawyer's vicarious liability for acts of firm lawyers is determined by general partnership law. On liability for independent contractors, see Comment *e* hereto. On the distinction between employees (referred to in agency law as servants) and independent contractors, see Restatement Second, Agency §§ 2 and 220.

Even though no traditional partnership exists, a person might be able to assert vicarious liability under the doctrine of partnership by estoppel, or purported partnership, against lawyers who represented themselves to be partners or consented to another's so representing them when the person relied on that representation.

Legislation allows lawyers to practice in professional corporations and, in many states, in limited-liability general partnerships or limited-liability companies. Such legislation generally contains language excluding liability of principals of the entity for negligence or misconduct in which they did not participate directly or as supervisors. The effect of such statutory language on lawyers may be limited by the state supreme court's rules and by statutory provisions concerning professional regulation. Thus, rules in some states require lawyers in professional corporations or other entities to accept specified vicarious liability, to maintain specified liability insurance, or to give notice to clients of the nature of the firm.

* * *

d. Ordinary course of business or actual or apparent authority. Even when liability results from the act of a firm's principal or employee that was not within actual or apparent authority, the firm (and, to the extent stated in Subsections (2) and (3), its principals) is liable if the act was in the ordinary course of the firm's business (see Revised Uniform Partnership Act § 305 (1993); Uniform Partnership Act § 13; Restatement Second, Agency § 219). When an actor has apparent authority to act for the firm and an injured person has relied on that authority, the firm is subject to liability for certain of the actor's torts, for example negligence and fraud, and on contracts the actor entered into. Restatement Second, Agency §§ 159, 219, 248, 254, 257, 261, 265, and 267.

The ordinary course of business of a law firm includes the practice of law and various activities normally related to it. Thus, liability is imposed for legal malpractice (see §§ 48–54) by any firm lawyer; indebtedness incurred by staff in purchasing services or supplies; misapplication of funds in the custody of the firm or its personnel (see Revised Uniform Partnership Act § 305 (1993); Uniform Partnership Act § 14); and torts committed by a principal or employee while acting in the scope of employment, for example for the negligent driving of an employee who is on firm business (see generally Restatement Second, Agency §§ 219–249). That an act or omission giving rise to liability violated specific instructions given to the actor by the firm, for example a set of detailed malpractice-avoidance rules, does not remove the act or omission from the ordinary course of business. But nonfirm business or other acts, such as entry by a law-firm principal into an unrelated business partnership that is not part of the firm's practice of law and its ancillary activities, are not within the ordinary course of a law firm's business. Also excluded are acts of nonprincipals that are not within the scope of their employment, for example the writing of a will by a nonlawyer firm librarian not authorized to do so. Jurisdictions disagree about whether, under general agency law, a principal is liable for intentional torts such as assaults that an agent commits without any purpose of serving a principal whose enterprise helped create the risk of the act. In the case of law firms, the grounds for such liability are stronger when the plaintiff is a client and a client-lawyer relationship facilitated the tort.

The scope of a firm's course of business is determined from its own activities; a particular firm may have an ordinary course of business broader or narrower than those of otherwise comparable firms. For example, if other lawyers in a firm know that a firm lawyer regularly makes investments for firm clients from the proceeds of recoveries or the like, that may warrant a fact finder in concluding that the firm's ordinary course of business includes making such investments for clients. Likewise, activities such as the provision of title insurance can be within the ordinary course of the business of a law firm. When a firm or its principals own an enterprise that is not engaged in the practice of law, the corporate or other form of that enterprise may limit the liability of its owners; the professional rules of the jurisdiction may nonetheless subject the firm's principals to obligations other than civil liability with respect to the enterprise (see § 10, Comment *g*).

When a firm principal or employee has actual authority to act or refrain from acting, under this Section the firm is subject to resulting liabilities even if the act or omission was not within the ordinary course of the firm's business. For example, a firm may authorize a lawyer to engage in business transactions with a client. Actual authority may be conferred by specific authorization, an employment agreement, general understandings reflected in past practice and other circumstances (see Restatement Second, Agency § 229). A firm may also authorize an act by subsequent ratification (see Restatement Second, Agency § 218).

* * *

e. Liability for conduct of an actor not within a firm. Whether a firm is vicariously liable for wrongful acts or omissions by independent contractors such as process servers is determined by general principles of agency (see Restatement Second, Agency §§ 212–218 & 250–267). On the distinction between agents who are servants and independent contractors, see id. §§ 2 and 220. On contractual liability, see id. §§ 140–211. On liability for the firm's own involvement in tortious activities of nonemployees, see Restatement Second, Torts §§ 875–881. A firm and its principals are not liable to the client for the acts and omissions of independent contractors except when a contractor is performing the firm's own nondelegable duty to the client, but the firm is liable for its own negligence in selecting or supervising such contractors and for directing tortious conduct (see Restatement Second, Agency §§ 351, 356, & 358).

A firm is not ordinarily liable under this Section for the acts or omissions of a lawyer outside the firm who is working with firm lawyers as co-counsel or in a similar arrangement. Such a lawyer is usually an independent agent of the client over whom the firm has no control, not a servant or independent contractor. That is especially likely to be the case when the second lawyer represents the client in another jurisdiction, in which that lawyer, but not the firm's lawyers, is a member of the bar. The firm may, however, be liable in some circumstances. Thus a firm may be liable to the client for the acts and omissions of the outside lawyer if the firm assumes responsibility to a client for a matter, for example pursuant to obligations in fee-sharing arrangements (see § 47) or by assigning work to a temporary lawyer who has no direct relationship with the client. Such arrangements make the outside lawyer the firm's subagent (see Restatement Second, Agency §§ 5 & 406). In such circumstances, the outside lawyer may be liable to the firm for contribution or indemnity. A firm is liable to its client for acts and omissions of its own principals and employees relating to the outside lawyer, for example when it undertakes to recommend or supervise the outside lawyer and does so negligently or when its lawyers advise or participate in the outside lawyer's actionable conduct (see Restatement Second, Agency § 405). A firm may also be liable to a nonclient for the acts and omissions of an outside lawyer, for example when principals or employees of the firm direct or help perform those acts or omissions (see Restatement Second, Torts §§ 875–881; Restatement Second, Agency §§ 351 & 358). For of-counsel lawyers, see Comment *c* hereto.

* * *

g. Joint and several liability; contribution. When firm principals are personally liable vicariously, they are jointly and severally liable (see Revised Uniform Partnership Act § 306 (1993); Uniform Partnership Act § 15). They may be entitled to contribution or indemnity under the firm's governing agreement or other contractual provision or general legal principles. Under the Revised Uniform Partnership Act (see id. § 307), a judgment creditor must exhaust the partnership's assets before enforcing a judgment against a partner's assets.

* * *

i. Effect of the termination of a client's relationship with a firm. A lawyer's vicarious liability, if any, does not extend to acts and omissions occurring after the lawyer ceased to be a firm principal, except to the extent that failure to give proper notice of a dissolution or withdrawal may result in continuing responsibility for the firm's affairs (see § 33, Comment *b*). A lawyer is likewise not vicariously liable for acts and omissions occurring before the lawyer became a principal of a firm.

A lawyer's ceasing to be a principal of a firm, whether because the firm dissolves or the lawyer withdraws, does not terminate the lawyer's vicarious liability, if any, for acts and omissions occurring prior thereto. Likewise, a lawyer's death does not terminate vicarious liability, if any, for prior acts and omissions, although the vicarious liability must then be asserted against the lawyer's estate.

* * *

CHAPTER 5

CONFIDENTIAL CLIENT INFORMATION

Introductory Note

Introductory Note

This Chapter considers the law protecting the confidentiality of client information. The rules derive from agency law and professional regulations (see Topic 1), the attorney-client privilege (see Topic 2), and the lawyer work-product immunity (see Topic 3). Confidentiality is of great significance in both litigation practice and office practice. Moreover, the rules governing conflicts of interest (see Chapter 8) are founded on concepts of confidentiality that go beyond the attorney-client privilege and work-product immunity.

* * *

TOPIC 1. CONFIDENTIALITY RESPONSIBILITIES OF LAWYERS

TITLE A. A LAWYER'S CONFIDENTIALITY DUTIES

§ 59. Definition of "Confidential Client Information"

Confidential client information consists of information relating to representation of a client, other than information that is generally known.

Comment:

* * *

b. Kinds of confidential client information. A client's approach to a lawyer for legal assistance implies that the client trusts the lawyer to advance and protect the interests of the client (see § 16(1)). The resulting duty of loyalty is the predicate of the duty of confidentiality. The information that a lawyer is obliged to protect and safeguard is called *confidential client information* in this Restatement.

This definition covers all information relating to representation of a client, whether in oral, documentary, electronic, photographic, or other forms. It covers information gathered from any source, including sources such as third persons whose communications are not protected by the attorney-client privilege (see § 70). It includes work product that the lawyer develops in representing the client, such as the lawyer's notes to a personal file, whether or not the information is immune from discovery as lawyer work product (see Topic 3). It includes information acquired by a lawyer in all client-lawyer relationships (see § 14), including functioning as inside or outside legal counsel, government or private-practice lawyer, counselor or litigator, advocate or intermediary. It applies whether or not the client paid a fee, and whether a lawyer learns the information personally or through an agent, for example information acquired by a lawyer's partners or associate lawyers or by an investigator, paralegal, or secretary. Information acquired by an agent is protected even if it was not thereafter communicated to the lawyer, such as material acquired by an investigator and kept in the investigator's files.

The definition includes information that becomes known by others, so long as the information does not become generally known. See Comment *d* hereto; compare § 71 (condition of attorney-client privilege that communication be made with reasonable expectation of confidentiality); § 79 (waiver of the attorney-client privilege by subsequent disclosure). The fact that information falls outside the attorney-client privilege or work-product immunity does not determine its confidentiality under this Section.

* * *

c. The time at which information is acquired. Information acquired during the representation or before or after the representation is confidential so long as it is not generally known (see Comment *d* hereto) and relates to the representation. Such information, for example, might be acquired by the lawyer in considering whether to undertake a representation. On the duties of a lawyer with respect to confidential information of a prospective client, see § 15, Comment *c*. Post-representation confidential client information might be acquired, for example, in the form of information on subsequent developments.

* * *

§ 60. A Lawyer's Duty to Safeguard Confidential Client Information

(1) Except as provided in §§ 61–67, during and after representation of a client:

(a) the lawyer may not use or disclose confidential client information as defined in § 59 if there is a reasonable prospect that doing so will adversely affect a material interest of the client or if the client has instructed the lawyer not to use or disclose such information;

(b) the lawyer must take steps reasonable in the circumstances to protect confidential client information against impermissible use or disclosure by the lawyer's associates or agents that may adversely affect a material interest of the client or otherwise than as instructed by the client.

(2) Except as stated in § 62, a lawyer who uses confidential information of a client for the lawyer's pecuniary gain other than in the practice of law must account to the client for any profits made.

Comment:

* * *

b. Conflicts between protection of confidential client information and other values. The broad prohibition against divulging confidential client information comes at a cost to both lawyers and society. Lawyers sometimes learn information that cannot be disclosed because of the rule of confidentiality but that would be highly useful to other persons. Those may include persons whose personal plight and character are much more sympathetic than those of the lawyer's client or who could accomplish great public good or avoid great public detriment if the information were disclosed. Moreover, the free-speech interests of lawyers is impinged by a broad rule of confidentiality. Nonetheless, despite those costs, the confidentiality rule reflects a considered judgment that high net social value justifies it. It is recognized that the rule better protects legitimate client expectations about communications to their lawyers and that permitting divulgence would be inconsistent with the goal of furthering the lawful objectives of clients (see § 16(1)).

Illustration:

> 1. Lawyer is appointed to represent Client, a person who has been accused of murder. During confidential conferences between them, Client informs Lawyer that Client in fact committed not only the murder charged but two others as well. Client gives Lawyer sufficient detail to confirm beyond question that Client's story is true. The two other murders involve victims whose bodies have not yet been discovered. Because of similarities between the circumstances of the murders, parents of one of the victims approach Lawyer and beg for any information about their child. Lawyer realizes the personal anguish of the victim's parents and the peace the information that he knows could bring them. Unless Client consents to disclosure (see § 62), Lawyer must respond that Lawyer has no information to give them.

* * *

c(i). Impermissible use or disclosure—a reasonable prospect of adverse effect on a material client interest. The duty of confidentiality is defined in terms of the risk of harm. Subject to exceptions provided in §§ 61–67, use or disclosure of confidential client information is generally prohibited if there is a reasonable prospect that doing so will adversely affect a material interest of the client or prospective client. Although the lawyer codes do not express this limitation, such is the accepted interpretation. For example, under a literal reading of ABA Model Rules of Professional Conduct, Rule 1.6(a) (1983), a lawyer would commit a disciplinary violation by telling an unassociated lawyer in casual conversation the identity of a firm client, even if mention of the client's identity creates no possible risk of harm. Such a strict interpretation goes beyond the proper interpretation of the rule.

* * *

Adverse effects include all consequences that a lawyer of reasonable prudence would recognize as risking material frustration of the client's objectives in the representation or material misfortune, disadvantage, or other prejudice to a client in other respects, either during the course of the present representation or in the future. It includes consequences such as financial or physical harm and personal embarrassment that could be caused to a person of normal susceptibility and a normal interest in privacy.

Both use and disclosure adverse to a client are prohibited. As the term is employed in the Section, *use* of information includes taking the information significantly into account in framing a course of action, such as in making decisions when representing another client or in deciding whether to make a personal investment. *Disclosure* of information is revealing the information to a person not authorized to receive it and in a form that identifies the client or client matter either expressly or through reasonably ascertainable inference. Revealing information in a way that cannot be linked to the client involved is not a disclosure prohibited by the Section if there is no reasonable likelihood of adverse effect on a material interest of the client. Use of confidential client information can be adverse without disclosure. For example, in representing a subsequent client against the interests of a former client in a related matter, a lawyer who shapes the subsequent representation by employing confidential client information gained about the original client violates the duty of § 60(1) not to use that information, even if the lawyer does not disclose the information to anyone else (see § 132).

[*c(ii). Impermissible use or disclosure—specific client instructions.*]

* * *

When a fee for a client is paid by a third person (see § 134(1)) and in the absence of different client agreement or instructions, the client and not the third person directs the lawyer with respect to such matters as the treatment of files or other confidential client information. For the special instance of liability insurers, compare § 134, Comment *f*.

d. A lawyer's duty to safeguard confidential client information. A lawyer who acquires confidential client information has a duty to take reasonable steps to secure the information against misuse or inappropriate disclosure, both by the lawyer and by the lawyer's associates or agents to whom the lawyer may permissibly divulge it (see Comment *e*). This requires that client confidential information be acquired, stored, retrieved, and transmitted under systems and controls that are reasonably designed and managed to maintain confidentiality. In responding to a discovery request, for example, a lawyer must exercise reasonable care against the risk that confidential client information not subject to the request is inadvertently disclosed (see § 79). A lawyer should so conduct interviews with clients and others that the benefit of the attorney-client privilege and work-product immunity are preserved (see § 70, Comment *f*). On the release of information to further a client's objectives, including the waiver of claims of privilege or immunity, see § 61, Comment *d*. On asserting objections to attempts to obtain the client's confidential information, see § 63, Comment *b*.

A lawyer must take reasonable steps so that law-office personnel and other agents such as independent investigators properly handle confidential client information. That includes devising and enforcing appropriate policies and practices concerning confidentiality and supervising such personnel in performing those duties (see § 11). A lawyer may act reasonably in relying on other responsible persons in the office or on reputable independent contractors to provide that instruction and supervision (see id.). The reasonableness of specific protective measures depends on such factors as the duties of the agent or other person, the extent to which disclosure would adversely affect the client, the extent of prior training or experience of the person, the existence of other assurances such as adequate supervision by senior employees, and the customs and reputation of independent contractors.

* * *

e. Postrepresentation safeguarding. The duty of confidentiality continues so long as the lawyer possesses confidential client information. It extends beyond the end of the representation and beyond the death of the client. Accordingly, a lawyer must take reasonable steps for the future safekeeping of client files, including files in closed matters, or the systematic destruction of nonessential closed files. A lawyer must also take reasonably appropriate steps to provide for return, destruction, or continued safekeeping of client files in the event of the lawyer's retirement, ill health, death, discipline, or other interruption of the lawyer's practice.

f. Divulgence to persons assisting a lawyer in representing a client. A lawyer generally has authority to use or disclose confidential client information to persons assisting the lawyer in representing the client. Those include other lawyers in the same firm and employees such as secretaries and paralegals. A lawyer also may disclose information to independent contractors who assist in the representation, such as investigators, lawyers in other firms, prospective expert witnesses, and public courier companies and photocopy shops, to the extent reasonably appropriate in the client's behalf (see also § 70, Comment *h*). Such disclosures are not permitted contrary to a client's instructions, even within the lawyer's firm (see Comment *c(ii)* hereto), or when screening is required to avoid imputed disqualification of the lawyer's firm (see § 124, Comment *d*, & § 133, Comment *g*).

A lawyer's authority to disclose information for purposes of carrying out the representation is implied and therefore does not require express client consent (see § 21(3)). Agents of a lawyer assisting in representing a client serve as subagents and as such independently owe a duty of confidentiality to the client. See generally Restatement Second, Agency § 428(1) (subagent's general duties to known principals); id. § 395 (agent's general duty of confidentiality).

g. Divulgence to facilitate law practice. A lawyer may disclose confidential client information for the purpose of facilitating the lawyer's law practice, where no reasonable prospect of harm to the client is thereby created and where appropriate safeguards against impermissible use or disclosure are taken. Thus, disclosure is permitted to other lawyers in the same firm and to employees and agents such as accountants, file clerks, office managers, secretaries, and similar office assistants in the lawyer's firm, and with confidential, independent consultants, such as computer technicians, accountants, bookkeepers, law-practice consultants, and others who assist in furthering the law-practice business of the lawyer or the lawyer's firm.

* * *

i. Divulgence concerning property dispositions by a deceased client. The attorney-client privilege does not apply to communications relevant to an issue between parties who claim an interest through the same decedent (see § 81). As a corollary, the lawyer may reveal confidential client information to contending heirs or other claimants to an interest through a deceased client, in advance of testifying, if there is a reasonable prospect that doing so would advance the interests of the client-decedent (see § 61). Authority to instruct the lawyer (see Comment *c(ii)* hereto) with respect to such divulgence is determined under the law of succession.

* * *

l. Use or disclosure of confidential information of co-clients. A lawyer may represent two or more clients in the same matter as co-clients either when there is no conflict of interest between them (see

§ 121) or when a conflict exists but the co-clients have adequately consented (see § 122). When a conflict of interest exists, as part of the process of obtaining consent, the lawyer is required to inform each co-client of the effect of joint representation upon disclosure of confidential information (see § 122, Comment *c(i)*), including both that all material information will be shared with each co-client during the course of the representation and that a communicating co-client will be unable to assert the attorney-client privilege against the other in the event of later adverse proceedings between them (see § 75).

Sharing of information among the co-clients with respect to the matter involved in the representation is normal and typically expected. As between the co-clients, in many such relationships each co-client is under a fiduciary duty to share all information material to the co-clients' joint enterprise. Such is the law, for example, with respect to members of a partnership. Limitation of the attorney-client privilege as applied to communications of co-clients is based on an assumption that each intends that his or her communications with the lawyer will be shared with the other co-clients but otherwise kept in confidence (see § 75, Comment *d*). Moreover, the common lawyer is required to keep each of the co-clients informed of all information reasonably necessary for the co-client to make decisions in connection with the matter (see § 20). The lawyer's duty extends to communicating information to other co-clients that is adverse to a co-client, whether learned from the lawyer's own investigation or learned in confidence from that co-client.

Co-clients may understand from the circumstances those obligations on the part of the lawyer and their own obligations, or they may explicitly agree to share information. Co-clients can also explicitly agree that the lawyer is not to share certain information, such as described categories of proprietary, financial, or similar information with one or more other co-clients (see § 75, Comment *d*). A lawyer must honor such agreements. If one co-client threatens physical harm or other types of crimes or fraud against the other, an exception to the lawyer's duty of confidentiality may apply (see §§ 66–67).

There is little case authority on the responsibilities of a lawyer when, in the absence of an agreement among the co-clients to restrict sharing of information, one co-client provides to the lawyer material information with the direction that it not be communicated to another co-client. The communicating co-client's expectation that the information be withheld from the other co-client may be manifest from the circumstances, particularly when the communication is clearly antagonistic to the interests of the affected co-client. The lawyer thus confronts a dilemma. If the information is material to the other co-client, failure to communicate it would compromise the lawyer's duties of loyalty, diligence (see § 16(1) & (2)), and communication (see § 20) to that client. On the other hand, sharing the communication with the affected co-client would compromise the communicating client's hope of confidentiality and risks impairing that client's trust in the lawyer.

Such circumstances create a conflict of interest among the co-clients (see § 121 & § 122, Comment *h*). The lawyer cannot continue in the representation without compromising either the duty of communication to the affected co-client or the expectation of confidentiality on the part of the communicating co-client. Moreover, continuing the joint representation without making disclosure may mislead the affected client or otherwise involve the lawyer in assisting the communicating client in a breach of fiduciary duty or other misconduct. Accordingly, the lawyer is required to withdraw unless the communicating client can be persuaded to permit sharing of the communication (see § 32(2)(a)). Following withdrawal, the lawyer may not, without consent of both, represent either co-client adversely to the other with respect to the same or a substantially related matter (see § 121, Comment *e(i)*).

In the course of withdrawal, the lawyer has discretion to warn the affected co-client that a matter seriously and adversely affecting that person's interests has come to light, which the other co-client refuses to permit the lawyer to disclose. Beyond such a limited warning, the lawyer, after consideration of all relevant circumstances, has the further discretion to inform the affected co-client of the specific communication if, in the lawyer's reasonable judgment, the immediacy and magnitude of the risk to the affected co-client outweigh the interest of the communicating client in continued secrecy. In making such determinations, the lawyer may take into account superior legal interests of the lawyer or of affected third persons, such as an interest implicated by a threat of physical harm to the lawyer or another person. See also § 66.

Illustration:

2. Lawyer has been retained by Husband and Wife to prepare wills pursuant to an arrangement under which each spouse agrees to leave most of their property to the other (compare § 130, Comment *c*, Illustrations 1–3). Shortly after the wills are executed, Husband (unknown to Wife) asks Lawyer to prepare an inter vivos trust for an illegitimate child whose existence Husband has kept secret from Wife for many years and about whom Husband had not previously informed Lawyer. Husband states that Wife would be distraught at learning of Husband's infidelity and of Husband's years of silence and that

disclosure of the information could destroy their marriage. Husband directs Lawyer not to inform Wife. The inter vivos trust that Husband proposes to create would not materially affect Wife's own estate plan or her expected receipt of property under Husband's will, because Husband proposes to use property designated in Husband's will for a personally favored charity. In view of the lack of material effect on Wife, Lawyer may assist Husband to establish and fund the inter vivos trust and refrain from disclosing Husband's information to Wife.

3. Same facts as Illustration 2, except that Husband's proposed inter vivos trust would significantly deplete Husband's estate, to Wife's material detriment and in frustration of the Spouses' intended testamentary arrangements. If Husband refuses to inform Wife or to permit Lawyer to do so, Lawyer must withdraw from representing both Husband and Wife. In the light of all relevant circumstances, Lawyer may exercise discretion whether to inform Wife either that circumstances, which Lawyer has been asked not to reveal, indicate that she should revoke her recent will or to inform Wife of some or all the details of the information that Husband has recently provided so that Wife may protect her interests. Alternatively, Lawyer may inform Wife only that Lawyer is withdrawing because Husband will not permit disclosure of relevant information.

* * *

Even if the co-clients have agreed that the lawyer will keep certain categories of information confidential from one or more other co-clients, in some circumstances it might be evident to the lawyer that the uninformed co-client would not have agreed to nondisclosure had that co-client been aware of the nature of the adverse information. For example, a lawyer's examination of confidential financial information, agreed not to be shown to another co-client to reduce antitrust concerns, could show in fact, contrary to all exterior indications, that the disclosing co-client is insolvent. In view of the co-client's agreement, the lawyer must honor the commitment of confidentiality and not inform the other client, subject to the exceptions described in § 67. The lawyer must, however, withdraw if failure to reveal would mislead the affected client, involve the lawyer in assisting the communicating client in a course of fraud, breach of fiduciary duty, or other unlawful activity, or, as would be true in most such instances, involve the lawyer in representing conflicting interests.

m. Use or disclosure of confidential information of a nonclient. A lawyer may come into possession of confidential information of a nonclient, such as that of an opposing party in litigation or in negotiations. Such information may come from the other person or the lawyer or other agent of the person. When the receiving lawyer reasonably concludes that the transmission was authorized, the lawyer may use the information for the client's benefit, for example, where an opposing lawyer has conveyed the information apparently to advance representation (see § 61). Otherwise, the receiving lawyer's responsibilities depend on the circumstances. If the disclosure operates to end legal protection for the information, the lawyer may use it for the benefit of the lawyer's own client and may be required to do so if that would advance the client's lawful objectives (see § 16(1)). That would follow, for example, when an opposing lawyer failed to object to privileged or immune testimony (compare §§ 78, 86(1)(b), & 91(3)). The same legal result may follow when divulgence occurs inadvertently outside of court (see §§ 79 & 91). The receiving lawyer may be required to consult with that lawyer's client (see § 20) about whether to take advantage of the lapse.

* * *

Where deceitful or illegal means were used to obtain the information, the receiving lawyer and that lawyer's client may be liable, among other remedies, for damages for harm caused or for injunctive relief against use or disclosure. The receiving lawyer must take steps to return such confidential client information and to keep it confidential from the lawyer's own client in the interim.

Similarly, if the receiving lawyer is aware that disclosure is being made in breach of trust by a lawyer or other agent of the opposing person, the receiving lawyer must not accept the information. An offending lawyer may be disqualified from further representation in a matter to which the information is relevant if the lawyer's own client would otherwise gain a substantial advantage (see § 6, Comment i). A tribunal may also order suppression or exclusion of such information.

* * *

TITLE B. USING OR DISCLOSING CONFIDENTIAL CLIENT INFORMATION

§ 61. Using or Disclosing Information to Advance Client Interests

A lawyer may use or disclose confidential client information when the lawyer reasonably believes that doing so will advance the interests of the client in the representation.

Comment:

* * *

d. Reasonable calculation of advantage to a client. A lawyer may use or disclose confidential client information when presenting evidence or argument or engaging in other proceedings before a court, governmental agency, or other forum in behalf of a client. Thus, a lawyer may disclose such information in pleadings or other submissions, in presenting the testimony of witnesses and other evidence, in submitting briefs and other memoranda, or in discussing the matter with potential witnesses. Information thus disclosed may be not entirely favorable to the client. For tactical reasons, a lawyer may reasonably decide to present partly unfavorable information, even though it is confidential. A lawyer may do so in the interest of mitigating its damaging effect (for example, to prevent it from being brought out first by an adversary) or in order to present a complete account and thus gain the confidence of the factfinder.

* * *

§ 62. Using or Disclosing Information with Client Consent

A lawyer may use or disclose confidential client information when the client consents after being adequately informed concerning the use or disclosure.

Comment:

* * *

c. Adequately informed client consent. A lawyer is required to consult with a client before the client gives consent under this Section. The legal effect of failure to consult depends upon whether the question concerns the lawyer's duty to the client or the rights or interests of third persons. When the question concerns the lawyer's duty to the client, the client's consent is effective only if given on the basis of information and consultation reasonably appropriate in the circumstances. When the question concerns the effect of consent with respect to the client's legal relationship with third persons, the principles of actual and apparent authority control. See §§ 26 and 27.

* * *

§ 63. Using or Disclosing Information When Required by Law

A lawyer may use or disclose confidential client information when required by law, after the lawyer takes reasonably appropriate steps to assert that the informa-

tion is privileged or otherwise protected against disclosure.

Comment:

* * *

b. A lawyer's obligation to invoke available protection. A lawyer
generally is required to raise any reasonably tenable objection to
another's attempt to obtain confidential client information (see § 59)
from the lawyer if revealing the information would disadvantage the
lawyer's client and the client has not consented (see § 62), unless
disclosure would serve the client's interest (see § 61). The duty follows
from the general requirement that the lawyer safeguard such information (see § 60) and act competently in advancing the client's objectives
(see § 16(1)). The duty to object arises when a nonfrivolous argument
(see § 110) can be made that the law does not require the lawyer to
disclose such information. Such an argument could rest on the attorney-client privilege (see § 86(1)(b)), the work-product immunity (see
§ 87), or a ground such as the irrelevance of the information or its
character as hearsay. When the client is represented by successor
counsel, a predecessor lawyer's decision whether to invoke the privilege is appropriately directed by successor counsel or the client.

* * *

§ 64. Using or Disclosing Information in a Lawyer's Self–Defense

A lawyer may use or disclose confidential client information when and to the extent that the lawyer reasonably
believes necessary to defend the lawyer or the lawyer's
associate or agent against a charge or threatened charge
by any person that the lawyer or such associate or agent
acted wrongfully in the course of representing a client.

Comment:

* * *

c. Kinds of charges within the exception. A lawyer may act in
self-defense under this Section only to defend against charges that
imminently threaten the lawyer or the lawyer's associate or agent with
serious consequences, including criminal charges, claims of legal malpractice, and other civil actions such as suits to recover overpayment
of fees, complaints in disciplinary proceedings, and the threat of
disqualification (see Comment *h*). Imminent threat arises not only
upon filing of such charges but also upon the manifestation of intent to

initiate such proceedings by persons in an apparent position to do so, such as a prosecutor or an aggrieved potential litigant. On responding to informal, public accusations made by a client, see Comment *f* hereto.

Illustrations:

1. Lawyer was employed by a Firm of lawyers that represented Client in a pending public stock offering. Lawyer had unsuccessfully objected to other lawyers in Firm about a secret finder's fee that Client paid to Firm in connection with the stock offering, but which neither Client nor the other Firm lawyers proposed to disclose in the offering documents. The stock offering went forward without such disclosure. Purchaser bought some of the shares. Lawyer learns that a regulatory agency has begun to investigate the activities of Client, Firm, and Lawyer and contemplates a regulatory proceeding that, among other sanctions, will seek to bar Lawyer from participating in transactions within the regulatory jurisdiction of the agency. Lawyer also learns that lawyers for Purchaser are about to file suit seeking substantial damages and naming Lawyer as a codefendant. To the extent necessary to gain exoneration from or to mitigate the charges imminently threatened, Lawyer may disclose confidential information about Client to the regulatory agency and to the lawyers for Purchaser.

2. Lawyers in a law firm of which Lawyer is a member file a charge with a lawyer-disciplinary agency that Lawyer has converted funds belonging to Client, whom Lawyer had represented. In order to defend against the charges, Lawyer reasonably believes that it is necessary to disclose confidential client information about Client to show that Client had consented to Lawyer's use of the funds. Client, however, refuses to discuss the charges, to testify, or to consent to Lawyer disclosing any matter about Client or Client's funds. The agency decides to file charges against Lawyer because it believes that it has sufficient evidence from other sources. To the extent reasonably necessary to obtain exoneration from or to mitigate the disciplinary charges, Lawyer may reveal otherwise confidential information about Client and the funds. Before doing so, Lawyer should inform Client of Lawyer's need to use the information and seek Client's consent to its use, unless Client has already made it clear that Client will not consent. In making the disclosure, Lawyer must limit the extent to which the information is disclosed (see Comment *e* hereto).

* * *

4. Lawyer is discharged by Law Firm and files suit against it, alleging damages for wrongful discharge. Law Firm defends on the ground that Lawyer's work was incompetent. Law Firm may, to the extent reasonably necessary, employ confidential client information to support its defense of incompetence in defending against Lawyer's claim. Lawyer may, to the extent reasonably necessary, also employ confidential client information to respond to Law Firm's charges of incompetence.

There is a risk that a government agency or other complainant may assert unfounded charges against a lawyer to induce the lawyer to supply the complainant with information inculpating the lawyer's client. The risk of such abuse is to some extent unavoidable. The lawyer must minimize the risk by objecting to such abusive tactics and invoking the discretion to disclose only when it reasonably appears to the lawyer that the charge, although false, will in fact be pressed. Governmental interference with the client-lawyer relationship by unwarranted accusations, when established, should lead to severe sanctions against the governmental lawyers involved.

* * *

e. *Proportionate and restrained use.* Use or disclosure of confidential client information under this Section is warranted only if and to the extent that the disclosing lawyer reasonably believes it necessary. The concept of necessity precludes disclosure in responding to casual charges, such as comments not likely to be taken seriously by others. The disclosure is warranted only when it constitutes a proportionate and restrained response to the charges. The lawyer must reasonably believe that options short of use or disclosure have been exhausted or will be unavailing or that invoking them would substantially prejudice the lawyer's position in the controversy.

The lawyer may divulge confidential client information only to those persons with whom the lawyer must deal in order to obtain exoneration or mitigation of the charges. When feasible, the lawyer must also invoke protective orders, submissions under seal, and similar procedures to limit the extent to which the information is disseminated. A lawyer may not invoke or threaten to invoke the exception without a reasonable basis, nor for an extraneous purpose such as inducing a client to forgo a disciplinary complaint or a complaint for damages (see § 42). When a client has made a public charge of wrongdoing, a lawyer is warranted in making a proportionate and restrained public response.

* * *

g. Defense against a charge by a nonclient. If a person other than a client asserts that a lawyer engaged in wrongdoing in the course of representing a client, this Section permits the lawyer to disclose otherwise confidential client information in self-defense, despite the fact that the client involved has not waived confidentiality or had any role in threatening or making the charges. The analogous exception to the attorney-client privilege permits a lawyer to testify to otherwise privileged communications in self-defense against such charges (see § 83, Comment *d*).

* * *

§ 65. Using or Disclosing Information in a Compensation Dispute

A lawyer may use or disclose confidential client information when and to the extent that the lawyer reasonably believes necessary to permit the lawyer to resolve a dispute with the client concerning compensation or reimbursement that the lawyer reasonably claims the client owes the lawyer.

Comment:

* * *

b. Rationale. Without this exception, a lawyer could be deprived of important evidence to prove a rightful claim. Clients would thus sometimes be immune from honest claims for legal fees. Moreover, at least some disclosures necessary to establish a fee will not involve information that a client would find embarrassing or prejudicial, other than in defeating the client's position in the dispute.

* * *

§ 66. Using or Disclosing Information to Prevent Death or Serious Bodily Harm

(1) A lawyer may use or disclose confidential client information when the lawyer reasonably believes that its use or disclosure is necessary to prevent reasonably certain death or serious bodily harm to a person.

(2) Before using or disclosing information under this Section, the lawyer must, if feasible, make a good-faith effort to persuade the client not to act. If the client or another person has already acted, the lawyer must, if feasible, advise the client to warn the victim or to take

other action to prevent the harm and advise the client of the lawyer's ability to use or disclose information as provided in this Section and the consequences thereof.

(3) A lawyer who takes action or decides not to take action permitted under this Section is not, solely by reason of such action or inaction, subject to professional discipline, liable for damages to the lawyer's client or any third person, or barred from recovery against a client or third person.

Comment:

a. Scope and cross-references. This Section states an exception to the general duty of confidentiality in § 60(1), recognizing discretion in a lawyer to prevent the consequences of threats to life or personal safety. The rule stated in this Section is distinguishable from financial-harm disclosure under § 67 in three principal ways. First, the threat here need not be the product of a client act (see Comment *c* hereto). Second, the threat need not be created by a criminal or otherwise unlawful act (see id.). Third, the lawyer's services need not have been used to bring about the threatened death or serious bodily harm. As with § 67, a lawyer has discretion under this Section even if the use or disclosure threatens harm to the lawyer's client (see id.).

* * *

b. Rationale. The exception recognized by this Section is based on the overriding value of life and physical integrity. Threats to life or body encompassed within this Section may be the product of an act of the client or a nonclient and may be created by wrongful acts, by accident, or by circumstances. See Comment *c.* In all such events, the ultimate threat is the same, and its existence suffices to warrant a lawyer's taking corrective steps to prevent the threatened death or serious bodily harm.

* * *

c. Use or disclosure to prevent death or serious bodily harm. Subsection (1) applies whenever a lawyer has a reasonable basis for believing that use or disclosure of a client's confidential information is necessary to prevent reasonably certain death or serious bodily harm to a person. On what constitutes reasonable belief, see § 67, Comment *h.* A threat within Subsection (1) need not be the product of a client act; an act of a nonclient threatening life or personal safety is also included, as is a threat created through accident or natural causes. It follows that if such a threat is created by a person, whether a client or a nonclient, there is no requirement that the act be criminal or otherwise unlawful.

Illustration:

1.   Lawyer is representing Defendant, a responding party in a suit by Plaintiff seeking damages for personal injuries arising out of a vehicle accident. Lawyer asks Doctor, as a consulting expert, to conduct an evaluation of medical evidence submitted by Plaintiff in support of a claim of personal injury. Following the examination, Doctor reports to Lawyer that Plaintiff has an undiagnosed aortal aneurism, which is serious and life-threatening but which can readily be repaired through surgery. Lawyer knows from work on the case that Plaintiff, as well as Plaintiff's treating physician, lawyer, and medical experts, are unaware of the condition. Lawyer is also aware that, if notified of the condition, Plaintiff will likely claim significant additional damages following corrective surgery. Despite Lawyer's urging, Defendant refuses to permit revelation of the condition to Plaintiff. Under this Section, Lawyer has discretion under Subsection (1) to reveal the condition to Plaintiff.

* * *

Illustrations:

2.   Client seeks legal advice from Lawyer about his dismissal from a maintenance position by Landlord and eviction from his apartment. In expressing his anger about Landlord, Client reveals that Client has set a mechanical device to ignite and burn down the building. Lawyer has reason to believe that there are people living in the building. Despite Lawyer's remonstration, Client refuses to take any action to prevent the fire or to warn others. Despite the risk that calling the fire department or police may result in serious criminal charges against Client, Lawyer has discretion under Subsection (1) to do so.

3.   As the result of confidential disclosures at a meeting with engineers employed by Client Corporation, Lawyer reasonably believes that one of the engineers released a toxic substance into a city's water-supply system. Lawyer reasonably believes that the discharge will cause reasonably certain death or serious bodily harm to elderly or ill persons within a short period and that Lawyer's disclosure of the discharge is necessary to permit authorities to remove that threat or lessen the number of its victims. Lawyer's efforts to persuade responsible Client Corporation personnel to take corrective action have been unavailing. Although the act creating the threat has already occurred, Lawyer has

discretion to disclose under Subsection (1) for the purpose of preventing the consequences of the act.

* * *

Serious bodily harm within the meaning of the Section includes life-threatening illness and injuries and the consequences of events such as imprisonment for a substantial period and child sexual abuse. It also includes a client's threat of suicide.

* * *

f. Appropriate action. A lawyer's use or disclosure under this Section is a last resort when no other available action is reasonably likely to prevent the threatened death or serious bodily harm. Use or disclosure, when made, should be no more extensive than the lawyer reasonably believes necessary to accomplish the relevant purpose.

Preventive steps that a lawyer may appropriately take include consulting with relatives or friends of the person likely to cause the death or serious bodily harm and with other advisers to that person. (The lawyer may also seek the assistance of such persons in efforts to persuade the person not to act or to warn the threatened victim (see Comment *e* hereto).) A lawyer may also consult with law-enforcement authorities or agencies with jurisdiction over the type of conduct involved in order to prevent it and warn a threatened victim.

* * *

When a lawyer has taken action under the Section, in all but extraordinary cases the relationship between lawyer and client would have so far deteriorated as to make the lawyer's effective representation of the client impossible. Generally, therefore, the lawyer is required to withdraw from the representation (see § 32(2)(a) & Comment *f* thereto), unless the client gives informed consent to the lawyer's continued representation notwithstanding the lawyer's adverse use or disclosure of information. In any event, the lawyer generally must inform the client of the fact of the lawyer's use or disclosure (see § 20(1)), unless the lawyer has a superior interest in not informing the client, such as to protect the lawyer from wrongful retaliation by the client, to effectuate permissible measures that are not yet complete, or to prevent the client from inflicting further harms on third persons.

* * *

§ 67. Using or Disclosing Information to Prevent, Rectify, or Mitigate Substantial Financial Loss

(1) A lawyer may use or disclose confidential client information when the lawyer reasonably believes that its use or disclosure is necessary to prevent a crime or fraud, and:

   (a) the crime or fraud threatens substantial financial loss;

   (b) the loss has not yet occurred;

   (c) the lawyer's client intends to commit the crime or fraud either personally or through a third person; and

   (d) the client has employed or is employing the lawyer's services in the matter in which the crime or fraud is committed.

(2) If a crime or fraud described in Subsection (1) has already occurred, a lawyer may use or disclose confidential client information when the lawyer reasonably believes its use or disclosure is necessary to prevent, rectify, or mitigate the loss.

(3) Before using or disclosing information under this Section, the lawyer must, if feasible, make a good-faith effort to persuade the client not to act. If the client or another person has already acted, the lawyer must, if feasible, advise the client to warn the victim or to take other action to prevent, rectify, or mitigate the loss. The lawyer must, if feasible, also advise the client of the lawyer's ability to use or disclose information as provided in this Section and the consequences thereof.

(4) A lawyer who takes action or decides not to take action permitted under this Section is not, solely by reason of such action or inaction, subject to professional discipline, liable for damages to the lawyer's client or any third person, or barred from recovery against a client or third person.

Comment:

* * *

b. Rationale. The exceptions recognized in this Section reflect a balance between the competing considerations of protecting interests in client confidentiality and lawyer loyalty to clients, on the one hand,

and protecting the interests of society and third persons in avoiding substantial financial consequences of crimes or frauds, on the other. The integrity, professional reputation, and financial interests of the lawyer can also be implicated under Subsections (1) and (2) in view of the requirement that the lawyer's services have been employed in commission of the crime or fraud. The exceptions are also justified on the ground that the client is not entitled to the protection of confidentiality when the client knowingly causes substantial financial harm through a crime or fraud and when, as required under Subsections (1) and (2), the client has in effect misused the client-lawyer relationship for that purpose. In most instances of unlawful client acts that threaten such consequences to others, it may be hoped that the client's own sober reflection and the lawyer's counseling (see Comment *i* hereto) will lead the client to refrain from the act or to prevent or mitigate its consequences.

* * *

The exceptions stated in this Section permit a lawyer to exercise discretion to prevent the described loss to third persons, even though adverse effects might befall the client as a result. The exceptions are extraordinary. The only acts covered under the Section are the described crimes or frauds that threaten substantial financial loss to others. Clients remain protected in consulting a lawyer concerning the legal consequences of any such act in which the lawyer's services were not employed, including acts constituting crimes or frauds.

* * *

e. Employment of the lawyer's services in the client's act. Use or disclosure under either Subsection (1) or (2) requires that the lawyer's services are being or were employed in commission of a criminal or fraudulent act. The lawyer's involvement need not be known to or discoverable by the victim or other person. Subsections (1) and (2) apply without regard either to the lawyer's prior knowledge of the client's intended use of the lawyer's services or to when the lawyer forms a reasonable basis for a belief concerning the nature of the client's act. Such employment may occur, for example, when a client has a document prepared by the lawyer for use in a criminal or fraudulent scheme, receives the lawyer's advice concerning the act to assist in carrying it out, asks the lawyer to appear before a court or administrative agency as part of a transaction, or obtains advice that will assist the client in avoiding detection or apprehension for the crime or fraud. It is not necessary that the lawyer's services have been critical to success of the client's act or that the services were specifically requested by the client. It suffices if the services were or are being employed in the commission of the act.

* * *

Legal assistance provided only after the client's crime or fraud has already been committed is not within this Section, whether or not loss to the victim has already occurred, if the lawyer's services are not employed for the purposes of a further crime or fraud, such as the crime of obstruction of justice or other unlawful attempt to cover up the prior wrongful act. While applicable law may provide that a completed act is regarded for some purposes as a continuing offense, the limitation of Subsection (1)(d) applies with attention to the time at which the client's acts actually occurred.

Illustrations:

> 3. Client has been charged by a regulatory agency with participation in a scheme to defraud Victim. Client seeks the assistance of Lawyer in defending against the charges. The loss to Victim has already occurred. During the initial interview and thereafter, Lawyer is provided with ample reason to believe that Client's acts were fraudulent and caused substantial financial loss to Victim. Because Lawyer's services were not employed by Client in committing the fraud, Lawyer does not have discretion under this Section to use or disclose Client's confidential information.

* * *

f. Use or disclosure to prevent (Subsection (1)) or to rectify or mitigate (Subsection (2)) a client wrongful act. A lawyer has discretion to use or disclose under this Section when necessary to achieve either of two different purposes—to prevent the act from occurring (Subsection (1)) or to prevent, rectify, or mitigate loss caused by the act (Subsection (2)). Under Subsection (1), a lawyer may take preventive measures even though some act has already occurred, if some material part of the crime or fraud has not yet occurred or has not yet been inflicted on a victim. For example, in a criminal or fraudulent transaction involving more than one step, a lawyer would have discretion to take preventive action under Subsection (1) if some acts remained to be accomplished. Further, if all steps in a transaction to be taken by the client have already occurred, but the intended victim has not taken a final step, such as dispatching funds to the client, action to warn the victim not to take final steps is permissible preventive action within Subsection (1).

* * *

Illustrations:

> 5. Lawyer has assisted Client in preparing documents by means of which Client will obtain a $5,000,000 loan from Bank. The loan closing occurred on Monday and Bank will make the funds available for Client's use on Wednesday. On Tuesday Client reveals to Lawyer for the first time that Client knowingly obtained the loan by means of a materially false statement of Client's assets. Assuming that the other conditions for application of Subsection (2) are present, while Client's fraudulent act of obtaining the loan has, in large part, already occurred, Lawyer has discretion under the Subsection to use or disclose Client's confidential information to prevent the consequences of the fraud (final release of the funds from Bank) from occurring.

> 6. The same facts as in Illustration 5, except that Lawyer learned of the fraud on Wednesday after Bank had already released the funds to Client. Under Subsection (2), Lawyer's use or disclosure would be permissible if necessary for the purpose, for example, of enabling Bank to seize assets of Client in its possession or control as an offset against the fraudulently obtained loan or to prevent Client from sending the funds overseas and thereby making it difficult or impossible to trace them.

g. Client's intent. It is not required that the client's requisite intent existed at the time the client consulted the lawyer. For example, the client may form a plan to employ the lawyer's former services in drafting documents in a scheme that the client devises after the lawyer's services have ended. The client need not be aware specifically that the contemplated act was a crime or fraud (see also § 82, Comment *c*). As stated in Subsection (1)(c), the client may act either directly or through a third person. The Section does not apply if the lawyer is aware that the client's purpose had been abandoned, because in that situation disclosure is no longer necessary as required by the Section.

* * *

j. Appropriate action. A lawyer's use or disclosure of information under the Section is a last resort when no other available action is reasonably likely to prevent the threatened financial loss or to rectify

172

or mitigate it. Use or disclosure, when made, should be no more extensive than the lawyer reasonably believes necessary to accomplish the relevant purpose. On consulting with suitable advisers to a client, the importance of the circumstances known to the lawyer in determining the reasonableness of measures taken, withdrawal by the lawyer, and informing the client after use or disclosure, see § 66, Comment *f.*

In using or disclosing under this Section, the lawyer may also withdraw or disaffirm opinion letters, affidavits, and other legal documents that had been prepared for the client or others that might be employed or that might have been employed in furthering the crime or fraud or contributed to its consequences. In addition, under § 64, a lawyer may take steps that are justified as reasonably appropriate to defend the lawyer and the lawyer's associates against a charge of wrongdoing arising from the representation. Other law may require a lawyer to use or disclose confidential client information in such circumstances (see § 63).

* * *

TOPIC 2.   THE ATTORNEY–CLIENT PRIVILEGE

TITLE A.   THE SCOPE OF THE PRIVILEGE

* * *

§ 68.   Attorney–Client Privilege

Except as otherwise provided in this Restatement, the attorney-client privilege may be invoked as provided in § 86 with respect to:

> **(1) a communication**
>
> **(2) made between privileged persons**
>
> **(3) in confidence**
>
> **(4) for the purpose of obtaining or providing legal assistance for the client.**

Comment:

* * *

[*c.   Rationale supporting the privilege.*]

* * *

The rationale for the privilege is that confidentiality enhances the value of client-lawyer communications and hence the efficacy of legal services. The rationale is founded on three related assumptions. First, vindicating rights and complying with obligations under the law and under modern legal processes are matters often too complex and uncertain for a person untrained in the law, so that clients need to consult lawyers. The second assumption is that a client who consults a lawyer needs to disclose all of the facts to the lawyer and must be able to receive in return communications from the lawyer reflecting those facts. It is assumed that, in the absence of such frank and full discussion between client and lawyer, adequate legal assistance cannot be realized. Many legal rules are complex and most are fact-specific in their application. Lawyers are much better situated than nonlawyers to appreciate the effect of legal rules and to identify facts that determine whether a legal rule is applicable. Full disclosure by clients facilitates efficient presentation at trials and other proceedings and in a lawyer's advising functions.

The third assumption supporting the privilege is controversial— that clients would be unwilling to disclose personal, embarrassing, or unpleasant facts unless they could be assured that neither they nor their lawyers could be called later to testify to the communication. Relatedly, it is assumed that lawyers would not feel free in probing client's stories and giving advice unless assured that they would not thereby expose the client to adverse evidentiary risk. Those assumptions cannot be tested but are widely believed by lawyers to be sound. The privilege implies an impairment of the search for truth in some instances. Recognition of the privilege reflects a judgment that this impairment is outweighed by the social and moral values of confidential consultations. The privilege provides a zone of privacy within which a client may more effectively exercise the full autonomy that the law and legal institutions allow.

* * *

d. Source of the law concerning the privilege. In most of the states, the privilege is defined by statute or rule, typically in an evidence code; in a few states, the privilege is common law. In the federal system, the definition of the privilege is left to the common-law process with respect to issues on which federal law applies. Federal Rule of Evidence 501 provides generally that questions of privilege "shall be governed by the principles of the common law as they may be interpreted by the courts of the United States in the light of reason and experience." On elements of a claim or defense as to which state law supplies the rule of decision, however, Rule 501 provides that the federal courts are to apply the attorney-client privilege of the relevant state.

* * *

§ 69.   Attorney–Client Privilege—"Communication"

A communication within the meaning of § 68 is any expression through which a privileged person, as defined in § 70, undertakes to convey information to another privileged person and any document or other record revealing such an expression.

Comment:

* * *

b.   Communications qualifying for the privilege. A communication can be in any form. Most confidential client communications to a lawyer are written or spoken words, but the privilege applies to communication through technologically enhanced methods such as telephone and telegraph, audio or video tape recording, film, telecopier, and other electronic means. However, communications through a public mode may suggest the absence of a reasonable expectation of confidentiality (see § 71, Comment *e*).

c.   Intercepted communications. The communication need not in fact succeed; for example, an intercepted communication is within this Section (see § 71, Comment *c* (eavesdroppers)).

Illustration:

1.   Lawyer represents Client in a pending criminal investigation. Lawyer directs Client to make a tape recording detailing everything that Client knows about an unlawful enterprise for Lawyer's review. Client makes the tape recording in secret. A cell mate, after learning of the tape recording, informs the prosecutor who causes the tape to be seized under a subpoena. The attorney-client privilege covers the tape recording.

* * *

d.   Distinction between the content of a communication and knowledge of facts. The attorney-client privilege protects only the content of the communication between privileged persons, not the knowledge of privileged persons about the facts themselves. Although a client cannot be required to testify about communications with a lawyer about a subject, the client may be required to testify about what the client knows concerning the same subject. The client thus may invoke the privilege with respect to the question "Did you tell your lawyer the light was red?" but not with respect to the question

"Did you see that the light was red?" Similarly, the privilege does not apply to preexisting documents or other tangible evidence (see Comment *j*), even if they concern the same subject as a privileged communication.

* * *

e. Communicative client acts. The privilege extends to nonverbal communicative acts intended to convey information. For example, a client may communicate with a lawyer through facial expressions or other communicative bodily motions or gestures (nodding or shaking the head or holding up a certain number of fingers to indicate number) or acting out a recalled incident. On the other hand, the privilege does not extend to a client act simply because the client performed the act in the lawyer's presence. The privilege applies when the purpose in performing the act is to convey information to the lawyer.

Illustrations:

3. Client, charged with a crime, retains Lawyer as defense counsel. Lawyer obtains a police report stating that the perpetrator of the crime had a tattooed right forearm. Lawyer asks Client whether Client's right arm is tattooed. In answer, Client rolls up his right sleeve revealing his forearm. The information that the lawyer thereby acquires derives from a protected communication.

4. The same facts as in Illustration 3, except that, shortly after the crime, Client appears at Lawyer's office wearing a short-sleeved shirt. The observation by Lawyer that Client had a tattoo on his arm is not a communication protected by the privilege.

* * *

g. Client identity, the fact of consultation, fee payment, and similar matters. Courts have sometimes asserted that the attorney-client privilege categorically does not apply to such matters as the following: the identity of a client; the fact that the client consulted the lawyer and the general subject matter of the consultation; the identity of a nonclient who retained or paid the lawyer to represent the client; the details of any retainer agreement; the amount of the agreed-upon fee; and the client's whereabouts. Testimony about such matters normally does not reveal the content of communications from the client. However, admissibility of such testimony should be based on the extent to which it reveals the content of a privileged communication. The privilege applies if the testimony directly or by reasonable inference would reveal the content of a confidential communication.

176

But the privilege does not protect clients or lawyers against revealing a lawyer's knowledge about a client solely on the ground that doing so would incriminate the client or otherwise prejudice the client's interests.

* * *

h.   A record of a privileged communication. The privilege applies both to communications when made and to confidential records of such communications, such as a lawyer's note of the conversation. The privilege applies to a record when a communication embodied in the record can be traced to a privileged person as its expressive source (see § 70) and the record was created (see § 71) and preserved (see § 79) in a confidential state.

i.   Lawyer communications to a client. Confidential communications by a lawyer to a client are also protected, including a record of a privileged communication such as a memorandum to a confidential file or to another lawyer or other person privileged to receive such a communication under § 71. Some decisions have protected a lawyer communication only if it contains or expressly refers to a client communication. That limitation is rejected here in favor of a broader rule more likely to assure full and frank communication (see § 68, Comment *c*). Moreover, the broader rule avoids difficult questions in determining whether a lawyer's communication itself discloses a client communication. A lawyer communication may also be protected by the work-product immunity (see Topic 3).

Illustration:

7.   Lawyer writes a confidential letter to Client offering legal advice on a tax matter on which Client had sought Lawyer's professional assistance. Lawyer's letter is based in part on information that Client supplied to Lawyer, in part on information gathered by Lawyer from third persons, and in part on Lawyer's legal research. Even if each such portion of the letter could be separated from the others, the letter is a communication under this Section, and neither Lawyer nor Client can be made to disclose or testify about any of its contents.

* * *

j.   Preexisting documents and records. A client may communicate information to a lawyer by sending writings or other kinds of documentary or electronic recordings that came into existence prior to the time that the client communicates with the lawyer. The privilege

177

protects the information that the client so communicated but not the preexisting document or record itself. A client-authored document that is not a privileged document when originally composed does not become privileged simply because the client has placed it in the lawyer's hands. However, if a document was a privileged preexisting document and was delivered to the lawyer under circumstances that otherwise would make its communication privileged, it remains privileged in the hands of the lawyer.

* * *

§ 70.　Attorney–Client Privilege—"Privileged Persons"

Privileged persons within the meaning of § 68 are the client (including a prospective client), the client's lawyer, agents of either who facilitate communications between them, and agents of the lawyer who facilitate the representation.

Comment:

* * *

b.　A privileged person as the expressive source. To qualify as privileged, a communication must originate from a person who may make privileged communications and be addressed to persons who may receive them. Those persons are referred to in this Restatement as privileged persons. Client and lawyer are, of course, included. Other privileged persons are those who serve to facilitate communication between client and lawyer and persons who aid the lawyer in representing the client.

* * *

c.　An initial consultation. The privilege protects prospective clients—persons who communicate with a lawyer in an initial consultation but whom the lawyer does not thereafter represent—as well as persons with whom a client-lawyer relationship is established (see § 72(1) & Comment *d* thereof; see also § 15).

d.　Third-party payment of a fee. A person who pays a lawyer's fee is not necessarily a client. The relevant question is whether the lawyer undertook to give legal advice or provide other legal assistance to that person (see § 14; see also § 134).

e.　Privileged agents for a client or lawyer: in general. The privilege normally applies to communications involving persons who on their own behalf seek legal assistance from a lawyer (see § 72). However, a client need not personally seek legal assistance, but may appoint a third person to do so as the client's agent (e.g., § 134, Comment *f*). Whether a third person is an agent of the client or lawyer or a nonprivileged "stranger" is critical in determining application of the attorney-client privilege. If the third person is an agent for the purpose of the privilege, communications through or in the presence of that person are privileged; if the third person is not an agent, then the communications are not in confidence (see § 71) and are not privileged. Accordingly, a lawyer should allow a nonclient to participate only upon clarifying that person's role and when it reasonably appears that the benefit of that person's presence offsets the risk of a later claim that the presence of a third person forfeited the privilege.

f. A client's agent for communication. A person is a confidential agent for communication if the person's participation is reasonably necessary to facilitate the client's communication with a lawyer or another privileged person and if the client reasonably believes that the person will hold the communication in confidence. Factors that may be relevant in determining whether a third person is an agent for communication include the customary relationship between the client and the asserted agent, the nature of the communication, and the client's need for the third person's presence to communicate effectively with the lawyer or to understand and act upon the lawyer's advice.

Illustrations:

    1. The police arrest Client and do not permit Client to communicate directly with Client's regular legal counsel, Lawyer. Client asks Friend, a person whom Client trusts to keep information confidential, to convey to Lawyer the message that Lawyer should not permit the police to search Client's home. Friend is an agent for communication.

    2. Client and Lawyer do not speak a language known by the other. Client uses Translator to communicate an otherwise privileged message to Lawyer. Translator is an acquaintance of Client. Translator is an agent for communication.

* * *

An agent for communication need not take a direct part in client-lawyer communications, but may be present because of the Client's psychological or other need. A business person may be accompanied by a business associate or expert consultant who can assist the client in interpreting the legal situation.

* * *

The privilege applies to communications to and from the client disclosed to persons who hire the lawyer as an incident of the lawyer's engagement. Thus, the privilege covers communications by a client-insured to an insurance-company investigator who is to convey the facts to the client's lawyer designated by the insurer, as well as communications from the lawyer for the insured to the insurer in providing a progress report or discussing litigation strategy or settlement (see § 134, Comment *f*). Such situations must be distinguished from communications by an insured to an insurance investigator who will report to the company, to which the privilege does not apply.

g. A lawyer's agent. A lawyer may disclose privileged communications to other office lawyers and with appropriate nonlawyer staff—secretaries, file clerks, computer operators, investigators, office managers, paralegal assistants, telecommunications personnel, and similar law-office assistants. On the duty of a lawyer to protect client information being handled by nonlawyer personnel, see § 60(1)(b). The privilege also extends to communications to and from the client that are disclosed to independent contractors retained by a lawyer, such as an accountant or physician retained by the lawyer to assist in providing legal services to the client and not for the purpose of testifying.

h. An incompetent person as a client. When a client is mentally or physically incapacitated from effectively consulting with a lawyer, a representative may communicate with the incompetent person's lawyer under the protection of the privilege. The privilege also extends to any communications between the incompetent person and the representative relating to the communication with the lawyer.

* * *

§ 71. Attorney–Client Privilege—"In Confidence"

A communication is in confidence within the meaning of § 68 if, at the time and in the circumstances of the communication, the communicating person reasonably believes that no one will learn the contents of the communication except a privileged person as defined in § 70 or another person with whom communications are protected under a similar privilege.

Comment:

* * *

b. Rationale. Given the objectives of the attorney-client privilege (see § 68, Comment *c*), a communication must be made in circumstances reasonably indicating that it will be learned only by the lawyer, client, or another privileged person (see § 70). The matter communicated need not itself be secret. For example, a privileged person receiving the communication may have known the same information from another source. The intent of the communicating person to communicate in confidence is relevant but not determinative. Thus, communication in a nonconfidential setting evidences that secrecy was not a consideration even if it is later protested that confidentiality was intended. Extending the privilege to a nonconfidential communication would not further the policy of the privilege and would result in excluding otherwise admissible and relevant evidence (see § 68, Comment *d*). If the communicating person did not intend that the communication be confidential, it is not privileged regardless of the circumstances otherwise attending its transmission.

The presence of a stranger to the lawyer-client relationship does not destroy confidentiality if another privilege protects the communications in the same way as the attorney-client privilege. Thus, in a jurisdiction that recognizes an absolute husband-wife privilege, the presence of a wife at an otherwise confidential meeting between the husband and the husband's lawyer does not destroy the confidentiality required for the attorney-client privilege.

c. Confidential and nonconfidential communications. The circumstances must indicate that the communicating persons reasonably believed that the communication would be confidential. Thus, a conversation between lawyer and client in the lawyer's offices is privileged. The same will not necessarily apply to a communication in offices of the client, inasmuch as not all agents of the client are privileged persons within the meaning of § 70 (compare Illustration 1 hereto & Comment *d*). For the delineation of privileged persons in the case of a client that is an organization, see § 73.

The circumstances may indicate that the communicating person knows that a nonprivileged person will learn of it, thus impairing its confidentiality. For example, a client may talk with a lawyer in a loud voice in a public place where nonprivileged persons could readily overhear. Communication over a medium from which it is impossible to exclude other listeners, such as radio, strongly suggests that secrecy is not reasonably expected. Whether the client or other communicating person knew that nonprivileged persons would learn of the communication depends on the specific circumstances. The relevant circumstances are those reasonably evident to the communicating person, not the auditor. Thus, the presence of a surreptitious eavesdropper does not destroy confidentiality.

Illustrations:

1. Client and Lawyer confer in Client's office about a legal matter. Client realizes that occupants of nearby offices can normally hear the sound of voices coming from Client's office but reasonably supposes they cannot intelligibly detect individual words. An occupant of an adjoining office secretly records the conference between Client and Lawyer and is able to make out the contents of their communications. Even if it violates no law in the jurisdiction, the secret recording ordinarily would not be anticipated by persons wishing to confer in confidence. Accordingly, the fact that the eavesdropper overheard the Client–Lawyer communications does not impair their confidential status.

2. During a recess in a trial, Client and Lawyer walk into a courthouse corridor crowded with other persons attending the trial and discuss Client's intended testimony in tones loud enough to be readily overheard by bystanders. As Lawyer knows, the courthouse premises include several areas more appropriate for a confidential conversation than the corridor. The corridor conversation is not in confidence for the purposes of the privilege, and the privilege does not bar examining either Client or Lawyer concerning it.

Confidentiality is a practical requirement. Exigent circumstances may require communications under conditions where ordinary precautions for confidentiality are impossible. The privilege applies if the communicating person has taken reasonable precautions in the circumstances.

* * *

§ 72. Attorney–Client Privilege—Legal Assistance as the Object of a Privileged Communication

A communication is made for the purpose of obtaining or providing legal assistance within the meaning of § 68 if it is made to or to assist a person:

> **(1) who is a lawyer or who the client or prospective client reasonably believes to be a lawyer; and**

> **(2) whom the client or prospective client consults for the purpose of obtaining legal assistance.**

182

Comment:

* * *

b. The scope of legal assistance. The claimant of privilege must have consulted the lawyer to obtain legal counseling or advice, document preparation, litigation services, or any other assistance customarily performed by lawyers in their professional capacity. A lawyer's assistance is legal in nature if the lawyer's professional skill and training would have value in the matter. Some early authority suggested that the attorney-client privilege extended only to legal assistance in litigation. That limitation has not been followed by modern American authority or in the Section.

Client-lawyer communications retrospectively reflecting on past legal services, such as remarks after a trial or signing of a contract, are included within the privilege. Also included are communications that refer only speculatively to future legal services.

c. A client's purpose. A client must consult the lawyer for the purpose of obtaining legal assistance and not predominantly for another purpose. That limitation follows from the objective of the privilege, which is to encourage client communications to enable lawyers to render legal assistance to the client and to encourage lawyers to convey advice and other information to their clients (see § 68, Comment *c*). Whether another privilege (for example, doctor-patient privilege, interspousal communication privilege, or trade-secret privilege) might protect a specific communication is beyond the scope of this Restatement.

A consultation with one admitted to the bar but not in that other person's role as lawyer is not protected. Thus, a communication with a friend is not protected simply because the friend is a lawyer. Also not privileged are communications with a person who is a lawyer but who performs a predominantly business function within an organization, for example as a director or nonlegal officer of a corporation. When a person in such a role performs legal services for the client organization, the privilege applies. Whether a purpose is significantly that of obtaining legal assistance or is for a nonlegal purpose depends upon the circumstances, including the extent to which the person performs legal and nonlegal work, the nature of the communication in question, and whether or not the person had previously provided legal assistance relating to the same matter. Inside legal counsel to a corporation or similar organization (see § 73, Comment *i*) is fully empowered to engage in privileged communications.

* * *

If a lawyer's services are of a kind performed commonly by both lawyers and nonlawyers or that otherwise include both legal and nonlegal elements, difficult questions of fact may be presented. So long as the client consults to gain advantage from the lawyer's legal skills and training, the communication is within this Section, even if the client may expect to gain other benefits as well, such as business advice or the comfort of friendship. The primary consideration is the reasonable expectations of the person in the position of putative client. Some situations are sufficiently familiar in practice to warrant treating them as presumptively legal services. Thus, preparing a will or preparing to conduct litigation should always be regarded as legal assistance.

Illustrations:

2. As Lawyer has done in past years, Lawyer prepares Client's federal tax returns, using records, receipts, and other information supplied by Client and without discussing any issues with Client. Client's tax returns are not complex, nor do they require a knowledge of tax law beyond that possessed by nonlawyer preparers of tax returns. Client knows that Lawyer is admitted to practice law but has never discussed with Lawyer any legal question concerning taxes or return preparation, nor has Lawyer offered such advice. Client pays Lawyer on a per-form basis and in an amount comparable to what nonlawyer tax preparers charge. The trier of fact may, but need not, infer that Client's purpose was not that of obtaining legal assistance.

3. Client frequently has consulted Lawyer about legal matters relating to Client's growing business. Lawyer drafts documents and provides other legal assistance relating to a complicated transaction having important tax implications that Client and Lawyer identify and discuss. Client later asks Lawyer to prepare Client's federal income-tax return for the tax year in which the transaction occurs. The circumstances indicate that Lawyer is providing legal services in preparing the tax return.

* * *

e. *"Lawyer."* As provided in Subsection (1), the privilege applies to communications to a person whom the client reasonably believes to be a lawyer. Thus, a lawyer admitted to practice in another jurisdiction or a lawyer admitted to practice in a foreign nation is a lawyer for the purposes of the privilege. On communications involving inside legal counsel of an organization, see Comment c hereto. Communications to a person who falsely poses as a lawyer are privileged, so long as the confiding client reasonably believes that the impostor is a lawyer. Although local practice by a lawyer admitted elsewhere or by an impostor may constitute unauthorized practice of law, depriving the client of the privilege is an inappropriate sanction. Clients should be

184

protected in dealing with legal advisers in good faith and not be exposed to the uncertainties of choice-of-law questions.

* * *

TITLE B. THE ATTORNEY–CLIENT PRIVILEGE FOR ORGANIZATIONAL AND MULTIPLE CLIENTS

§ 73. The Privilege for an Organizational Client

When a client is a corporation, unincorporated association, partnership, trust, estate, sole proprietorship, or other for-profit or not-for-profit organization, the attorney-client privilege extends to a communication that:

(1) otherwise qualifies as privileged under §§ 68–72;

(2) is between an agent of the organization and a privileged person as defined in § 70;

(3) concerns a legal matter of interest to the organization; and

(4) is disclosed only to:

(a) privileged persons as defined in § 70; and

(b) other agents of the organization who reasonably need to know of the communication in order to act for the organization.

Comment:

* * *

b. Rationale. The attorney-client privilege encourages organizational clients to have their agents confide in lawyers in order to realize the organization's legal rights and to achieve compliance with law (Comment *d* hereto). Extending the privilege to corporations and other organizations was formerly a matter of doubt but is no longer questioned. However, two pivotal questions must be resolved.

The first is defining the group of persons who can make privileged communications on behalf of an organization. Balance is required. The privilege should cover a sufficiently broad number of organizational communications to realize the organization's policy objectives, but not insulate ordinary intraorganizational communications that may later have importance as evidence. Concern has been expressed, for example, that the privilege would afford organizations "zones of silence" that would be free of evidentiary scrutiny. A subsidiary problem is whether persons who would be nonprivileged occurrence witnesses with respect to communications to a lawyer representing a natural person can be conduits of privileged communications when the client is an organization. That problem has been addressed in terms of the "subject-matter" and "control-group" tests for the privilege (see Comment *d*).

Second is the problem of defining the types of organizations treated as clients for purposes of the privilege. It is now accepted that the privilege applies to corporations, but some decisions have questioned whether the privilege should apply to unincorporated associations, partnerships, or sole proprietorships. Neither logic nor principle supports limiting the organizational privilege to the corporate form (see Comment *c* hereto).

c. Application of the privilege to an organization. As stated in the Section, the privilege applies to all forms of organizations. A corporation with hundreds of employees could as well be a sole proprietorship if its assets were owned by a single person rather than its shares being owned by the same person. It would be anomalous to accord the privilege to a business in corporate form but not if it were organized as a sole proprietorship. In general, an organization under this Section is a group having a recognizable identity as such and some permanency. Thus, an organization under this Section ordinarily would include a law firm, however it may be structured (as a professional corporation, a partnership, a sole proprietorship, or otherwise). The organization need not necessarily be treated as a legal entity for any other legal purpose. The privilege extends as well to charitable, social, fraternal, and other nonprofit organizations such as labor unions and chambers of commerce.

d. An agent of an organizational client. As stated in Subsection (2), the communication must involve an agent of the organization, on one hand, and, on the other, a privileged person within the meaning of § 70, such as the lawyer for the organization. Persons described in Subsection (4)(b) may disclose the communication under a need-to-know limitation (see Comment *g* hereto). The existence of a relationship of principal and agent between the organizational client and the privileged agent is determined according to agency law (see generally Restatement Second, Agency §§ 1–139).

Some decisions apply a "control group" test for determining the scope of the privilege for an organization. That test limits the privilege to communications from persons in the organization who have authority to mold organizational policy or to take action in accordance with the lawyer's advice. The control-group circle excludes many persons within an organization who normally would cooperate with an organization's lawyer. Such a limitation overlooks that the division of functions within an organization often separates decisionmakers from those knowing relevant facts. Such a limitation is unnecessary to prevent abuse of the privilege (see Comment *g*) and significantly frustrates its purpose.

Other decisions apply a "subject matter" test. That test extends the privilege to communications with any lower-echelon employee or agent so long as the communication relates to the subject matter of the representation. In substance, those decisions comport with the need-to-know formulation in this Section (see Comment *g*).

* * *

Agents of the organization who may make privileged communications under this Section include the organization's officers and employees. For example, a communication by any employee of a corporation to the corporation's lawyer concerning the matter as to which the lawyer was retained to represent the corporation would be privileged, if other conditions of the privilege are satisfied. The concept of agent also includes independent contractors with whom the corporation has a principal-agent relationship and extends to agents of such persons when acting as subagents of the organizational client. For example, a foreign-based corporation may retain a general agency (perhaps a separate corporation) in an American city for the purpose of retaining counsel to represent the interests of the foreign-based corporation. Communications by the general agency would be by an agent for the purpose of this Section.

* * *

In the case of a partnership, general partners and employees and other agents and subagents of the partnership may serve as agents of the organization for the purpose of making privileged communications (see generally Restatement Second, Agency § 14A). Limited partners who have no other relationship (such as employee) with the limited partnership are analogous to shareholders of a corporation and are not such agents.

* * *

[*g. The need-to-know limitation on disclosing privileged communications.*]

* * *

The need-to-know limitation of Subsection (4)(b) permits disclosing privileged communications to other agents of the organization who reasonably need to know of the privileged communication in order to act for the organization in the matter. Those agents include persons who are responsible for accepting or rejecting a lawyer's advice on behalf of the organization or for acting on legal assistance, such as general legal advice, provided by the lawyer. Access of such persons to privileged communications is not limited to direct exchange with the lawyer. A lawyer may be required to take steps assuring that attorney-client communications will be disseminated only among privileged persons who have a need to know. Persons defined in Subsection (4)(b) may be apprised of privileged communications after they have been made, as by examining records of privileged communications previously made, in order to conduct the affairs of the organization in light of the legal services provided.

Illustration:

1. Lawyer for Organization makes a confidential report to President of Organization, describing Organization's contractual relationship with Supplier, and advising that Organization's contract with Supplier could be terminated without liability. President sends a confidential memorandum to Manager, Organization's purchasing manager, asking whether termination of the contract would nonetheless be inappropriate for business reasons. Because Manager's response would reasonably depend on several aspects of Lawyer's advice, Manager would have need to know the justifying reason for Lawyer's advice that the contract could be terminated. Lawyer's report to President remains privileged notwithstanding that President shared it with Manager.

The need-to-know concept properly extends to all agents of the organization who would be personally held financially or criminally liable for conduct in the matter in question or who would personally benefit from it, such as general partners of a partnership with respect to a claim for or against the partnership. It extends to persons, such as members of a board of directors and senior officers of an organization, whose general management and supervisory responsibilities include wide areas of organizational activities and to lower-echelon agents of the organization whose area of activity is relevant to the legal advice or service rendered.

* * *

h. Directed and volunteered agent communications. It is not necessary that a superior organizational authority specifically direct an agent to communicate with the organization's lawyer. Unless instructed to the contrary, an agent has authority to volunteer information to a lawyer when reasonably related to the interests of the organization.

An agent has similar authority to respond to a request for information from a lawyer for the organization. And the lawyer for the organization ordinarily may seek relevant information directly from employees and other agents without prior direction from superior authorities in the organization.

* * *

j. Invoking and waiving the privilege of an organizational client. The privilege for organizational clients can be asserted and waived only by a responsible person acting for the organization for this purpose. On waiver, see §§ 78–80. Communications involving an organization's director, officer, or employee may qualify as privileged, but it is a separate question whether such a person has authority to invoke or waive the privilege on behalf of the organization. If the lawyer was representing both the organization and the individual as co-clients, the question of invoking and waiving the privilege is determined under the rule for co-clients (see § 75, Comment *e*). Whether a lawyer has formed a client-lawyer relationship with a person affiliated with the organization, as well as with the organization, is determined under § 14. Communications of such a person who approaches a lawyer for the organization as a prospective client are privileged as provided in § 72. Unless the person's contrary intent is reasonably manifest to a lawyer for the organization, the lawyer acts properly in assuming that a communication from any such person is on behalf and in the interest of the organization and, as such, is privileged in the interest of the organization and not of the individual making the communication. When the person manifests an intention to make a communication privileged against the organization, the lawyer must resist entering into such a client-lawyer relationship and receiving such a communication if doing so would constitute an impermissible conflict of interest (see § 131, Comment *e*).

* * *

k. Succession in legal control of an organization. When ownership of a corporation or other organization as an entity passes to successors, the transaction carries with it authority concerning asserting or waiving the privilege. After legal control passes in such a transaction, communications from directors, officers, or employees of the acquired organization to lawyers who represent only the predecessor organization, if it maintains a separate existence from the acquiring organization, may no longer be covered by the privilege. When a corporation or other organization has ceased to have a legal existence such that no person can act in its behalf, ordinarily the attorney-client privilege terminates (see generally § 77, Comment *c*).

Illustration:

> 3. X, an officer of Ajax Corporation, communicates in confidence with Lawyer, who represents Ajax, concerning dealings between Ajax and one of its creditors, Vendor Corporation. Ajax later is declared bankrupt and a bankruptcy court appoints Trustee as the trustee in bankruptcy for Ajax. Thereafter, Lawyer is called to the witness stand in litigation between Vendor Corporation and Trustee. Trustee has authority to determine whether the attorney-client privilege should be asserted or waived on behalf of the bankrupt Ajax Corporation with respect to testimony by Lawyer about statements by X. X cannot assert a privilege because X was not a client of Lawyer in the representation. Former officers and directors of Ajax cannot assert the privilege because control of the corporation has passed to Trustee.

* * *

§ 74. The Privilege for a Governmental Client

Unless applicable law otherwise provides, the attorney-client privilege extends to a communication of a governmental organization as stated in § 73 and of an individual employee or other agent of a governmental organization as a client with respect to his or her personal interest as stated in §§ 68–72.

Comment:

* * *

b. Rationale. The objectives of the attorney-client privilege (see § 68, Comment *c*), including the special objectives relevant to organizational clients (see § 73, Comment *b*), apply in general to governmental clients. The privilege aids government entities and employees in obtaining legal advice founded on a complete and accurate factual picture. Communications from such persons should be correspondingly privileged.

A narrower privilege for governmental clients may be warranted by particular statutory formulations. Open-meeting and open-files statutes reflect a public policy against secrecy in many areas of governmental activity. Moreover, unlike persons in private life, a public agency or employee has no autonomous right of confidentiality in communications relating to governmental business.

Nonetheless, the legal system has recognized the strategic concerns of a public agency or officer in establishing and asserting public legal rights. Even public legal rights are contingent at their boundaries and subject to argumentation and dispute as to their precise extent. Members of the public who assert legal interests against a public agency or officer act not in the general public interest but in their private interest or in what they assert is the public interest. The public acting through its public agencies is entitled to resist claims and contentions that the agency considers legally or factually unwarranted. To that end, a public agency or employee is entitled to engage in confidential communications with counsel to establish and maintain legal positions. Accordingly, courts generally have construed open-meeting, open-files, whistle-blower, and similar statutes as subject to the attorney-client privilege, recognizing that otherwise governments would be at unfair disadvantage in litigation, in handling claims and in negotiations.

* * *

e. Invoking and waiving the privilege of a governmental client. The privilege for governmental entities may be asserted or waived by the responsible public official or body. The identity of that responsible person or body is a question of local governmental law. In some states, for example, the state's attorney general decides matters of litigation policy for state agencies, including decisions about the privilege. In other states, such decisions are made by another executive officer or agency in suits in which the attorney general otherwise conducts the litigation. As a general proposition, the official or body that is empowered to assert or forego a claim or defense is entitled to assert or forego the privilege for communications relating to the claim or defense. Waiver of the privilege is determined according to the standards set forth in § 73, Comment *j*. See also Comment *d* hereto.

* * *

§ 75. The Privilege of Co–Clients

(1) If two or more persons are jointly represented by the same lawyer in a matter, a communication of either co-client that otherwise qualifies as privileged under §§ 68–72 and relates to matters of common interest is privileged as against third persons, and any co-client may invoke the privilege, unless it has been waived by the client who made the communication.

(2) Unless the co-clients have agreed otherwise, a communication described in Subsection (1) is not privi-

191

leged as between the co-clients in a subsequent adverse proceeding between them.

Comment:

* * *

d. The subsequent-proceeding exception to the co-client privilege. As stated in Subsection (2), in a subsequent proceeding in which former co-clients are adverse, one of them may not invoke the attorney-client privilege against the other with respect to communications involving either of them during the co-client relationship. That rule applies whether or not the co-client's communication had been disclosed to the other during the co-client representation, unless they had otherwise agreed.

Rules governing the co-client privilege are premised on an assumption that co-clients usually understand that all information is to be disclosed to all of them. Courts sometimes refer to this as a presumed intent that there should be no confidentiality between co-clients. Fairness and candor between the co-clients and with the lawyer generally precludes the lawyer from keeping information secret from any one of them, unless they have agreed otherwise (see § 60, Comment *l*).

* * *

Co-clients may agree that the lawyer will not disclose certain confidential communications of one co-client to other co-clients. If the co-clients have so agreed and the co-clients are subsequently involved in adverse proceedings, the communicating client can invoke the privilege with respect to such communications not in fact disclosed to the former co-client seeking to introduce it. In the absence of such an agreement, the lawyer ordinarily is required to convey communications to all interested co-clients (see § 60, Comment *l*). A co-client may also retain additional, separate counsel on the matter of the common representation; communications with such counsel are not subject to this Section.

e. Standing to assert the co-client privilege; waiver. If a third person attempts to gain access to or to introduce a co-client communication, each co-client has standing to assert the privilege. The objecting client need not have been the source of the communication or previously have known about it.

* * *

One co-client does not have authority to waive the privilege with respect to another co-client's communications to their common lawyer.

If a document or other recording embodies communications from two or more co-clients, all those co-clients must join in a waiver, unless a nonwaiving co-client's communication can be redacted from the document.

* * *

§ 76. The Privilege in Common–Interest Arrangements

(1) If two or more clients with a common interest in a litigated or nonlitigated matter are represented by separate lawyers and they agree to exchange information concerning the matter, a communication of any such client that otherwise qualifies as privileged under §§ 68–72 that relates to the matter is privileged as against third persons. Any such client may invoke the privilege, unless it has been waived by the client who made the communication.

(2) Unless the clients have agreed otherwise, a communication described in Subsection (1) is not privileged as between clients described in Subsection (1) in a subsequent adverse proceeding between them.

Comment:

* * *

b. Rationale. The rule in this Section permits persons who have common interests to coordinate their positions without destroying the privileged status of their communications with their lawyers. For example, where conflict of interest disqualifies a lawyer from representing two co-defendants in a criminal case (see § 129), the separate lawyers representing them may exchange confidential communications to prepare their defense without loss of the privilege. Clients thus can elect separate representation while maintaining the privilege in cooperating on common elements of interest.

c. Confidentiality and common-interest rules. The common-interest privilege somewhat relaxes the requirement of confidentiality (see § 71) by defining a widened circle of persons to whom clients may disclose privileged communications. As a corollary, the rule also limits what would otherwise be instances of waiver by disclosing a communication (compare § 79). Communications of several commonly interested clients remain confidential against the rest of the world, no matter how many clients are involved. However, the known presence of a stranger negates the privilege for communications made in the stranger's presence.

Exchanging communications may be predicated on an express agreement, but formality is not required. It may pertain to litigation or to other matters. Separately represented clients do not, by the mere fact of cooperation under this Section, impliedly undertake to exchange all information concerning the matter of common interest.

d. The permissible extent of common-interest disclosures. Under the privilege, any member of a client set—a client, the client's agent for communication, the client's lawyer, and the lawyer's agent (see § 70)—can exchange communications with members of a similar client set. However, a communication directly among the clients is not privileged unless made for the purpose of communicating with a privileged person as defined in § 70. A person who is not represented by a lawyer and who is not himself or herself a lawyer cannot participate in a common-interest arrangement within this Section.

e. Extent of common interests. The communication must relate to the common interest, which may be either legal, factual, or strategic in character. The interests of the separately represented clients need not be entirely congruent.

Illustration:

1. Lawyer One separately represents Corporation A and Lawyer Two represents Corporation B in defending a products-liability action brought by a common adversary, Plaintiff X. The two lawyers agree to exchange otherwise privileged communications of their respective clients concerning settlement strategies. Plaintiff Y later sues Corporation A and Corporation B for damages for alleged defects involving the same products and attempts to obtain discovery of the communications between Lawyer One and Lawyer Two. The communications exchanged between the lawyers for Corporation A and Corporation B are privileged and cannot be discovered.

Unlike the relationship between co-clients, the common-interest relationship does not imply an undertaking to disclose all relevant information (compare § 75, Comment *d*). Confidential communications disclosed to only some members of the arrangement remain privileged against other members as well as against the rest of the world.

f. Subsequent adverse proceedings. Disclosing privileged communications to members of a common-interest arrangement waives the privilege as against other members in subsequent adverse proceedings between them, unless they have agreed otherwise. In that respect, the common-interest exception operates in the same way as the exception

194

for subsequent adverse proceedings as between co-clients (see § 75, Comment *d*). Disclosing information does not waive the privilege with respect to other communications that might also be germane to the matter of common interest but that were not in fact disclosed.

There is no waiver between the members exchanging a communication if they have agreed that it will remain privileged as against each other in subsequent adverse proceedings.

g. Standing to assert the privilege; waiver. Any member of a common-interest arrangement may invoke the privilege against third persons, even if the communication in question was not originally made by or addressed to the objecting member.

In the absence of an agreement to the contrary, any member may waive the privilege with respect to that person's own communications. Correlatively, a member is not authorized to waive the privilege for another member's communication. If a document or other recording embodies communications from two or more members, a waiver is effective only if concurred in by all members whose communications are involved, unless an objecting member's communication can be redacted.

* * *

TITLE C. DURATION OF THE ATTORNEY–CLIENT PRIVILEGE; WAIVERS AND EXCEPTIONS

Introductory Note

The attorney-client privilege must be asserted to maintain its protection. The privileged status of the communication can be waived in several ways (see §§ 78–80). Waivers are sometimes classified as "express" or "implied." Most instances result from inaction that the law treats as inconsistent with maintaining the privilege. The term "implied" waiver suggests advertent client purpose, but this is not required. Indeed, the client may waive the privilege even though entirely ignorant of its application. In this respect, the law's attitude toward the privilege is unsympathetic. Moreover, in certain limited instances the law recognizes exceptions to the privilege (see §§ 81–85).

Although the privilege for a client communication may be waived or lost, the information may remain confidential for other purposes. Application of waiver or exception to a communication does not relieve a lawyer of the legal duty otherwise to protect the communication against further disclosure or use adverse to the client.

§ 77. Duration of the Privilege

Unless waived (see §§ 78–80) or subject to exception (see §§ 81–85), the attorney-client privilege may be invoked as provided in § 86 at any time during or after termination of the relationship between client or prospective client and lawyer.

Comment:

* * *

b. Termination of the client-lawyer relationship. The attorney-client privilege continues indefinitely. Termination of the client-lawyer relationship, even for cause, does not terminate the privilege.

c. Death of a client or cessation of existence of an organization. The privilege survives the death of the client. A lawyer for a client who has died has a continuing obligation to assert the privilege (see § 63, Comment *b*). On standing to assert the privilege, see § 86, Comments *c* and *d.*

The privilege is subject to exception in a controversy concerning a deceased client's disposition of property (see § 81). When ownership or control of an organizational client is transferred or when the organization ceases to exist, the right to invoke the privilege in behalf of the organization may also shift to others or terminate (see § 73, Comment *k*).

* * *

§ 78. Agreement, Disclaimer, or Failure to Object

The attorney-client privilege is waived if the client, the client's lawyer, or another authorized agent of the client:

    (1) agrees to waive the privilege;

    (2) disclaims protection of the privilege and

        (a) another person reasonably relies on the disclaimer to that person's detriment; or

        (b) reasons of judicial administration require that the client not be permitted to revoke the disclaimer; or

    (3) in a proceeding before a tribunal, fails to object properly to an attempt by another person to give or exact testimony or other evidence of a privileged communication.

Comment:

* * *

c. Client agreement. Subsection (1) recognizes that the privilege can be waived by consent of a client, the client's lawyer, or another authorized agent. A lawyer generally has implied authority to waive a client's confidentiality rights in the course of representing the client (see § 61). That authority is especially important in litigation, where the lawyer is empowered to deal with evidentiary issues (see § 16(3) & § 26). A lawyer may be required in some circumstances to advise a client concerning waiver (see § 22). Whether a client can contract away the privilege by consent to a conflict of interest is considered in § 122.

Illustration:

1. A and B were partners in a business enterprise experiencing financial difficulties. Each retained a lawyer. A agreed to send B communications that he had received from his lawyer analyzing financial arrangements between them if B would forbear from filing suit against A. B delayed filing suit, but A refused to honor his agreement. In subsequent litigation, B seeks discovery of the information communicated to A by A's lawyer. A's agreement waives the protection of the attorney-client privilege.

The power of an agent, such as an employee of an organization, to waive the privilege is determined under the law of agency.

* * *

[*e. Failure to object to evidence.*]

* * *

In pretrial discovery, excessive concern with avoiding waiver can unduly delay and encumber the proceeding. Accordingly, procedural rules commonly permit parties to stipulate that privilege is not waived by failure to object during pretrial discovery (see Federal Rules of Civil Procedure, Rule 29).

* * *

§ 79. Subsequent Disclosure

The attorney-client privilege is waived if the client, the client's lawyer, or another authorized agent of the client voluntarily discloses the communication in a non-privileged communication.

197

Comment:

* * *

b. Subsequent disclosure. Voluntary disclosure of a privileged communication is inconsistent with a later claim that the communication is to be protected. When the disclosure has been made voluntarily, it is unnecessary that there have been detrimental reliance (compare § 78(2)).

c. Authorized disclosure by a lawyer or other agent. The privilege is waived if the client's lawyer or another authorized agent of the client discloses the communication acting under actual or apparent authority. A lawyer generally has implied authority to disclose confidential client communications in the course of representing a client (see § 27, Comment *c*; see also § 61). Ratification of the agent's authority has the same effect (see § 26, Comment *e*). Whether a subagent of the client or lawyer has authority to waive is governed by agency law. A file clerk in a law firm, for example, does not have implied authority.

* * *

d. A privileged subsequent disclosure. A subsequent disclosure that is itself privileged does not result in waiver. Thus, a client who discloses a communication protected by the attorney-client privilege to a second lawyer does not waive the privilege if the attorney-client privilege or work-product immunity protects the second communication. So also, showing a confidential letter from the client's lawyer to the client's spouse under circumstances covered by the marital privilege preserves the attorney-client privilege.

e. Extent of disclosure. Waiver results only when a nonprivileged person learns the substance of a privileged communication. Knowledge by the nonprivileged person that the client consulted a lawyer does not result in waiver, nor does disclosure of nonprivileged portions of a communication or its general subject matter. Public disclosure of facts that were discussed in confidence with a lawyer does not waive the privilege if the disclosure does not also reveal that they were communicated to the lawyer. See § 69, Comment *d* (distinction between communications and facts).

Illustrations:

2. Client, a defendant in a personal-injury action, makes a privileged communication to Lawyer concerning the circumstances of the accident. In a later judicial proceeding, Client, under questioning by Lawyer, testifies about the occurrence but

not about what Client told Lawyer about the same matter. On cross-examination, the lawyer for Plaintiff inquires whether the Client's testimony is consistent with the account Client gave to Lawyer in confidence. Client's testimony did not waive the privilege.

3. The same facts as in Illustration 2, except that Client states that "I've testified exactly as I told Lawyer just a week after the accident happened. I told Lawyer that the skid marks made by Plaintiff's car were 200 feet long. And I've said the same things here." Such testimony waives the privilege by subsequent disclosure. On the extent of waiver, see Comment *f* hereto.

In the circumstances of Illustration 3, if the client merely testifies that the subject of skid marks was discussed with the client's lawyer, the privilege is not waived.

* * *

g. Voluntary subsequent disclosure. To constitute waiver, a disclosure must be voluntary. The disclosing person need not be aware that the communication was privileged, nor specifically intend to waive the privilege. A disclosure in obedience to legal compulsion or as the product of deception does not constitute waiver.

Illustrations:

4. A burglar ransacks Client's confidential files and carries away copies of communications from Client to Lawyer protected by the attorney-client privilege. The police apprehend the burglar, recover the copies, and examine them in order to identify their owner. Client's right to invoke the privilege is not lost.

5. At a hearing before a tribunal, the presiding officer erroneously overrules Lawyer's objection to a question put to Client that calls for a communication protected by the attorney-client privilege. Client then testifies. By testifying, Client has not waived objection to efforts to elicit additional privileged communications in the litigation nor to claim on appeal that the hearing officer incorrectly overruled Lawyer's objection. Client also can seek protection of the attorney-client privilege in subsequent litigation.

* * *

199

h. Inadvertent disclosure. A subsequent disclosure through a voluntary act constitutes a waiver even though not intended to have that effect. It is important to distinguish between inadvertent waiver and a change of heart after voluntary waiver. Waiver does not result if the client or other disclosing person took precautions reasonable in the circumstances to guard against such disclosure. What is reasonable depends on circumstances, including: the relative importance of the communication (the more sensitive the communication, the greater the necessary protective measures); the efficacy of precautions taken and of additional precautions that might have been taken; whether there were externally imposed pressures of time or in the volume of required disclosure; whether disclosure was by act of the client or lawyer or by a third person; and the degree of disclosure to nonprivileged persons.

Once the client knows or reasonably should know that the communication has been disclosed, the client must take prompt and reasonable steps to recover the communication, to reestablish its confidential nature, and to reassert the privilege. Otherwise, apparent acceptance of the disclosure may reflect indifference to confidentiality. Even if fully successful retrieval is impracticable, the client must nonetheless take feasible steps to prevent further distribution.

* * *

§ 80. Putting Assistance or a Communication in Issue

(1) The attorney-client privilege is waived for any relevant communication if the client asserts as to a material issue in a proceeding that:

(a) the client acted upon the advice of a lawyer or that the advice was otherwise relevant to the legal significance of the client's conduct; or

(b) a lawyer's assistance was ineffective, negligent, or otherwise wrongful.

(2) The attorney-client privilege is waived for a recorded communication if a witness:

(a) employs the communication to aid the witness while testifying; or

(b) employed the communication in preparing to testify, and the tribunal finds that disclosure is required in the interests of justice.

Comment:

* * *

b. Putting a privileged communication into issue. The exceptions stated in Subsection (1) are based on considerations of forensic fairness (compare § 79). If the communication could not be introduced, a client could present the justification of legal advice in an inaccurate, incomplete, and self-serving way. The issue of reliance on legal advice can be interjected through pleadings or testimony. Waiver extends to all communications relevant to the issue asserted by the client. A tribunal may control discovery to postpone or pretermit the issue. For example, if legal advice is presented as an alternative defense, discovery with respect to that issue may be postponed to allow the client opportunity to determine whether to withdraw that defense.

* * *

§ 81. A Dispute Concerning a Decedent's Disposition of Property

The attorney-client privilege does not apply to a communication from or to a decedent relevant to an issue between parties who claim an interest through the same deceased client, either by testate or intestate succession or by an inter vivos transaction.

Comment:

* * *

b. A dispute between claimants through the same decedent. The exception in the Section is sometimes justified on the ground that the decedent would have wished full disclosure to facilitate carrying out the client's intentions. The dispute might involve either testate or intestate succession or claims arising from inter vivos transactions to which the decedent was a party. The witness will most often be the decedent's lawyer, who is in a position to know the client's intentions and whose testimony ordinarily will not be tainted by personal interest. Suppressing such testimony would hamper the fair resolution of questions of testator intent in will-contest and similar types of cases. It is therefore probable that the exception does little to lessen the inclination to communicate freely with lawyers (see § 68, Comment *c*).

* * *

§ 82.   Client Crime or Fraud

The attorney-client privilege does not apply to a communication occurring when a client:

(a) consults a lawyer for the purpose, later accomplished, of obtaining assistance to engage in a crime or fraud or aiding a third person to do so, or

(b) regardless of the client's purpose at the time of consultation, uses the lawyer's advice or other services to engage in or assist a crime or fraud.

Comment:

* * *

b.   Rationale. When a client consults a lawyer intending to violate elemental legal obligations, there is less social interest in protecting the communication. Correlatively, there is a public interest in preventing clients from attempting to misuse the client-lawyer relationship for seriously harmful ends. Denying protection of the privilege can be founded on the additional moral ground that the client's wrongful intent forfeits the protection. The client can choose whether or not to commit or aid the act after consulting the lawyer and thus is able to avoid exposing secret communications. The exception does not apply to communications about client crimes or frauds that occurred prior to the consultation. Whether a communication relates to past or ongoing or future acts can be a close question. See Comment *e* hereto.

c.   Intent of the client and lawyer. The client need not specifically understand that the contemplated act is a crime or fraud. The client's purpose in consulting the lawyer or using the lawyer's services may be inferred from the circumstances. It is irrelevant that the legal service sought by the client (such as drafting an instrument) was itself lawful.

Illustrations:

1.   Client is a member of a group engaged in the ongoing enterprise of importing and distributing illegal drugs. Client has agreed with confederates, as part of the consideration for participating in the enterprise, that Client will provide legal representation for the confederates when necessary. Client and Lawyer agree that, for a substantial monthly retainer, Lawyer will stand ready to provide legal services in the event that Client or Client's associates encounter legal difficulties during the operation of the

enterprise. In a communication that otherwise qualifies as privileged under § 68, Client informs Lawyer of the identities of confederates in the enterprise. Client continues to engage in the criminal enterprise following the communication. The crime-fraud exception renders nonprivileged the communications between Client and Lawyer, including identification of Client's confederates.

2. Client, who is in financial difficulty, consults Lawyer A concerning the sale of a parcel of real estate owned by Client. Lawyer A provides legal services in connection with the sale. Client then asks Lawyer A to represent Client in petitioning for bankruptcy. Lawyer A advises Client that the bankruptcy petition must list the sale of the real estate because it occurred within the year previous to the date of filing the petition. Client ends the representation. Client shortly thereafter hires Lawyer B. Omitting to tell Lawyer B about the land sale, Client directs Lawyer B to file a bankruptcy petition that does not disclose the proceeds of the sale. In a subsequent proceeding in which Client's fraud in filing the petition is in issue, a tribunal would be warranted in inferring that Client consulted Lawyer A with the purpose of obtaining assistance to defraud creditors in bankruptcy and thus that the communications between Client and Lawyer A concerning report of the land sale in the bankruptcy petition are not privileged. It would also suffice should the tribunal find that Client attempted to use Lawyer A's advice about the required contents of a bankruptcy petition to defraud creditors by withholding information about the land sale from Lawyer B.

A client could intend criminal or fraudulent conduct but not carry through the intended act. The exception should not apply in such circumstances, for it would penalize a client for doing what the privilege is designed to encourage—consulting a lawyer for the purpose of achieving law compliance. By the same token, lawyers might be discouraged from giving full and candid advice to clients about legally questionable courses of action. On the other hand, a client may consult a lawyer about a matter that constitutes a criminal conspiracy but that is later frustrated—and, in that sense, not later accomplished (cf. Subsection (a))—or, similarly, about a criminal attempt. Such a crime is within the exception stated in the Section if its elements are established.

* * *

d. Kinds of illegal acts included within the exception. The authorities agree that the exception stated in this Section applies to client conduct defined as a crime or fraud. Fraud, for the purpose of the exception, requires a knowing or reckless misrepresentation (or nondisclosure when applicable law requires disclosure) likely to injure another (see Restatement Second, Torts §§ 525–530 (defining elements of fraudulent misrepresentation)).

The evidence codes and judicial decisions are divided on the question of extending the exception to other wrongs such as intentional torts, which, although not criminal or fraudulent, have hallmarks of clear illegality and the threat of serious harm. Legislatures and courts classify illegal acts as crimes and frauds for purposes and policies different from those defining the scope of the privilege. Thus, limiting the exception to crimes and frauds produces an exception narrower than principle and policy would otherwise indicate. Nonetheless, the prevailing view limits the exception to crimes and frauds. The actual instances in which a broader exception might apply are probably few and isolated, and it would be difficult to formulate a broader exception that is not objectionably vague.

* * *

[e. *Continuing crimes and frauds.*]

* * *

The exception does apply to client crimes or frauds that are ongoing or continuing. With respect to past acts that have present consequences, such as the possession of stolen goods, consultation of lawyer and client is privileged if it addresses how the client can rectify the effects of the illegal act—such as by returning the goods to their rightful owner—or defending the client against criminal charges arising out of the offense.

Illustration:

4. Client consults Lawyer about Client's indictment for the crimes of theft and of unlawfully possessing stolen goods. Applicable law treats possession of stolen goods as a continuing offense. Client is hiding the goods in a secret place, knowing that they are stolen. Confidential communications between Client and Lawyer concerning the indictment for theft and possession and the facts underlying those offenses are privileged. Confidential communications concerning ways in which Client can continue to possess the stolen goods, including information supplied by Client about their present location, are not protected by the privilege because of the crime-fraud exception. Confidential communications about ways in

which Client might lawfully return the stolen goods to their owner are privileged.

* * *

f. Invoking the crime-fraud exception. The crime-fraud exception is relevant only after the attorney-client privilege is successfully invoked. The person seeking access to the communication then must present a prima facie case for the exception. A prima facie case need show only a reasonable basis for concluding that the elements of the exception (see Comment *d*) exist. The showing must be made by evidence other than the contested communication itself. Once a prima facie showing is made, the tribunal has discretion to examine the communication or hear testimony about it in camera, that is, without requiring that the communications be revealed to the party seeking to invoke the exception (see § 86, Comment *f*).

Unless the crime-fraud exception plainly applies to a client-lawyer communication, a lawyer has an obligation to assert the privilege (see § 63, Comment *b*).

* * *

§ 83. Lawyer Self–Protection

The attorney-client privilege does not apply to a communication that is relevant and reasonably necessary for a lawyer to employ in a proceeding:

(1) to resolve a dispute with a client concerning compensation or reimbursement that the lawyer reasonably claims the client owes the lawyer; or

(2) to defend the lawyer or the lawyer's associate or agent against a charge by any person that the lawyer, associate, or agent acted wrongfully during the course of representing a client.

Comment:

* * *

b. Rationale. The exceptions to the duty of confidentiality (see § 72) for lawyer disclosure in self-defense (see § 64) and in pursuing a compensation claim (see § 65) and that stated in this Section rest on considerations of fairness (see § 64, Comment *b*; § 65, Comment *b*). To exclude such evidence would leave lawyers uniquely defenseless against false charges, and leave them unable to assert well-founded claims for fee compensation or oppose disqualification motions and disciplinary charges.

* * *

§ 84. Fiduciary–Lawyer Communications

In a proceeding in which a trustee of an express trust or similar fiduciary is charged with breach of fiduciary duties by a beneficiary, a communication otherwise within § 68 is nonetheless not privileged if the communication:

(a) is relevant to the claimed breach; and

(b) was between the trustee and a lawyer (or other privileged person within the meaning of § 70) who was retained to advise the trustee concerning the administration of the trust.

Comment:

* * *

b. Rationale. In litigation between a trustee of an express trust and beneficiaries of the trust charging breach of the trustee's fiduciary duties, the trustee cannot invoke the attorney-client privilege to prevent the beneficiaries from introducing evidence of the trustee's communications with a lawyer retained to advise the trustee in carrying out the trustee's fiduciary duties. The exception applies in suits brought directly by a beneficiary or by a representative of the beneficiary. It does not apply to communications between the trustee and a lawyer specifically retained by the trustee to represent, not the trust or the trustee with respect to executing trust duties, but the trustee in the trustee's personal capacity, such as to assist the trustee in a dispute with a beneficiary or to assert a right against the beneficiary.

* * *

§ 85. Communications Involving a Fiduciary Within an Organization

In a proceeding involving a dispute between an organizational client and shareholders, members, or other constituents of the organization toward whom the directors, officers, or similar persons managing the organization bear fiduciary responsibilities, the attorney-client privilege of the organization may be withheld from a communication otherwise within § 68 if the tribunal finds that:

(a) those managing the organization are charged with breach of their obligations toward the shareholders, members, or other constituents or toward the organization itself;

(b) the communication occurred prior to the assertion of the charges and relates directly to those charges; and

(c) the need of the requesting party to discover or introduce the communication is sufficiently compelling and the threat to confidentiality sufficiently confined to justify setting the privilege aside.

Comment:

* * *

c. Application of the organizational-fiduciary exception. A court applying this Section weighs the benefits of disclosure against the benefits of continuing confidentiality. The determination should be guided by the following considerations: (1) the extent to which beneficiaries seeking the information have interests that conflict with those of opposing or silent beneficiaries; (2) the substantiality of the beneficiaries' claim and whether the proceeding was brought for ulterior purpose; (3) the relevance of the communication to the beneficiaries' claim and the extent to which information it contains is available from nonprivileged sources; (4) whether the beneficiaries' claim asserts criminal, fraudulent, or similarly illegal acts; (5) whether the communication relates to future conduct of the organization that could be prejudiced; (6) whether the communication concerns the very litigation brought by the beneficiaries; (7) the specificity of the beneficiaries' request; (8) whether the communication involves trade secrets or other information that has value beyond its character as a client-lawyer communication; (9) the extent to which the court can employ protective orders to guard against abuse if the communication is revealed; and (10) whether the determination not to waive the privilege made in behalf of the organization was by a disinterested group of directors or officers.

* * *

TITLE D. INVOKING THE PRIVILEGE AND ITS EXCEPTIONS

§ 86. Invoking the Privilege and Its Exceptions

(1) When an attempt is made to introduce in evidence or obtain discovery of a communication privileged under § 68:

(a) A client, a personal representative of an incompetent or deceased client, or a person succeeding to the interest of a client may invoke or waive the privilege, either personally or through counsel or another authorized agent.

(b) A lawyer, an agent of the lawyer, or an agent of a client from whom a privileged communication is sought must invoke the privilege when doing so appears reasonably appropriate, unless the client:

(i) has waived the privilege; or

(ii) has authorized the lawyer or agent to waive it.

(c) Notwithstanding failure to invoke the privilege as specified in Subsections (1)(a) and (1)(b), the tribunal has discretion to invoke the privilege.

(2) A person invoking the privilege must ordinarily object contemporaneously to an attempt to disclose the communication and, if the objection is contested, demonstrate each element of the privilege under § 68.

(3) A person invoking a waiver of or exception to the privilege (§§ 78–85) must assert it and, if the assertion is contested, demonstrate each element of the waiver or exception.

Comment:

* * *

c. Objection by a lawyer or agent. A client's lawyer has both standing and usually a duty to assert the privilege (see § 63, Comment *b*). Under the law of agency, a similar duty might also rest upon an agent of the lawyer (see § 70, Comment *g*) and an agent of the client (see § 70, Comment *f*). See generally Restatement Second, Agency §§ 395–396. A person in position to invoke the privilege should be cognizant that under some circumstances testimony as to a portion of a communication waives the privilege with respect to related communications (see § 79, Comment *f*).

* * *

g. Redaction. The privilege might apply to only a part of a communication. The communication may be edited (redacted) to remove the privileged portion and the remainder admitted. Redaction is proper if it can be achieved without either disclosing privileged communication or distorting the remainder as evidence.

* * *

TOPIC 3. THE LAWYER WORK–PRODUCT IMMUNITY

Introductory Note

* * *

Work-product immunity is a relatively recent development in American jurisprudence. The Federal Rules of Civil Procedure of 1938, with their expansion of pretrial discovery, gave impetus to the work-product doctrine, first in the Supreme Court's 1947 decision in *Hickman v. Taylor.* The Federal Rules were extensively amended in 1970 to incorporate *Hickman v. Taylor* and related common-law decisions. Every American jurisdiction now provides some protection for trial-preparation materials. Because *Hickman* and the federal discovery rules have been widely emulated in state systems, this Topic focuses primarily on the work-product doctrine articulated for federal courts.

* * *

TITLE A. THE SCOPE OF THE LAWYER WORK–PRODUCT IMMUNITY

§ 87. Lawyer Work–Product Immunity

(1) **Work product consists of tangible material or its intangible equivalent in unwritten or oral form, other than underlying facts, prepared by a lawyer for litigation then in progress or in reasonable anticipation of future litigation.**

(2) **Opinion work product consists of the opinions or mental impressions of a lawyer; all other work product is ordinary work product.**

(3) **Except for material which by applicable law is not so protected, work product is immune from discovery**

or other compelled disclosure to the extent stated in §§ 88
(ordinary work product) and 89 (opinion work product)
when the immunity is invoked as described in § 90.

Comment:

* * *

[b.   Rationale.]

* * *

Protection of lawyer thought processes (see § 89) is at the core of
work-product rationale; accordingly, those are accorded the broadest
protection. A lawyer's analysis can readily be replicated by an opposing lawyer and, in any event, would usually be inadmissible in evidence. Factual information gathered by a lawyer usually relates
directly to controverted issues and generally is discoverable in forms
that do not reveal the lawyer's thought processes.

* * *

*d.   The relationship of the work-product immunity to the attor-
ney-client privilege.* The attorney-client privilege is limited to communications between a client and lawyer and certain of their agents (see
§ 70); in contrast, work product includes many other kinds of materials (see Comment *f*), even when obtained from sources other than the
client. Application of the attorney-client privilege absolutely bars
discovery or testimonial use; in contrast, the work-product immunity is
a qualified protection that, in various circumstances, can be overcome
on a proper showing (see §§ 88 & 89). The attorney-client privilege
protects communications between client and lawyer regarding all kinds
of legal services (see § 72); in contrast, the work-product immunity is
limited to materials prepared for or in anticipation of litigation (see
Comments *h-j*).

* * *

e.   The source of the law concerning work-product immunity. In
the federal system, work-product immunity is recognized both under
Rule 26(b)(3) of the Federal Rules of Civil Procedure and as a
common-law rule following the decision in *Hickman v. Taylor.* In a
few states work-product immunity is established by common law, but
in most states it is defined by statute or court rule. Some state
statutes mirror Federal Rule of Civil Procedure 26(b)(3); others codify
the principles of *Hickman v. Taylor* more broadly; and others codify
pre-*Hickman* rules that were not adopted for the federal courts. State
courts, in construing their statutes, often look to federal case law in
applying work-product immunity.

f. Types of work-product materials. Work product includes tangible materials and intangible equivalents prepared, collected, or assembled by a lawyer. Tangible materials include documents, photographs, diagrams, sketches, questionnaires and surveys, financial and economic analyses, hand-written notes, and material in electronic and other technologically advanced forms, such as stenographic, mechanical, or electronic recordings or transmissions, computer data bases, tapes, and printouts. Intangible work product is equivalent work product in unwritten, oral or remembered form. For example, intangible work product can come into question by a discovery request for a lawyer's recollections derived from oral communications.

* * *

g. The distinction between protected materials and nonprotected underlying facts. Work-product immunity does not apply to underlying facts of the incident or transaction involved in the litigation, even if the same information is contained in work product. For a comparison to the nonprivileged status accorded to facts under the attorney-client privilege, see § 69, Comment *d.*

* * *

i. Anticipation of litigation: the reasonableness standard. Work-product immunity attaches when litigation is then in progress or there is reasonable anticipation of litigation by the lawyer at the time the material was prepared. On what constitutes litigation, see Comment *h* hereto. The fact that litigation did not actually ensue does not affect the immunity.

In one sense, almost all of a lawyer's work anticipates litigation to some degree, because preparing documents or arranging transactions is aimed at avoiding future litigation or enhancing a client's position should litigation occur. However, the immunity covers only material produced when apprehension of litigation was reasonable in the circumstances. The reasonableness of anticipation is determined objectively by considering the factual context in which materials are prepared, the nature of the materials, and the expected role of the lawyer in ensuing litigation.

Illustrations:

1. Employer's Lawyer writes to Physician, setting out circumstances of an employee's death and asking for Physician's opinion as to the cause, stating that Lawyer is preparing for a "possible claim" by the employee's executor for worker-compensation benefits. Lawyer's letter is protected work product.

2. Informed that agents of the Justice Department are questioning Publisher's customers, Lawyer for Publisher prepared a memorandum analyzing the antitrust implications of Publisher's standard contract form with commercial purchasers. Publisher's employees testify before a grand jury investigating antitrust issues in the publishing industry. Lawyer, reasonably believing there is a risk that the grand jury will indict Publisher, interviews the employees and prepares a debriefing memorandum. Both Lawyer's memorandum analyzing the contract form and Lawyer's debriefing memorandum were prepared in anticipation of litigation. The grand-jury proceeding is itself litigation for this purpose (see Comment *h*).

* * *

§ 88. Ordinary Work Product

When work product protection is invoked as described in § 90, ordinary work product (§ 87(2)) is immune from discovery or other compelled disclosure unless either an exception recognized in §§ 91–93 applies or the inquiring party:

> **(1) has a substantial need for the material in order to prepare for trial; and**

> **(2) is unable without undue hardship to obtain the substantial equivalent of the material by other means.**

Comment:

* * *

[*b. The need-and-hardship exception—in general.*]

* * *

Demonstrating the requisite need and hardship requires the inquiring party to show that the material is relevant to the party's claim or defense, and that the inquiring party will likely be prejudiced in the absence of discovery. As a corollary, it must be shown that substantially equivalent material is not available or, if available, only through cost and effort substantially disproportionate to the amount at stake in the litigation and the value of the information to the inquiring party. The necessary showing is more easily made after other discovery has been completed.

The most common situation involves a prior statement by a witness who is absent, seriously ill, or deceased and thus now unavailable. See Federal Rule of Evidence 804(a). Another common situation concerns statements made contemporaneously with an event. Such statements are often the most reliable recording of recollections of that event and in that sense unique. A third situation is where the passage of time has dulled the memory of the witness.

Illustration:

1.   Several witnesses testify before a grand jury investigating the publishing industry. Shortly afterward, Lawyer for Publisher debriefs the witnesses and writes memoranda of those interviews in anticipation of the possible indictment of Publisher and later civil suits. Six years later, Plaintiffs, representing a class of consumers, file an antitrust class action against Publisher and seek discovery of the non-opinion work-product portions of Lawyer's debriefing memoranda. Plaintiffs have been diligent in preparing their case and gathering evidence through other means and demonstrate that the witnesses now are unable to recall the events to which they testified. The court may order the memorandum produced. If the memorandum contains both ordinary and opinion work product, see § 89, Comment *c*.

Substantial need also exists when the material consists of tests performed nearly contemporaneously with a litigated event and substantially equivalent testing is no longer possible.

c.   Material for impeachment. Need is shown when a requesting party demonstrates that there is likely to be a material discrepancy between a prior statement of a witness reflected in a lawyer's notes and a statement of the same person made later during discovery, such as during a deposition. The discrepancy must be of an impeaching quality. A clear case exists when the witness admits to such a discrepancy. However, the inquiring party may demonstrate a reasonable basis by inference from circumstances. In camera inspection of the statement may be appropriate to determine whether the material should be produced.

* * *

§ 89.   Opinion Work Product

   When work product protection is invoked as described in § 90, opinion work product (§ 87(2)) is immune

from discovery or other compelled disclosure unless either the immunity is waived or an exception applies (§§ 91–93) or extraordinary circumstances justify disclosure.

Comment:

* * *

b. Rationale. Mental impressions, opinions, conclusions, and legal theories form the core of work product. As impressions formed after the event or transaction in issue, they are also not of the same evidentiary value as percipient witness observation or contemporaneous recording of the event. Disclosure of ordinary work product in cases of need and hardship facilitates trial preparation, but no comparable utility ordinarily attends discovery of a lawyer's theories, conclusions, and other opinions. Strict protection for opinion work product effectuates functioning of the adversary system (see § 87, Comment *b*). Moreover, analysis expressed in opinion work product can be carried out by the requesting party's lawyer.

The protection for opinion work product is qualified by discovery rules requiring disclosure of legal contentions on which a party intends to rely (see Federal Rules of Civil Procedure 33(b) and 36(a); cf. id., Rule 16 (pretrial conference)). Also, an advocate is required under certain circumstances to inform a tribunal of adverse legal authority (see § 111).

* * *

TITLE B.   PROCEDURAL ADMINISTRATION OF THE LAWYER WORK–PRODUCT IMMUNITY

§ 90.   Invoking the Lawyer Work–Product Immunity and Its Exceptions

(1) Work-product immunity may be invoked by or for a person on whose behalf the work product was prepared.

(2) The person invoking work-product immunity must object and, if the objection is contested, demonstrate each element of the immunity.

(3) Once a claim of work product has been adequately supported, a person entitled to invoke a waiver or exception must assert it and, if the assertion is contested, demonstrate each element of the waiver or exception.

Comment:

* * *

c. Objection by a lawyer. A lawyer has implied authority to invoke the immunity. So long as doing so is not inconsistent with the interests of the client, a lawyer may invoke immunity on the basis of the lawyer's independent interest in privacy. When lawyer and client have conflicting wishes or interests with respect to work-product material, the lawyer must follow instruction of the client (see § 21).

* * *

TITLE C. WAIVERS AND EXCEPTIONS TO THE WORK–PRODUCT IMMUNITY

Introductory Note

The rules governing waiver and exception applicable to work-product material generally parallel those for the attorney-client privilege (see §§ 78–85).

* * *

§ 91. Voluntary Acts

Work-product immunity is waived if the client, the client's lawyer, or another authorized agent of the client:

(1) agrees to waive the immunity;

(2) disclaims protection of the immunity and:

(a) another person reasonably relies on the disclaimer to that person's detriment; or

(b) reasons of judicial administration require that the client not be permitted to revoke the disclaimer; or

(3) in a proceeding before a tribunal, fails to object properly to an attempt by another person to give or exact testimony or other evidence of work product; or

(4) discloses the material to third persons in circumstances in which there is a significant likelihood that an adversary or potential adversary in anticipated litigation will obtain it.

Comment:

* * *

b. Waiver of the work-product immunity by voluntary disclosure. Work-product protection is waived by disclosure to third parties if it occurs in circumstances in which there is a significant likelihood that an adversary in litigation will obtain the materials. For analogous waiver of the attorney-client privilege by subsequent disclosure, see § 79. Cf. also § 92(2) (waiver of work-product immunity by use of materials in preparing nonparty witness to testify). Indifference to such a consequence indicates that protection of the immunity was not important to the person claiming the protection. However, the privacy requirement for work-product material is in some situations less exacting than the corresponding requirement for the attorney-client privilege. Effective trial preparation often entails disclosing work product to coparties and nonparties. Work product, including opinion work product, may generally be disclosed to the client, the client's business advisers or agents, the client's lawyer or other representative, associated lawyers and other professionals working for the client, or persons similarly aligned on a matter of common interest (compare § 76). On disclosure to a client's liability insurer, see § 134, Comment *f.* Disclosure permitted by a protective order or made subject to the parties' confidential agreement does not destroy the immunity.

* * *

§ 92. Use of Lawyer Work Product in Litigation

(1) Work-product immunity is waived for any relevant material if the client asserts as to a material issue in a proceeding that:

(a) the client acted upon the advice of a lawyer or that the advice was otherwise relevant to the legal significance of the client's conduct; or

(b) a lawyer's assistance was ineffective, negligent, or otherwise wrongful.

(2) The work-product immunity is waived for recorded material if a witness

(a) employs the material to aid the witness while testifying, or

(b) employed the material in preparing to testify, and the tribunal finds that disclosure is required in the interests of justice.

Comment:

* * *

c. A client's attack on a lawyer's services. A party who asserts that a lawyer's assistance was defective may not invoke work-product immunity to prevent an opposing party's access to information concerning the claim. See § 80, Comment *c* (analogous waiver of attorney-client privilege). Where the interests of the lawyer and the client conflict (see § 83 & § 90, Comment *c*), the lawyer may not use the work-product protection to deny the client access to relevant work-product materials (see § 90, Comment *c*).

* * *

§ 93. Client Crime or Fraud

Work-product immunity does not apply to materials prepared when a client consults a lawyer for the purpose, later accomplished, of obtaining assistance to engage in a crime or fraud or to aid a third person to do so or uses the materials for such a purpose.

Comment:

* * *

b. Rationale. Like the crime-fraud exception to the attorney-client privilege (see § 82, Comment *b*), the crime-fraud exception for work-product immunity recognizes that crime and fraud do not warrant such protection. The exception applies to ongoing or future crimes or frauds but not to work product prepared in a representation concerning completed client acts. Whether work product relates to past acts or future or ongoing acts requires close analysis (see § 82, Comment *e*).

[*c. The intents of the client and the lawyer.*]

* * *

If the client alone has the requisite criminal or fraudulent intent, work-product immunity is lost despite the innocence of the lawyer (see § 82, Comment *c*). The public interest in deterring wrongful acts outweighs the innocent lawyer's interest in privacy. The rule also prevents a client from advancing an illegal scheme through a noncomplicit lawyer. Once the required showing is made, opinion work product of an innocent lawyer is subject to disclosure along with opinion work product of the client and ordinary work product of both client and lawyer. Conversely, the exception does not apply when a lawyer representing an innocent client commits or is complicit in another's crime or fraud (see § 82, Comment *c*, Illustration 3).

* * *

CHAPTER 6

REPRESENTING CLIENTS—IN GENERAL

* * *

TOPIC 1. LAWYER FUNCTIONS IN REPRESENTING CLIENTS—IN GENERAL

* * *

§ 94. Advising and Assisting a Client—In General

(1) **A lawyer who counsels or assists a client to engage in conduct that violates the rights of a third person is subject to liability:**

218

(a) to the third person to the extent stated in §§ 51 and 56–57; and

(b) to the client to the extent stated in §§ 50, 55, and 56.

(2) For purposes of professional discipline, a lawyer may not counsel or assist a client in conduct that the lawyer knows to be criminal or fraudulent or in violation of a court order with the intent of facilitating or encouraging the conduct, but the lawyer may counsel or assist a client in conduct when the lawyer reasonably believes:

(a) that the client's conduct constitutes a good-faith effort to determine the validity, scope, meaning, or application of a law or court order; or

(b) that the client can assert a nonfrivolous argument that the client's conduct will not constitute a crime or fraud or violate a court order.

(3) In counseling a client, a lawyer may address nonlegal aspects of a proposed course of conduct, including moral, reputational, economic, social, political, and business aspects.

Comment:

* * *

c. Counseling about activity of doubtful legality. Lawyers are occupationally engaged in advising clients about activities on which law has an often uncertain bearing. A lawyer who proceeds reasonably to advise a client with the intent of providing the client with legal advice on how to comply with the law does not act wrongfully, even if the client employs that advice for wrongful purposes or even if a tribunal later determines that the lawyer's advice was incorrect. As stated in Subsection (2)(b), a lawyer acts appropriately for purposes of professional discipline so long as the lawyer reasonably believes that the client can assert a nonfrivolous argument that the client's intended action will not constitute a crime or fraud or violate a court order (see also Comment *e*). The requirement of a nonfrivolous argument is measured by an objective test. In such circumstances, if the lawyer's advice or other assistance proves to be inaccurate as a result of the lawyer's negligence, the lawyer may be liable to the client for harm caused (see Subsection (1)(b) & § 50), but the lawyer is not susceptible to professional discipline (other than for incompetence) for counseling wrongful conduct. On the extent to which the lawyer may be civilly liable to nonclients who may be injured, see § 51.

Under Subsection (2), a lawyer who counsels or assists a client to engage in activity that the lawyer knows to be criminal or fraudulent or in violation of a court order, other than as described in the Subsection, is subject to professional discipline. Such a rule (applicable to crime and fraud) is stated in the widely adopted ABA Model Rules of Professional Conduct, Rule 1.2(d) (1983); on violation of a court order, see Comment *d*. "Fraud" is defined in the Terminology section of the ABA Model Rules as denoting "conduct having a purpose to deceive and not merely negligent misrepresentation or failure to apprise another of relevant information." Failure to apprise another of relevant information may constitute such fraud, as when a lawyer purposefully fails to disclose information necessary to render a statement of the lawyer not materially deceptive (see § 98 & Comment *e*). A lawyer's intent to facilitate or encourage wrongful action may be inferred if in the circumstances it should have been apparent to the lawyer that the client would employ the assistance to further the client's wrongful conduct and the lawyer nonetheless provided the assistance.

* * *

d. Violation of a court order. Violation of a court order directly challenges the rule of law. Rule 1.2(d) of the ABA Model Rules of Professional Conduct (1983), prohibiting assistance to a client's crime or fraud, omits explicit reference to the client's violation of a court order. However, decisional law treats it as equally wrongful for a lawyer knowingly to counsel or assist a client to violate a court order. The decisions often employ the prohibition stated in ABA Model Rule 8.4(d) against conduct prejudicial to the administration of justice. Moreover, in many circumstances a client's violation of a court order constitutes the crime of contempt, and a lawyer's assistance may thus directly violate ABA Model Rule 1.2(d). A lawyer also may be guilty of contempt of court as a principal with respect to the lawyer's own acts in assisting a client to violate a valid court order.

Accordingly, a lawyer counseling or assisting a client who contemplates violating a court order is legally constrained in much the same manner as when the client's conduct is a crime or fraud (see Comment *c*). The lawyer may contest a request for such an order before it is entered or seek later clarification, modification, vacatur, or appellate review. However, as stated in Subsection (2), a lawyer may not knowingly counsel or assist the client to violate a court order. On a good-faith challenge to a court order of doubtful validity, see Comment *e*.

e. A reasonable test of a legal obligation. The scope of legal obligations is in many instances unclear, calling for the exercise by the lawyer of legal skill and judgment in assessing the limits of legality (see Comment c). Moreover, even if an obligation is clearly stated, an invalid statute or regulation ordinarily need not be obeyed; in other instances, as with some court orders, law may require that the statute or regulation be obeyed until it is set aside by a reviewing tribunal. The terms of such law are in general beyond the scope of the Restatement.

* * *

f. Advice about enforcement policy. A lawyer's advice to a client about the degree of risk that a law violation will be detected or prosecuted violates the rule of Subsection (2) when the circumstances indicate that the lawyer thereby intended to counsel or assist the client's crime, fraud, or violation of a court order. No bright-line rule immunizes the lawyer from adverse legal consequences. In many borderline situations, the lawyer's intent will be a disputable question of fact (see Comments *a* & *c*), as will be questions of the lawyer's knowledge (see Comment *g*). Such questions will be determined from all the circumstances. In general, a lawyer may advise a client about enforcement policy in areas of doubtful legality so long as the lawyer does not knowingly counsel or assist the client to engage in criminal or fraudulent activity or activity that violates a court order. Clearly, such advice is permissible when the lawyer knows that nonenforcement amounts to effective abandonment of the prohibition and not simply temporary dereliction on the part of enforcing authorities or ignorance on their part of sufficient facts to bring an enforcement proceeding.

Illustrations:

1. Client plays cards with friends in Client's home and asks Lawyer whether it would be illegal for the players to place small bets on the games. Lawyer knows that a criminal statute prohibiting gambling literally applies to such betting. Lawyer also knows that as a matter of long-standing policy and practice, persons who gamble on social games played in private homes for small stakes are not prosecuted. Lawyer may advise Client about the nonenforcement policy and practice.

2. Lawyer reasonably believes that Client has a nonfrivolous basis for asserting on state income-tax returns that Client's use of a personal automobile is for a business purpose and thus that related expenses are a proper deduction. Among other things, Lawyer has advised Client concerning the likelihood of an audit by tax authorities if Client takes the intended deduction. Lawyer bases the assessment of audit likelihood on published figures

showing the incidence of audits for automobile use for taxpayers at Client's income level. In the course of that discussion, Client also asks Lawyer what the average taxpayer at Client's income level deducts for charitable contributions in a year without incurring an audit. From prior dealings with Client, Lawyer knows that Client seldom makes charitable contributions and in past years has not made contributions of more than a few dollars. In the circumstances, Lawyer's advice about enforcement policy concerning the automobile use was appropriate within Subsection (2). While the facts stated above suggest that advice concerning enforcement policy for charitable deductions would not be permissible, whether under all the facts Lawyer may so advise Client depends on whether Lawyer reasonably believes that Client will likely use Lawyer's advice to claim false deductions.

g. A lawyer's knowledge of the wrongful nature of a client's conduct. A lawyer's disciplinary liability under Subsection (2) turns on client activity that the lawyer knows to be criminal or fraudulent or in violation of a court order. On other, nondisciplinary-law definitions of the kind of knowledge that will incur liability, see Comment *a.* In general, actual knowledge of the client's wrongful purpose is required (see § 56, Comment *f*). Knowledge under Subsection (2) may be inferred from circumstances and determining the issue is generally for the finder of fact.

When a lawyer's state of knowledge is relevant, in the absence of circumstances indicating otherwise, a lawyer may assume that a client will use the lawyer's counsel for proper purposes. Mere suspicion on the part of the lawyer that the client might intend to commit a crime or fraud is not knowledge. Under the actual knowledge standard of Subsection (2), a lawyer is not required to make a particular kind of investigation in order to ascertain more certainly what the facts are, although it will often be prudent for the lawyer to do so. Only information known to the lawyer at the time the lawyer provides the assistance is relevant, not information learned afterwards. On the other hand, the prohibitions of Subsection (2) apply at whatever point the lawyer does know that the client's intended conduct is criminal, fraudulent, or in violation of a court order. On withdrawal in such circumstances, see § 32(3); see also §§ 66–67 (disclosure to prevent certain injuries) and § 51, Comment *h* (duty based on lawyer's knowledge of client's breach of fiduciary duty).

* * *

§ 95. An Evaluation Undertaken for a Third Person

(1) In furtherance of the objectives of a client in a representation, a lawyer may provide to a nonclient the results of the lawyer's investigation and analysis of facts or the lawyer's professional evaluation or opinion on the matter.

(2) When providing the information, evaluation, or opinion under Subsection (1) is reasonably likely to affect the client's interests materially and adversely, the lawyer must first obtain the client's consent after the client is adequately informed concerning important possible effects on the client's interests.

(3) In providing the information, evaluation, or opinion under Subsection (1), the lawyer must exercise care with respect to the nonclient to the extent stated in § 51(2) and not make false statements prohibited under § 98.

Comment:

a. Scope and cross-references. This Section deals with disparate activities, including audit response letters (see Comment *f*), internal investigations, and third-party legal opinions. Each has a separate purpose and attendant circumstances. An audit letter provides an outside check on management representations in preparing financial statements relied upon by investors and the financial community. A report on an internal investigation reviews management conduct for the protection of shareholders, the investment community, and sometimes regulators. In audit-letter-response and internal-investigation situations, the interests protected are largely or entirely unrepresented. On the other hand, in most third-party-opinion situations, those who rely on the opinion are typically represented by counsel who negotiate the opinion to be given and review it when received. Custom and practice determining the scope of diligence in represented situations is articulated in bar-association reports, treatises, and articles.

* * *

c. A lawyer's duties to a third-party recipient of an evaluation. A lawyer providing an evaluation purporting to be a fair and objective evaluation does not function as an advocate for the legal or factual position of the lawyer's client. Unless otherwise required or permitted by the terms under which the evaluation is given, the lawyer's duty is to provide a fair and objective opinion. On the extent of a lawyer's liability in tort to a third-person recipient of an evaluation for failure

223

to exercise care in providing the evaluation, see § 51 and Comment *e* thereto. By statements in the evaluation, the lawyer may undertake to exercise a higher or lesser standard of care. As stated in Subsection (3), the lawyer is prohibited by the requirement of § 98 from making false representations to the addressee, a duty included within but less extensive than the lawyer's duty under § 51.

The third-person recipient of a lawyer's evaluation does not thereby become the client of the lawyer, and the lawyer does not thereby undertake all duties owed to a client, such as confidentiality or avoidance of conflicting interests (compare § 14). In rendering an evaluation, a lawyer does not undertake to advise the third person except with respect to the questions actually covered by the evaluation. For example, if a seller's lawyer renders a title opinion to the purchaser, the lawyer does not thereby undertake to record the resulting deed or to take other steps to protect the interests of the purchaser in the transaction, such as by advising whether the recipient should proceed with the transaction, accept title in a different form, or seek alteration of other terms of the transaction. However, to the extent stated in § 14, a lawyer may incur the duties of the client-lawyer relationship with the addressee, such as when the lawyer specifically invites the addressee to rely on the lawyer to provide services beyond those involved in furnishing the evaluation (see § 51, Comment *e*; see also § 14).

The factual basis of an evaluation is that which it states, expressly or by implication from the circumstances. In all events, unless stated or agreed otherwise, a lawyer's evaluation does not entail a guarantee by the lawyer that facts stated in it are accurate. In some circumstances, such as when the lawyer purports to be making a report of a factual investigation undertaken by the lawyer, a reasonable reader of the report would assume that the lawyer is reporting facts known by the lawyer to be accurate. A lawyer normally may rely on facts provided by corporate officers and other agents of a client that the lawyer reasonably believes to be appropriate sources for such facts without further investigation or specific disclosure, unless the recipient of the opinion objects or the version of the facts provided or other circumstances indicate that further verification is required.

A lawyer may not without express disclosure rely for purposes of a legal opinion or other evaluation report on a fact or factual assumption that the lawyer knows to be inaccurate or, in the case of a factual representation, to have been provided under circumstances making reliance unwarranted. Express disclosure is unnecessary if the inaccuracy is known by or apparent to the recipient or its counsel. When an evaluation report is stated to be predicated upon a factual investigation by the lawyer, unless the report otherwise describes the investigation, issuance of the report implies that an investigation has been conducted that is consistent with customary practice and otherwise reasonable in the circumstances, having regard to the understanding of the parties, the facts to be ascertained, the reliance likely to be placed on the lawyer's report by the addressee, and the stakes at risk.

* * *

Unless effectively stated or agreed otherwise, a legal opinion or similar evaluation constitutes an assurance that it is based on legal research and analysis customary and reasonably appropriate in the circumstances and that it states the lawyer's professional opinion as to how any legal question addressed in the opinion would be decided by the courts in the applicable jurisdiction on the date of the evaluation. The lawyer is not required to state reservations or doubts about legal issues unless they are of a nature that prevents the lawyer from reasonably concluding that the opinion reflects the result that would be reached by the highest court of the applicable jurisdiction.

* * *

[d.   *Risks to a client in providing an evaluation report.*]

* * *

However, in some circumstances it will be reasonably likely that providing the evaluation may require the lawyer to disclose confidential client information in a way inconsistent with the client's interests or otherwise to incur significant risk of material harm to the client. For example, disclosure of facts in an evaluation report may cause such harm by waiving the client's attorney-client privilege (see § 79) or the work-product immunity (see § 91(4)). In some circumstances, it will be apparent from the outset that the evaluation undertaking is reasonably likely to affect the client's interests materially and adversely. For example, when a lawyer is commissioned to conduct an investigation of questioned client activities in anticipation of providing a report to a regulatory agency, preliminary inquiry may indicate the likely need to report substantial wrongdoing by the client. In other circumstances, it may appear at the outset that evaluation will incur no significant risk to the client, but facts later ascertained may indicate unanticipated information or legal conclusions whose disclosure would be likely to affect the client's interests materially and adversely, but whose omission from the report would be misleading or otherwise violate the lawyer's duty under § 51 to exercise care.

In such a situation, the lawyer must appropriately consult with the client (see § 20) and obtain the client's consent (see § 62) before undertaking or continuing the evaluation. The lawyer must abide by the client's decision whether preparation of the evaluation should either be discontinued or be completed and the adverse evaluation provided to the third person (see § 21(2)). Alternatively, the lawyer and client may determine it appropriate to negotiate with the intended addressee of the evaluation to modify its scope or terms, thus removing the adverse effect to the client.

* * *

TOPIC 2. REPRESENTING ORGANIZATIONAL CLIENTS

* * *

§ 96. Representing an Organization as Client

(1) When a lawyer is employed or retained to represent an organization:

> (a) the lawyer represents the interests of the organization as defined by its responsible agents acting pursuant to the organization's decision-making procedures; and

> (b) subject to Subsection (2), the lawyer must follow instructions in the representation, as stated in § 21(2), given by persons authorized so to act on behalf of the organization.

(2) If a lawyer representing an organization knows of circumstances indicating that a constituent of the organization has engaged in action or intends to act in a way that violates a legal obligation to the organization that will likely cause substantial injury to it, or that reasonably can be foreseen to be imputable to the organization and likely to result in substantial injury to it, the lawyer must proceed in what the lawyer reasonably believes to be the best interests of the organization.

(3) In the circumstances described in Subsection (2), the lawyer may, in circumstances warranting such steps, ask the constituent to reconsider the matter, recommend that a second legal opinion be sought, and seek review by appropriate supervisory authority within the organization, including referring the matter to the highest authority that can act in behalf of the organization.

Comment:

* * *

b. Rationale: an organization as client. A lawyer who has been employed or retained to represent an organization as a client owes professional duties of loyalty and competence to the organization. By representing the organization, a lawyer does not thereby also form a client-lawyer relationship with all or any individuals employed by it or who direct its operations or who have an ownership or other beneficial interest in it, such as its shareholders. However additional circumstances may result in a client-lawyer relationship with constituents while the lawyer concurrently represents the organization (see Comment *h* hereto).

A lawyer representing only an organization does not owe duties of care (see § 52), diligence (see § 16), or confidentiality (see § 60) to constituents of the organization. Compare § 132, Comment *g(ii)* (duties of confidentiality to persons about whom lawyer learned confidential information in prior representation of client). Correspondingly, although a lawyer for the organization acts at the direction of its officers, the lawyer for an organization does not possess, solely in that capacity, power to act for officers as their lawyer. Thus, third persons may not reasonably conclude, solely from that capacity, that a lawyer for the organization represents officers individually (compare §§ 26 & 27). Similarly, a lawyer representing only a constituent does not, by virtue of that representation, owe either to the organization employing the constituent or to other constituents obligations that would arise only from a client-lawyer relationship with the organization.

* * *

A lawyer representing an organization deals with individuals such as its officers, directors, and employees, who serve as constituents of the organization. Such individuals acting under the organization's authority retain and direct the lawyer to act on behalf of the organization (see Comment *d* hereto). Nonetheless, personal dealings with such persons do not lessen the lawyer's responsibilities to the organization as client, and the lawyer may not let such dealings hinder the lawyer in the performance of those responsibilities.

A "constituent" of an organization within the meaning of the Section has the same meaning as in Rule 1.13 of the ABA Model Rules of Professional Conduct (1983). A constituent includes an officer, director, or employee of the organization. A shareholder of a stock corporation or a member of a membership corporation is also a constituent within the meaning of this Section, as under Rule 1.13.

* * *

c. Forms of client organizations. In general, this Section applies to representation of formally constituted organizations. In all events, whether a client-lawyer relationship is formed is to be determined in light of the considerations stated in § 14. Such organizations include for-profit and nonprofit corporations, limited-liability companies, unincorporated associations (such as trade associations and labor unions), general and limited partnerships, professional corporations, business trusts, joint ventures, and similar organizations. An organization client may also be an informal entity such as a social club or an informal group that has established an investment pool. For the purposes of this Section, whether the organization is a formal legal entity is relevant but not determinative. For example, while a sole proprietorship is not treated as an entity for many legal purposes, such an organization may be of sufficient size and complexity to warrant treatment as an organizational client under this Section.

* * *

e. A constituent's breach of a legal obligation to the client organization. A lawyer representing an organization is required to act with reasonable competence and diligence in the representation (see § 16(2)) and to use care in representing the organizational client (see § 50). The lawyer thus must not knowingly or negligently assist any constituent to breach a legal duty to the organization. However, a lawyer's duty of care to the organization is not limited to avoidance of assisting acts that threaten injury to a client. A lawyer is also required to act diligently and to exercise care by taking steps to prevent reasonably foreseeable harm to a client. Thus, Subsection (2) requires a lawyer to take action to protect the interests of the client organization with respect to certain breaches of legal duty to the organization by a constituent.

The lawyer is not prevented by rules of confidentiality from acting to protect the interests of the organization by disclosing within the organization communications gained from constituents who are not themselves clients. That follows even if disclosure is against the interests of the communicating person, of another constituent whose breach of duty is in issue, or of other constituents (see § 131, Comment *e*). Such disclosure within the organization is subject to direction of a constituent who is authorized to act for the organization in the matter and who is not complicit in the breach (see Comment *d*). The lawyer may withdraw any support that the lawyer may earlier have provided the intended act, such as by withdrawing an opinion letter or draft transaction documents prepared by the lawyer.

Illustration:

1. Lawyer represents Charity, a not-for-profit corporation. Charity promotes medical research through tax-deductible contri-

butions made to it. President as chief executive officer of Charity retained Lawyer to represent Charity as outside general counsel and has extensively communicated in confidence with Lawyer on a variety of matters concerning Charity. President asks Lawyer to draft documents by which Charity would make a gift of a new luxury automobile to a social friend of President. In that and all other work, Lawyer represents only Charity and not President as a client. Lawyer concludes that such a gift would cause financial harm to Charity in violation of President's legal duties to it. Lawyer may not draft the documents. If unable to dissuade President from effecting the gift, Lawyer must take action to protect the interests of Charity (see Subsection (2) & Comment f). Lawyer may, for example, communicate with members of Charity's board of directors in endeavoring to prevent the gift from being effectuated.

f. Proceeding in the best interests of the client organization. Within the meaning of Subsection (2), a wrongful act of a constituent threatening substantial injury to a client organization may be of two types. One is an act or failure to act that violates a legal obligation to the organization and that would directly harm the organization, such as by unlawfully converting its assets. The other is an act or failure to act by the constituent that, although perhaps intended to serve an interest of the organization, will foreseeably cause injury to the client, such as by exposing the organization to criminal or civil liability.

In either circumstance, as stated in Subsection (2), if the threatened injury is substantial the lawyer must proceed in what the lawyer reasonably believes to be the best interests of the organization. Those interests are normally defined by appropriate managers of the organization in the exercise of the business and managerial judgment that would be exercised by a person of ordinary prudence in a similar position. The lawyer's duty of care is that of an ordinarily prudent lawyer in such a position (see ALI Principles of Corporate Governance: Analysis and Recommendations § 4.01, at 148–149 (1994)). In the face of threats of substantial injury to the organization of the kind described in Subsection (2), the lawyer must assess the following: the degree and imminence of threatened financial, reputational, and other harms to the organization; the probable results of litigation that might ensue against the organization or for which it would be financially responsible; the costs of taking measures within the organization to prevent or correct the harm; the likely efficaciousness of measures that might be taken; and similar considerations.

The measures that a lawyer may take are those described in Subsection (3), among others. Whether a lawyer has proceeded in the best interests of the organization is determined objectively, on the basis of the circumstances reasonably apparent to the lawyer at the time. Not all lawyers would attempt to resolve a problem defined in Subsection (2) in the same manner. Not all threats to an organization are of the same degree of imminence or substantiality. In some instances the constituent may be acting solely for reasons of self-interest. In others, the constituent may act on the basis of a business judgment whose utility or prudence may be doubtful but that is within the authority of the constituent. The lawyer's assessment of those factors may depend on the constituent's credibility and intentions, based on prior dealings between them and other information available to the lawyer.

* * *

In a situation arising under Subsection (2), a lawyer does not fulfill the lawyer's duties to the organizational client by withdrawing from the representation without attempting to prevent the constituent's wrongful act. However, the lawyer's threat to withdraw unless corrective action is taken may constitute an effective step in such an attempt.

If a lawyer has attempted appropriately but unsuccessfully to protect the best interests of the organizational client, the lawyer may withdraw if permissible under § 32. Particularly when the lawyer has unsuccessfully sought to enlist assistance from the highest authority within the organization, the lawyer will be warranted in withdrawing either because the client persists in a course of action involving the lawyer's services that the lawyer reasonably believes is criminal or fraudulent (see § 32(3)(d)) or because the client insists on taking action that the lawyer considers repugnant or imprudent (see § 32(3)(f)). On proportionality between certain grounds for withdrawal and possible harm to the organizational client that would be caused by withdrawal, see § 32, Comment h(i). On the circumstances in which a lawyer is required to withdraw, see § 32(2). Following withdrawal, if the lawyer had fulfilled applicable duties prior to withdrawal, the lawyer has no further duty to initiate action to protect the interests of the client organization with respect to the matter. The lawyer continues to be subject to the duties owed to any former client, such as the duty not to become involved in subsequent adverse representations (see § 132) or otherwise to use or disclose the former client's confidential information adversely to the former client (see § 60).

* * *

§ 97. Representing a Governmental Client

A lawyer representing a governmental client must proceed in the representation as stated in § 96, except that the lawyer:

(1) possesses such rights and responsibilities as may be defined by law to make decisions on behalf of the governmental client that are within the authority of a client under §§ 22 and 21(2);

(2) except as otherwise provided by law, must proceed as stated in §§ 96(2) and 96(3) with respect to an act of a constituent of the governmental client that violates a legal obligation that will likely cause substantial public or private injury or that reasonably can be foreseen to be imputable to and thus likely result in substantial injury to the client;

(3) if a prosecutor or similar lawyer determining whether to file criminal proceedings or take other steps in such proceedings, must do so only when based on probable cause and the lawyer's belief, formed after due investigation, that there are good factual and legal grounds to support the step taken; and

(4) must observe other applicable restrictions imposed by law on those similarly functioning for the governmental client.

Comment:

[*a. Scope and cross-references.*]

* * *

This Section covers a lawyer employed full time by a governmental client as well as a lawyer in private practice who provides legal services to a governmental client. With respect to such governmental-representation matters, see Comment *i* hereto.

* * *

b. Rationale. Although similar in many respects to representation of a client in private practice (see Comment *a* hereto), representation of a governmental client may significantly differ in three principal respects. First, the goals of a governmental client necessarily include pursuit of the public interest, as identified by law and as determined by decisions of government officials in the course of their duties. Second, both government lawyers and governmental officials directing the activities of government lawyers are often subject to greater legal constraint (for example, under state and federal constitutions) than is true of lawyers representing nongovernmental persons or entities. Third, and conversely, a government lawyer may possess powers beyond those possessed by a lawyer representing a nongovernmental client, such as the power to select those persons who will be charged with serious crimes (see Comment *h*). Some government lawyers, such as an elected state attorney general or similar officer, have discretionary powers under law that have no parallel in representation of nongovernmental clients (see Comment *g*).

* * *

    c. Identity of a governmental client. No universal definition of the client of a governmental lawyer is possible. For example, it has been asserted that government lawyers represent the public, or the public interest. However, determining what individual or individuals personify the government requires reference to the need to sustain political and organizational responsibility of governmental officials, as well as the organizational arrangements structured by law within which governmental lawyers work. Those who speak for the governmental client may differ from one representation to another. The identity of the client may also vary depending on the purpose for which the question of identity is posed. For example, when government lawyers negotiate a disputed question of departmental jurisdiction between two federal agencies, it is not helpful to refer to the client of each of the lawyers as "the federal government" or "the public" when considering who is empowered to direct the lawyers' activities. For many purposes, the preferable approach on the question presented is to regard the respective agencies as the clients and to regard the lawyers working for the agencies as subject to the direction of those officers authorized to act in the matter involved in the representation (see Subsection (3)).

* * *

    When a lawyer is retained to represent a specific individual, either in that person's public (see Comment *b*) or private (nongovernmental) capacity, the person (in the appropriate capacity) is the client, unless the use of the individual's name is merely nominal and the government is the interested party. As described above with respect to multiple agencies, the identity and the specification of the capacity of the person represented by the lawyer is determined by the undertaking and reasonable expectations of both the lawyer and individual (see § 14). A lawyer who represents a governmental official in the person's public capacity must conduct the representation to advance public interests as determined by appropriate governmental officers and not, if different, the personal interests of the occupant of the office (see generally Comment *f*).

d. Confidentiality. Some limitations on the scope of confidentiality may apply in the case of a governmental client under statutory or constitutional provisions. See § 74, Comment *b* (open-files, open-meeting, and similar statutes); Comment *h* hereto (duty of prosecutor to turn over exculpatory evidence to accused). Apart from such limitations, a lawyer for a governmental client must protect confidential client information of the governmental client, as provided in Chapter 5 (see § 60), to the same extent as would be required of a lawyer in a private-practice representation. When a lawyer is the responsible governmental officer determining whether the government will waive the protection of confidentiality, the lawyer must proceed as stated in Comment *g*.

* * *

[*f. Advancing a governmental client's objectives.*]

* * *

Courts have stressed that a lawyer representing a governmental client must seek to advance the public interest in the representation and not merely the partisan or personal interests of the government entity or officer involved (see Comment *c* hereto). In many instances, the factor is stressed for hortatory rather than definitional purposes. A government lawyer must follow lawful directions of authorized superiors with respect to the scope and implementation of the representation (see generally § 21(2); see Comment *j* hereto).

* * *

h. A government lawyer's responsibility when litigating on behalf of a governmental client. Unlike lawyers in private practice, a government lawyer with power to file and conduct criminal or civil proceedings against citizens is subject to special limitations in doing so.

Lawyers empowered by law to bring and press criminal charges have an authority that must be exercised with care to protect the rights of both the innocent and the guilty. Comparable limitations apply to governmental lawyers prosecuting civil enforcement proceedings that bear significant traits of criminal proceedings and that are similarly stigmatizing, such as a proceeding to forfeit ownership of goods that are allegedly the fruits or instrumentalities of crime or to enjoin an allegedly criminal activity. Constitutional considerations concerning separation of powers limit the extent to which tribunals may scrutinize prosecutorial discretion concerning the nature of charges brought and the selection of persons who are charged.

The traditional standard is that prosecutors must bring charges only if based on probable cause. While it is not believed that there is any substantive difference, the applicable requirement stated in Subsection (3) is that the prosecutor must possess the belief, formed after due investigation, that there are good factual and legal grounds to support the charge. As required by constitutional law and the lawyer codes, in conducting a prosecution a prosecutor must make timely disclosure to an accused of all evidence or information known to the prosecutor that tends to negate the guilt of the accused or mitigate the offense. In connection with sentencing, a prosecutor must disclose to the defense and to the tribunal all mitigating information known to the prosecutor, except when the prosecutor is relieved of this responsibility by a valid privilege or a protective order of the tribunal. A prosecutor must exercise reasonable care to prevent investigators and similar employees of the prosecutor's office from making an extrajudicial statement that the prosecutor would be prohibited from making under § 109. In presenting a matter ex parte to a grand jury, a prosecutor is governed by § 112.

* * *

j. Wrongdoing by a constituent of a governmental client. When a constituent of a governmental client has acted, failed to act, or proposes to act as stated in Subsection (2), the lawyer must proceed as stated in § 96(2) and (3). In addition, legislation or regulations may prescribe different conditions for the lawyer's actions, conferring broader authority on a governmental lawyer to prevent or rectify constituent wrongdoing.

* * *

If a constituent's acts fall within Subsection (2), a lawyer representing a governmental client must proceed as stated in § 96(3) and (4) with respect to those acts. With respect to referral of a matter to a higher authority, such a referral can often be made to allied governmental agencies, such as the government's general legal office, such as a state's office of attorney general.

* * *

TOPIC 3. LAWYER DEALINGS WITH A NONCLIENT

* * *

TITLE A. DEALINGS WITH A NONCLIENT—GENERALLY

* * *

§ 98. Statements to a Nonclient

A lawyer communicating on behalf of a client with a nonclient may not:

(1) knowingly make a false statement of material fact or law to the nonclient,

(2) make other statements prohibited by law; or

(3) fail to make a disclosure of information required by law.

Comment:

* * *

[b. Rationale.]

* * *

This Section applies equally to statements made to a sophisticated person, such as to a lawyer representing another client, as well as to an unsophisticated person. However, the sophistication in similar transactions of a person to whom a representation is made is relevant in determining such issues as the reasonableness of the person's reliance on the representation.

c. Knowing misrepresentation. The law of misrepresentation applies to lawyers. See generally Restatement Second, Contracts § 159 and following; Restatement Second, Torts § 525 and following. For purposes of common-law damage recovery, reckless as well as knowing misrepresentation by a lawyer may be actionable. On negligent misrepresentation, see also § 51(2). A misrepresentation can occur through direct statement or through affirmation of a misrepresentation of another, as when a lawyer knowingly affirms a client's false or misleading statement. A statement can also be false because only partially true. If constrained from conveying specific information to a nonclient, for example due to confidentiality obligations to the lawyer's client, the lawyer must either make no representation or make a representation that is not false.

For purposes of professional discipline, the lawyer codes generally incorporate the definition of misrepresentation employed in the civil law of tort damage liability for knowing misrepresentation, including the elements of falsity, scienter, and materiality. However, for disciplinary purposes, reliance by and injury to another person are not

235

required. The lawyer codes of many jurisdictions also prohibit a lawyer from engaging in "conduct involving dishonesty, fraud, deceit, or misrepresentation" (see § 5, Comment c). Some courts have interpreted these provisions to impose a more exacting standard of disclosure than the prohibition against knowing misrepresentation (compare id.).

A knowing misrepresentation may relate to a proposition of fact or law. Certain statements, such as some statements relating to price or value, are considered nonactionable hyperbole or a reflection of the state of mind of the speaker and not misstatements of fact or law (see Restatement Second, Contracts § 168; Restatement Third, Unfair Competition § 3, Comment d). Whether a misstatement should be so characterized depends on whether it is reasonably apparent that the person to whom the statement is addressed would regard the statement as one of fact or based on the speaker's knowledge of facts reasonably implied by the statement or as merely an expression of the speaker's state of mind. Assessment depends on the circumstances in which the statement is made, including the past relationship of the negotiating persons, their apparent sophistication, the plausibility of the statement on its face, the phrasing of the statement, related communication between the persons involved, the known negotiating practices of the community in which both are negotiating, and similar circumstances. In general, a lawyer who is known to represent a person in a negotiation will be understood by nonclients to be making nonimpartial statements, in the same manner as would the lawyer's client. Subject to such an understanding, the lawyer is not privileged to make misrepresentations described in this Section.

A lawyer may also be liable under civil or criminal law for aiding and abetting a client's misrepresentation (see § 8). A lawyer representing a client in a transaction with respect to which the client has made a misrepresentation is not free, after the lawyer learns of the misrepresentation, to continue providing assistance to the client as if the misrepresentation had not been made when the lawyer's continued representation of the client would induce the nonclient reasonably to believe that no such misrepresentation has occurred.

Illustration:

> 1. Client has contracted to sell interests in Client's business to Buyer. As part of the arrangement, Lawyer for Client prepares an offering statement to be presented to Buyer. Lawyer knows that information in the statement, provided by Client, is materially misleading; the information shows Client's business as profitable and growing, but Lawyer knows that its assets are heavily encumbered, business is declining and unprofitable, and the com-

pany has substantial debts. Lawyer's knowing actions assisted Client's fraud.

d. Subsequently discovered falsity. A lawyer who has made a representation on behalf of a client reasonably believing it true when made may subsequently come to know of its falsity. An obligation to disclose before consummation of the transaction ordinarily arises, unless the lawyer takes other corrective action. See Restatement Second, Agency § 348, Comment *c*; Restatement Second, Contracts § 161(a) (nondisclosure as equivalent to assertion when person "knows that disclosure of the fact is necessary to prevent some previous assertion from being a misrepresentation or from being fraudulent or material"). Disclosure, being required by law (see § 63), is not prohibited by the general rule of confidentiality (see § 60). Disclosure should not exceed what is required to comply with the disclosure obligation, for example by indicating to recipients that they should not rely on the lawyer's statement. On permissive disclosure to prevent or rectify a client's wrongful act, see §§ 66–67.

e. Affirmative disclosure. In general, a lawyer has no legal duty to make an affirmative disclosure of fact or law when dealing with a nonclient. Applicable statutes, regulations, or common-law rules may require affirmative disclosure in some circumstances, for example disciplinary rules in some states requiring lawyers to disclose a client's intent to commit life-threatening crimes or other wrongful conduct (see § 66, Comment *b*, and Reporter's Note thereto; on permissive disclosure, see §§ 66–67).

* * *

f. Other wrongful statements. Beyond the law of misrepresentation, other civil or criminal law may constrain a lawyer's statements, for example, the criminal law of extortion. In some jurisdictions, lawyer codes prohibit a lawyer negotiating a civil claim from referring to the prospect of filing criminal charges against the opposing party. On the extent of lawyer liability for defamatory statements concerning nonclients, see § 57(1).

* * *

TITLE B.   CONTACT WITH A REPRESENTED NONCLIENT

* * *

§ 99.   A Represented Nonclient—The General Anti–Contact Rule

(1) A lawyer representing a client in a matter may not communicate about the subject of the representation with a nonclient whom the lawyer knows to be represented in the matter by another lawyer or with a representative of an organizational nonclient so represented as defined in § 100, unless:

> (a) the communication is with a public officer or agency to the extent stated in § 101;

> (b) the lawyer is a party and represents no other client in the matter;

> (c) the communication is authorized by law;

> (d) the communication reasonably responds to an emergency; or

> (e) the other lawyer consents.

(2) Subsection (1) does not prohibit the lawyer from assisting the client in otherwise proper communication by the lawyer's client with a represented nonclient.

Comment:

* * *

b.   Rationale. The rules stated in §§ 99–103, protect against overreaching and deception of nonclients. The rule of this Section also protects the relationship between the represented nonclient and that person's lawyer and assures the confidentiality of the nonclient's communications with the lawyer (see also § 102).

The general exception to the rule stated in Subsection (1)(e) requires consent of the opposing lawyer; consent of the client alone does not suffice (see Comment *j*). The rule accordingly has been criticized for requiring three-stage communications (from client, through lawyer, through another lawyer, or vice versa) that are often more expensive, delayed, and inconvenient than direct communication. In addition, the rule limits client autonomy by requiring that both communication and consent be given by the lawyer (see Comment *j* hereto). Notwithstanding such criticism, the rule is universally followed in American jurisdictions.

* * *

The anti-contact rule constrains a lawyer who represents another person in the matter. The rule also applies to nonlawyer employees and other agents of a lawyer, such as an investigator. On agents of a client, see Comment *k* hereto.

  c.   Persons protected by the anti-contact rule. As stated in Subsection (1), the anti-contact prohibition extends to any nonclient that the contacting lawyer knows to be represented by counsel in the matter in which the lawyer is representing a client. It is not limited to situations of opposing parties in litigation or in which persons otherwise have adverse interests. Thus, the rule covers a represented co-party and a nonparty fact witness who is represented by counsel with respect to the matter, as well as a nonclient so represented prior to any suit being filed and regardless of whether such suit is contemplated or eventuates. A lawyer represented by other counsel is a represented person and hence covered by this Section. On inside legal counsel for a corporation or similar organization, see § 100, Comment *c.*

  A lawyer who does not represent a person in the matter and who is approached by an already-represented person seeking a second professional opinion or wishing to discuss changing lawyers or retaining additional counsel, may, without consent from or notice to the original lawyer, respond to the request, including giving an opinion concerning the propriety of the first lawyer's representation. If such additional or substituted counsel is retained, an opposing lawyer may, of course, communicate and otherwise deal with new counsel for the nonclient. Thus, a lawyer representing a claimant in an injury case may approach a lawyer personally retained in the matter by an insured defendant even if other counsel have been designated by the defendant's insurer to represent the person in the matter.

  d.   A communication on an unrelated matter. This Section does not prohibit communications with a represented nonclient in the course of social, business, or other relationships or communications that do not relate to the matter involved in the representation. What matter or matters are involved in a representation depends on the circumstances. For example, a lawyer might know that a witness at a deposition was represented by a lawyer for an opposing party only for purposes of attending the deposition. The lawyer may contact that nonclient following the deposition when representation has ended.

* * *

  e.   A lawyer communicating in a nonrepresentational situation. A lawyer representing his or her own interests pro se may communicate with an opposing represented nonclient on the same basis as other principals (see Subsection (1)(b)). A lawyer representing both a client and the lawyer's own interests in the same matter is subject to the anti-contact rule of the Section.

* * *

f. Prohibited forms of communication. Under the anti-contact rule of this Section, a lawyer ordinarily is not authorized to communicate with a represented nonclient even by letter with a copy to the opposite lawyer or even if the opposite lawyer wrongfully fails to convey important information to that lawyer's client (see § 20), such as a settlement offer. The rule prohibits all forms of communication, such as sending a represented nonclient a copy of a letter to the nonclient's lawyer or causing communication through someone acting as the agent of the lawyer (see § 5(2) & Comment *f* thereto) (prohibition against violation of duties through agents). The anti-contact rule applies to any communication relating to the lawyer's representation in the matter, whoever initiates the contact and regardless of the content of the ensuing communication.

Illustration:

4. Wife is represented by Lawyer A in a marriage-dissolution action. Husband is represented by Lawyer B. Meeting without Lawyer A or Lawyer B, Wife and Husband negotiate the outlines of an agreement providing for property division and child support. Wife then brings Husband to Lawyer A's office to have the agreement reduced to writing. Lawyer A welcomes both Wife and Husband and engages in a discussion of provisions of the agreement with both of them. Lawyer A has violated the rule of this Section.

g. A communication authorized by law. As stated in Subsection (1)(c), direct communication with a represented nonclient is permissible, without consent of the nonclient's lawyer (cf. Comment *j* hereto), when authorized by law. Where such communication is permissible, it may extend no further than reasonably necessary. No complete list of such authorizations is stated here. Several of the important interests are described below. See also § 101 (contact with officers or employees of represented governmental agency). Whether direct communication is authorized depends on the legal justification for the contact in the situation, having regard for the interest in protecting client-lawyer relationships and avoiding overreaching of represented nonclients (see Comment *b*).

An interest sometimes recognized by law is that of transmitting notice directly to a represented nonclient of certain legally significant matters. Among other things, such notice eliminates the possibility of disputes as to the authority of the nonclient's lawyer to receive such notice. For example, law commonly provides for service of process on a defendant, even in instances where the lawyer for the plaintiff knows that the defendant is represented by a lawyer in the matter. However, after initial notice has been transmitted directly to the represented nonclient, the authority of the defendant's lawyer to act on the defendant's behalf can readily be determined (see § 25). Thereafter, communication with the nonclient ordinarily must be conducted through the nonclient's lawyer.

Direct communication may occur pursuant to court order or under the supervision of a court. Thus, a lawyer is authorized by law to interrogate as a witness an opposing represented nonclient during the course of a duly noticed deposition or at a trial or other hearing. It may also be appropriate for a tribunal to order transmittal of documents, such as settlement offers, directly to a represented client.

* * *

i. A communication reasonably responding to an emergency. Communication with a represented nonclient is authorized to protect life or personal safety and to deal with other emergency situations. As provided in Subsection (1)(d), communication in such situations is permissible to the extent reasonably necessary to deal with the emergency.

Illustration:

5. Lawyer A represents Husband in a divorce action. Wife has retained Lawyer B in connection with the action. Late at night, Wife calls Lawyer A, saying that Husband is threatening to harm her and that she cannot reach Lawyer B. Lawyer A advises Wife to leave the house and that Lawyer A will immediately attempt to calm down Husband. Lawyer A has not violated the rule of this Section.

j. A communication with the consent of the lawyer for the represented nonclient. As stated in Subsection (1)(e), a lawyer otherwise subject to the rule of this Section may communicate with a represented nonclient when that person's lawyer has consented to or acquiesced in the communication. An opposing lawyer may acquiesce, for example, by being present at a meeting and observing the communication. Similarly, consent may be implied rather than express, such as where such direct contact occurs routinely as a matter of custom, unless the opposing lawyer affirmatively protests.

* * *

k. A communication by a client with a represented nonclient. No general rule prevents a lawyer's client, either personally or through a nonlawyer agent, from communicating directly with a represented nonclient. Thus, while neither a lawyer nor a lawyer's investigator or other agent (see Comment *b* hereto) may contact the represented nonclient, the same bar does not extend to the client of the lawyer or the client's investigator or other agent.

As stated in Subsection (2), the anti-contact rule does not prohibit a lawyer from advising the lawyer's own client concerning the client's communication with a represented nonclient, including communications that may occur without the prior consent (compare Comment *j*) or knowledge of the lawyer for the nonclient.

The lawyer for a client intending to make such a communication may advise the client regarding legal aspects of the communication, such as whether an intended communication is libelous or would otherwise create risk for the client. Prohibiting such advice would unduly restrict the client's autonomy, the client's interest in obtaining important legal advice, and the client's ability to communicate fully with the lawyer. The lawyer may suggest that the client make such a communication but must not assist the client inappropriately to seek confidential information, to invite the nonclient to take action without the advice of counsel, or otherwise to overreach the nonclient.

Illustration:

6. Lawyer represents Owner, who has a worsening business relationship with Contractor. From earlier meetings, Lawyer knows that Contractor is represented by a lawyer in the matter. Owner drafts a letter to send to Contractor stating Owner's position in the dispute, showing a copy of the draft to Lawyer. Viewing the draft as inappropriate, Lawyer redrafts the letter, recommending that Client send out the letter as redrafted. Client does so, as Lawyer knew would occur. Lawyer has not violated the rule of this Section.

l. A communication with class members. A lawyer who represents a client opposing a class in a class action is subject to the anti-contact rule of this Section. For the purposes of this Section, according to the majority of decisions, once the proceeding has been certified as a class action, the members of the class are considered clients of the lawyer for the class; prior to certification, only those class members with whom the lawyer maintains a personal client-lawyer relationship are clients. Prior to certification and unless the court orders otherwise, in the case of competing putative class actions a lawyer for one set of representatives may contact class members who are only putatively represented by a competing lawyer, but not class representatives or members known to be directly represented in the matter by the other lawyer.

* * *

§ 100. Definition of a Represented Nonclient

Within the meaning of § 99, a represented nonclient includes:

(1) a natural person represented by a lawyer; and:

(2) a current employee or other agent of an organization represented by a lawyer:

(a) if the employee or other agent supervises, directs, or regularly consults with the lawyer concerning the matter or if the agent has power to compromise or settle the matter;

(b) if the acts or omissions of the employee or other agent may be imputed to the organization for purposes of civil or criminal liability in the matter; or

(c) if a statement of the employee or other agent, under applicable rules of evidence, would have the effect of binding the organization with respect to proof of the matter.

Comment:

* * *

b. Rationale. Operation of the anti-contact rule with respect to natural persons ordinarily involves no questions of agency authority. However, with respect to organizational clients, difficult questions of the scope of the rule are presented.

An organization acts only through agents. Thus, certain employees and perhaps other persons are properly regarded as nonclients who may not be contacted under § 99. The definition of Subsection (2)

243

applies whether or not the employee or other representative is personally represented by counsel for the organization. (With respect to the scope of the anti-contact rule when a representative of an organization is personally represented, see Comment *h* hereto.) A very broad definition of such persons, for example one including all present and former employees, would be easily administered but at an unacceptably high cost. Under such a rule, the organization's lawyer (as permitted under § 99 & Comment *j* thereto) could deny permission for the inquiring lawyer to speak to any employee. The opposing party would thus be required to resort to the burdensome process of filing suit (based on less information than would otherwise be available) and obtaining discovery to gain access to relevant information. Moreover, employees may be unwilling to speak as freely or candidly at a deposition in the presence of the lawyers for their employer as in an informal, pretrial interview. There is no justification for permitting one party thus to control entirely the flow of information to opposing parties. Such control is not available to an individual party, whose friends and colleagues may be approached without infringing the rule. The anti-contact rule stated in the Section therefore reflects a balance among the considerations pertinent to the anti-contact rule (see § 99, Comment *b*).

* * *

c. A person who regularly consults with an organization's lawyer (Subsection (2)(a)). As stated in Subsection (2)(a), the anti-contact rule of § 99 applies to persons connected with an organization who supervise, direct, or regularly consult with a lawyer for the organization in the matter or who have power to compromise or settle the matter in consultation with the lawyer. Such persons are likely to have confidential information concerning the matter, much of which would be immune from discovery under the attorney-client privilege (§ 68 and following) and the work-product doctrine (§ 87 and following) (see also Subsection (2)(b) & Comment *f* hereto). While such a person may also know discoverable facts, ex parte contact would incur the risk that the person would be unable to distinguish between properly discoverable facts and protected information. In addition, with respect to persons in the organization who supervise or direct the lawyer or who have power to settle or compromise the matter on behalf of the organization, the anti-contact rule also seeks to prevent improvident settlements and impairment of the relationship of trust and confidence with the lawyer (see § 99, Comment *b*).

Agents and others who are in contact with the organization's lawyer may bear different levels of responsibility, for example, a corporate vice president dealing with patent counsel on a patent challenge, a corporate clerk assigned to collect documents for the lawyer, or a production employee providing expert information to the lawyer about a mechanical process that is in issue. On the other hand, agents and others (including managerial employees) who are not within the definition of this Section may be contacted without consent regardless of their position in the organization.

Illustrations:

> 1. Manager heads the transportation department of Corporation, which is defending against a claim for personal injuries by Plaintiff. Plaintiff, represented by Lawyer A, seeks damages resulting from a traffic accident allegedly caused by Corporation's negligence in hiring Driver who had a bad driving record. Lawyer A knows that Corporation is represented by Lawyer B in defending against the claim. Manager has power to authorize settlement of the matter with Plaintiff on behalf of Corporation. Lawyer A may not contact Manager except with the consent of Lawyer B or as otherwise permitted under § 99.

> 2. Same facts as stated in Illustration 1, except that authorization to settle claims is reserved to Executive Vice President of Corporation and is not part of Manager's responsibilities. Lawyer A may contact Manager without the consent of Lawyer B, unless contact with Manager is otherwise prohibited by Subsection (2) or by § 102. On the other hand, if the facts were that Manager had responsibility for the allegedly negligent hiring, Manager would be a represented nonclient within Subsection (2)(b).

* * *

d. A person whose act or omission may be imputed to an organization for purposes of liability (Subsection (2)(b)). As stated in Subsection (2)(b), the anti-contact rule of § 99 also extends to persons connected with an organization, regardless of their rank, whose acts or omissions in the matter may be imputed to the organization for purposes of civil or criminal liability with respect to the matter involved in the representation. Such a person has acted in the matter on behalf of the organization and, save for the separate legal character of the organizational form, would often be directly named as a party in a lawsuit involving the matter. The Subsection applies even if facts are disputed concerning the person's actions, such as whether they are properly imputed to the organization or whether they were the cause of the harm alleged.

245

Illustrations:

3.   Same facts as stated in Illustration 1, except that Lawyer A wishes to interview Driver. Under applicable agency and tort law, Driver has allegedly committed an act for which civil or criminal liability may be imputed to Corporation in the matter involved in Lawyer B's representation of Corporation. Lawyer A may not contact Driver without the consent of Lawyer B or as otherwise permitted under § 99. The result does not change if Corporation has filed an answer asserting that Driver's actions were beyond the scope and course of Driver's duties and thus not imputable to Corporation.

* * *

When an individual employee or agent falls within Subsection (2)(b), there may be a conflict of interest between the organizational client and the person. A lawyer for the organization who is requested to represent the individual must comply with conflict-of-interest requirements before undertaking such a representation (see § 131, Comment e).

e.   An employee or agent whose statement binds an organization under applicable evidence law (Subsection (2)(c)). Under evidence law generally applied a century ago and still in force in some jurisdictions for certain purposes, some employees and agents have the power to make statements that bind the principal, in the sense that the principal may not introduce evidence contradicting the binding statement. When such a binding-admission rule applies, under Subsection (2)(c) an employee or agent with power to make such a statement is a represented nonclient within the anti-contact rule of § 99. Such a person is analogous to a person who possesses power to settle a dispute on behalf of the organization (see Comment c).

However, under modern evidence law, employees and agents who lack authority to enter into binding contractual settlements on behalf of the organization have no power to make such binding statements. Modern evidence rules make certain statements of an employee or agent admissible notwithstanding the hearsay rule, but allow the organization to impeach or contradict such statements. Employees or agents are not included within Subsection (2)(c) solely on the basis that their statements are admissible evidence. A contrary rule would essentially mean that most employees and agents with relevant information would be within the anti-contact rule, contrary to the policies described in Comment b.

f. Instructing an employee or agent not to communicate with an opposing lawyer. A principal or the principal's lawyer may inform employees or agents of their right not to speak with opposing counsel and may request them not to do so (see § 116(4) & Comment *e* thereto). In certain circumstances, a direction to do so could constitute an obstruction of justice or a violation of other law. However, even when lawful, such an instruction is a matter of intra-organizational policy and not a limitation against a lawyer for another party who is seeking evidence. Thus, even if an employer, by general policy or specific directive, lawfully instructs all employees not to cooperate with another party's lawyer, that does not enlarge the scope of the anti-contact rule applicable to that lawyer.

g. A former employee or agent. Contact with a former employee or agent ordinarily is permitted, even if the person had formerly been within a category of those with whom contact is prohibited. Denial of access to such a person would impede an adversary's search for relevant facts without facilitating the employer's relationship with its counsel. A former employee or agent of a party may in some circumstances be within the anti-contact rule of § 99 or within the prohibited class of persons described in § 102, Comment *d.* For example a former employee who, as the lawyer knows, continues regularly to consult about the matter with the lawyer for the ex-employer is within Subsection (2)(a); thus no such employee may be contacted except as permitted under § 99. See also § 102, Comment *d.*

* * *

i. Limitations on otherwise permissible contact with an employee or agent. A lawyer may not seek confidential information during the course of an otherwise permissible communication (see § 102). After beginning to communicate with a nonclient, a lawyer may learn that the nonclient is represented in the matter. The lawyer must then cease further communication, unless an exception stated in § 99 applies.

* * *

§ 101. A Represented Governmental Agency or Officer

(1) Unless otherwise provided by law (see § 99(1)(c)) and except as provided in Subsection (2), the prohibition stated in § 99 against contact with a represented nonclient does not apply to communications with employees of a represented governmental agency or with a governmental officer being represented in the officer's official capacity.

(2) In negotiation or litigation by a lawyer of a specific claim of a client against a governmental agency or against a governmental officer in the officer's official capacity, the prohibition stated in § 99 applies, except that the lawyer may contact any officer of the government if permitted by the agency or with respect to an issue of general policy.

Comment:

* * *

b. Rationale. This Section takes the position that the application of the anti-contact rule to representations against the government should be limited to those instances in which the government stands in a position closely analogous to that of a private litigant and with respect to contact where potential for abuse is clear (see Comment *c*). Jurisdictions differ considerably concerning the extent to which direct lawyer contact with a government officer or employee is permitted under the general anti-contact rule. All jurisdictions accept, of course, that direct contact is permissible when protected by the right of the client or lawyer under the First Amendment to petition the government for redress of grievances. On the other hand, there is little authority providing guidance on what contact is thus protected. California, in which there is much representation against governmental bodies, expressly provides in its lawyer code that the anti-contact rule is generally inapplicable in all such representations. The rule in most jurisdictions is unclear. While no explicit exception permitting contact, such as stated in Subsection (1), is stated, commentary in most of the lawyer codes suggests a limited anti-contact rule, although one of indefinite scope. Ethics-committee opinions in some of the jurisdictions construe the anti-contact rule quite narrowly for such representations.

Were the broad anti-contact rule of § 99 routinely applied in dealings with governmental agencies, any matter disputed with a governmental agency could be pursued with safety only through the agency's lawyer. Such a result would require in each instance that a lawyer intending to make a direct contact first accurately determine the reach of the First Amendment. It would also compromise the public interest in facilitating direct communication between representatives of citizens and government officials reflected in open-government, open-file, freedom-of-information, and similar enactments.

The practical need of the government for the broad protection of the anti-contact rule also seems dubious. Concern based on client vulnerability (see § 99, Comment *b*) will often be misplaced with respect to officers who are selected and trained for service to the public and who will often have an established relationship with and ready access to government counsel. The governmental interest in guarding against overreaching is independently protected by law in many respects, including the general rule against waivers of governmental rights by individual governmental employees and regulations specifying procedures that must be followed in settling government litigation. A lawyer contacting a represented governmental agency or official remains subject to other restrictions on such contact, including the limitations of § 98 on misrepresentation in general and those of § 103 on misrepresentations of the lawyer's capacity and the nature of the interests of the lawyer's client. See also, e.g., § 113(1) (prohibition against ex parte contact with adjudicative officer). Protection against such threats of overreaching by opposing lawyers as may be thought to exist despite those protections can readily be afforded through individual-officer reaction or administrative policies. For example, unless limited by law a represented governmental agency or officer may refuse to speak to a lawyer, instead referring the lawyer to government counsel. The government may also adopt organizational directives or policies requiring employees to refuse to speak to opposition lawyers without consent or the presence of the organization's counsel (see § 100, Comment *f*). In an extreme situation, a tribunal may be empowered to enter an order prohibiting or limiting contact (see § 99, Comment *m*).

* * *

c. Negotiation or litigation involving a specific claim. When the government is represented in a dispute involving a specific claim, the status of the government as client may be closely analogous to that of any other organizational party (see § 100). Where such a close analogy exists, as stated in Subsection (2), the anti-contact rule of § 99 applies, although with reduced scope. Thus, in prosecuting a tort claim against a governmental agency based on the activities of an agency employee in operating a motor vehicle, a personal interview with the employee is subject to the anti-contact rule (see § 100(2)(b)). In any specific-claims representation, contact is permissible with officers of governmental agencies other than the agency specifically involved and with officers of the governmental agency in question who do not have power to bind the agency with respect to the specific matter.

Even litigation over a specific claim may involve general policy issues, as when the litigation involves a novel question of the applicability or validity of a regulation. In such instances, this Section permits direct contact with any governmental officer with power to affect the policy, contact that may be protected under the First Amendment in any event. Alternatively, the contact may be in a context where such is regarded as customary or expected by the government agency, and as such is permissible.

* * *

§ 102. Information of a Nonclient Known to Be Legally Protected

A lawyer communicating with a nonclient in a situation permitted under § 99 may not seek to obtain information that the lawyer reasonably should know the nonclient may not reveal without violating a duty of confidentiality to another imposed by law.

Comment:

* * *

b. Rationale. Agents may possess information that is confidential under an evidentiary privilege or under a law providing specific confidentiality protection to the principal. For example, the information may be protected under the attorney-client privilege (see § 68), work-product immunity (see § 87), or the doctor-patient privilege (see Comment *d*). The agent may not disclose the information to a stranger to the principal-agent relationship when doing so would impair substantial interests of the principal (see generally Restatement Second, Agency §§ 395 (during employment) & 396 (postemployment)). Moreover, a third person who obtains such information, knowing it to be such, from an incautious or complicit agent commits an actionable wrong against the principal (see id. § 312). Thus, the rules of this Section flow from the law of agency, evidence, and unfair competition and similar bodies of law. As such, they may also apply to nonlawyers, a subject that is beyond the scope of this Restatement.

* * *

c. The prohibition against seeking confidential information in the course of an otherwise permissible communication. The Section assumes that a lawyer is communicating with an agent permissibly, in that the anti-contact rule of § 99 is inapplicable, but that the agent possesses confidential information of a principal that the agent could not lawfully divulge. The lawyer's inquiry may not extend to matters whose disclosure would violate the agent's legal duty.

When the confidentiality duty does not extend to the subject matter of the confidential information itself (as it does extend, for example, to the subject matter of state secrets or business secrets), the lawyer may inquire into factual information even though the agent may also have conveyed that information to a lawyer in a confidential communication. For example, the inquiring lawyer may inquire into the same facts the agent discussed in confidence with the principal's lawyer. However, the lawyer may not seek to examine, for example, the agent's copy of correspondence with such a lawyer (if privileged) or otherwise ask the agent what the agent told a lawyer for the principal. The point corresponds to one of the corollaries to the attorney-client privilege—that confidential client-lawyer communication does not immunize even a client from being required to testify to facts that may be contained in the communication (see § 69, Comment *d*).

Illustration:

1. A governmental environmental-protection Agency is investigating whether Manufacturer had violated law by releasing certain toxic substances. Agency's Lawyer A is assisting in the investigation. Learning of the investigation, Manufacturer directs all its employees to cooperate in providing information to Lawyer B, who is representing Manufacturer in the matter. Employee is a production-line worker with no responsibility for directing or otherwise extensively assisting in Lawyer B's work, whose acts or omissions are not suspected to have caused the release of the substances, whose statements are not binding on Manufacturer, and who is thus not a representative of Manufacturer within the definition of § 100. Accordingly, Lawyer A may interview or otherwise contact Employee without the consent of Lawyer B (cf. § 99). Under this Section, in doing so Lawyer A may not seek to learn of Employee's privileged statements to Lawyer B or any privileged communication from Lawyer B to Employee. However, Lawyer A may seek to obtain from Employee, among other information, facts about the same topics that Employee may also have discussed with Lawyer B.

d. Prohibited contact with a nonclient agent extensively exposed to confidential information. Several decisions have held that a lawyer representing a client in a matter may not communicate concerning the representation with a nonclient agent who the lawyer knows is likely to possess extensive and relevant confidential and privileged information, or similar legally protected information of another nonclient interested in the matter that is confidential with respect to the lawyer's client. Those decisions typically involve a person—for example, an expert witness or paralegal assisting opposing counsel—whose employment has entailed exposure to extensive confidential information about the principal, who likely possesses little information that is not privileged, and whose role as confidential agent should have been apparent to the inquiring lawyer. They also involve situations in which confidentiality occurs by operation of law and not solely, for example, through a contractual undertaking of the agent. They are based on communication with such an agent alone and do not require a further demonstration that the agent in fact impermissibly conveyed confidential information to the lawyer (cf. § 132, Comment *d(iii)*) or that the agent or the agent's principal was represented in the matter.

* * *

Illustrations:

2. Lawyer, representing Plaintiff, attends a deposition in the offices of Law Firm, representing Defendant. During a recess in the deposition, Lawyer strikes up a conversation with Paralegal who is employed by Law Firm and who, as Lawyer knows, is performing significant work on the matter. The conversation leads to a later social occasion, when Lawyer and Paralegal discuss the background of several matters covered during the depositions, including work product of Law Firm that Paralegal is not privileged to reveal to Lawyer. Lawyer has impermissibly communicated with a confidential agent of Defendant.

* * *

e. Communication with an opposing lawyer. A lawyer may not induce another lawyer to violate that lawyer's duty of confidentiality to a client or accept confidential information known to have been imparted in breach of trust by the communicating lawyer (see § 60, Comment *m*). It is not a violation to accept the advantage of inadvertent, and even negligent, disclosure of confidential information by the other lawyer, if the effect of the other lawyer's action is to waive the right of that lawyer's client to assert confidentiality. See §§ 78–80 (waiver of attorney-client privilege by consent, disclaimer, defective assertion, subsequent disclosure, or by putting legal assistance or communication into issue); §§ 91–92 (waiver of work-product immunity by voluntary acts or use in litigation).

* * *

TITLE C. DEALINGS WITH AN UNREPRESENTED NONCLIENT

* * *

§ 103. Dealings with an Unrepresented Nonclient

In the course of representing a client and dealing with a nonclient who is not represented by a lawyer:

(1) the lawyer may not mislead the nonclient, to the prejudice of the nonclient, concerning the identity and interests of the person the lawyer represents; and

(2) when the lawyer knows or reasonably should know that the unrepresented nonclient misunderstands the lawyer's role in the matter, the lawyer must make reasonable efforts to correct the misunderstanding when failure to do so would materially prejudice the nonclient.

Comment:

a. Scope and cross-references. This Section states the rule prohibiting a lawyer from misrepresenting material matters concerning the lawyer's representational role when dealing with an unrepresented nonclient. The rule is drawn primarily from the lawyer codes, except that they do not require the element of prejudice to the nonclient. That element is, however, usually required for the purposes of civil liability.

* * *

[*b. Rationale.*]

* * *

This Section states two general requirements. First, the lawyer must not mislead the unrepresented nonclient to that person's detriment concerning the identity and interests of the person whom the lawyer represents. For example, the lawyer may not falsely state or imply that the lawyer represents no one, that the lawyer is disinterestedly protecting the interests of both the client and the unrepresented nonclient, or that the nonclient will suffer no harm by speaking freely. Such a false statement could disarm the unrepresented nonclient and result in unwarranted advantage to the lawyer's client. Second, the lawyer is subject to a duty of disclosure when the lawyer knows or reasonably should know that the unrepresented nonclient misunderstands the lawyer's role in the matter and when failure to correct the misunderstanding would prejudice the nonclient or the nonclient's principal.

* * *

[*d. A transaction on behalf of a client with an unrepresented nonclient.*]

Formerly, a lawyer-code rule prohibited a lawyer from giving "legal advice" to an unrepresented nonclient. That restriction has now been omitted from most lawyer codes in recognition of the implicit representations that a lawyer necessarily makes in such functions as providing transaction documents to an unrepresented nonclient for signature, seeking originals or copies of documents and other information from the nonclient, and describing the legal effect of actions taken or requested.

Illustrations:

1. Lawyer represents Insurer in a wrongful-death claim asserted by Personal Representative, who is not represented by a lawyer. The claim concerns the death of Decedent assertedly caused by an insured of Insurer. Under applicable law, a settlement by Personal Representative must be approved by a tribunal. Personal Representative and Insurer's claims manager have agreed on a settlement amount. Lawyer prepares the necessary documents and presents them to Personal Representative for signature. Personal Representative, who is aware that Lawyer represents the interests of Insurer, asks Lawyer why the documents are necessary. Lawyer responds truthfully that to be effective, the documents must be executed and filed for court approval. Lawyer's conduct is permissible under this Section.

2. Lawyer represents the financing Bank in a home sale. Buyer, the borrower, is not represented by another lawyer. Under the terms of the transaction, Buyer is to pay the legal fees of Lawyer. Buyer sends Lawyer a letter stating, "I have several questions about legal issues in the house purchase on which you are representing me." Buyer also has several telephone conversations with Lawyer in which Buyer makes similar statements. In the circumstances, it should be apparent to Lawyer that Buyer is assuming, perhaps mistakenly, that Lawyer represents Buyer in the transaction. It is also apparent that Buyer misunderstands Lawyer's role as lawyer for Bank. Lawyer must inform Buyer that Lawyer represents only Bank and that Buyer should not rely on Lawyer to protect Buyer's interests in the transaction.

e. Dealings with an unrepresented constituent of an organization client. A lawyer for an organizational client, whether inside or outside legal counsel (see § 96), may have important responsibilities in investigating relevant facts within the organization. In doing so, the lawyer may interview constituents of the organization, who in some instances might have interests that differ from those of the organization and might be at personal risk of criminal prosecution or civil penalties. A constituent may mistakenly assume that the lawyer will act to further the personal interests of the constituent, perhaps even against the interests of the organization. Such a mistake on the part of the constituent can occur after an extended period working with the lawyer on matters of common interest to the organization and the constituent, particularly if the lawyer has formerly provided personal counsel to the constituent, and may be more likely to occur with inside legal counsel due to greater personal acquaintanceship. Such an assumption, although erroneous, may be harmless so long as the interests of the constituent and the organization do not materially conflict. However, when those interests do materially conflict, the lawyer's failure to warn the constituent of the nature of the lawyer's role could prejudicially mislead the constituent, impair the interests of the organization, or both.

An adequate clarification may in some instances be required to protect the interest of the organization client in unencumbered representation. Failing to clarify the lawyer's role and the client's interests may redound to the disadvantage of the organization if the lawyer, even if unwittingly, thereby undertakes concurrent representation of both the organization and the constituent. Such a finding could be based in part on a finding that the lawyer's silence had reasonably induced the constituent to believe that the lawyer also represented the constituent. On forming a client-lawyer relationship with a constituent of an organization client, see § 96, Comment *h*; see generally § 14. Among other consequences, the lawyer may be required to withdraw from representing both clients because of the conflict (see § 121, Comment *e(i)*).

* * *

When the lawyer does not have a reasonable belief that the constituent is adequately informed, the lawyer must take reasonable steps to correct the constituent's reasonably apparent misunderstanding, particularly when the risk confronting the constituent is severe. For example, the constituent's expression of a belief that the lawyer will keep their conversation confidential from others with decisionmaking authority in the organization or that the interests of the constituent and the organization are the same, when they are not, would normally require a warning by the lawyer. In all events, as required under this Section, a lawyer must not mislead an unrepresented nonclient about such matters as the lawyer's role and the nature of the client organization's interests with respect to the constituent.

* * *

TOPIC 4. LEGISLATIVE AND ADMINISTRATIVE MATTERS

* * *

§ 104. Representing a Client in Legislative and Administrative Matters

A lawyer representing a client before a legislature or administrative agency:

(1) must disclose that the appearance is in a representative capacity and not misrepresent the capacity in which the lawyer appears;

(2) must comply with applicable law and regulations governing such representations; and

(3) except as applicable law otherwise provides:

(a) in an adjudicative proceeding before a government agency or involving such an agency as a participant, has the legal rights and responsibilities of an advocate in a proceeding before a judicial tribunal; and

(b) in other types of proceedings and matters, has the legal rights and responsibilities applicable in the lawyer's dealings with a private person.

Comment:

* * *

b. Rationale. A lawyer's work may involve representing clients in their dealings with legislative bodies or administrative agencies. That work may occur at the level of a village office or town council or at the executive levels of a federal agency and can range over a wide array of legal services. Some such representations partake of many of the same characteristics as litigation in courts. Other work is more like negotiation between private parties, as where a lawyer negotiates with a government officer over the terms of an agency permit. Still other representations have no direct counterpart in the representation of clients in nongovernmental matters, as where a lawyer provides legal services to a client in attempting to achieve compliance with regulatory requirements. The interests of third parties beyond the governmental agency may or may not be directly involved.

* * *

c. Misrepresentation of a lawyer's representative capacity. A self-introduction that a lawyer appears in a representative capacity is common in many legislative and administrative proceedings and is required by the lawyer codes and Subsection (1). The rule is enforced through professional discipline (see § 5). Legislation requiring lawyers functioning as lobbyists to register and file disclosure statements concerning their representative capacity may also apply (see Subsection (2)) and may provide for other remedies, as may a governmental agency's rules of practice.

d. A lawyer's representation of a client before a legislature or administrative agency—adjudicative or nonadjudicative proceeding. A lawyer's representation of a client before some legislative and administrative bodies is governed by statutes and regulations. For example, a federal statute applicable to lawyers as well as others requires that a person serving as representative of a foreign government must register with a federal agency, describing the representative relationship in some detail. Certain agencies, such as the federal Treasury Department and Patent and Trademark Office, have regulations applicable to lawyers practicing before them. Agency rules sometimes require that a lawyer submitting an application to the agency certify the accuracy of factual presentations in the application and make affirmative disclosures of described facts (compare § 98). As stated in Subsection (2), a lawyer providing representation subject to such laws must comply with them.

* * *

CHAPTER 7

REPRESENTING CLIENTS IN LITIGATION

TOPIC 1. ADVOCACY IN GENERAL

---

* * *

TOPIC 1. ADVOCACY IN GENERAL

* * *

§ 105. Complying with Law and Tribunal Rulings

In representing a client in a matter before a tribunal, a lawyer must comply with applicable law, including rules of procedure and evidence and specific tribunal rulings.

Comment:

* * *

d. Compliance with an applicable court order. An advocate takes steps in litigation in conformity with law of general application (see Comment *c*). Judicial officers are generally empowered to impose additional restrictions to control the course of a proceeding before them. Once a judicial ruling has been made, a lawyer ordinarily must either conform or risk contempt or other sanction (see Comment *e*). An order directed to a lawyer's client is generally binding on the client's lawyer if the latter has notice of the order.

e. Advocacy and contempt. Courts are generally empowered (see § 1, Comment *b*) to control conduct in the courtroom, including that of lawyers, so that judicial business may be conducted fairly and expeditiously. Courts also possess the power to punish advocates for contempt. On sanctions for aiding and abetting a client's contempt, see § 94, Comment *d*. However, the power to punish a lawyer for contempt is susceptible to abuse, particularly if used precipitously or by a judicial officer personally embroiled in controversy with an advocate or with the advocate's client.

Because of the potential for abuse, the contempt power usually is constrained by procedural requirements such as notice of charges, the right to counsel, opportunity for hearing, and the right to call witnesses. Those procedures vary depending on whether the contempt is punished summarily or after a hearing, whether the proceeding seeks criminal or civil contempt sanctions, and, if criminal sanctions are sought, the degree of their severity. Some procedures are required under the federal Constitution. The requirements of contempt procedure are beyond the scope of this Restatement. However, in general a judicial officer determining whether a lawyer has committed contempt needs to balance the objective of according lawyers necessary scope for effective advocacy and that of keeping proceedings fair and fairly conducted. Advocacy ordinarily should not be punished as criminal contempt unless the lawyer's conduct substantially and intentionally disrupts the proceeding. While the general standard is the same in both civil and criminal cases, a lawyer representing a person accused of crime has special constitutionally based duties of diligent advocacy.

* * *

§ 106. Dealing with Other Participants in Proceedings

In representing a client in a matter before a tribunal, a lawyer may not use means that have no substantial purpose other than to embarrass, delay, or burden a third person or use methods of obtaining evidence that are prohibited by law.

Comment:

* * *

b. Investigating and tape recording witnesses. A lawyer may conduct an investigation of a witness to gather information from or about the witness. Such an investigation may legitimately address potentially relevant aspects of the finances, associations, and personal life of the witness. In conducting such investigations personally or through others, however, a lawyer must observe legal constraints on intrusion on privacy. The law of some jurisdictions, for example, prohibits recording conversations with another person without the latter's consent. When secret recording is not prohibited by law, doing so is permissible for lawyers conducting investigations on behalf of their clients, but should be done only when compelling need exists to obtain evidence otherwise unavailable in an equally reliable form. Such a need may exist more readily in a criminal-defense representation. In conducting such an investigation, a lawyer must comply with the limitations of § 99 prohibiting contact with represented person, of § 102 restricting communication with persons who owe certain duties of confidentiality to others, and of § 103 prohibiting misleading an unrepresented person.

[*c. Calling and examining witness.*]

* * *

Distinguishing between permissible and impermissible examination is normally left to the discretion of the officer presiding at the hearing. A client may instruct a lawyer how to proceed in examining witnesses, subject to the lawyer's obligations to the tribunal (see § 21(2) & Comment *d* thereto & § 23). A particularly difficult problem is presented when a lawyer has an opportunity to cross-examine a witness with respect to testimony that the lawyer knows to be truthful, including harsh implied criticism of the witness's testimony, character, or capacity for truth-telling. Even if legally permissible, a lawyer would presumably do so only where that would not cause the lawyer to lose credibility with the tribunal or alienate the factfinder. Moreover, a lawyer is never required to conduct such examination, and the lawyer may withdraw if the lawyer's client insists on such a course of action in a setting in which the lawyer considers it imprudent or repugnant (see § 32(3)(f) & Comment *j* thereto).

A lawyer who asks irrelevant or otherwise objectionable questions or employs other means that have no purpose other than to harass the witness may be subjected to judicial sanctions or professional discipline. Rules of permissible questioning under the evidence law applied in a particular tribunal regulate such questions and appropriate judicial responses to them.

A lawyer other than a prosecutor (see § 97, Comment *h*) is not required to inform any nonclient witness or prospective witness of the right to invoke privileges against answering, including the privilege against self-incrimination. On the prohibition against misleading a nonclient witness or other person, see § 99; see also § 103.

d. Opposing counsel and other participants. The professional ideal for the relationship between opposing advocates is that they bear toward each other a respectful and cooperative attitude marked by civility, consistent with their primary responsibilities to their clients. Similar respect and cooperativeness should characterize a lawyer's interactions with all participants in a proceeding. Certain conduct toward other participants, including opposing lawyers, is prohibited, including unlawful physical force or its threat, racial or gender or similar slurs, and charges of wrongdoing made recklessly or knowing them to be without foundation. Also prohibited are legally impermissible forms of partisanship, such as misrepresenting the record (see § 120, Comment *f*). However, a lawyer is permitted to make vigorous argument and to attack an opposing position on all legally available grounds (see § 110). On limitations on calling opposing counsel as a witness, see § 108(4).

* * *

§ 107. Prohibited Forensic Tactics

In representing a client in a matter before a tribunal, a lawyer may not, in the presence of the trier of fact:

(1) state a personal opinion about the justness of a cause, the credibility of a witness, the culpability of a civil litigant, or the guilt or innocence of an accused, but the lawyer may argue any position or conclusion adequately supported by the lawyer's analysis of the evidence; or

(2) allude to any matter that the lawyer does not reasonably believe is relevant or that will not be supported by admissible evidence.

Comment:

* * *

b. A lawyer's assertion of a personal opinion. Subsection (1), prohibiting a lawyer from asserting to a tribunal the lawyer's personal

261

opinion about various matters, is designed to prevent interjection of the lawyer's own credibility into the issues to be decided (cf. § 108 (advocate-witness rule)). The rule also preserves the advocate's role as an independent professional agent. Permitting advocates to make personal affirmations would by implication disparage the causes of a client for whom the chosen advocate could not conscientiously vouch, prejudicing the rights of those with unpopular or difficult cases.

It may be difficult in practice to maintain the line between permissible zealous argument about facts and inferences to be drawn from them and impermissible personal endorsement. Latitude is left to the advocate in doubtful cases, subject to the superintending power of the presiding officer to prevent improper or misleading argument.

c. *"Backdoor" methods of proof of an inadmissible matter.* Trial maneuvers can be calculated to suggest to the factfinder (especially a jury) legally irrelevant and otherwise inadmissible evidence or considerations. A classic example is asking a witness a question that calls for an inadmissible response, knowing that the question will have suggested the response, even if objection to it is sustained. For example, a prosecutor may not ask a nonparty defense witness a question when the prosecutor knows the witness will invoke the privilege against self-incrimination and refuse to testify. A lawyer may not offer evidence on the representation that a proper foundation will be laid for its admission when the lawyer has no reasonable basis for believing that the such a foundation can be provided. However, when, under applicable law, invoking a privilege or asserting an objection is a permissible basis for arguing an inference to the jury, the fact that such a privilege or objection will be invoked does not make it improper to ask the question for the purpose of arguing such an inference.

* * *

§ 108. An Advocate as a Witness

(1) Except as provided in Subsection (2), a lawyer may not represent a client in a contested hearing or trial of a matter in which:

(a) the lawyer is expected to testify for the lawyer's client; or

(b) the lawyer does not intend to testify but (i) the lawyer's testimony would be material to establishing a claim or defense of the client, and (ii) the client has not consented as stated in § 122 to the lawyer's intention not to testify.

(2) A lawyer may represent a client when the lawyer will testify as stated in Subsection (1)(a) if:

(a) the lawyer's testimony relates to an issue that the lawyer reasonably believes will not be contested or to the nature and value of legal services rendered in the proceeding;

(b) deprivation of the lawyer's services as advocate would work a substantial hardship on the client; or

(c) consent has been given by (i) opposing parties who would be adversely affected by the lawyer's testimony and, (ii) if relevant, the lawyer's client, as stated in § 122 with respect to any conflict of interest between lawyer and client (see § 125) that the lawyer's testimony would create.

(3) A lawyer may not represent a client in a litigated matter pending before a tribunal when the lawyer or a lawyer in the lawyer's firm will give testimony materially adverse to the position of the lawyer's client or materially adverse to a former client of any such lawyer with respect to a matter substantially related to the earlier representation, unless the affected client has consented as stated in § 122 with respect to any conflict of interest between lawyer and client (see § 125) that the testimony would create.

(4) A tribunal should not permit a lawyer to call opposing trial counsel as a witness unless there is a compelling need for the lawyer's testimony.

Comment:

* * *

b. Rationale. Combining the role of advocate and witness creates several risks. The lawyer's role as witness may hinder effective advocacy on behalf of the client. The combined roles risk confusion on the part of the factfinder and the introduction of both impermissible advocacy from the witness stand and impermissible testimony from counsel table. Concomitantly, an advocate may not interfere with an opposing counsel's function as advocate by calling him or her to the witness stand, except for compelling reasons (see Subsection (4) & Comment *l*). When a lawyer will give testimony adverse to the lawyer's client, a conflict of interest is presented that must either be avoided by withdrawal of the lawyer and the lawyer's firm or, where permitted, consented to by the client as provided in § 122 (see Subsection (3) & Comment *f*).

c. *The basic prohibition against an advocate testifying.* The advocate-witness rule applies in all contested proceedings in which a lawyer appears as both advocate and witness, including trials, hearings on motions for preliminary injunction and for summary judgment, and trial-type hearings before administrative agencies. The rule applies whether the case is being tried to a judge or jury. In trials to a judge, less need may exist for exacting application of the rule in some situations, such as when dealing with contested pretrial matters, particularly where the testimony of the advocate will not be lengthy (see also Comment *g*).

A lawyer serving in a capacity other than that of a courtroom advocate is not precluded from being a witness for the lawyer's client. For example, a lawyer is not subject to the rule who does not appear on a list of counsel, or will not sit at counsel table or otherwise physically appear in support of advocacy. The rule does not require disqualification if the lawyer gives testimony in a proceeding separate from the matter in which the lawyer appears as advocate. Similarly, a lawyer who testifies before a judicial officer concerning only a preliminary motion is not thereby disqualified from serving as advocate at a subsequent trial before a jury.

* * *

e. *The effect of an advocate's announced intent or status as a material witness.* Subsection (1)(a) generally prohibits a lawyer from being both advocate and witness. Prohibition is not affected by the character of the testimony as cumulative.

As recognized in Subsection (1)(b), in certain circumstances a lawyer is a necessary witness and subject to the prohibition against advocacy, regardless of the lawyer's possible inclination not to testify. A lawyer's testimony is material within the meaning of the Subsection when a reasonable lawyer, viewing the circumstances objectively, would conclude that failure of the lawyer to testify would have a substantially adverse effect on the client's cause. The forensic value of evidence must be assessed in practical terms. If other evidence is significantly less probative or credible or the issue is critical and contested, the lawyer's testimony, although cumulative, may be of significant forensic value and thus material.

Illustration:

> 1. Lawyer One represented Seller in negotiating the sale of Seller's real estate and at the closing of the transaction. In each

negotiating session and at the closing, the only parties present were Seller, Lawyer One, Buyer, and Buyer's lawyer. Buyer has now filed suit against Seller to rescind the transaction for fraud, alleging that Seller and Lawyer One made misrepresentations during the negotiations and at the closing. The evidence of what was said is sharply conflicting. Lawyer One would be regarded as a material witness for Seller.

The decision whether a lawyer whose testimony is material should continue in the matter as advocate is one for the client (see § 22). Since the lawyer might be disinclined to testify in order to remain as advocate, a conflict of interest is presented (see § 125). The conflict is consentable when the lawyer can adequately represent the client in the litigation without providing the testimony (see § 122(2)(c)), and when the client gives informed consent to the conflict (see § 122(1)). The client must understand the implications of consent. See also Comment *k* hereto.

f. An advocate's testimony adverse to a client's interest. The advocate-witness rule usually involves intended testimony favorable to the lawyer's client. When the lawyer's testimony would be adverse to an important interest of a present or former client, the broader rule of Subsection (3) applies. In such a representation, a conflict exists between the lawyer's duty to testify truthfully and the client's interest in avoiding adverse testimony (see, e.g., §§ 125 & 132). In the absence of client consent, such adverse testimony requires disqualification not only of the lawyer but of the lawyer's firm as well (compare Comment *i*). Although effective client consent removes the conflict between client and lawyer, an opposing party has standing to object to the lawyer's continued advocacy when the advocate personally will testify.

* * *

g. The exception for uncontested testimony or to establish the value of legal services (Subsection (2)(a)). An advocate may testify for the lawyer's client to establish a necessary fact that is not significantly contested, for example, to establish the chain of custody or genuineness of a document. Thus, it is customary for advocates to attest to the genuineness of documents when supporting a motion based on facts. Even at a trial, counsel ordinarily may assume that the opposing party will stipulate to apparently uncontested facts. Refusal of an opposing party to do so should not put the advocate's client to the risks and expense of obtaining either other witnesses or other counsel.

The value of legal services rendered in the proceeding may be testified to by an advocate. The exception applies only with respect to legal services rendered in the proceeding in which the testimony will be given and in ancillary proceedings. The exception rests on the need for testimony on such questions by lawyers who participated in providing the services and on the assumption that the issue will normally be tried before a judge in a collateral proceeding rather than before the jury hearing the merits, such as in many fee-shifting situations. However, the exception also applies to jury-tried issues.

h. The exception due to substantial hardship (Subsection (2)(b)). Disqualification of an advocate ordinarily works hardship on the client. Substantial hardship warrants the lawyer in continuing as advocate while also testifying. Relevant factors include the length of time the lawyer has represented the client, the complexity of the issues, the client's economic resources, the lawyer's care in attempting to anticipate or avoid the necessity of testifying, the extent of harm to the lawyer's client and opposing parties from the blending of the roles of advocate and witness, additional expense that disqualification would entail, and the effect of delay upon the interests of the parties and the tribunal.

i. Representation by an advocate affiliated with a testifying lawyer. Any other lawyer in a testifying lawyer's firm may serve as advocate for a party in the proceeding, despite disqualification of one or more firm lawyers as advocates under Subsection (1)(a), so long as the representation would not involve a conflict of interest under Subsection (3). In the typical case in which the lawyer's testimony will be favorable to the client, another firm lawyer may serve as advocate. However, on a lawyer's testimony adverse to the interests of the firm's client, see Comment *f*.

j. Testimony by nonlawyer employee or agent of an advocate. The rule of Subsection (1) does not apply to an advocate's nonlawyer employees or agents who do not sit at counsel table or otherwise visibly function in support of advocacy before the factfinder. The exception applies to paralegals, investigators, secretaries, accountants, or other nonlawyer employees, agents, or independent contractors such as investigators. Under rules of evidence, the relationship between such a witness and an advocate may be shown to impeach the person's testimony.

* * *

l. Calling an opposing advocate as a witness. As provided in Subsection (4), a lawyer may call opposing counsel to the witness stand only when doing so is justified by compelling need (see also § 106, Comment *e*). A lawyer called as a witness may be seriously disrupted in functioning as an advocate (see Comment *b*). Calling opposing counsel may also create the false impression in the eyes of a jury that the lawyer was improperly involved in the underlying transaction. An adversary who wishes to make an issue of an opposing advocate's role as a prospective witness normally should promptly move for disqualification (see Comment *k*).

* * *

§ **109.** An Advocate's Public Comment on Pending Litigation

(1) In representing a client in a matter before a tribunal, a lawyer may not make a statement outside the proceeding that a reasonable person would expect to be disseminated by means of public communication when the lawyer knows or reasonably should know that the statement will have a substantial likelihood of materially prejudicing a juror or influencing or intimidating a prospective witness in the proceeding. However, a lawyer may in any event make a statement that is reasonably necessary to mitigate the impact on the lawyer's client of substantial, undue, and prejudicial publicity recently initiated by one other than the lawyer or the lawyer's client.

(2) A prosecutor must, except for statements necessary to inform the public of the nature and extent of the prosecutor's action and that serve a legitimate law-enforcement purpose, refrain from making extrajudicial comments that have a substantial likelihood of heightening public condemnation of the accused.

Comment:

* * *

[*b. Rationale.*]

* * *

Professional limitations on trial publicity responded to recurring instances of prejudicial publicity, primarily in sensational criminal cases. Modern attempts to regulate date from the decision of the United States Supreme Court in Sheppard v. Maxwell, 384 U.S. 333, 86 S.Ct. 1507, 16 L.Ed.2d 600 (1966), in which the Court reversed a criminal conviction because of highly prejudicial publicity adverse to the accused. On the other hand, restrictive provisions of the lawyer codes have sometimes also been successfully attacked on constitutional grounds.

Restrictions on the out-of-court speech of advocates seek to balance three interests. First, the public and the media have an interest in access to facts and opinions about litigation because litigation has important public dimensions. Second, litigants may have an interest in placing a legal dispute before the public or in countering adverse publicity about the matter, and their lawyers may feel a corresponding duty to further the client's goals through contact with the media. Third, the public and opposing parties have an interest in ensuring that the process of adjudication will not be distorted by statements carried in the media, particularly in criminal cases. The free-expression rights of advocates, because of their role in the ongoing litigation, are not as extensive as those of either nonlawyers or lawyers not serving as advocates in the proceeding.

Regulation of advocate comment must be justified by a compelling state interest and narrowly tailored to achieve that interest. One such compelling state interest is preventing pretrial and trial comment from becoming an improper basis for factfinders' decisions. That concern is largely irrelevant in matters to be decided by judges. Judicial officers are expected to be immune from the influences of inadmissible evidence and similar sources of information and from the potentially distorting effects of inflamed public opinion. Thus, media comments by a lawyer outside a nonjury proceeding will pose a significant and direct threat to the administration of justice and thus warrant application of the rule of Subsection (1) only in extreme situations. Accordingly, concern has focused mainly on prejudicial trial comment that has a substantial likelihood of contaminating a jury (see Comment c). A second compelling state interest is preventing pretrial and trial comment that will influence a prospective witness, such as by inducing reluctance to testify out of fear of retaliation.

c. *A substantial likelihood of material prejudice to a litigated matter.* Subsection (1) prohibits trial comment only in circumstances in which the lawyer's statement entails a substantial likelihood of material prejudice, that is, where lay factfinders or a witness would likely learn of the statement and be influenced in an inappropriate way. If the same information is available to the media from other sources, the lawyer's out-of-court statement alone ordinarily will not cause prejudice. For example, if the lawyer for a criminal defendant simply repeats to the media outside the courthouse what the lawyer said before a jury, the lawyer's out-of-court statement cannot be said to have caused prejudice. However, the fact that information is available from some other source is not controlling; the information must be both available and likely in the circumstances to be reported by the media.

There may be a likelihood of prejudice even if the tribunal can sequester the jury because sequestration may be imposed too late and, in any event, inflicts hardship on members of a jury. Taint of a lay jury is of most concern prior to trial, when publicity will reach the population from which the jury will be called. When a statement is made after a jury has rendered a decision that is not set aside, taint is unlikely, regardless of the nature of the statement. Additional considerations of timing may be relevant. For example, a statement made long before a jury is to be selected presents less risk than the same statement made in the heat of intense media publicity about an imminent or ongoing proceeding.

Several ABA model lawyer codes attempted to detail presumptively prohibited comments. However, such lists may be misleadingly broad or include prohibitions that are invalid as undue infringements of free speech in particular circumstances. Correlatively, ABA Model Rules of Professional Conduct, Rule 3.6 (1983) specifies categories of "safe harbor" statements that may be made to the media by an advocate, without regard to their possibly prejudicial effect in the circumstances. Unless prohibited by a specific court order, a lawyer statement falling within such a "safe harbor" provision does not violate this Section. As ABA Model Rule 3.6 recognizes, statements beyond those listed are also permissible unless they fall within the prohibitions of the rule. Similarly, a 1994 amendment to ABA Model Rule 3.6 recognizes, in words similar to those in Subsection (1), the right of a lawyer to make corrective public statements necessary to combat recent publicity prejudicial to the lawyer's client, so long as the lawyer or the lawyer's client is not the source of the prejudicial publicity.

* * *

e.   Prosecutors and other government lawyers. Lawyers who serve as prosecutors or otherwise as government lawyers have significantly diminished free-expression rights to comment publicly on matters in which they are officially involved as advocates. Accordingly, prohibitions against pretrial and trial comment by such lawyers can be more extensive. When the position of the governmental lawyer is filled by popular election, restriction may be particularly necessary to prevent improper extrajudicial comment made for vote-getting purposes. In all events, prosecutors must observe the heightened limitations on extrajudicial comment stated in Subsection (2).

* * *

TOPIC 2.   LIMITS ON ADVOCACY

* * *

§ 110.   Frivolous Advocacy

(1) A lawyer may not bring or defend a proceeding or assert or controvert an issue therein, unless there is a

basis for doing so that is not frivolous, which includes a good-faith argument for an extension, modification, or reversal of existing law.

(2) Notwithstanding Subsection (1), a lawyer for the defendant in a criminal proceeding or the respondent in a proceeding that could result in incarceration may so defend the proceeding as to require that the prosecutor establish every necessary element.

(3) A lawyer may not make a frivolous discovery request, fail to make a reasonably diligent effort to comply with a proper discovery request of another party, or intentionally fail otherwise to comply with applicable procedural requirements concerning discovery.

Comment:

* * *

b.   Rationale. Frivolous advocacy inflicts distress, wastes time, and causes increased expense to the tribunal and adversaries and may achieve results for a client that are unjust. Nonetheless, disciplinary enforcement against frivolous litigation is rare. Most bar disciplinary agencies rely on the courts in which litigation occurs to deal with abuse. Tribunals usually sanction only extreme abuse. Administration and interpretation of prohibitions against frivolous litigation should be tempered by concern to avoid overenforcement.

c.   Procedural sanction against unfounded assertions in litigation. Procedural rules modeled on Rule 11 of the Federal Rules of Civil Procedure impose affirmative obligations going beyond a requirement of minimally plausible position. In addition, courts have inherent power to impose sanctions against frivolous or otherwise abusive litigation tactics (see generally § 1, Comment *b*).

Such procedural rules generally have four elements, although jurisdictions differ on particulars. First, a lawyer may file a pleading, motion, or other paper only after making an inquiry about facts and law that is reasonable in the circumstances. Second, the lawyer's conclusions as to the facts and law must meet an objective, minimal standard of supportability. Third, litigation measures may not be taken for an improper purpose, even in instances in which they are otherwise minimally supportable. Finally, remedies provided for violations may include sanctions such as fee shifting, which in appropriate cases may be imposed directly on an offending lawyer (see Comment *g*).

Federal Rule 11 and corresponding state procedural rules generally are applicable only to positions asserted in writings signed by a lawyer, such as a pleading or motion. Other sources of law may extend a court's power to other activities of an advocate. For example, in the federal system, § 1927 of Title 28 of the United States Code prohibits actions of a lawyer, not limited to writings, that unduly multiply proceedings. A similar authority is conferred on federal appellate courts under Federal Rule of Appellate Procedure 38. Many courts also recognize a residual inherent power to impose sanctions on lawyers for bad-faith litigation. Detailed consideration of Federal Rule 11 and similar procedural rules is beyond the scope of this Restatement.

d. Frivolous positions in litigation. A frivolous position is one that a lawyer of ordinary competence would recognize as so lacking in merit that there is no substantial possibility that the tribunal would accept it. A nonfrivolous argument includes a good-faith argument for an extension, modification, or reversal of existing law. Whether good faith exists depends on such factors as whether the lawyer in question or another lawyer established a precedent adverse to the position being argued (and, if so, whether the lawyer disclosed that precedent), whether new legal grounds of plausible weight can be advanced, whether new or additional authority supports the lawyer's position, or whether for other reasons, such as a change in the composition of a multi-member court, arguments can be advanced that have a substantially greater chance of success.

* * *

§ 111. Disclosure of Legal Authority

In representing a client in a matter before a tribunal, a lawyer may not knowingly:

(1) make a false statement of a material proposition of law to the tribunal; or

(2) fail to disclose to the tribunal legal authority in the controlling jurisdiction known to the lawyer to be directly adverse to the position asserted by the client and not disclosed by opposing counsel.

Comment:

* * *

b. An advocate's false statement of law. Tribunals must be able to rely upon advocates for reasonably accurate statements of law. No worthwhile purpose is served by permitting misstatements of law. The rule of the Section prohibits direct misstatement, such as misquotation of precedent or asserting the existence of authority known to have been repealed. The rule also prohibits implicit misrepresentations, such as making an apparently complete recital of relevant authorities but omitting an adverse decision that should be considered by the tribunal for a fair determination of the point.

   c. *An advocate's duty to disclose adverse legal authority.* Subsection (2) states the rule requiring an advocate to disclose adverse legal authority in defined circumstances. Failure to do so may have the same effect as a misstatement of the law (cf. Subsection (1)). It deprives the court of useful information and serves no interest of the client other than obtaining a result not provided for by the law. It is sometimes argued that the rule requires the advocate to act against the client's interest and that it draws a dubious distinction between legal authority and facts. (Facts unknown to an adversary generally need not be disclosed, even if they are critical to the outcome (see § 120, Comment *b;* but cf., e.g., § 97, Comment *h*).) However, the advocate's role is to present the client's cause within the framework of the law, which requires common terms of legal reference with the court and opposing counsel.

   A lawyer need not cite all relevant and adverse legal authority; citation of principal or representative "directly adverse" legal authorities suffices. In determining what authority is "directly adverse," a lawyer must follow the jurisprudence of the court before which the legal argument is being made. In most jurisdictions, such legal authority includes all decisions with holdings directly on point, but it does not include dicta.

   When relying on a statute or regulation, a lawyer is similarly required by Subsection (2) to indicate when it has been amended or otherwise substantially limited by subsequent legislation or declared invalid or given a substantial narrowing construction by an authoritative court ruling or interpretative regulation. The lawyer may, of course, challenge the soundness of the adverse authority, attempt to distinguish it, or present other reasons why it should not be followed (see § 110).

* * *

   d. *"Adverse legal authority" in the "controlling jurisdiction."* "Legal authority" includes case-law precedents as well as statutes, ordinances, and administrative regulations. Legal authority is within the "controlling jurisdiction" according to the established hierarchy of legal authority in the federal system. In a matter governed by state law, it is the relevant state law as indicated by the established hierarchy of law within that state, taking into account, if applicable, conflict-of-laws rules. Ordinarily, it does not include decisions of courts of coordinate jurisdiction. In a federal district court, for example, a decision of another district court or of the court of appeals from another circuit would not ordinarily be considered authority from the controlling jurisdiction by the sitting tribunal. However, in those jurisdictions in which a decision of a court of coordinate jurisdiction is controlling, such a decision is subject to the rule of the Section.

* * *

§ 112. Advocacy in Ex Parte and Other Proceedings

In representing a client in a matter before a tribunal, a lawyer applying for ex parte relief or appearing in another proceeding in which similar special requirements of candor apply must comply with the requirements of § 110 and §§ 118–120 and further:

(1) must not present evidence the lawyer reasonably believes is false;

(2) must disclose all material and relevant facts known to the lawyer that will enable the tribunal to reach an informed decision; and

(3) must comply with any other applicable special requirements of candor imposed by law.

Comment:

* * *

b. Required disclosure in an ex parte proceeding. An ex parte proceeding is an exception to the customary methods of bilateral presentation in the adversary system. A potential for abuse is inherent in applying to a tribunal in absence of an adversary. That potential is partially redressed by special obligations on a lawyer presenting a matter ex parte.

* * *

To the extent the rule of this Section requires a lawyer to disclose confidential client information, disclosure is required by law within the meaning of § 62. On the other hand, the rule of the Section does not require the disclosure of privileged evidence.

c. Other proceedings requiring a special degree of candor. In some special proceedings, public policy requires unusual candor from an advocate. The candor required is determined by the legal requirements applicable to such a proceeding. In some jurisdictions, for example, unusual candor is required in proceedings seeking custody of a child, in applications for the involuntary commitment of a person for

273

mental disability, and in reports by trustees or executors. Similarly, a lawyer representing a class in a class action has duties of care toward the class and may be taking a position that requires an informed decision by the tribunal. In such circumstances (as in an application for a fee to be awarded out of the class recovery), the lawyer must disclose information necessary for the tribunal to make an adequately informed decision. That may be particularly true where the lawyer's position is supported by the opposing party, as following a settlement agreement between the parties.

* * *

TOPIC 3. ADVOCATES AND TRIBUNALS

* * *

§ 113. Improperly Influencing a Judicial Officer

(1) A lawyer may not knowingly communicate ex parte with a judicial officer before whom a proceeding is pending concerning the matter, except as authorized by law.

(2) A lawyer may not make a gift or loan prohibited by law to a judicial officer, attempt to influence the officer otherwise than by legally proper procedures, or state or imply an ability so to influence a judicial officer.

Comment:

* * *

b. Rationale. Ex parte communication with a judicial official before whom a matter is pending violates the right of the opposing party to a fair hearing and may constitute a violation of the due-process rights of the absent party. A communication made secretly may not withstand scrutiny. Ex parte communication also threatens to embarrass the parties' relationship with the judicial officer, requiring the officer either improperly to acquiesce in the conduct or to make a censorious response.

c. Prohibited ex parte communications. An ex parte communication is one that concerns the matter, that is between a lawyer representing a client and a judicial officer, and that occurs outside of the presence and without the consent of other parties to the litigation or their representatives. A written communication to a judicial officer with a copy sent timely to opposing parties or their lawyers is not ex parte. The prohibition applies to communication about the merits of the cause and to communications about a procedural matter the resolution of which will provide the party making the communication substantial tactical or strategic advantage. The prohibition does not apply to routine and customary communications for the purpose of scheduling a hearing or similar communications, but does apply to communications for the purpose of having a matter assigned to a particular court or judge.

The prohibition applies regardless of who initiates the communication and whether it occurs in person or over the telephone, through mail or electronic communication, or directly or through a third person, such as the lawyer's client. If a judicial officer initiates an impermissible ex parte communication with an advocate, the advocate must refuse to continue the communication. However, the form of communication may be important in determining whether the lawyer was aware that it was ex parte. The prohibition becomes effective when the lawyer knows that the judicial officer has assumed or will assume any responsibility in the matter and continues until responsibility is terminated. Thus, communication in knowing anticipation of a proceeding also violates the rule of this Section.

d. The officers covered by the prohibition against ex parte communications. The prohibition applies to a judge, master, hearing officer, arbitrator, or other officer authorized to rule upon evidence or argument about a disputed matter. It also applies to other officials who have decisionmaking authority in the litigation, such as a jury commissioner or a clerk with responsibility to assign cases to judges. It also applies to indirect communications, as through a judge's clerk. Ex parte communications with officials with decisionmaking authority in nonadjudicative matters, such as a legislator or the policymaking head of a government department, are frequently the subject of professional and regulatory restrictions. Such communications are beyond the scope of this Restatement.

e. Permissible ex parte communications. A lawyer is authorized to communicate with a judicial officer ex parte when doing so is permitted by law. For example, if applicable law so provides, a lawyer may seek a temporary restraining order without notice to the opposing party. On the special obligation of candor in making such applications, see § 112. Law permits some ex parte presentations not to be revealed to an opposing party. For example, a lawyer claiming that a communication is protected from disclosure by a privilege may be permitted to submit the contested material for in camera review by a judicial officer (see § 86, Comment *f*). A request for a search warrant is made ex parte for reasons of surprise and security; the application, if successful, will typically result in a prompt opportunity to challenge the warrant. In an emergency involving a matter of vital importance, such as a threat to the life or safety of the presiding officer, a juror, or a witness, necessary communication may be made without notice.

* * *

§ 114. A Lawyer's Statements Concerning a Judicial Officer

A lawyer may not knowingly or recklessly make publicly a false statement of fact concerning the qualifications or integrity of an incumbent of a judicial office or a candidate for election to such an office.

Comment:

[a. *Scope and cross-references.*]

* * *

Within the meaning of this Section, a judicial officer includes any person engaged in adjudicating disputes, including a judge, hearing officer, magistrate, or similar official.

b. *Rationale.* Lawyers are specially situated to assess the official performance of judges and other judicial and legal officers. Accordingly, both constitutional law and sound social policy require that lawyers have broad latitude in criticizing such officers. Under the rule of New York Times v. Sullivan, 376 U.S. 254, 84 S.Ct. 710, 11 L.Ed.2d 686 (1964), and its progeny, judges and other public legal officers are "public officials," so that an action by a judge or public legal officer against a lawyer for damages for defamation would require a showing of actual malice. Similar considerations should also lead to application of the standard in *New York Times v. Sullivan* in lawyer-discipline cases.

* * *

§ 115. Lawyer Contact with a Juror

A lawyer may not:

(1) except as allowed by law, communicate with or seek to influence a person known by the lawyer to be a member of a jury pool from which the jury will be drawn;

(2) except as allowed by law, communicate with or seek to influence a member of a jury; or

(3) communicate with a juror who has been excused from further service:

(a) when that would harass the juror or constitute an attempt to influence the juror's actions as a juror in future cases; or

(b) when otherwise prohibited by law.

Comment:

* * *

b. Communication with a prospective juror. The rules concerning jury trial undertake to ensure that no juror will have a predisposition toward either party. Prohibition of pretrial communication with prospective jurors both prevents improper influence and avoids the necessity of inquiry concerning such contacts.

c. Communication with a juror during sitting. A lawyer involved in a jury trial properly has extensive communication with members of a jury during the trial through contact that is closely regulated. As provided in Subsection (2), a lawyer may not otherwise communicate with or seek to influence sitting jurors except as allowed by law. As with the prohibition against ex parte communication with a judicial officer (see § 113, Comment *c*), a lawyer is required to refuse communication with a juror who attempts to initiate it.

d. Posttrial communication with a juror. In some jurisdictions, a lawyer is permitted to interview jurors after they have completed service. Other jurisdictions forbid all posttrial interviews except pursuant to court supervision. Subsection (3) requires a lawyer to comply with such requirements. In any event, a lawyer must not harass the juror or attempt to influence the person as a juror in a future proceeding.

e. Jury tampering. Subsections (1) and (2) prohibit unlawful attempts to influence a juror or prospective member of a jury, such as through bribery or coercion.

* * *

TOPIC 4. ADVOCATES AND EVIDENCE

* * *

§ 116. Interviewing and Preparing a Prospective Witness

(1) A lawyer may interview a witness for the purpose of preparing the witness to testify.

(2) A lawyer may not unlawfully obstruct another party's access to a witness.

(3) A lawyer may not unlawfully induce or assist a prospective witness to evade or ignore process obliging the witness to appear to testify.

(4) A lawyer may not request a person to refrain from voluntarily giving relevant testimony or information to another party, unless:

> (a) the person is the lawyer's client in the matter; or

> (b) (i) the person is not the lawyer's client but is a relative or employee or other agent of the lawyer or the lawyer's client, and (ii) the lawyer reasonably believes compliance will not materially and adversely affect the person's interests.

Comment:

* * *

b.   Preparing a witness to testify. Under litigation practice uniformly followed in the United States, a lawyer may interview prospective witnesses prior to their testifying. A prospective witness is generally under no obligation to submit to such an interview. As a practical matter, rules requiring inquiry to support factual allegations in a complaint or other document (see § 110, Comment *c*) may require a lawyer to interview witnesses to gain the necessary factual foundation. Competent preparation for trial (see generally § 52(1)) (general negligence standard might also require pre-testimonial interviews with witnesses).

* * *

In preparing a witness to testify, a lawyer may invite the witness to provide truthful testimony favorable to the lawyer's client. Preparation consistent with the rule of this Section may include the following: discussing the role of the witness and effective courtroom demeanor; discussing the witness's recollection and probable testimony; revealing to the witness other testimony or evidence that will be presented and asking the witness to reconsider the witness's recollection or recounting of events in that light; discussing the applicability of law to the events in issue; reviewing the factual context into which the witness's observations or opinions will fit; reviewing documents or other physical evidence that may be introduced; and discussing probable lines of hostile cross-examination that the witness should be prepared to meet. Witness preparation may include rehearsal of testimony. A lawyer may suggest choice of words that might be employed to make the

278

witness's meaning clear. However, a lawyer may not assist the witness to testify falsely as to a material fact (see § 120(1)(a)).

c. Obstructing another party's access to a witness. Except as stated in Subsection (4) and discussed in Comment *e,* a lawyer generally may not attempt to prevent a witness from being interviewed by another party. The rule applies whether the interview would produce testimony favorable to the party or otherwise. A lawyer may not offer threats or financial or other inducements to a witness not to cooperate with another party. However, a lawyer is under no obligation to reveal the identity or probable testimony of a potential witness except as required by rules governing pretrial discovery or by other law.

The rule of Subsection (2) is limited to attempts to obstruct access to a witness "unlawfully." In limited circumstances, such obstruction may be lawful. For example, a prosecutor may be legally entitled to place an eligible person in a witness-protection program.

d. Inducing or assisting a witness to evade or ignore a subpoena or similar process. A lawyer may not attempt unlawfully to induce a witness to ignore a subpoena or similar order to appear for testimony or unlawfully counsel the witness to evade service of the order, as by leaving the jurisdiction or hiding out (see generally § 105). Misleading a witness for the purpose of inducing the witness not to provide testimony is also wrongful.

A lawyer may advise a client to resist testifying on any nonfrivolous ground (see § 110), if doing so is in the client's interest. A lawyer for a party may properly inform a nonclient witness of the right to resist an unlawful order to testify, the privilege against self-incrimination, or other basis for objection to testifying, but the lawyer may not attempt unlawfully to persuade the nonclient witness not to testify on those or other grounds. Such activities may constitute the crime of obstruction of justice or a similar offense. In communicating with a prospective witness, a lawyer must also observe limitations on dealings with an unrepresented person (see § 99).

e. Requesting a person not to cooperate with another party. A lawyer may inform any person of the right not to be interviewed by any other party, but a lawyer may not request that a person exercise that right or attempt otherwise to induce noncooperation, except as permitted under Subsection (4). A lawyer may also advise of the right to insist on conditions, such as that the lawyer or the person's own lawyer be present during any interview or that the interview be recorded. It is also permissible in the course of preparing a friendly witness for testimony at a deposition or hearing (see Comment *b* hereto) to warn the witness not to volunteer testimony not directly responsive to a question.

Only in the circumstances stated in Subsection (4) may a lawyer seek to have a witness refrain from voluntarily giving relevant information to another party. A lawyer may properly demand that a person who is not otherwise excepted from the Subsection observe a legal obligation of confidentiality to the lawyer's client. For example, a physician or member of the clergy who is considered to be an independent contractor may nonetheless owe a legal duty of confidentiality to the client, which the client's lawyer may properly insist that the person observe.

* * *

§ 117. Compensating a Witness

A lawyer may not offer or pay to a witness any consideration:

(1) in excess of the reasonable expenses of the witness incurred and the reasonable value of the witness's time spent in providing evidence, except that an expert witness may be offered and paid a noncontingent fee;

(2) contingent on the content of the witness's testimony or the outcome of the litigation; or

(3) otherwise prohibited by law.

Comment:

* * *

b. *Reasonable payments to a witness.* A lawyer may pay a witness or prospective witness the reasonable expenses incurred by the witness in providing evidence. Such expenses may include the witness's reasonable expenses of travel to the place of a deposition or hearing or to the place of consultation with the lawyer and for reasonable out-of-pocket expenses, such as for hotel, meals, or child care. Under Subsection (1), a lawyer may also compensate a witness for the reasonable value of the witness's time or for expenses actually incurred in preparation for and giving testimony, such as lost wages caused by the witness's absence from employment.

* * *

As stated in Subsections (2) and (3), the offer or payment of allowable expenses may not be contingent on the content of the witness's testimony or the outcome of the litigation or otherwise prohibited by law. In some jurisdictions, a witness need not obey a subpoena unless tendered statutory witness fees and travel expenses.

c.   Compensating an expert witness. A fee paid an expert witness may not be contingent on the content of the witness's testimony or the result in the litigation. On a lawyer's liability for an expert's fee, see § 30(2)(b). On a lawyer's advancing the costs of litigation, see § 36(2). An opposing party may inquire into the fee paid to an expert or other witness in order to impeach the testimony of the witness. The prohibition against contingent compensation does not apply to an expert retained only to consult and not to testify or otherwise provide evidence.

d.   The prohibition against a contingent fee to a witness. A witness may not be bribed or offered compensation that is contingent on the witness's testimony or the result in the litigation. If a necessary witness in a case is also serving as advocate with a contingent-fee arrangement with a party, the lawyer is subject to possible disqualification as counsel because of the lawyer's status as witness (see § 108).

* * *

§ **118.**   Falsifying or Destroying Evidence

(1) **A lawyer may not falsify documentary or other evidence.**

(2) **A lawyer may not destroy or obstruct another party's access to documentary or other evidence when doing so would violate a court order or other legal requirements, or counsel or assist a client to do so.**

Comment:

[*a.   Scope and cross-references.*]

* * *

For purposes of Subsection (2), "evidence" is usually defined as documentary or other physical material (including material stored in electronically retrievable form) that a reasonable lawyer would understand may be relevant to an official proceeding. It does not include exhibits and the like that an advocate or client constructs for illustrative purposes at a proceeding, even if the exhibit would be regarded as evidence for some other purpose.

b.   Falsifying documentary and other evidence. Advocates in the adversary system are primarily responsible for assembling documentary and other evidence to be presented. A lawyer thereby may serve as custodian of evidentiary material, which ordinarily should reach the proceeding in its original condition. A lawyer may not alter such material in any way that impairs its evidentiary value for other parties. Rules of procedure may permit alteration of evidence in the course of reasonable scientific tests by experts.

A lawyer may not forge a document or alter a document with the purpose of misleading another, such as by back-dating the document, removing the document to another file to create a false impression of its provenance, deleting or adding language or other characters to the document so as to alter its effect, or materially changing its physical appearance.

A document, such as an affidavit or declaration, prepared by a lawyer for verification by another person must include only factual statements that the lawyer reasonably believes the person would make if testifying in person before the factfinder. On a submission to a tribunal based on the lawyer's personal knowledge, such as the lawyer's own affidavit or declaration, see § 120.

    c. Destroying documentary or other physical evidence. Unlawful destruction or concealment of documents or other evidence during or in anticipation of litigation may subvert fair and full exposition of the facts. On the other hand, it would be intolerable to require retention of all documents and other evidence against the possibility that an adversary in future litigation would wish to examine them. Accordingly, it is presumptively lawful to act pursuant to an established document retention-destruction program that conforms to existing law and is consistently followed, absent a supervening obligation such as a subpoena or other lawful demand for or order relating to the material. On a lawyer's advice to a client on such matters as document retention or suppression, see generally § 94. If the client informs the lawyer that the client intends to destroy a document unlawfully or in violation of a court order, the lawyer must not advise or assist the client to do so (id.).

It may be difficult under applicable criminal law to define the point at which legitimate destruction becomes unlawful obstruction of justice. Under criminal law, a lawyer generally is subject to constraints no different from those imposed on others. Obstruction of justice and similar statutes generally apply only when an official proceeding is ongoing or imminent. For example, The American Law Institute Model Penal Code § 241.7 (1985) provides that the offense of tampering with or fabricating physical evidence occurs only if "an official proceeding or investigation is pending or about to be instituted.…"

A lawyer may not destroy evidence or conceal or alter it when a discovery demand, subpoena, or court order has directed the lawyer or the lawyer's client to turn over the evidence. Difficult questions of interpretation can arise with respect to destruction of documents in anticipation of a subpoena or similar process that has not yet issued at the time of destruction. For example, a company manufacturing a product that may cause injuries in the future is not, in the absence of specific prohibition, prohibited from destroying all manufacturing records after a period of time; but difficult questions of interpretation of obstruction-of-justice statutes may arise concerning such practices as culling incriminating documents while leaving others in place. No general statement can accurately describe the legality of record destruction; statutes and decisions in the particular jurisdiction must be consulted. In many jurisdictions, there is no applicable precedent. Legality may turn on such factual questions as the state of mind of the client or a lawyer.

Particular statutes and regulations may impose special obligations to retain records and files and to make them accessible to governmental officials. Procedural law or a tribunal ruling may impose other or additional obligations. For example, a lawyer may not knowingly withhold a document that has been properly requested in discovery unless the lawyer does so in procedurally proper form (see § 110, Comment *e*). Conversely, a lawyer responding to a request for discovery of documents may not mix responsive and nonresponsive documents together in a way designed to obstruct detection of responsive documents (see id.).

Some jurisdictions have recognized an action for damages by a litigant who suffers loss from "spoliation"—an opposing party's or lawyer's unwarranted and injurious suppression of evidence. In some jurisdictions, an unfavorable evidentiary inference may be drawn from failure to produce material that was at one time in the possession and under the control of a party to litigation. The inference may be invoked even in circumstances in which destruction is otherwise lawful. Section 51 does not provide for a lawyer's liability to a nonclient for negligence in such a situation. Falsification or unlawful destruction of evidence may also constitute contempt or may be subject to the tribunal's inherent power to impose a suitable sanction (see § 1, Comment *c*).

* * *

§ 119. Physical Evidence of a Client Crime

With respect to physical evidence of a client crime, a lawyer:

(1) may, when reasonably necessary for purposes of the representation, take possession of the evidence and retain it for the time reasonably necessary to examine it and subject it to tests that do not alter or destroy material characteristics of the evidence; but

(2) following possession under Subsection (1), the lawyer must notify prosecuting authorities of the lawyer's possession of the evidence or turn the evidence over to them.

Comment:

[*a. Scope and cross-references.*]

* * *

This Section applies to evidence of a client crime, contraband, weapons, and similar implements used in an offense. It also includes such material as documents and material in electronically retrievable form used by the client to plan the offense, documents used in the course of a mail-fraud violation, or transaction documents evidencing a crime.

* * *

b. Physical evidence of a client crime; retention for reasonably necessary examination. As stated in Subsection (1), a lawyer may legitimately need to possess evidence relating to a crime for the purpose of examining it to prepare a defense. A lawyer has the same privilege as prosecutors to possess and examine such material for the lawful purpose of assisting in the trial of criminal cases. Such an examination may include scientific tests, so long as they do not alter or destroy the value of the evidence for possible use by the prosecution. So long as the lawyer's possession is for that purpose, criminal laws that generally prohibit possession of contraband or other evidence of crimes are inapplicable to the lawyer. Nonetheless, possession of such material otherwise than in strict compliance with the requirements stated in this Section may subject the lawyer to risk of prosecution as an accessory after the fact for accepting evidence that might otherwise be found. A lawyer's office may also thereby be subject to search. In dealing with such evidence, a lawyer may not unlawfully alter, destroy, or conceal it (see § 118). On the prohibition against advising or assisting another person, including the client, to do so, see § 94.

c. Disposition of evidence of a client crime. Once a lawyer's reasonable need for examination of evidence of a client crime has been satisfied, a lawyer's responsibilities with respect to further possession of the evidence are determined under the criminal law and the law affecting confidentiality of client information (see generally Chapter 5). Under the general criminal law, physical evidence of a client crime in possession of the lawyer may not be retained to a point at which its utility as evidence for the prosecution is significantly impaired, such as by waiting until after the trial.

Some decisions have alluded to an additional option—returning the evidence to the site from which it was taken, when that can be accomplished without destroying or altering material characteristics of the evidence. That will often be impossible. The option would also be unavailable when the lawyer reasonably should know that the client or another person will intentionally alter or destroy the evidence.

Evidence subject to this Section will come to the attention of the authorities either through being turned over by the lawyer to them or through notification by the lawyer or another. In the latter case, the authorities may obtain the evidence from the lawyer by proper process. The prosecution and defense should make appropriate arrangements for introduction and authentication of the evidence at trial. Because of the risk of prejudice to the client, that should be done without improperly revealing the source of the evidence to the finder of fact. The parties may also agree that the tribunal may instruct the jury, without revealing the lawyer's involvement, that an appropriate chain of possession links the evidence to the place where it was located before coming into the lawyer's possession. In the absence of agreement to such an instruction by the defense, the prosecutor may offer evidence of the lawyer's possession if necessary to establish the chain of possession.

* * *

§ 120. False Testimony or Evidence

(1) A lawyer may not:

(a) knowingly counsel or assist a witness to testify falsely or otherwise to offer false evidence;

(b) knowingly make a false statement of fact to the tribunal;

(c) offer testimony or other evidence as to an issue of fact known by the lawyer to be false.

(2) If a lawyer has offered testimony or other evidence as to a material issue of fact and comes to know of its falsity, the lawyer must take reasonable remedial measures and may disclose confidential client information when necessary to take such a measure.

(3) A lawyer may refuse to offer testimony or other evidence that the lawyer reasonably believes is false, even if the lawyer does not know it to be false.

Comment:

* * *

b. Rationale. An advocate seeks to achieve the client's objectives (see § 16(1)) but in doing so may not distort factfinding by the tribunal by knowingly offering false testimony or other evidence.

* * *

The procedural rules concerning burden of proof allocate responsibility for bringing forward evidence. A lawyer might know of testimony or other evidence vital to the other party, but unknown to that party or their advocate. The advocate who knows of the evidence, and who has complied with applicable rules concerning pretrial discovery and other applicable disclosure requirements (see, e.g, § 118), has no legal obligation to reveal the evidence, even though the proceeding thereby may fail to ascertain the facts as the lawyer knows them.

c. A lawyer's knowledge. A lawyer's obligations under Subsection (2) depend on what the lawyer knows and, in the case of Subsection (3), on what the lawyer reasonably believes (see Comment *j*). A lawyer's knowledge may be inferred from the circumstances. Actual knowledge does not include unknown information, even if a reasonable lawyer would have discovered it through inquiry. However, a lawyer may not ignore what is plainly apparent, for example, by refusing to read a document (see § 94, Comment *g*). A lawyer should not conclude that testimony is or will be false unless there is a firm factual basis for doing so. Such a basis exists when facts known to the lawyer or the client's own statements indicate to the lawyer that the testimony or other evidence is false.

d. Offer of false testimony or other false evidence. False testimony includes testimony that a lawyer knows to be false and testimony from a witness who the lawyer knows is only guessing or reciting what the witness has been instructed to say. This Section employs the terms "false testimony" and "false evidence" rather than "perjury" because the latter term defines a crime, which may require elements not relevant for application of the requirements of the Section in other contexts. For example, although a witness who testifies in good faith but contrary to fact lacks the mental state necessary for the crime of perjury, the rule of the Section nevertheless applies to a lawyer who knows that such testimony is false. When a lawyer is charged with the criminal offense of suborning perjury, the more limited definition appropriate to the criminal offense applies.

A lawyer's responsibility for false evidence extends to testimony or other evidence in aid of the lawyer's client offered or similarly sponsored by the lawyer. The responsibility extends to any false testimony elicited by the lawyer, as well as such testimony elicited by another lawyer questioning the lawyer's own client, another witness favorable to the lawyer's client, or a witness whom the lawyer has substantially prepared to testify (see § 116(1)). A lawyer has no responsibility to correct false testimony or other evidence offered by an opposing party or witness. Thus, a plaintiff's lawyer, aware that an adverse witness being examined by the defendant's lawyer is giving false evidence favorable to the plaintiff, is not required to correct it (compare Comment *e*). However, the lawyer may not attempt to reinforce the false evidence, such as by arguing to the factfinder that the false evidence should be accepted as true or otherwise sponsoring or supporting the false evidence (see also Comment *e*).

Illustrations:

1.   Lawyer, representing Defendant, knows that a contract between Plaintiff's decedent and Defendant had been superseded by a materially revised version that was executed and retained by Defendant. Plaintiff's Counsel is unaware of the revised contract and has failed to seek information about it in discovery. At trial, Lawyer elicits testimony from Defendant by inquiring about "the contract that you and Plaintiff's decedent signed" and presents Defendant with the original contract, asking, "Is this the contract that you and Plaintiff's decedent signed?" Defendant responds affirmatively. Lawyer has violated Subsection (1)(c).

* * *

e.   Counseling or assisting a witness to offer false testimony or other false evidence. A lawyer may not knowingly counsel or assist a witness to testify falsely or otherwise to offer false evidence as to a material issue of fact (Subsection (1)(a)). With respect to the right of a criminal defendant to testify and application of the rule to criminal-defense counsel, see Comment *i* hereto. If a lawyer knows that a witness will provide truthful evidence as to some matters but false evidence as to others, the lawyer must not elicit the false evidence. On affirmative remedial steps that a lawyer must take when a lawyer knows that a witness has offered false evidence, see Comment *h*.

* * *

The prohibitions against false evidence address matters offered in aid of the lawyer's client (see Comment *d*). It is not a violation to elicit from an adversary witness evidence known by the lawyer to be false and apparently adverse to the lawyer's client. The lawyer may have sound tactical reasons for doing so, such as eliciting false testimony for the purpose of later demonstrating its falsity to discredit the witness. Requiring premature disclosure could, under some circumstances, aid the witness in explaining away false testimony or recasting it into a more plausible form.

Illustration:

4. Lawyer, representing Plaintiff, takes the deposition of Witness, who describes the occurrence in question in a way unfavorable to Plaintiff. From other evidence, Lawyer knows that Witness is testifying falsely. Subsequently, the case is settled, and Lawyer never discloses the false nature of Witness's deposition testimony. Lawyer's conduct does not violate this Section.

f. A lawyer's statement of fact to a tribunal. A lawyer may make a submission to a tribunal based on the lawyer's personal knowledge, such as the lawyer's own affidavit or declaration or a representation made on the lawyer's own knowledge. For example, the lawyer may state during a scheduling conference that a conflict exists in the lawyer's trial schedule or state on appeal that certain evidence appears of record. In such statements the lawyer purports to convey information based on personal knowledge. A tribunal or another party should be able to rely on such a statement. Such a statement must have a reasonable basis for belief.

* * *

For the purpose of Subsection (1)(b) a knowing false statement of fact includes a statement on which the lawyer then has insufficient information from which reasonably to conclude that the statement is accurate. A lawyer may make conditional or suppositional statements so long as they are so identified and are neither known to be false nor made without a reasonable basis in fact for their conditional or suppositional character.

* * *

For purposes of professional discipline, the lawyer codes prohibit a lawyer from making only a false statement of "material" fact. A similar condition attaches to the crime of perjury (although often not to the related crime of false swearing or false statements.) However, other procedural or substantive rules may contain no such qualification.

g.   *Remonstrating with a client or witness.* Before taking other steps, a lawyer ordinarily must confidentially remonstrate with the client or witness not to present false evidence or to correct false evidence already presented. Doing so protects against possibly harsher consequences. The form and content of such a remonstration is a matter of judgment. The lawyer must attempt to be persuasive while maintaining the client's trust in the lawyer's loyalty and diligence. If the client insists on offering false evidence, the lawyer must inform the client of the lawyer's duty not to offer false evidence and, if it is offered, to take appropriate remedial action (see Comment *h*).

h.   *Reasonable remedial measures.* A lawyer who has taken appropriate steps to avoid offering false evidence (see Comment *g*) may be required to take additional measures. A lawyer may be surprised by unexpected false evidence given by a witness or may come to know of its falsity only after it has been offered.

If the lawyer's client or the witness refuses to correct the false testimony (see Comment *g*), the lawyer must take steps reasonably calculated to remove the false impression that the evidence may have made on the finder of fact (Subsection (2)). Alternatively, a lawyer could seek a recess and attempt to persuade the witness to correct the false evidence (see Comment *g*). If such steps are unsuccessful, the lawyer must take other steps, such as by moving or stipulating to have the evidence stricken or otherwise withdrawn, or recalling the witness if the witness had already left the stand when the lawyer comes to know of the falsity. Once the false evidence is before the finder of fact, it is not a reasonable remedial measure for the lawyer simply to withdraw from the representation, even if the presiding officer permits withdrawal (see Comment *k* hereto). If no other remedial measure corrects the falsity, the lawyer must inform the opposing party or tribunal of the falsity so that they may take corrective steps.

To the extent necessary in taking reasonable remedial measures under Subsection (2), a lawyer may use or reveal otherwise confidential client information (see § 63). However, the lawyer must proceed so that, consistent with carrying out the measures (including, if necessary, disclosure to the opposing party or tribunal), the lawyer causes the client minimal adverse effects. The lawyer has discretion as to which measures to adopt, so long as they are reasonably calculated to correct the false evidence. If the lawyer makes disclosure to the opposing party or tribunal, thereafter the lawyer must leave further steps to the opposing party or tribunal. Whether testimony concerning client-lawyer communications with respect to the false evidence can be elicited is determined under § 82 (crime-fraud exception to attorney-client privilege). The lawyer's disclosure may give rise to a conflict between the lawyer and client requiring the lawyer to withdraw from the representation (see Comment k hereto).

Responsibilities of a lawyer under this Section extend to the end of the proceeding in which the question of false evidence arises. Thus, a lawyer representing a client on appeal from a verdict in a trial continues to carry responsibilities with respect to false evidence offered at trial, particularly evidence discovered to be false after trial (see Comment i). If a lawyer is discharged by a client or withdraws, whether or not for reasons associated with the false evidence, the lawyer's obligations under this Section are not thereby terminated. In such an instance, a reasonable remedial measure may consist of disclosing the matter to successor counsel.

* * *

i. *False evidence in a criminal-defense representation.* The rules stated in the Section generally govern defense counsel in criminal cases. The requirement stated in Comment g with respect to remonstrating with a client may often be relevant. However, because of the right to the effective assistance of counsel, withdrawal (see Comment k) may be inappropriate in response to threatened client perjury in a criminal case. If defense counsel withdraws, normally it will be necessary for the accused to retain another lawyer or for the court to appoint one, unless the accused proceeds without counsel. Replacement counsel also may have to deal with the same client demand to take the stand to testify falsely. A tribunal may also be concerned that controversy over false evidence may be contrived to delay the proceeding. In criminal cases many courts thus are strongly inclined not to permit withdrawal of defense counsel, particularly if trial is underway or imminent. Withdrawal may be required, however, if the accused denies defense counsel's assertion that presentation of false evidence is threatened.

Some courts permit an accused in such circumstances to give "open narrative" testimony, without requiring defense counsel to take affirmative remedial action as required under Subsection (2). Defense counsel asks only a general question about the events, provides no guidance through additional questions, and does not refer to the false evidence in subsequent argument to the factfinder. Counsel does not otherwise indicate to the presiding officer or opposing counsel that the testimony or other evidence is false, although such indication may be necessary to deal with a prosecutor's objection to use of the open-narrative form of testimony. From the unusual format of examination, prosecutor and presiding officer are likely to understand that the accused is offering false testimony, but an unguided jury may be unaware of or confused about its significance. That solution is not consistent with the rule stated in Subsection (2) or with the requirements of the lawyer codes in most jurisdictions.

However, the defendant may still insist on giving false testimony despite defense counsel's efforts to persuade the defendant not to testify or to testify accurately (see Comment *g*). The accused has the constitutional rights to take the witness stand and to offer evidence in self-defense (see § 22). Unlike counsel in a civil case, who can refuse to call a witness (including a client) who will offer false evidence (see Comment *e*), defense counsel in a criminal case has no authority (beyond persuasion) to prevent a client-accused from taking the witness stand. (Defense counsel does possess that authority with respect to nonclient witnesses and must exercise it consistent with this Section (see § 23).) If the client nonetheless insists on the right to take the stand, defense counsel must accede to the demand of the accused to testify. Thereafter defense counsel may not ask the accused any question if counsel knows that the response would be false. Counsel must also be prepared to take remedial measures, including disclosure, in the event that the accused indeed testifies falsely (see Comment *h*).

In one situation, disclosure of client perjury to the tribunal may not be feasible. When a criminal case is being tried without a jury, informing the judge of perjury by an accused might be tantamount to informing the factfinder of the guilt of the accused. In such an instance, disclosure to the prosecutor might suffice as a remedial measure. The prosecutor may not refer in the judge's presence to the information provided by defense counsel under this Section.

* * *

k.   False evidence and the client-lawyer relationship. A lawyer's actions in accordance with this Section may impair the trust and respect that otherwise would exist between lawyer and client. A lawyer may be discharged by the client or withdraw from the representation (see § 32).

If a difference between lawyer and client over falsity occurs just before or during trial, a tribunal may refuse to permit a lawyer to withdraw when withdrawal would require the client to proceed without counsel (see § 32(4)).

* * *

291

CHAPTER 8

CONFLICTS OF INTEREST

---

* * *

TOPIC 1.   CONFLICTS OF INTEREST—IN GENERAL

* * *

§ 121. The Basic Prohibition of Conflicts of Interest

Unless all affected clients and other necessary persons consent to the representation under the limitations and conditions provided in § 122, a lawyer may not repre-

292

sent a client if the representation would involve a conflict of interest. A conflict of interest is involved if there is a substantial risk that the lawyer's representation of the client would be materially and adversely affected by the lawyer's own interests or by the lawyer's duties to another current client, a former client, or a third person.

Comment:

[*a. Scope and cross-references.*]

* * *

The Section refers to consent by clients "and other necessary persons" in view of the possible need for consent by nonclients, for example former clients under § 132 or persons who were never in a lawyer-client relationship with the lawyer under § 132, Comment *g(ii)*.

b. Rationale. The prohibition against lawyer conflicts of interest reflects several competing concerns. First, the law seeks to assure clients that their lawyers will represent them with undivided loyalty. A client is entitled to be represented by a lawyer whom the client can trust. Instilling such confidence is an objective important in itself. For example, the principle underlying the prohibition against a lawyer's filing suit against a present client in an unrelated matter (see § 128, Comment *e*) may also extend to situations, not involving litigation, in which significant impairment of a client's expectation of the lawyer's loyalty would be similarly likely. Contentious dealings, for example involving charges of bad faith against the client whom the lawyer represents in another matter would raise such a concern. So also would negotiating on behalf of one client when a large proportion of the lawyer's other client's net worth is at risk.

Second, the prohibition against conflicts of interest seeks to enhance the effectiveness of legal representation. To the extent that a conflict of interest undermines the independence of the lawyer's professional judgment or inhibits a lawyer from working with appropriate vigor in the client's behalf, the client's expectation of effective representation (see § 16) could be compromised.

Third, a client has a legal right to have the lawyer safeguard the client's confidential information (see § 60). Preventing use of confidential client information against the interests of the client, either to benefit the lawyer's personal interest, in aid of some other client, or to foster an assumed public purpose is facilitated through conflicts rules that reduce the opportunity for such abuse.

Fourth, conflicts rules help ensure that lawyers will not exploit clients, such as by inducing a client to make a gift to the lawyer (see § 127).

Finally, some conflict-of-interest rules protect interests of the legal system in obtaining adequate presentations to tribunals. In the absence of such rules, for example, a lawyer might appear on both sides of the litigation, complicating the process of taking proof and compromising adversary argumentation (see § 128).

On the other hand, avoiding conflicts of interest can impose significant costs on lawyers and clients. Prohibition of conflicts of interest should therefore be no broader than necessary. First, conflict avoidance can make representation more expensive. To the extent that conflict-of-interest rules prevent multiple clients from being represented by a single lawyer, one or both clients will be required to find other lawyers. That might entail uncertainty concerning the successor lawyers' qualifications, usually additional cost, and the inconvenience of separate representation. In matters in which individual claims are small, representation of multiple claimants might be required if the claims are effectively to be considered at all. Second, limitations imposed by conflicts rules can interfere with client expectations. At the very least, one of the clients might be deprived of the services of a lawyer whom the client had a particular reason to retain, perhaps on the basis of a long-time association with the lawyer. In some communities or fields of practice there might be no lawyer who is perfectly conflict-free. Third, obtaining informed consent to conflicted representation itself might compromise important interests. As discussed in § 122, consent to a conflict of interest requires that each affected client give consent based on adequate information. The process of obtaining informed consent is not only potentially time-consuming; it might also be impractical because it would require the disclosure of information that the clients would prefer not to have disclosed, for example, the subject matter about which they have consulted the lawyer. Fourth, conflicts prohibitions interfere with lawyers' own freedom to practice according to their own best judgment of appropriate professional behavior. It is appropriate to give significant weight to the freedom and professionalism of lawyers in the formulation of legal rules governing conflicts.

c. The general conflict-of-interest standard. The standard adopted in this Chapter answers the four questions to which any conflicts-of-interest standard must respond. Those are (i) What kind of effect is prohibited? (ii) How significant must the effect be? (iii) What probability must there be that the effect will occur? (iv) From whose perspective are conflicts of interest to be determined? The standard adopted here incorporates elements common to all three of the major lawyer codes developed in this century. It casts the answer to each question in terms of factual predicates and practical consequences that are reasonably susceptible of objective assessment by lawyers subject to the rules, by clients whom the rules affect, and by tribunals.

[*c(i). Prohibited effects.*]

* * *

"Adverse" effect relates to the quality of the representation, not necessarily the quality of the result obtained in a given case. The standard refers to the incentives faced by the lawyer before or during the representation because it often cannot be foretold what the actual result would have been if the representation had been conflict-free.

Illustration:

1.   Lawyer has been retained by A and B, each a competitor for a single broadcast license, to assist each of them in obtaining the license from Agency. Such work often requires advocacy by the lawyer for an applicant before Agency. Lawyer's representation will have an adverse effect on both A and B as that term is used in this Section. Even though either A or B might obtain the license and thus arguably not have been adversely affected by the joint representation, Lawyer will have duties to A that restrict Lawyer's ability to urge B's application and vice versa. In most instances, informed consent of both A and B would not suffice to allow the dual representation (see § 122).

* * *

c(iii). Likelihood of effect. There is no conflict of interest within the meaning of this Section unless there is a "substantial risk" that a material adverse effect will occur. In many cases the material adverse effect on the representation will be immediate, actual, and apparent. Other situations, however, might present a risk that is only potential or contingent. In this context, "substantial risk" means that in the circumstances the risk is significant and plausible, even if it is not certain or even probable that it will occur. The standard requires more than a mere possibility of adverse effect.

Illustration:

3.   Clients A and B have come to Lawyer for help in organizing a new business. Lawyer is satisfied that both clients are committed to forming the enterprise and that an agreement

can be prepared that will embody their common undertaking. Nonetheless, because a substantial risk of future conflict exists in any such arrangement, Lawyer must explain to the clients that because of future economic uncertainties inherent in any such undertaking, the clients' interests could differ in material ways in the future. Lawyer must obtain informed consent pursuant to § 122 before undertaking the common representation.

Some conflicts can be eliminated by an agreement limiting the scope of the lawyer's representation if the limitation can be given effect without rendering the remaining representation objectively inadequate (see § 19 & § 122, Comment *g(iv)*).

* * *

General antagonism between clients does not necessarily mean that a lawyer would be engaged in conflicted representations by representing the clients in separate, unrelated matters. A conflict for a lawyer ordinarily exists only when there is conflict in the interests of the clients that are involved in the matters being handled by the lawyer or when unrelated representations are of such a nature that the lawyer's relationship with one or both clients likely would be adversely affected.

Illustration:

5. For many years Law Firm has represented Bank in mortgage foreclosures and does so currently. Other lawyers in Law Firm have continuously represented Manufacturer as outside general counsel and do so currently. Bank and Manufacturer entered into an agreement under which Bank would loan a sum of money to Manufacturer. Lawyers from Law Firm did not represent either client in negotiating the loan agreement. A dispute arose between the parties to the agreement, and Manufacturer announced that it would file suit against Bank for breach of the loan contract. Absent client consent as provided in § 122, Law Firm lawyers may not represent either Bank or Manufacturer in the litigation (see § 128(2)). Law Firm may not withdraw from representing either client in order to file or defend a suit on the loan agreement against the other (see § 132, Comment *c*). Law Firm may, however, continue to provide legal services to both clients in matters unrelated to the litigation because as to those matters the clients' interests are not in conflict.

c(iv). The perspective for determining conflict of interest. This Section employs an objective standard by which to assess the adverseness, materiality, and substantiality of the risk of the effect on representation. The standard of this Section is not the "appearance of impropriety" standard formerly used by some courts to define the scope of impermissible conflicts. That standard could prohibit not only conflicts as defined in this Section, but also situations that might appear improper to an uninformed observer or even an interested party.

The propriety of the lawyer's action should be determined based only on facts and circumstances that the lawyer knew or should have known at the time of undertaking or continuing a representation. It should not be evaluated in light of information that became known only later and that could not reasonably have been anticipated.

* * *

d. Representation of a client. The prohibition of conflicts of interest ordinarily restricts a lawyer's activities only where those activities materially and adversely affect the lawyer's ability to represent a client including such an effect on a client's reasonable expectation of the lawyer's loyalty. The formation of a client-lawyer relationship is considered in § 14. Obligations to nonclients might be imposed on a lawyer by other principles of law, see § 135. That a formal client-lawyer relationship has come to an end does not terminate all conflict-of-interest restrictions, such as the prohibition against a lawyer accepting representation contrary to the interest of a former client (see § 132).

For purposes of identifying conflicts of interest, a lawyer's client is ordinarily the person or entity that consents to the formation of the client-lawyer relationship, see § 14. For example, when a lawyer is retained by Corporation A, Corporation A is ordinarily the lawyer's client; neither individual officers of Corporation A nor other corporations in which Corporation A has an ownership interest, that hold an ownership interest in Corporation A, or in which a major shareholder in Corporation A has an ownership interest, are thereby considered to be the lawyer's client.

In some situations, however, the financial or personal relationship between the lawyer's client and other persons or entities might be such that the lawyer's obligations to the client will extend to those other persons or entities as well. That will be true, for example, where financial loss or benefit to the nonclient person or entity will have a direct, adverse impact on the client.

Illustrations:

> 6. Lawyer represents Corporation A in local real-estate transactions. Lawyer has been asked to represent Plaintiff in a products-liability action against Corporation B claiming substantial damages. Corporation B is a wholly owned subsidiary of Corporation A; any judgment obtained against Corporation B will have a material adverse impact on the value of Corporation B's assets and on the value of the assets of Corporation A. Just as Lawyer could not file suit against Corporation A on behalf of another client, even in a matter unrelated to the subject of Lawyer's representation of Corporation A (see § 128, Comment *e*), Lawyer may not represent Plaintiff in the suit against Corporation B without the consent of both Plaintiff and Corporation A under the limitations and conditions provided in § 122.

> 7. The same facts as in Illustration 6, except that Corporation B is not a subsidiary of Corporation A. Instead, 51 percent of the stock of Corporation A and 60 percent of the stock of Corporation B are owned by X Corporation. The remainder of the stock in both Corporation A and Corporation B is held by the public. Lawyer does not represent X Corporation. The circumstances are such that an adverse judgment against Corporation B will have no material adverse impact on the financial position of Corporation A. No conflict of interest is presented; Lawyer may represent Plaintiff in the suit against Corporation B.

Similar problems could arise where the client and nonclient are individuals and representation adverse to the nonclient could have direct material effect on the client's interest. Such a situation would exist, for example, where a lawyer representing one spouse was asked to bring suit against the other, or where a lawyer representing one holder of an interest in property was asked by someone else to bring suit against the other holder in circumstances where the suit could materially and adversely affect the interest of the lawyer's client.

In yet other situations, the conflict of interest arises because the circumstances indicate that the confidence that a client reasonably reposes in the loyalty of a lawyer would be compromised due to the lawyer's relationship with another client or person whose interests would be adversely affected by the representation.

* * *

Significant control of the nonclient by the client also might suffice to require a lawyer to treat the nonclient as if it were a client in determining whether a conflict of interest exists in a lawyer's representation of another client with interests adverse to the nonclient.

* * *

A conflict of interest can also arise because of specific obligations, such as the obligation to hold information confidential, that the lawyer has assumed to a nonclient.

* * *

e. Withdrawal from conflicting representations—in general. A conflict can be avoided by declining to represent a new client or, when appropriate, by obtaining effective consent (see § 122). However, a lawyer might undertake representation before realizing that a conflict exists. In addition, subsequent events might create conflicts. For example, a merger of law firms or a merger of a corporate client with a nonclient enterprise might create conflicts after the representation begins (see Comment *e(v)* hereto). The appropriate course of action in such situations might vary with the circumstances, as indicated in the following Comments.

e(i). Withdrawal or consent in typical cases of postrepresentation conflict. If a lawyer withdraws from representation of multiple clients because of a conflict of interest (or for any other reason), the rule stated in § 132 prohibits representation in the same or a substantially related matter of a remaining client whose interests in the matter are materially adverse to the interests of a now-former client. For example, two clients previously represented by lawyers in a firm in the same transaction pursuant to effective consent might thereafter have a falling out such that litigation is in prospect (see §§ 130 & 128). The firm may not withdraw from representing one client and take an adversary position against that client in behalf of the other in the subsequent litigation (see § 132, Comment *c*). The firm must obtain informed consent from both clients (see § 122) or withdraw entirely. Consent in advance to such continued representation may also be provided as stated in § 122, Comment *d*. The fact that neither joint client could assert the attorney-client privilege in subsequent litigation between them (see § 75) does not by itself negate the lawyer's more extensive obligations of confidentiality under § 60 and loyalty under § 16(1).

e(ii). Successive representations involving no conflict. A lawyer or firm might be in a position to withdraw from fewer than all the representations in a joint-client representation and thereby remove a conflict if it is possible after withdrawal for the lawyer to continue representation only with respect to matters not substantially related to the former representation (compare § 132) or with respect to related matters for clients that are not adverse to the now-former client.

* * *

e(iii). Withdrawal due to revocation of consent. On the effect of one client's revocation of consent on a lawyer's ability to continue representing other clients, see § 122, Comment *f.*

e(iv). Withdrawal from representing an "accommodation" client. On representing a regular client after withdrawal from representation of another client undertaken for a limited purpose and as an accommodation to the clients, see § 132, Comment *i.*

* * *

g. Detecting conflicts. For the purpose of identifying conflicts of interest, a lawyer should have reasonable procedures, appropriate for the size and type of firm and practice, to detect conflicts of interest, including procedures to determine in both litigation and nonlitigation matters the parties and interests involved in each representation.

* * *

§ 122. Client Consent to a Conflict of Interest

(1) A lawyer may represent a client notwithstanding a conflict of interest prohibited by § 121 if each affected client or former client gives informed consent to the lawyer's representation. Informed consent requires that the client or former client have reasonably adequate information about the material risks of such representation to that client or former client.

(2) Notwithstanding the informed consent of each affected client or former client, a lawyer may not represent a client if:

(a) the representation is prohibited by law;

(b) one client will assert a claim against the other in the same litigation; or

(c) in the circumstances, it is not reasonably likely that the lawyer will be able to provide adequate representation to one or more of the clients.

Comment:

* * *

b.　Rationale. The prohibition against lawyer conflicts of interest is intended to assure clients that a lawyer's work will be characterized by loyalty, vigor, and confidentiality (see § 121, Comment *b*). The conflict rules are subject to waiver through informed consent by a client who elects less than the full measure of protection that the law otherwise provides. For example, a client in a multiple representation might wish to avoid the added costs that separate representation often entails. Similarly, a client might consent to a conflict where that is necessary in order to obtain the services of a particular law firm.

Other considerations, however, limit the scope of a client's power to consent to a conflicted representation. A client's consent will not be effective if it is based on an inadequate understanding of the nature and severity of the lawyer's conflict (Comment *c* hereto), violates law (Comment *g(i)*), or if the client lacks capacity to consent (Comment *c*). Client consent must also, of course, be free of coercion. Consent will also be insufficient to permit conflicted representation if it is not reasonably likely that the lawyer will be able to provide adequate representation to the affected clients, or when a lawyer undertakes to represent clients who oppose each other in the same litigation (Comment *g(iii)*).

* * *

c(i).　The requirement of informed consent—adequate information. Informed consent requires that each affected client be aware of the material respects in which the representation could have adverse effects on the interests of that client. The information required depends on the nature of the conflict and the nature of the risks of the conflicted representation. The client must be aware of information reasonably adequate to make an informed decision.

Information relevant to particular kinds of conflicts is considered in several of the Sections hereafter. In a multiple-client situation, the information normally should address the interests of the lawyer and other client giving rise to the conflict; contingent, optional, and tactical considerations and alternative courses of action that would be foreclosed or made less readily available by the conflict; the effect of the representation or the process of obtaining other clients' informed consent upon confidential information of the client; any material reservations that a disinterested lawyer might reasonably harbor about the arrangement if such a lawyer were representing only the client being advised; and the consequences and effects of a future withdrawal of consent by any client, including, if relevant, the fact that the lawyer would withdraw from representing all clients (see § 121, Comment *e*). Where the conflict arises solely because a proposed representation will be adverse to an existing client in an unrelated matter, knowledge of the general nature and scope of the work being performed for each client normally suffices to enable the clients to decide whether or not to consent.

When the consent relates to a former-client conflict (see § 132), it is necessary that the former client be aware that the consent will allow the former lawyer to proceed adversely to the former client. Beyond that, the former client must have adequate information about the implications (if not readily apparent) of the adverse representation, the fact that the lawyer possesses the former client's confidential information, the measures that the former lawyer might undertake to protect against unwarranted disclosures, and the right of the former client to refuse consent. The former client will often be independently represented by counsel. If so, communication with the former client ordinarily must be through successor counsel (see § 99 and following).

The lawyer is responsible for assuring that each client has the necessary information. A lawyer who does not personally inform the client assumes the risk that the client is inadequately informed and that the consent is invalid. A lawyer's failure to inform the clients might also bear on the motives and good faith of the lawyer. On the other hand, clients differ as to their sophistication and experience, and situations differ in terms of their complexity and the subtlety of the conflicts presented. The requirements of this Section are satisfied if the client already knows the necessary information or learns it from other sources. A client independently represented—for example by inside legal counsel or by other outside counsel—will need less information about the consequences of a conflict but nevertheless may have need of information adequate to reveal its scope and severity. When several lawyers represent the same client, responsibility to make disclosure and obtain informed consent may be delegated to one or more of the lawyers who appears reasonably capable of providing adequate information.

Disclosing information about one client or prospective client to another is precluded if information necessary to be conveyed is confidential (see § 60). The affected clients may consent to disclosure (see § 62), but it also might be possible for the lawyer to explain the nature of undisclosed information in a manner that nonetheless provides an adequate basis for informed consent. If means of adequate disclosure are unavailable, consent to the conflict may not be obtained.

The requirement of consent generally requires an affirmative response by each client. Ambiguities in a client's purported expression of consent should be construed against the lawyer seeking the protection of the consent (cf. § 18). In general, a lawyer may not assume consent from a client's silent acquiescence. However, consent may be inferred from active participation in a representation by a client who has reasonably adequate information about the material risks of the representation after a lawyer's request for consent. Even in the absence of consent, a tribunal applying remedies such as disqualification (see § 121, Comment *f*) will apply concepts of estoppel and waiver when an objecting party has either induced reasonable reliance on the absence of objection or delayed an unreasonable period of time in making objection.

* * *

c(ii). The requirement of informed consent—the capacity of the consenting person. Each client whose consent is required must have the legal capacity to give informed consent. Consent purportedly given by a client who lacks legal capacity to do so is ineffective. Consent of a person under a legal disability normally must be obtained from a guardian or conservator appointed for the person. Consent of a minor normally is effective when given by a parent or guardian of the minor. In class actions certification of the class, determination that the interests of its members are congruent, and assessment of the adequacy of representation are typically made by a tribunal.

* * *

d. Consent to future conflicts. Client consent to conflicts that might arise in the future is subject to special scrutiny, particularly if the consent is general. A client's open-ended agreement to consent to all conflicts normally should be ineffective unless the client possesses sophistication in the matter in question and has had the opportunity to receive independent legal advice about the consent. A client's informed consent to a gift to a lawyer (see § 127) ordinarily should be given contemporaneously with the gift.

On the other hand, particularly in a continuing client-lawyer relationship in which the lawyer is expected to act on behalf of the client without a new engagement for each matter, the gains to both lawyer and client from a system of advance consent to defined future conflicts might be substantial. A client might, for example, give informed consent in advance to types of conflicts that are familiar to the client. Such an agreement could effectively protect the client's interest while assuring that the lawyer did not undertake a potentially disqualifying representation.

Illustrations:

2. Law Firm has represented Client in collecting commercial claims through Law Firm's New York office for many years.

Client is a long-established and sizable business corporation that is sophisticated in commercial matters generally and specifically in dealing with lawyers. Law Firm also has a Chicago office that gives tax advice to many companies with which Client has commercial dealings. Law Firm asks for advance consent from Client with respect to conflicts that otherwise would prevent Law Firm from filing commercial claims on behalf of Client against the tax clients of Law Firm's Chicago office (see § 128). If Client gives informed consent the consent should be held to be proper as to Client. Law Firm would also be required to obtain informed consent from any tax client of its Chicago office against whom Client wishes to file a commercial claim, should Law Firm decide to undertake such a representation.

3. The facts being otherwise as stated in Illustration 2, Law Firm seeks advance consent from each of its Chicago-office corporate-tax clients to its representation of any of its other clients in matters involving collection of commercial claims adverse to such tax clients if the matters do not involve information that Law Firm might have learned in the tax representation. To provide further assurance concerning the protection of confidential information, the consent provides that, should Law Firm represent any client in a collection matter adverse to a tax client, a procedure to protect confidential information of the tax client will be established (compare § 124, Comment *d*). Unless such a tax client is shown to be unsophisticated about legal matters and relationships with lawyers, informed consent to the arrangement should be held to be proper.

If a material change occurs in the reasonable expectations that formed the basis of a client's informed consent, the new conditions must be brought to the attention of the client and new informed consent obtained (see also Comment *f* hereto (client revocation of consent)). If the new conflict is not consentable (see Comment *g* hereto), the lawyer may not proceed.

* * *

f. Revocation of consent through client action or a material change of circumstances. A client who has given informed consent to an otherwise conflicted representation may at any time revoke the consent (see § 21(2)). Revoking consent to the client's own representation, however, does not necessarily prevent the lawyer from continuing to represent other clients who had been jointly represented along with the revoking client. Whether the lawyer may continue the other representation depends on whether the client was justified in revoking the consent (such as because of a material change in the factual basis on which the client originally gave informed consent) and whether material detriment to the other client or lawyer would result. In addition, if the client had reserved the prerogative of revoking consent, that agreement controls the lawyer's subsequent ability to continue representation of other clients.

* * *

A client who has given informed consent to be represented as a joint client with another would be justified in revoking the consent if the common lawyer failed to represent that client with reasonable loyalty (see Comment *h* hereto). The client would also be justified in revoking consent if a co-client materially violated the express or implied terms of the consent, such as by abusing the first client's confidential information through disclosing important information to third persons without justification. Improper behavior of the other client or the lawyer might indicate that one or both of them cannot be trusted to respect the legitimate interests of the consenting client.

Illustration:

> 4. Client A and Client B validly consent to be represented by Lawyer in operating a restaurant in a city. After a period of amicable and profitable collaboration, Client A reasonably concludes that Lawyer has begun to take positions against Client A and consistently favoring the interests of Client B in the business. Reasonably concerned that Lawyer is no longer properly serving the interests of both clients, Client A withdraws consent. Withdrawal of consent is effective and justified (see Comment *h* hereto). Lawyer may not thereafter continue representing either Client A or Client B in a matter adverse to the other and substantially related to Lawyer's former representation of the clients (see § 121, Comment *e(i)*).

In the absence of valid reasons for a client's revocation of consent, the ability of the lawyer to continue representing other clients depends on whether material detriment to the other client or lawyer would result and, accordingly, whether the reasonable expectations of those persons would be defeated. Once the client or former client has given informed consent to a lawyer's representing another client, that other client as well as the lawyer might have acted in reliance on the consent. For example, the other client and the lawyer might already have invested time, money, and effort in the representation. The other client might already have disclosed confidential information and developed a relationship of trust and confidence with the lawyer. Or, a client relying on the consent might reasonably have elected to forgo opportunities to take other action.

Illustrations:

5. On Monday, Client A and Client B validly consent to being represented by Lawyer in the same matter despite a conflict of interest. On Wednesday, before either Client B or Lawyer has taken or forgone any significant action in reliance, Client A withdraws consent. Lawyer is no longer justified in continuing with the joint representation. Lawyer also may not continue to represent Client B alone without A's renewed informed consent to Lawyer's representation of B if doing so would violate other Sections of this Chapter, for example because A's and B's interests in the matter would be antagonistic or because Lawyer had learned confidential information from A relevant in the matter (see § 132; see also § 15, Comment *c*, & § 121, Comment *e(i)*). Similarly, if Client A on Wednesday did not unequivocally withdraw consent but stated to Lawyer that on further reflection Client A now had serious doubts about the wisdom of the joint representation, Lawyer could not reasonably take material steps in reliance on the consent. Before proceeding, Lawyer must clarify with Client A whether A indeed gives informed consent and whether the joint representation may thereby continue.

6. Clients A and B validly consent to Lawyer representing them jointly as co-defendants in a breach-of-contract action. On the eve of trial and after months of pretrial discovery on the part of all parties, Client A withdraws consent to the joint representation for reasons not justified by the conduct of Lawyer or Client B and insists that Lawyer cease representing Client B. At this point it would be difficult and expensive for Client B to find separate representation for the impending trial. Client A's withdrawal of consent is ineffective to prevent the continuing representation of B in the absence of compelling considerations such as harmful disloyalty by Lawyer.

7. Client A, who consulted Lawyer about a tax question, gave informed advance consent to Lawyer's representing any of Lawyer's other clients against Client A in matters unrelated to Client A's tax question. Client B, who had not theretofore been a client of Lawyer, wishes to retain Lawyer to file suit against Client A for personal injuries suffered in an automobile accident. After Lawyer informs Client B of the nature of Lawyer's work for

Client A, and the nature and risks presented by any conflict that might be produced, Client B consents to the conflict of interest. After Lawyer has undertaken substantial work in preparation of Client B's case, Client A seeks to withdraw the advance consent for reasons not justified by the conduct of Lawyer or Client B. Even though Client A was Lawyer's client before Client B was a client, the material detriment to both Lawyer and Client B would render Client A's attempt to withdraw consent ineffective.

* * *

g. *Nonconsentable conflicts.* Some conflicts of interest preclude adverse representation even if informed consent is obtained.

g(i). *Representations prohibited by law.* As stated in Subsection (2)(a), informed consent is unavailing when prohibited by applicable law. In some states, for example, the law provides that the same lawyer may not represent more than one defendant in a capital case and that informed consent does not cure the conflict (see § 129, Comment *c*). Under federal criminal statutes, certain representations by a former government lawyer (cf. § 133) are prohibited, and informed consent by the former client is not recognized as a defense.

* * *

g(iii). *Conflicts between adversaries in litigation.* When clients are aligned directly against each other in the same litigation, the institutional interest in vigorous development of each client's position renders the conflict nonconsentable (see § 128, Comment *c*, & § 129). The rule applies even if the parties themselves believe that the common interests are more significant in the matter than the interests dividing them. While the parties might give informed consent to joint representation for purposes of negotiating their differences (see § 130, Comment *d*), the joint representation may not continue if the parties become opposed to each other in litigation.

Illustration:

     8. A and B wish to obtain an amicable dissolution of their marriage. State law treats marriage dissolution as a contested judicial proceeding. Lawyer is asked to represent both A and B in negotiation of the property settlement to be submitted to the court in the proceeding. Informed consent can authorize Lawyer to represent both parties in the property-settlement negotiations (subject to exceptions in some jurisdictions, where interests of children are involved, for example), but consent does not authorize

Lawyer to represent both A and B if litigation is necessary to obtain the final decree. The parties may agree that Lawyer will represent only one of them in the judicial proceeding. The other party would either be represented by another lawyer or appear pro se (see §§ 128 & 130).

* * *

g(iv). Other circumstances rendering a lawyer incapable of providing adequate representation. Concern for client autonomy generally warrants respecting a client's informed consent. In some situations, however, joint representation would be objectively inadequate despite a client's voluntary and informed consent. In criminal cases, for example, joint representation of co-defendants with irreconcilable or unreconciled interests might render their representation constitutionally inadequate and thus require a court to prohibit the joint representation (see § 129, Comment *c*). Similarly, a conflict of interest among class members might render a lawyer's representation in a class action inadequate despite informed consent by the class representatives (see § 128, Comment *d*; see also, e.g., § 131, Comment *f*, Illustration 5).

The general standard stated in Subsection (2)(c) assesses the likelihood that the lawyer will, following consent, be able to provide adequate representation to the clients. The standard includes the requirements both that the consented-to conflict not adversely affect the lawyer's relationship with either client and that it not adversely affect the representation of either client. In general, if a reasonable and disinterested lawyer would conclude that one or more of the affected clients could not consent to the conflicted representation because the representation would likely fall short in either respect, the conflict is nonconsentable.

Decisions holding that a conflict is nonconsentable often involve facts suggesting that the client, who is often unsophisticated in retaining lawyers, was not adequately informed or was incapable of adequately appreciating the risks of the conflict (compare Comments *c(i)* & *c(ii)* hereto). Decisions involving clients sophisticated in the use of lawyers, particularly when advised by independent counsel, such as by inside legal counsel, rarely hold that a conflict is nonconsentable.

The nature of the conflict is also important. The professional rules and court decisions indicate that informed consent will always suffice with respect to a former-client conflict of interest (§ 132). With respect to simultaneous-representation conflicts (Topic 3), when the matters are unrelated it would only be in unusual circumstances that a lawyer could not provide adequate representation with consent of all affected clients. On the other hand, when the representation involves the same matter or the matters are significantly related, it may be more difficult for the lawyer to provide adequate legal assistance to multiple clients (see, e.g., § 131, Comment *e*, Illustration 4).

Illustrations:

> 9. Lawyer occasionally represents Bank in collection matters and is doing so currently in one lawsuit. Employee requests Lawyer to file an employment-discrimination charge against Bank. Bank, acting through its inside legal counsel, gives informed consent to Lawyer's representation of Employee against Bank with respect to the matter. Employee, following discussion with Lawyer concerning the nature of Lawyer's collection representations of Bank, freely gives informed consent as well. The circumstances indicate no basis for concluding that Lawyer would be unable to provide adequate representation to Bank in the collection matters and to Employee in the discrimination claim against Bank.

> 10. Lawyer has been asked by Buyer and Seller to represent both of them in negotiating and documenting a complex real-estate transaction. The parties are in sharp disagreement on several important terms of the transaction. Given such differences, Lawyer would be unable to provide adequate representation to both clients.

> 11. The facts being otherwise as stated in Illustration 10, the parties are both in agreement on terms and possess comparable knowledge and experience in such transactions, but, viewed objectively, the transaction is such that both parties should receive extensive counseling concerning their rights in the transaction and possible optional arrangements, including security interests, guarantees, and other rights against each other and in resisting the claims of the other party for such rights. Given the scope of legal representation that each prospective client should receive, Lawyer would be unable to provide adequate representation to both clients.

A conflict can be rendered nonconsentable because of personal circumstances affecting the lawyer's ability in fact to provide adequate representation. For example, if the lawyer has such strong feelings of friendship toward one of two prospective joint clients that the lawyer could not provide adequate representation to the other client (compare

Comment *h* hereto), the lawyer may not proceed with the joint representation.

* * *

§ 123. Imputation of a Conflict of Interest to an Affiliated Lawyer

Unless all affected clients consent to the representation under the limitations and conditions provided in § 122 or unless imputation hereunder is removed as provided in § 124, the restrictions upon a lawyer imposed by §§ 125–135 also restrict other affiliated lawyers who:

(1) are associated with that lawyer in rendering legal services to others through a law partnership, professional corporation, sole proprietorship, or similar association;

(2) are employed with that lawyer by an organization to render legal services either to that organization or to others to advance the interests or objectives of the organization; or

(3) share office facilities without reasonably adequate measures to protect confidential client information so that it will not be available to other lawyers in the shared office.

Comment:

* * *

b. Rationale. Imputation of conflicts of interest to affiliated lawyers reflects three concerns. First, lawyers in a law firm or other affiliation described in this Section ordinarily share each other's interests. A fee for one lawyer in a partnership, for example, normally benefits all lawyers in the partnership. Where a lawyer's relationship with a client creates an incentive to violate an obligation to another client, an affiliated lawyer will often have similar incentive to favor one client over the other. Second, lawyers affiliated as described in this Section ordinarily have access to files and other confidential information about each other's clients. Indeed, clients might assume that their confidential information will be shared among affiliated lawyers (compare § 60, Comment *f*). Sharing confidential client information among affiliated lawyers might compromise the representation of one or both clients if the representations conflict. Third, a client would often have difficulty proving that the adverse representation by an affiliated lawyer was wholly isolated. Duties of confidentiality on the part of the

310

affiliated lawyers prevents adequate disclosure of the interactions among them. Moreover, to demonstrate that the lawyer misused confidential information the client often would be forced to reveal the very information whose confidentiality the client seeks to protect. However, considerations of free choice of lawyers by clients and the free mobility of lawyers between firms or other employers caution against extending imputation further than necessary (see § 124, Comment *b*).

c. Lawyers associated in a law partnership, professional corporation, sole proprietorship, or similar association. This Section most commonly applies to lawyers associated in various forms of organization engaged in the private practice of law.

c(i). Law-firm members and employees. The rule of imputation applies to both owner-employer and associate-employees of a sole-proprietorship law practice, to partners and associates in a partnership for the practice of law, and to shareholder-principals and nonequity lawyer employees of a professional corporation or similar organization conducting a law practice. The lawyers in all such organizations typically have similar access to confidential client information. Owners, partners, and shareholder-principals have a shared economic interest. Associates and nonequity lawyer employees have both a stake in the continued viability of their employer and an incentive to keep the employer's good will.

Illustration:

> 1. Lawyer A and Lawyer B are partners in a law firm. Client is considering filing suit against a commercial enterprise in which Lawyer A has a 30 percent ownership interest. Without the informed consent of Client, Lawyer A may not represent Client in the matter (see § 125). Under the rule of imputation described in this Section, Lawyer B also may not represent Client.

A form of lawyer-employee is the lawyer temporary—a lawyer who temporarily works for a firm needing extra professional help. The rules barring representation adverse to a former client (see § 132) and imputing conflicts to all lawyers associated in a firm generally apply to such lawyer temporaries.

c(ii). Of-counsel relationships. The rule of imputation of this Section ordinarily applies due to the association of lawyers who are "of counsel." A lawyer is of counsel if designated as having that relationship with a firm or when the relationship is regular and continuing although the lawyer is neither a partner in the firm nor employed by it on a full-time basis. A lawyer who is of counsel to a firm often has more limited access to confidential client information than firm partners and associates and usually a smaller financial stake in the firm. Nonetheless, the incentive to misuse confidential information, the difficulty of determining when it has been misused, the ostensible professional relationship, as well as the administrative ease of a definite rule, justify extending imputation to lawyers having an of-counsel status. In unusual situations, the relationship between an "of counsel" lawyer and the firm may be shown to be so attenuated, despite typical connotations of the term, that there is no significant risk of compromising client confidentiality or otherwise providing a basis for imputation.

c(iii). Associated lawyers or law firms. Two or more lawyers or law firms might associate for purposes of handling a particular case. A common example is a lawyer who appears as local counsel in litigation principally handled by another firm. Each lawyer must comply with the rules concerning conflict of interest, and other lawyers in their respective firms are governed by the rules of imputation. However, a conflict imputed within a firm does not extend by imputation to lawyers in another firm working on another matter.

Similarly, when a lawyer consults with other lawyers in specialized areas of the law, the consultant lawyer may not personally represent clients with conflicting interests. However, the normal consulting relationship is essentially an association for purposes of the matter in question between lawyers otherwise practicing separately. Hence, the rule of this Comment applies.

Illustration:

> 2. Firm X is about to file a patent-infringement action on behalf of Client against Opponent. Firm X has no patent lawyers in its office, so it wishes to affiliate with Firm Y, a patent firm, to handle the representation. Firm Y has had no connection with Opponent but Lawyer A in Firm Y represents P against D, another of Firm X's clients, in an unrelated matter. Lawyer A's adverse representation of P is not imputed to Firm X, nor is Firm X's relationship with D imputed to Firm Y. The fact that Firms X and Y represent opposing clients in a different matter would not prevent their affiliation in the patent matter.

d. Lawyers employed by an organization to render legal services to it. Section 123(2) applies the rule of imputation to certain situations in which lawyers are employed by an organization.

d(i). Corporate legal offices. Lawyers employed by the legal department of a corporation or similar organization commonly represent only the organization as a client. However, such a lawyer might sometimes be asked to represent officers, directors, or employees of the organization. A lawyer so employed might also have continuing obligations to clients formerly represented in previous employment. Furthermore, lawyers in corporate legal offices will often have access to confidential information in the possession of other lawyers in the same office. The possibility of misuse of information in such situations can be as great as in private law firms. The lawyer-employees are to that extent comparable to partners and associates in a private law firm. Thus, as provided in this Section, the principles of imputed prohibition apply.

* * *

d(ii). Government legal offices—in general. Government legal offices often present the same potential for access to confidential information and motivation to direct the representations as exist in a corporate legal office or private law firm. Government lawyers thus are subject to imputed prohibition under this Section when they are employed by a government agency to render legal services to that agency as stated in Subsection (2) or are officed in physical proximity to each other as stated in Subsection (3). However, measures taken within a governmental law office can adequately assure that confidential client information will not be shared by various lawyers within the office (see § 124).

d(iii). Prosecutor offices. When one member of a prosecutor's office is personally prohibited from acting because of a conflict of interest, the question arises whether the entire office is disqualified, so that outside counsel must be retained to prosecute the case. If prosecutor staff lawyers commonly discuss cases with each other and have physical access to each other's files, Subsection (3) imputes conflicts to all such prosecutors (see Comment *e* hereto). If there is no such access, the issue under Subsection (2) is whether the lawyers in the prosecutor offices should be said to work for the same "organization." If prosecutor offices are organized by county, for example, the county might be regarded as the common organizational employer, so that if one assistant prosecutor in the county were prohibited from acting, all other prosecutors in that county would be prohibited as well. However, if the office is operated so as to avoid material risk that confidential information will be inadequately safeguarded, the formal organization of the prosecutor's office should not inevitably require imputation. Establishing procedures for removal of imputation like those in § 124 can in appropriate circumstances ameliorate otherwise serious practical problems created by imputation.

* * *

d(iv). Public-defender offices. In a public-defender office, conflict-of-interest questions commonly arise when the interests of two or more defendants so conflict that lawyers in a private-practice defense firm could not represent both or all the defendants (see § 129). The rules on imputed conflicts and screening of this Section apply to a public-defender organization as they do to a law firm in private practice in a similar situation.

d(v). Nonprofit legal-services agencies. Lawyers in some nonprofit legal-services agencies might be affected by conflicting interests in much the same manner as lawyers in any other legal office. As with a public defender (see Comment *d(iv)* hereto), the rules on imputed conflicts and screening apply to a nonprofit legal-services organization. If more than one party in such a matter is in need of legal assistance and their interests conflict, either a private lawyer or a lawyer from an autonomous legal-services agency must provide the representation.

e. Lawyers sharing office space. When lawyers share office space, they typically share some common costs such as rent, library, and office salaries, but not income from work on cases. Subsection (3) governs imputation of conflicts in such arrangements. The key inquiry is whether the physical organization and actual operation of the office space is such that the confidential client information of each lawyer is secure from the others. Where such security is provided and where no other plausible risks to confidentiality and loyalty are presented, the conflicts of the lawyers are not imputed to each other by reason of their office-sharing arrangement. On the other hand, lawyers who do associate in a matter, share fee income, or hold themselves out as partners or members of a professional corporation (even if that is not a fact) are held to the stricter rule applicable to members of a firm (see Comment *c(i)* hereto).

f. Imputed conflicts through nonlawyer employees. Nonlawyer employees of a law office owe duties of confidentiality by reason of their employment (see Restatement Second, Agency § 396). However, their duty of confidentiality is not imputed to others so as to prohibit representation of other clients at a subsequent employer. Even if the person learned the information in circumstances that would disqualify a lawyer and the person has become a lawyer, the person should not be regarded as a lawyer for purposes of the imputation rules of this Section.

314

Law students who clerk in firms, like other nonlawyer employees, typically have limited responsibilities and thus might acquire little sensitive confidential information about matters. Absent special circumstances, they should be considered nonlawyer employees for the purposes of this Section. Persons who have completed their legal education and are awaiting admission to practice at the time of providing services to a client of a law firm typically have duties comparable to admitted lawyers and accordingly should ordinarily be treated as lawyers for purposes of imputation.

Some risk is involved in a rule that does not impute confidential information known by nonlawyers to lawyers in the firm. For example, law students might work in several law offices during their law-school careers and thereby learn client information at Firm A that could be used improperly by Firm B. Experienced legal secretaries and paralegal personnel similarly often understand the significance and value of confidential material with which they work. Incentives exist in many such cases for improper disclosure or use of the information in the new employment.

On the other hand, nonlawyers ordinarily understand less about the legal significance of information they learn in a law firm than lawyers do, and they are often not in a position to articulate to a new employer the nature of the information gained in the previous employment. If strict imputation were applied, employers could protect themselves against unanticipated disqualification risks only by refusing to hire experienced people. Further, nonlawyers have an independent duty as agents to protect confidential information, and firms have a duty to take steps designed to assure that the nonlawyers do so (see § 60, Comment d). Adequate protection can be given to clients, consistent with the interest in job mobility for nonlawyers, by prohibiting the nonlawyer from using or disclosing the confidential information (see § 124) but not extending the prohibition on representation to lawyers in the new firm or organization. If a nonlawyer employee in fact conveys confidential information learned about a client in one firm to lawyers in another, a prohibition on representation by the second firm would be warranted.

g. *Family relationships among lawyers.* The fact that lawyers are related by blood or marriage does not, in itself, require imputation under the rule described in this Section. Like lawyers in the same firm, however, the degree of financial interdependence, sharing of information, and loyalty between spouses, for example, is ordinarily high. Yet, if the rule were that a spouse and the spouse's firm are disqualified from any case in which the other spouse was disqualified, law firms would be reluctant to hire either spouse. Thus, in general, the law does not impute conflicts between firms of lawyers by virtue of family relationship alone. However, in the absence of informed consent by all affected clients (see § 122), lawyers who are married to each other—or lawyers similarly related such as parent-lawyers and their lawyer children—may not personally represent clients adverse to the interests of clients of the other spouse or relative. Each must also observe prohibitions against misuse of confidential client information (see § 60). Conflicts arising out of relationships in which financial resources are pooled and living quarters shared in circumstances closely approximating marriage should be treated in the same way as spousal conflicts.

* * *

§ 124. Removing Imputation

(1) Imputation specified in § 123 does not restrict an affiliated lawyer when the affiliation between the affiliated lawyer and the personally prohibited lawyer that required the imputation has been terminated, and no material confidential information of the client, relevant to the matter, has been communicated by the personally prohibited lawyer to the affiliated lawyer or that lawyer's firm.

(2) Imputation specified in § 123 does not restrict an affiliated lawyer with respect to a former-client conflict under § 132, when there is no substantial risk that confidential information of the former client will be used with material adverse effect on the former client because:

(a) any confidential client information communicated to the personally prohibited lawyer is unlikely to be significant in the subsequent matter;

(b) the personally prohibited lawyer is subject to screening measures adequate to eliminate participation by that lawyer in the representation; and

(c) timely and adequate notice of the screening has been provided to all affected clients.

(3) Imputation specified in § 123 does not restrict a lawyer affiliated with a former government lawyer with respect to a conflict under § 133 if:

(a) the personally prohibited lawyer is subject to screening measures adequate to eliminate involvement by that lawyer in the representation; and

> (b) timely and adequate notice of the screening
> has been provided to the appropriate government
> agency and to affected clients.

Comment:

* * *

b. Rationale. Imputation creates burdens both for clients and lawyers. Some clients who wish to be represented by a trusted or highly recommended lawyer or law firm must forgo the engagement. A single personally prohibited lawyer can conflict out literally hundreds of lawyers in a firm. Prospective imputed prohibition inhibits mobility of lawyers from one firm or employer to another. The burden of prohibition should end when material risks to confidentiality and loyalty resulting from shared income and access to information have been avoided by appropriate measures (see Comment *d* hereto).

c. Imputation after the termination of an affiliation.

c(i). Personally prohibited lawyer terminates the affiliation. During the time that a personally prohibited lawyer is associated with another lawyer, law firm, or other organization to which prohibition is imputed under § 123, the lawyer could reveal confidential information to any other lawyer within the organization. Accordingly, imputed prohibition of all lawyers in the firm is appropriately required by § 123. However, after the personally prohibited lawyer has left the firm, an irrebuttable presumption of continued sharing of client confidences or continued disloyalty induced by the affiliation is no longer justified.

The lawyers remaining in the affiliation may rebut the presumption that confidential information was shared during the period of actual affiliation. They have the burden of persuasion concerning three facts: (1) that no material confidential client information relevant to the matter was revealed to any lawyer remaining in the firm; (2) that the firm does not now possess or have access to sources of client confidential information, particularly client documents or files; and (3) that the personally prohibited lawyer will not share fees in the matter so as to have an interest in the representation.

Illustration:

1. Lawyer A is a partner in ABC law firm, and Lawyer B formerly was a partner. Client X has sought to retain Lawyer A to file suit on behalf of X against Y. Before joining the ABC firm, Lawyer B had represented Y at an earlier stage of the current

dispute. Lawyer B has now resigned from the ABC firm, disclosed no confidential information about Y relevant to the matter to other lawyers in ABC, left no files at ABC that relate to the proposed suit, and will not share in fees derived by the ABC firm from the representation of X. The limitation governing B, resulting from the proposed representation being substantially related to the prior representation of Y by B (see § 132), is no longer imputed to A. Hence A may represent Client X against Y.

A personally prohibited lawyer who enters a new law firm or other affiliation causes imputed prohibition of all affiliated lawyers as stated in § 123. Such imputation is subject to removal under Subsection (2) or (3).

c(ii). A non-personally-prohibited lawyer terminates the affiliation. When a lawyer leaves a firm or other organization whose lawyers were subject to imputed prohibition owing to presence in the firm of another lawyer, the departed lawyer becomes free of imputation so long as that lawyer obtained no material confidential client information relevant to the matter. Similarly, lawyers in the new affiliation are free of imputed prohibition if they can carry the burden of persuading the finder of fact that the arriving lawyer did not obtain confidential client information about a questioned representation by another lawyer in the former affiliation.

Illustration:

2. Client X has sought to retain Lawyer A, a partner in the firm of ABC, to represent X in a suit against Y. The suit has not yet been filed. Lawyer A is required to decline the representation because Y is also a client of Lawyer B in ABC. Lawyer A resigns from the ABC firm without having learned material confidential information of Y relevant to X's claim. The imputed disqualification is thereby removed, and Lawyer A may now represent Client X.

d. Screening against the risk of misuse of confidential information.

d(i). Screening—in general. Three situations must be distinguished. First, a lawyer's minor involvement in a matter for a former client might have involved no or so little exposure to confidential information that no conflict should be found (see § 132, Comment *h*). Second, the lawyer's involvement might have been more substantial,

318

rendering the lawyer personally prohibited from the representation by reason of a former-client conflict of interest (see § 132), but screening may be appropriate under Subsection (2). A common instance in which this may be true is that of a junior lawyer in a law firm who provides minimal assistance on a peripheral element of a transaction, thereby gaining little confidential information that would be relevant in the later matter. Third, in the circumstances the lawyer's involvement and the nature and relevance of confidential information in the lawyer's possession might be such that screening will not remove imputation under Subsection (2). Determining which result is appropriate requires careful analysis of the particular facts.

If the requirements of either Subsection (2) or (3) are met, imputation is removed and consent to the representation by the former client is not required. The required screening measures must be imposed in the subsequent representation at the time the conflict is discovered or reasonably should have been discovered, and they must be of sufficient scope, continuity, and duration to assure that there will be no substantial risk to confidential client information.

Lawyer codes generally recognize the screening remedy in cases involving former government lawyers who have returned to private practice (see Comment *e* hereto). Screening to prevent imputation from former private-client representations has similar justification, giving clients wider choice of counsel and making it easier for lawyers to change employers. The rule in Subsection (2) thus permits screening as a remedy in situations in which the information possessed by a personally prohibited lawyer is not likely to be significant. The lawyer or firm seeking to remove imputation has the burden of persuasion that there is no substantial risk that confidential information of the former client will be used with material adverse effect on the former client.

Significance of the information is determined by its probable utility in the later representation, including such factors as the following: (1) whether the value of the information as proof or for tactical purposes is peripheral or tenuous; (2) whether the information in most material respects is now publicly known; (3) whether the information was of only temporary significance; (4) the scope of the second representation; and (5) the duration and degree of responsibility of the personally prohibited lawyer in the earlier representation.

The lawyer codes in most states impose disciplinary responsibility in a wider range of circumstances of former private-client representations. Specifically, most codes do not recognize that screening can preclude disqualification of a law firm by imputation from a personally prohibited lawyer, even if the screening is timely and effective and the client information involved is innocuous. The issue typically arises under motions to disqualify, not in disciplinary proceedings. A tribunal has discretion whether or not to require disqualification. Subsection (2) states a rule to guide exercise of that discretion.

Illustrations:

3. As can readily be shown from contemporaneous time records, when Lawyer was an associate in Law Firm ABC, Lawyer spent one-half hour in conversation with another associate about research strategies involving a narrow issue of venue in federal court in the case of *Developer v. Bank*, in which the firm represented Bank. The conversation was based entirely on facts pleaded in the complaint and answer, and Lawyer learned no confidential information about the matter. Lawyer then left Firm ABC and became an associate in Firm DEF. Two years later, Lawyer was asked to represent Developer against Bank in a matter substantially related to the matter in which Firm ABC represented Bank. In the circumstances, due to the proven lack of exposure of Lawyer to confidential information of Bank, Bank should not be regarded as the former client of Lawyer for the purpose of applying § 132 (see § 132, Comment *h*). Alternatively, a tribunal may require that Lawyer be screened from partic-ipation in the matter as provided in this Section and, on that basis, permit other lawyers affiliated with Lawyer in Firm DEF to represent the client against Bank.

4. The same facts as Illustration 3, except that Lawyer while representing Bank in Firm ABC was principally in charge of developing factual information about the underlying dispute. The dispute involved a loan Bank made to Developer on Tract A in the city in which both conduct business. The dispute was resolved after extensive discovery and a full trial before Lawyer left Firm ABC. An affiliated lawyer in Lawyer's new firm, Firm DEF, has been asked to represent Developer in a dispute with Bank over a loan on Tract B. Because of the similarity of facts in the two disputes—involving both tracts, both loans, and both parties to them—a tribunal finds the matters are substantially related and accordingly that Lawyer is personally prohibited from representing Developer against Bank with respect to Tract B (see § 132). However, the tribunal also finds that, despite that factual overlap, the information Lawyer might have acquired about Bank would have little significance in the later dispute because it concerned only an earlier period of time so that any importance it might have had was significantly diminished by the time of the

second dispute, because it mainly involves information already a matter of public record in the earlier trial, and because all factual information will be largely irrelevant in view of the fact that the pleadings indicate that the only contested issue in the second dispute involves a matter of contract interpretation. In the circumstances, the tribunal should further find that Firm DEF may represent Developer against Bank if Lawyer has been screened as provided in Subsection (2).

5. The same facts as Illustration 4, except that the earlier dispute was settled after Lawyer had conducted extensive examination of Bank's files but without any discovery by Developer's then counsel or trial. Little time has passed since Lawyer acquired the information from Bank, and the information remains highly relevant in the later dispute. The pleadings in the second dispute indicate that a large number of important factual issues similar to those in the earlier dispute remain open. In the circumstances, the likelihood that the information possessed by Lawyer will be significant in the second matter renders screening under this Section inappropriate.

d(ii). Screening—adequacy of measures. Screening must assure that confidential client information will not pass from the personally prohibited lawyer to any other lawyer in the firm. The screened lawyer should be prohibited from talking to other persons in the firm about the matter as to which the lawyer is prohibited, and from sharing documents about the matter and the like. Further, the screened lawyer should receive no direct financial benefit from the firm's representation, based upon the outcome of the matter, such as a financial bonus or a larger share of firm income directly attributable to the matter. However, it is not impermissible that the lawyer receives compensation and benefits under standing arrangements established prior to the representation. An adequate showing of screening ordinarily requires affidavits by the personally prohibited lawyer and by a lawyer responsible for the screening measures. A tribunal can require that other appropriate steps be taken.

* * *

d(iii). Screening—timely and adequate notice of screening to all affected clients. An affected client will usually have difficulty demonstrating whether screening measures have been honored. Timely and adequate notice of the screening must therefore be given to the affected clients, including description of the screening measures reasonably sufficient to inform the affected client of their adequacy.

Notice will give opportunity to protest and to allow arrangements to be made for monitoring compliance.

* * *

 e. *Screening a former government lawyer.* As stated in Comment *d* hereto, avoidance of imputation by screening of former government lawyers is permitted in most lawyer codes. If hiring a former government lawyer would disqualify an entire firm from cases arising before that lawyer's agency, the lawyer would not likely be hired. That, in turn, would make it more difficult for the government to hire able lawyers at the outset.

 The personally prohibited lawyer must be screened from any participation in the matter and should receive no direct financial benefit from the firm's representation as stated in Comment *d(ii)*. Written notice must be given to the appropriate government agency so that it can ascertain compliance with the screening requirement. Those precautions prevent imputation even if the confidential information communicated to the lawyer in the prior matter is significant (see § 74 & § 133, Comment *b*).

* * *

TOPIC 2. CONFLICTS OF INTEREST BETWEEN A LAWYER AND A CLIENT

* * *

§ 125. A Lawyer's Personal Interest Affecting the Representation of a Client

 Unless the affected client consents to the representation under the limitations and conditions provided in § 122, a lawyer may not represent a client if there is a substantial risk that the lawyer's representation of the client would be materially and adversely affected by the lawyer's financial or other personal interests.

Comment:

* * *

 c. *A lawyer with a personal or financial interest adverse to an interest of a client.* Client interests include all those that a reasonable lawyer, unaffected by a conflicting personal interest, would protect or advance. Perhaps the clearest case of a conflict is where the lawyer has a significant adverse financial interest in the object of the representation. Such a financial interest, other than one so insignificant that a person of normal sensibility would be unaffected by it, ordinarily constitutes a conflict of interest. A lawyer having such an interest is prohibited from accepting or continuing the representation unless the affected client gives informed consent.

A conflict under this Section need not be created by a financial interest. Included are interests that might be altruistic, such as an interest in furthering a charity favored by the lawyer, and matters of personal relationship, for example where the opposing party is the lawyer's spouse or a long-time friend or an institution with which the lawyer has a special relationship of loyalty. Such a conflict may also result from a lawyer's deeply held religious, philosophical, political, or public-policy beliefs. (On the limited imputation of such conflicts, see Comment *g* hereto.) A conflict exists if such an interest would materially impair the lawyer's ability to consider alternative courses of action that otherwise might be available to a client, to discuss all relevant aspects of the subject matter of the representation with the client, or otherwise to provide effective representation to the client. In some cases, a conflict between the personal or financial interests of a lawyer and those of a client will be so substantial that client consent will not suffice to remove the disability (see § 122, Comment *g*).

Illustrations:

    1. Lawyer owns a 25 percent interest in a restaurant. Client was a customer at the restaurant and suffered severe food poisoning. Client has asked Lawyer to file suit against the restaurant for damages substantially in excess of insurance coverage. Lawyer's interest as investor in the restaurant might materially and adversely affect Lawyer's representation of Client. Because Client's recovery could significantly affect the value of Lawyer's investment interest, Lawyer may not represent Client even if Client were to give informed consent (see § 122(2)).

    2. Same facts as in Illustration 1, except that Lawyer's child owns a five percent interest in the restaurant. Even though Lawyer owns no interest personally, concern about injuring the financial position or reputation of Lawyer's child might materially and adversely affect Lawyer's representation of Client. If Lawyer concludes that Lawyer can overcome the personal concerns involved and represent Client effectively, the representation may proceed if Client gives informed consent to the representation (see § 122).

3.   Lawyer owns stock in a publicly held mutual fund that, in turn, carries in its diversified portfolio an interest of less than one percent in the common stock of Ajax Corporation, a publicly held corporation that produces frozen foods. The value of Lawyer's indirect interest in Ajax Corporation is less than $25.00. Client developed food poisoning after eating frozen peas that had been processed by Ajax Corporation and has asked Lawyer to file suit for damages against it. The described interest is so small, and the possibility of an effect on Lawyer's representation is so remote, that Lawyer need not raise the possibility of a conflict of interest with Client.

* * *

d. A lawyer seeking employment with an opposing party or law firm. This Section applies when a lawyer seeks to discuss the possibility of the lawyer's future employment with an adversary or an adversary's law firm. The conflict arises whether the discussions about future employment are initiated by the lawyer or by the other side. If discussion of employment has become concrete and the interest in such employment is mutual, the lawyer must promptly inform the client. Without effective client consent (see § 122), the lawyer must terminate all further discussions concerning the employment, or withdraw from representing the client (see § 32(2) & (3)). The same protocol is required with respect to a merger of law firms or similar change (see § 123).

* * *

e. A lawyer openly expressing public-policy views inconsistent with a client's position. In general, a lawyer may publicly take personal positions on controversial issues without regard to whether the positions are consistent with those of some or all of the lawyer's clients. Consent of the lawyer's clients is not required. Lawyers usually represent many clients, and professional detachment is one of the qualities a lawyer brings to each client. Moreover, it is a tradition that a lawyer's advocacy for a client should not be construed as an expression of the lawyer's personal views. Resolution of many public questions is benefited when independent legal minds are brought to bear on them. For example, if tax lawyers advocating positions about tax reform were obliged to advocate only positions that would serve the positions of their present clients, the public would lose the objective contributions to policy making of some persons most able to help.

However, a lawyer's right to freedom of expression is modified by the lawyer's duties to clients. Thus, a lawyer may not publicly take a policy position that is adverse to the position of a client that the lawyer is currently representing if doing so would materially and adversely affect the lawyer's representation of the client in the matter. The requirement that a lawyer not misuse a client's confidential information (see § 60) similarly applies to discussion of public issues. On the right of a lawyer to withdraw from a representation because of disagreement with a client's views, see § 32.

* * *

f. Initiation and settlement of class actions and other multiple-client representations. Class actions and similar proceedings can raise a number of personal-interest conflict-of-interest questions. A class action can transform a modest claim into a set of claims of large consequence and often has potential for magnifying attorney's fees. An individual plaintiff usually begins with a concern about an individual wrong, and prompt and complete redress of that wrong is often the client's goal. A class action might be the only practical means of vindicating the client interest. However, a class action can substitute a longer, more complex proceeding for one more beneficial for the client's individual interests. Where bringing a claim as a class action might materially and adversely affect the interests of the individual client, that possibility must be disclosed to that client. On the determination of client-lawyer relationships in class actions, see § 14, Comment *f.*

Settlement of a class action or similar suit can also create a conflict concerning the lawyer's fee. The defendant, for example, might offer to settle the matter for an amount or kind of relief that is relatively generous to the lawyer's client if the lawyer will agree to accept a low fee award. Conversely, the defendant might acquiesce in a generous award of attorney's fees in exchange for relatively modest relief for the client's substantive claim. The latter arrangement must be rejected by the class lawyer as subordinating the interests of the lawyer's client to the lawyer's own interest.

* * *

§ 126. Business Transactions Between a Lawyer and a Client

A lawyer may not participate in a business or financial transaction with a client, except a standard commercial transaction in which the lawyer does not render legal services, unless:

(1) the client has adequate information about the terms of the transaction and the risks presented by the lawyer's involvement in it;

(2) the terms and circumstances of the transaction are fair and reasonable to the client; and

(3) the client consents to the lawyer's role in the transaction under the limitations and conditions provided in § 122 after being encouraged, and given a reasonable opportunity, to seek independent legal advice concerning the transaction.

Comment:

[*a.   Scope and cross-references.*]

* * *

The requirements of this Section do not apply to ordinary client-lawyer fee agreements providing, for example, for hourly, lump-sum, or contingent fees. They do apply when a lawyer takes an interest in the client's business as payment of all or part of a legal fee. Other financial arrangements are examined in Chapter 3, including the reasonableness of legal fees (see § 34; see also § 135 (acting as officer or director of a client)). With respect to conflict-of-interest issues that arise out of transactions involving a client and a business in which a lawyer has an interest, see § 125, Comment *c*.

In any civil proceeding between a lawyer and a client or their successors, the lawyer has the burden of persuading the tribunal that requirements stated in this Section have been satisfied. In a disciplinary, criminal, or similar proceeding, the burden of persuasion rests on the prosecution (see § 5 (lawyer discipline)). In a discipline case, once proof has been introduced that the lawyer entered into a business transaction with a client, the burden of persuasion is on the lawyer to show that the transaction was fair and reasonable and that the client was adequately informed.

b.   Rationale. A lawyer's legal skill and training, together with the relationship of trust that arises between client and lawyer, create the possibility of overreaching when a lawyer enters into a business transaction with a client. Furthermore, a lawyer who engages in a business transaction with a client is in a position to arrange the form of the transaction or give legal advice to protect the lawyer's interests rather than advancing the client's interests. Proving fraud or actual overreaching might be difficult. Hence, the law does not require such a showing on the part of a client.

Illustration:

1. Lawyer, Investor, and Developer agree to form a corporation for the purpose of developing a residential subdivision. At the time, Lawyer represents both Investor and Developer as clients in other matters. Stock allocations are to be based on the agreed value of Investor's contributed land, the value of Developer's design and development services, and the value of Lawyer's legal services in organizing the enterprise and representing it thereafter. The arrangement constitutes a business transaction with a client and is subject to the requirements of this Section throughout the period during which the parties continue the arrangement.

* * *

c. Standard commercial transactions. The requirements of informed consent and objective fairness are satisfied when lawyer and client enter into standard commercial transactions in the regular course of business of the client, involving a product or service as to which the lawyer provides no legal services. This Section therefore does not apply to such transactions. Standard commercial transactions are those regularly entered into between the client and the general public, typically in which the terms and conditions are the same for all customers. In such circumstances, the client's interests in the transaction with the lawyer need no special protection. On the other hand, where a lawyer engages in the sale of goods or services ancillary to the practice of law, for example, the sale of title insurance, the requirements of this Section do apply.

d. A client's knowledge of the terms and the lawyer's role. A lawyer violates the standard of candor by entering into a transaction with a client as undisclosed principal, or without disclosing information or terms that might materially affect the client's bargain (see Restatement Second, Trusts § 170(2)).

Illustrations:

2. Lawyer represents the surviving Spouse of a long-time client. Lawyer advises Spouse that farmland owned by the estate should be sold to pay taxes. Using the name of a business associate as purported buyer, Lawyer purchases the land from Spouse without disclosing Lawyer's involvement in the purchase.

Even if the price is objectively fair, Lawyer has violated the requirement that Lawyer's identity be disclosed to the client.

* * *

e. The requirement that the terms of the transaction be fair. The requirement that the transaction be fair from the perspective of an objective observer derives from the general fiduciary requirement of fair dealing with a client (see § 16(3); Restatement Second, Trusts § 170(2) & Comment *w* thereto). Unintended overreaching is a possibility in transactions involving lawyers and their clients. Accordingly a lawyer must overcome a presumption that overreaching occurred by demonstrating the fairness of the transaction. Fairness is determined based on facts that reasonably could be known at the time of the transaction, not as the facts later develop. The relative ability of lawyer and client to foresee how the facts might develop, however, is relevant in determining fairness. An appropriate test is whether a disinterested lawyer would have advised the client not to enter the transaction with some other party.

Illustrations:

4. Lawyer and Client agree to purchase a parcel of land together. Because Client lacks sufficient cash, Client borrows the money from Lawyer at an interest rate of 10 percent. That was the general market rate of interest on the date of the loan, but Lawyer knew from discussions with another client, Banker, that Client would be able to borrow the same amount from several financial institutions at a lower rate of interest. Lawyer violated Lawyer's obligations to deal fairly with Client. Lawyer had reliable information, relevant to a material element of the transaction, that Lawyer failed to convey to Client.

[*f. Consent only after encouragement and opportunity to obtain independent legal advice.*]

* * *

An opportunity to obtain competent independent advice tends to assure that the client has time to consider the transaction and that the lawyer is not applying undue pressure on the client. By the same token, evidence that a lawyer has not allowed the client opportunity to obtain independent counsel is evidence of overreaching. An independent adviser also can bring an objective eye to the proposed arrangement.

* * *

g. The requirement of written notice and consent. Lawyer codes commonly require that notice to the client and the client's consent to a business transaction with the client's lawyer be in writing. When required by law, disclosure to the client of the terms of the transaction must also be in writing. Absence of the required writing renders the transaction voidable at the client's option. Written notice focuses the client's attention upon the right to withhold consent and has important evidentiary value if a dispute later arises concerning the client's consent. The notice should provide the client sufficient time to enable the client to study the transaction and obtain independent advice.

* * *

§ 127. A Client Gift to a Lawyer

(1) A lawyer may not prepare any instrument effecting any gift from a client to the lawyer, including a testamentary gift, unless the lawyer is a relative or other natural object of the client's generosity and the gift is not significantly disproportionate to those given other donees similarly related to the donor.

(2) A lawyer may not accept a gift from a client, including a testamentary gift, unless:

(a) the lawyer is a relative or other natural object of the client's generosity;

(b) the value conferred by the client and the benefit to the lawyer are insubstantial in amount; or

(c) the client, before making the gift, has received independent advice or has been encouraged, and given a reasonable opportunity, to seek such advice.

Comment:

[*a. Scope and cross-references.*]

* * *

The law of undue influence treats client gifts as presumptively fraudulent, so that the lawyer-donee bears a heavy burden of persuasion that the gift is fair and not the product of overreaching or otherwise an imposition upon the client. See Restatement Second,

Trusts § 343, Comments *l* and *m* (voidability of gifts from beneficiary to trustee); cf. Restatement Second, Contracts § 177 (contracts voidable on ground of undue influence). This Section assumes, but does not restate fully, the law of undue influence. The Section is stricter than the general law of undue influence in some jurisdictions. For example, the Section prohibits a lawyer from accepting a gift from a client (apart from the three stated exceptions) even if the lawyer has not engaged in undue influence.

b. Rationale. A client's valuable gift to a lawyer invites suspicion that the lawyer overreached or used undue influence. It would be difficult to reach any other conclusion when a lawyer has solicited the gift. Testamentary gifts are a subject of particular concern, both because the client is often of advanced age at the time the will is written and because it will often be difficult to establish the client's true intentions after the client's death. At the same time, the client-lawyer relationship in which a gift is made is often extended and personal. A genuine feeling of gratitude and admiration can motivate a client to confer a gift on the lawyer. The rule of this Section respects such genuine wishes while guarding against overreaching by lawyers.

c. Gifts subject to this Section. For the purposes of this Section, a gift is any transfer by the client to the lawyer of a thing of value made without consideration (compare § 126). A client's gift to a member of the lawyer's family, or to a person or institution designated by the lawyer, is treated as a gift to the lawyer if it was made under circumstances manifesting an intent to evade the rule of this Section.

d. Solicitation of a client gift. Even with respect to a gift not otherwise in violation of the lawyer's duty to the client under Subsection (2), a lawyer may not improperly induce the gift to the lawyer or to a spouse, child, or similar beneficiary of the lawyer (see generally Restatement Second, Property (Donative Transfers) § 34.7). Even bargain exchanges between lawyer and client are subject to a high level of scrutiny (see § 126, Comment *b*); it follows that gratuitous transfers conferring benefits on the lawyer are at least as subject to scrutiny. Accordingly, a client may void the client's gift to a lawyer or to the lawyer's beneficiary, unless the lawyer can demonstrate that the gift was not improperly induced by undue influence or otherwise. A lawyer's suggestion that a client make a gift to a charity favored by a lawyer would not ordinarily be improper, so long as the lawyer informs the client that the lawyer favors the charity and employs no improper means such as misrepresentation or other means of overreaching. A lawyer's suggestion to a client that the client employ the lawyer's services in the future does not constitute the solicitation of a gift.

e. A lawyer as a relative or other natural object of a client-donor's generosity. The general prohibition against a lawyer's receipt of a gift from a client is subject to exception when the lawyer is so related to the client that the gift should not cause suspicion (Subsection (2)(a)). Thus, a client-parent's gift to a lawyer-child is permissible. Such gifts are permissible even in the absence of independent legal advice (compare Subsection (2)(c)). In many families, one of whose members is a lawyer, it would be thought unusual for a family member to go outside the family for legal advice, for example, to write a will or create a trust for a family member. That the lawyer receives a gift under such a will or trust would, in context, ordinarily not indicate overreaching. However, if the lawyer receives significantly more benefit from a donative transfer of the family-member client than others in the family who are similarly related to the client, in the event of a challenge the lawyer bears the burden of persuading the tribunal that the gift was not the product of overreaching.

* * *

g. The effect of the client's opportunity to obtain independent advice. When a competent and independent person other than the lawyer-donee acts as the client's adviser with respect to a particular gift, there is less reason to be concerned with overreaching by the lawyer. A lawyer's encouragement to a client to seek independent advice also evidences concern for fairness on the lawyer's part. Whether the lawyer may prepare an instrument effecting the gift from the client to the lawyer is determined by Subsection (1), under which independent advice is irrelevant. If the lawyer does not prepare such an instrument, the lawyer is not precluded from receiving a gift subject to the limitations of Subsection (2)(c), including that of independent advice. Such a gift also remains subject to invalidation if the circumstances warrant under the law of fraud, duress, undue influence, or mistake (see Restatement Second, Trusts § 141 & § 343, Comments *l* & *m*).

Illustrations:

3. Client has come to Lawyer for preparation of Client's will. "I do not have living relatives and you have been my trusted friend and adviser for most of my adult life," Client tells Lawyer. "I want you to have a bequest of $50,000 from my estate." Lawyer urges Client to ask another lawyer to advise Client about such a gift and prepare any will effecting it. Client refuses, saying "I do not want anyone else to know my business." Lawyer may not draft Client's will containing the proposed gift to Lawyer.

4. The same facts as in Illustration 3, except that Client, professing the same wish to benefit Lawyer, tells Lawyer that Client is going to make a $50,000 cash gift to Lawyer. Lawyer encourages and gives Client a reasonable opportunity to seek independent advice about making a gift to Lawyer. Client does not do so. Lawyer may accept the inter vivos gift of $50,000 from Client, so long as Lawyer did not solicit the gift or prepare an instrument effecting the gift from Client.

5. On behalf of Client, a corporation assisted in the matter by Inside Legal Counsel, Lawyer has obtained satisfaction of a judgment in an amount significantly surpassing what Client and Inside Legal Counsel thought possible. Lawyer receives payment of Lawyer's final statement with a covering letter from Inside Legal Counsel stating that Client, on the recommendation of Inside Legal Counsel, was also enclosing an additional check in a substantial amount in gratitude for the outstanding result obtained by Lawyer. Lawyer may accept the gift of the additional check, reasonably assuming that Client has been appropriately advised in the matter by Inside Legal Counsel.

The recommendation of independent advice must be more than perfunctory. The independent adviser may not be affiliated with the lawyer-donee. It is not necessary that the person consulted as adviser be a lawyer. Any person qualifies who is mature and appropriately experienced in personal financial matters, trusted by the client, not a beneficiary of the gift, and not selected by or affiliated with the lawyer.

A lawyer-donee bears the burden of showing that reasonable effort was made to persuade the client to obtain independent advice and that the lawyer did not otherwise unduly influence or overreach the client. If the lawyer-donee has tried but failed to persuade the client to seek such help, or if the client rejects the independent adviser's counsel, the presumption of overreaching can be overcome and the gift upheld.

* * *

TOPIC 3.   CONFLICTS OF INTEREST AMONG CURRENT CLIENTS

* * *

§ 128.   Representing Clients with Conflicting Interests in Civil Litigation

Unless all affected clients consent to the representation under the limitations and conditions provided in § 122, a lawyer in civil litigation may not:

> (1) represent two or more clients in a matter if there is a substantial risk that the lawyer's representation of one client would be materially and adversely affected by the lawyer's duties to another client in the matter; or

> (2) represent one client to assert or defend a claim against or brought by another client currently represented by the lawyer, even if the matters are not related.

Comment:

* * *

b. Rationale. Dealing with a conflict of interest among current clients requires reconciling four fundamental and sometimes competing values. First, confidential information of one client must not be used, intentionally or inadvertently, on behalf of another client in ways that would have material and adverse consequences for the disadvantaged client. Although such use violates the requirement of § 60(1), the fact of use will often be difficult to detect and therefore requires preventive measures. Second, the client's faith in the lawyer's loyalty to the client's interests will be severely tried whenever the lawyer must be loyal to another client whose interests are materially adverse. Third, a tribunal properly wishes assurance that its own processes not be compromised by less than vigorous advocacy, delayed by a necessary change of counsel in the course of the proceeding, or later reversed because a litigant was inadequately represented. Even if the parties would give informed consent to being represented by one lawyer, in some cases the parties' positions cannot be effectively presented through the same advocate (see § 122(2)(b) & Comment *g(iii)* thereto). Fourth, clients might want to reduce the costs of litigation and achieve the benefits of a coordinated position in their cases. Clients normally are allowed to give informed consent to a representation that otherwise would violate this Section.

c(i). Clients aligned in opposition to each other—in general. Fundamental conflicts of loyalty and threats to client confidentiality would be inevitable if a lawyer were to represent clients opposing each other in the same litigation. Many actions that the lawyer took on behalf of one client would have the potential for being at the expense of the other. Furthermore, the public interest in the orderly management of litigation could be seriously compromised. Thus, the same lawyer may not represent both plaintiff and defendant in a breach-of-contract lawsuit, for example. A similar rule applies, as stated in Subsection (2), when the clients are involved in two or more lawsuits that are otherwise unrelated. The rule of Subsection (2) applies without regard to the specific inquiries relevant in assessing a conflict under Subsection (1). See Comment *e* hereto.

* * *

d.   Clients nominally aligned on the same side in the litigation. Multiple representation is precluded when the clients, although nominally on the same side of a lawsuit, in fact have such different interests that representation of one will have a material and adverse effect on the lawyer's representation of the other. Such conflicts can occur whether the clients are aligned as co-plaintiffs or co-defendants, as well as in complex and multiparty litigation.

d(i).   Clients aligned as co-plaintiffs. No conflict of interest is ordinarily presented when two or more of a lawyer's clients assert claims against a defendant. However, sometimes two parties aligned on the same side of a case as co-claimants might wish to characterize the facts differently. The client-claimants might also have a potential lawsuit against each other. For example, a passenger in an automobile damage action might be a co-plaintiff with the driver of the car in a suit alleging negligence of the driver of the other car, but also be able to contend that the driver of the passenger's car was negligent as well, a conclusion that the driver would be motivated to deny. Where there are such possible claims, the lawyer must warn clients about the possibilities of such differences and obtain the consent of each before agreeing to represent them as co-claimants (see § 122).

When multiple claimants assert claims against a defendant who lacks sufficient assets to meet all of the damage claims, a conflict of interest might also be presented. Indeed, whether or not the defendant has assets sufficient to pay all claims, a proposed settlement might create conflicts because the plaintiffs differ in their willingness to accept the settlement. Before any settlement is accepted on behalf of multiple clients, their lawyer must inform each of them about all of the terms of the settlement, including the amounts that each of the other claimants will receive if the settlement is accepted. A similar conflict of interest can arise for a lawyer representing multiple defending parties.

Illustrations:

1. Lawyer represents A and B, pedestrians struck by an automobile as they stood at a street corner. Each has sued C, the owner-driver, for $150,000. C has $100,000 in liability insurance coverage and no other assets with which to satisfy a judgment. Neither A nor B can be paid the full amount of their claims and any sum recovered by one will reduce the assets available to pay the other's claim. Because of the conflict of interest, Lawyer can continue to represent both A and B only with the informed consent of each (see § 122).

2. The same facts as in Illustration 1, except that C offers to settle A's claim for $60,000 and B's claim for $40,000. Lawyer must inform both A and B of all of the terms of the proposed settlement, including the amounts offered to each client. If one client wishes to accept and the other wishes to reject the proposed settlement, Lawyer may continue to represent both A and B only after a renewal of informed consent by each.

d(ii). Clients aligned as co-defendants in civil case. Clients aligned as co-defendants also can have conflicting interests. Each would usually prefer to see the plaintiff defeated altogether, but if the plaintiff succeeds, each will often prefer to see liability deflected mainly or entirely upon other defendants. Indeed, a plaintiff often sues multiple defendants in the hope that each of the defendants will take the position that another of them is responsible, thus enhancing the likelihood of the plaintiff's recovering. Such conflicts preclude joint representation, absent each co-defendant's informed consent (see § 122).

A contract between the parties can eliminate the conflict. When an employee injures someone in an incident arising out of the employment, for example, an employer that is capable of paying the judgment might agree in advance to hold the employee harmless in the matter so that only the employer will bear any judgment ultimately entered. If only one of the parties will ultimately be liable to the plaintiff, there is little reason to incur the expense of separate counsel. However, the initial conflict must be understood by both defendants and each must consent, particularly if the clients must negotiate an agreement governing who will bear ultimate liability (see § 130).

* * *

e. Suing a present client in an unrelated matter. A lawyer's representation of Client A might require the lawyer to file a lawsuit against Client B whom the lawyer represents in an unrelated matter.

Because the matters are unrelated, no confidential information is likely to be used improperly, nor will the lawyer take both sides in a single proceeding. However, the lawyer has a duty of loyalty to the client being sued. Moreover, the client on whose behalf suit is filed might fear that the lawyer would pursue that client's case less effectively out of deference to the other client. Thus, a lawyer may not sue a current client on behalf of another client, even in an unrelated matter, unless consent is obtained under the conditions and limitations of § 122. On identifying who is a present client, see § 14 and § 121, Comment *d*. On the possibility of informed consent in advance to such suits in certain cases, see § 122, Comment *d*.

Illustrations:

> 3. Lawyer represents Client B in seeking a tax refund. Client A wishes to file suit against Client B in a contract action unrelated to the tax claim. Lawyer may not represent Client A in the suit against Client B as long as Lawyer represents Client B in the tax case, unless both clients give informed consent. On withdrawal, see § 121, Comment *e*.

* * *

f. Concurrently taking adverse legal positions on behalf of different clients. A lawyer ordinarily may take inconsistent legal positions in different courts at different times. While each client is entitled to the lawyer's effective advocacy of that client's position, if the rule were otherwise law firms would have to specialize in a single side of legal issues.

However, a conflict is presented when there is a substantial risk that a lawyer's action in Case A will materially and adversely affect another of the lawyer's clients in Case B. Factors relevant in determining the risk of such an effect include whether the issue is before a trial court or an appellate court; whether the issue is substantive or procedural; the temporal relationship between the matters; the practical significance of the issue to the immediate and long-run interests of the clients involved; and the clients' reasonable expectations in retaining the lawyer. If a conflict of interest exists, absent informed consent of the affected clients under § 122, the lawyer must withdraw from one or both of the matters. Informed client consent is provided for in § 122. On circumstances in which informed client consent would not allow the lawyer to proceed with representation of both clients, see § 122(2)(c) and Comment *g(iv)* thereto.

Illustrations:

5. Lawyer represents two clients in damage actions pending in different United States District Courts. In one case, representing the plaintiff, Lawyer will attempt to introduce certain evidence at trial and argue there for its admissibility. In the other case, representing a defendant, Lawyer will object to an anticipated attempt by the plaintiff to introduce similar evidence. Even if there is some possibility that one court's ruling might be published and cited as authority in the other proceeding, Lawyer may proceed with both representations without obtaining the consent of the clients involved.

6. The same facts as in Illustration 5, except that the cases have proceeded to the point where certiorari has been granted in each by the United States Supreme Court to consider the common evidentiary question. Any position that Lawyer would assert on behalf of either client on the legal issue common to each case would have a material and adverse impact on the interests of the other client. Thus, a conflict of interest is presented. Even the informed consent of both Client A and Client B would be insufficient to permit Lawyer to represent each before the Supreme Court.

* * *

§ 129. Conflicts of Interest in Criminal Litigation

Unless all affected clients consent to the representation under the limitations and conditions provided in § 122, a lawyer in a criminal matter may not represent:

(1) two or more defendants or potential defendants in the same matter; or

(2) a single defendant, if the representation would involve a conflict of interest as defined in § 121.

Comment:

* * *

b. Rationale. The rules in this Section, like those examined in § 128, seek to protect confidential client information, enhance clients' sense of lawyers' loyalty, assist a court's effort to assure fairness and the finality of results, and minimize the cost of legal assistance for clients. In addition, criminal litigation is governed by constitutional protections not applicable in civil litigation. The Sixth Amendment, for example, guarantees that "In all criminal prosecutions, the accused shall enjoy the right . . . to have the Assistance of Counsel for his defense." That guarantee and its implied right to the effective assistance of counsel impose special constraints on the representation of multiple clients in criminal matters. However, the same guarantee cautions that a tribunal not disturb a fully informed selection of counsel absent compelling circumstances.

* * *

c. Multiple criminal-defense representations. Subsection (1) recognizes that the representation of co-defendants in criminal cases involves at least the potential for conflicts of interest. For example, if one defendant is offered favorable treatment in return for testimony against a co-defendant, a single lawyer could not give advice favorable to one defendant's interests while adhering to the duty of loyalty to the other. Similarly, individual defendants might have had different motives for and understandings of events, so that establishing a common position among them is difficult. Witnesses who would be favorable to one defendant might be subject to cross-examination that would be unfavorable to another defendant. In closing argument, counsel must choose which facts to stress. For example, stressing the minor role of one defendant might imply the major role of another.

Because of such potential conflicts and the constitutional significance of the issues they raise, joint representation in criminal cases often has a material and adverse effect on the representation of each defendant and thus cannot be undertaken in the absence of client consent under the limitations and conditions stated in § 122.

Criminal defendants might nonetheless consider it in their interest to be represented by a single lawyer even when the financial cost of separate counsel is not a factor. A single lawyer can help assure a common position and increase the likelihood that none of the co-defendants will cooperate with the prosecution against the others. For such reasons, a criminal conviction involving joint representation ordinarily is not impeachable absent a showing of timely objection and actual prejudice. Were the rule otherwise, defendants could avoid raising a conflict issue before trial so as to create an issue for later appeal.

On the other hand, both the prosecutor and the trial judge have a responsibility to assure a fair trial for each defendant. When a defense lawyer would be required to assume an adverse position with respect to one or more of the clients, the conflict is nonconsentable (see

§ 122(2)(b) & Comment *g(iii)* thereto). Efficient operation of the judicial system requires that a verdict not be vulnerable to contentions that a defendant was disadvantaged by an undisclosed conflict of interest. A prosecutor might object to joint-representation arrangements to assure that a conflict possibility is resolved before trial. Even without objection by the prosecutor or defendant, the tribunal may raise the issue on its own initiative and refuse to permit joint representation where there is a significant threat to the interest in the finality of judgments.

Illustrations:

    1. A and B are co-defendants charged with a felony offense of armed robbery. They are both represented by Lawyer. The prosecutor believes that A planned the crime and was the only one carrying a weapon. The prosecutor offers to accept B's plea of guilty to a misdemeanor if B will testify against A. Lawyer's loyalty to A causes Lawyer to persuade B that the prosecutor's proposal should be rejected. Following a trial, both A and B are convicted of the felony. When plea negotiations involving B's separate interests began, B should have received independent counsel. In the circumstances, Lawyer could not properly represent A and B even with the informed consent of both clients (see § 122, Comment *g(iii)*).

* * *

    d. A criminal-defense lawyer with conflicting duties to other clients. As required in Subsection (2), a conflict exists when a defense lawyer in a criminal matter has duties to clients in other matters that might conflict. A conflict exists, for example, if the lawyer also represents either a prosecutor or a prosecution witness in an unrelated matter. The conflict could lead the lawyer to be less vigorous in defending the criminal case in order to avoid offending the other client, or the lawyer might be constrained in cross-examining the other client (see § 60(1)). A lawyer who represents a criminal defendant may not represent the state in unrelated civil matters when such representation would have a material and adverse effect on the lawyer's handling of the criminal case.

    Ordinarily, these conflicts may be waived by client consent under the limitations and conditions in § 122. Because the defendant's constitutional rights are implicated, court procedures often require that

339

consent be made part of the formal record in the criminal case (see Comment *c* hereto).

* * *

§ 130. Multiple Representation in a Nonlitigated Matter

Unless all affected clients consent to the representation under the limitations and conditions provided in § 122, a lawyer may not represent two or more clients in a matter not involving litigation if there is a substantial risk that the lawyer's representation of one or more of the clients would be materially and adversely affected by the lawyer's duties to one or more of the other clients.

Comment:

[*a. Scope and cross-references.*]

* * *

The conflicts considered in this Section generally arise in two contexts. The multiple clients might seek the lawyer's assistance on achieving a common goal, such as forming a corporation, recognizing that they have common interests with respect to major elements of the relationship but also interests concerning which there might be differences and potential for conflict. Second, multiple clients might seek the lawyer's assistance to resolve a recognized area of difference, such as the settlement outside litigation of a business dispute. The latter conflicts include those considered under the heading of "intermediation" in ABA Model Rules of Professional Conduct, Rule 2.2 (1983). Although its terminology might be thought to imply otherwise, Rule 2.2 addresses a particular setting for applying the general rules governing conflicts. "Intermediation" is a term that has not passed into general professional usage and is not employed here.

* * *

b. Rationale. As in litigated cases, multiple representation not involving litigation requires a lawyer to remain loyal to clients and protect their confidential information (see § 60(1)). Providing economical legal services is also a relevant concern (see § 128 & § 129, Comment *b*). The orderly administration of tribunals is, by definition, not a relevant factor for the issues in this Section.

Whether a lawyer can function in a situation of conflict (see § 121) depends on whether the conflict is consentable (see § 122(2)), which in turn depends on whether it is "reasonably likely that the lawyer will be able to provide adequate representation" to all affected clients (see

§ 122(2)). Conflicted but unconsented representation of multiple clients, for example of the buyer and seller of property, is sometimes defended with the argument that the lawyer was performing the role of mere "scrivener" or a similarly mechanical role. The characterization is usually inappropriate. A lawyer must accept responsibility to give customary advice and customary range of legal services, unless the clients have given their informed consent to a narrower range of the lawyer's responsibilities. On limitations of a lawyer's responsibilities, see § 19(1).

c. Assisting multiple clients with common objectives, but conflicting interests. When multiple clients have generally common interests, the role of the lawyer is to advise on relevant legal considerations, suggest alternative ways of meeting common objectives, and draft instruments necessary to accomplish the desired results. Multiple representations do not always present a conflict of interest requiring client consent (see § 121). For example, in representing spouses jointly in the purchase of property as co-owners, the lawyer would reasonably assume that such a representation does not involve a conflict of interest. A conflict could be involved, however, if the lawyer knew that one spouse's objectives in the acquisition were materially at variance with those of the other spouse.

Illustrations:

    1.   Husband and Wife consult Lawyer for estate-planning advice about a will for each of them. Lawyer has had professional dealings with the spouses, both separately and together, on several prior occasions. Lawyer knows them to be knowledgeable about their respective rights and interests, competent to make independent decisions if called for, and in accord on their common and individual objectives. Lawyer may represent both clients in the matter without obtaining consent (see § 121). While each spouse theoretically could make a distribution different from the other's, including a less generous bequest to each other, those possibilities do not create a conflict of interest, and none reasonably appears to exist in the circumstances.

    2.   The same facts as in Illustration 1, except that Lawyer has not previously met the spouses. Spouse A does most of the talking in the initial discussions with Lawyer. Spouse B, who owns significantly more property than Spouse A, appears to disagree with important positions of Spouse A but to be uncomfortable in expressing that disagreement and does not pursue them when Spouse A appears impatient and peremptory. Representation of both spouses would involve a conflict of interest. Lawyer may

proceed to provide the requested legal assistance only with consent given under the limitations and conditions provided in § 122.

3.   The same facts as in Illustration 1, except that Lawyer has not previously met the spouses. But in this instance, unlike in Illustration 2, in discussions with the spouses, Lawyer asks questions and suggests options that reveal both Spouse A and Spouse B to be knowledgeable about their respective rights and interests, competent to make independent decisions if called for, and in accord on their common and individual objectives. Lawyer has adequately verified the absence of a conflict of interest and thus may represent both clients in the matter without obtaining consent (see § 122).

Clients might not fully understand the potential for conflict in their interests as the result of ignorance about their legal rights, about possible alternatives to those that the clients have considered prior to retaining the lawyer, or about the uncommunicated plans or objectives of another client. In other situations, prospective clients might agree on objectives when they first approach the common lawyer, but it should be reasonably apparent that a conflict is likely to develop as the representation proceeds. A client's right to communicate in confidence with the attorney should not be constrained by concern that discord might result (cf. § 75). A lawyer is not required to suggest or assume discord where none exists, but when a conflict is reasonably apparent or foreseeable, the lawyer may proceed with multiple representation only after all affected clients have consented as provided in § 122.

Illustration:

4.   A, B, and C are interested in forming a partnership in which A is to provide the capital, B the basic patent, and C the management skill. Only C will spend significant amounts of time operating the business. A, B, and C jointly request Lawyer to represent them in creating the partnership. The different contributions to be made to the partnership alone indicate that the prospective partners have conflicts of interest with respect to the structure and governance of the partnership (see § 121). With the informed consent of each (see § 122), Lawyer may represent all three clients in forming the business. Lawyer may assist the clients in valuing their respective contributions and suggest arrangements to protect their respective interests. With respect to conflicts and informed consent in representing the partnership as

well as the partners once the business is established, see § 131, Comment *e*.

d. Clients with known differences to be resolved. Multiple prospective clients might already be aware that their interests and objectives are antagonistic to some degree. The lawyer must ascertain at the outset what kind of assistance the clients require. Service by the lawyer or another person as an arbitrator or mediator (and not as a lawyer representing clients), for example, might well serve the clients' interests.

When circumstances reasonably indicate that the prospective clients might be able to reach a reasonable reconciliation of their differences by agreement and with the lawyer's assistance, the lawyer may represent them after obtaining informed consent (see § 122). In particular, the lawyer should explain the effect of joint representation on the lawyer's ability to protect each client's confidential information (see § 75). If the joint representation is undertaken, the lawyer should help the clients reach agreement on outstanding issues but should not advance the interests of one of the clients to the detriment of another (see § 122, Comment *h*).

Relations among multiple clients can develop into adversarial, even litigated, matters. Even if the possibility of litigation is substantial and even though the consent does not permit the lawyer to represent one client against the other if litigation does ensue (see § 122(2)(b) & § 128), with informed consent a lawyer could accept multiple representation in an effort to reconcile the differences of the clients short of litigation. The lawyer should inform the clients that the effort to overcome differences might ultimately fail and require the lawyer's complete withdrawal from the matter, unless the clients agreed that the lawyer thereafter could continue to represent less than all clients (see § 121, Comment *e(i)*). The lawyer is not required to encourage each client to obtain independent advice about being jointly represented, but the lawyer should honor any client request for such an opportunity.

Illustrations:

5. The same facts as in Illustration 4, except that the partnership of A, B, and C is formed and commences business. The business encounters difficulty in securing customers and controlling costs, and it shortly appears that the business will fail unless additional funding is obtained. No outside funds are available, and A announces unwillingness to provide additional capital

unless B and C agree to increase A's interest in the business. B and C believe that A is requesting an unreasonably large additional share. A, B, and C seek Lawyer's assistance in resolving their disagreements. A conflict clearly exists between the clients (§ 121). Lawyer may agree to represent the three clients in seeking to arrive at a mutually satisfactory resolution, but only after Lawyer obtains the informed consent of each client and there is a clear definition of the services that Lawyer will provide. In representing the clients, Lawyer may not favor the position of any client over the others (see § 122, Comment *h*).

6. Husband and Wife have agreed to obtain an uncontested dissolution of their marriage. They have consulted Lawyer to help them reach an agreement on disposition of their property. A conflict of interest clearly exists between the prospective clients (§ 121). If reasonable prospects of an agreement exist, Lawyer may accept the joint representation with the effective consent of both (see § 122). However, in the later dissolution proceeding, Lawyer may represent only one of the parties (see § 128, Comment *c*), and Lawyer must withdraw from representing both clients if their efforts to reach an agreement fail (see § 121, Comment *e(i)*).

* * *

§ 131. Conflicts of Interest in Representing an Organization

Unless all affected clients consent to the representation under the limitations and conditions provided in § 122, a lawyer may not represent both an organization and a director, officer, employee, shareholder, owner, partner, member, or other individual or organization associated with the organization if there is a substantial risk that the lawyer's representation of either would be materially and adversely affected by the lawyer's duties to the other.

Comment:

* * *

b. Rationale. An organization with more than a single owner-employee is an aggregation of multiple interests, if only because it is made up of multiple persons or entities. Persons initially forming an organization are linked by a common interest that partly transcends their individual interests. The individuals might have separate lawyers for their other activities and for negotiating the question of their shares or other forms of control in the organization. However, a lawyer might be retained for representation relating to the organization separate from that of any individual associated with the enterprise. An organization's lawyer thus is said to represent the entity and not the elements that make it up. A lawyer for an organization serves whatever lawful interest the organization defines as its interest, acting through its responsible agents and in accordance with its decisionmaking procedures (see § 96(1) and Comment *d* thereto).

* * *

[*e. Representation of an organization and an individual constituent.*]

* * *

When a lawyer proposes to represent both an organization and a person associated with it, such as an officer, director, or employee, whether a conflict exists is determined by an analysis of the interests of the organization as an entity and those of the individuals involved. That is true whether the multiple representation involves civil (see § 128) or criminal (see § 129) litigation or a nonlitigated matter (see § 130). The interests of the organization are those defined by its agents authorized to act in the matter (see § 96, Comment *d*). For example, when an organization is accused of wrongdoing, an individual such as a director, officer, or other agent will sometimes be charged as well, and the lawyer representing the organization might be asked also to represent the individual. Such representation would constitute a conflict of interest when the individual's interests are materially adverse to the interests of the organization (see § 121). When there is no material adversity of interest, such as when the individual owns all of the equity in the organization or played a routine role in the underlying transaction, no conflict exists. In instances of adversity, concurrent representation would be permissible with the consent of all affected clients under the limitations and conditions stated in § 122.

Consent by an organization can be given in any manner consistent with the organization's lawful decisionmaking procedures. Applicable corporate law may provide that an officer who is personally interested in the matter may not provide consent in the matter. In deciding whether to consent to multiple representation by outside counsel, the organization might rely upon the advice of inside legal counsel. Issues concerning informed consent by public organizations to otherwise conflicted representations are discussed in § 122, Comment *c*.

Illustrations:

3. President, the chief executive officer of Corporation, has been charged with discussing prices with the president of a competing firm. If found guilty, both President and Corporation will be subject to civil and criminal penalties. Lawyer, who is representing Corporation, has concluded after a thorough investigation that no such pricing discussions occurred. Both Corporation and President plan to defend on that ground. President has asked Lawyer to represent President as well as Corporation in the proceedings. Although the factual and legal defenses of President and Corporation appear to be consistent at the outset, the likelihood of conflicting positions in such matters as plea bargaining requires Lawyer to obtain the informed consent of both clients before proceeding with the representation (see § 129, Comment *c*).

4. The same facts as in Illustration 3, except that after further factual investigation both President and Corporation now concede that the pricing discussions took place. One of President's defenses will be that the former general counsel of Corporation told President that discussion of general pricing practices with a competitor was not illegal. Corporation denies that such was the advice given and asserts that President acted without authority. The conflict between President and Corporation is so great that the same lawyer could not provide adequate legal services to both in the matter. Thus, continued representation of both is not subject to consent (see § 122, Comment *g(iii)*, & §§ 128 & 129).

If a person affiliated with an organization makes an unsolicited disclosure of information to a lawyer who represents only the organization, indicating the person's erroneous expectation that the lawyer will keep the information confidential from the organization, the lawyer must inform the person that the lawyer does not represent the person (see § 103, Comment *e*). The lawyer generally is not prohibited from sharing the communication with the organization. However, the requirements stated in § 15, Comment *c*, with respect to safeguarding confidential information of a prospective client may apply. That would occur when the person reasonably appeared to be consulting the lawyer as present or prospective client with respect to the person's individual interests, and the lawyer failed to warn the associated person that the lawyer represents only the organization and could act against the person's interests as a result (see § 103, Comment *e*). With respect to a lawyer's duties when a person associated with the organization expressed an intent to act wrongfully and thereby threatens harm to the organization client, see § 96(2) and Comment *f* thereto.

Issues considered in this Comment may be particularly acute in the case of close corporations, small partnerships, and similar organizations in which, for example, one person with substantial ownership interests also manages. Such a manager may have a corresponding tendency to treat corporate and similar entity distinctions as mere formalities. In such instances, when ownership is so concentrated that no nonmanaging owner exists and in the absence of material impact on the interests of other nonclients (such as creditors in the case of an insolvent corporation), a lawyer acts reasonably in accepting in good faith a controlling manager's position that the interests of all controlling persons and the entity should be treated as if they were the same. Similar considerations apply when a close corporation or similar organization is owned and managed by a small number of owner-managers whose interests are not materially in conflict.

* * *

TOPIC 4. CONFLICTS OF INTEREST WITH A FORMER CLIENT

* * *

§ 132. A Representation Adverse to the Interests of a Former Client

Unless both the affected present and former clients consent to the representation under the limitations and conditions provided in § 122, a lawyer who has represented a client in a matter may not thereafter represent another client in the same or a substantially related matter in which the interests of the former client are materially adverse. The current matter is substantially related to the earlier matter if:

(1) the current matter involves the work the lawyer performed for the former client; or

(2) there is a substantial risk that representation of the present client will involve the use of information acquired in the course of representing the former client, unless that information has become generally known.

Comment:

* * *

b. Rationale. The rule described in this Section accommodates four policies. First, absent the rule, a lawyer's incentive to serve a present client might cause the lawyer to compromise the lawyer's continuing duties to the former client (see § 33). Specifically, the lawyer might use confidential information of the former client contrary to that client's interest and in violation of § 60. The second policy consideration is the converse of the first. The lawyer's obligations to the former client might constrain the lawyer in representing the present client effectively, for example, by limiting the questions the lawyer could ask the former client in testimony. Third, at the time the lawyer represented the former client, the lawyer should have no incentive to lay the basis for subsequent representation against that client, such as by drafting provisions in a contract that could later be construed against the former client. Fourth, and pointing the other way, because much law practice is transactional, clients often retain lawyers for service only on specific cases or issues. A rule that would transform each engagement into a lifetime commitment would make lawyers reluctant to take new, relatively modest matters.

c. The relationship between current-client and former-client conflicts rules. The difference between a former-client conflict under this Section and a present-client conflict considered in Topic 3 (§§ 128–130) is that this Section applies only to representation in the same or a substantially related matter. The present-client conflict rules prohibit adverse representation regardless of the lack of any other relationship between them. If the two representations overlap in time, the rules of §§ 128–130 apply.

* * *

If a lawyer is approached by a prospective client seeking representation in a matter adverse to an existing client, the present-client conflict may not be transformed into a former-client conflict by the lawyer's withdrawal from the representation of the existing client. A premature withdrawal violates the lawyer's obligation of loyalty to the existing client and can constitute a breach of the client-lawyer contract of employment (see § 32, Comment *c*). On withdrawal when a dispute arises between two or more of the lawyer's clients, see § 121, Comment *e(i)*. On advance consent, see id. and § 122, especially Comment *d*.

d. The same or a substantially related matter. As indicated in the Section, three types of former-client conflicts are prohibited.

d(i). Switching sides in the same matter. Representing one side and then switching to represent the other in the same matter clearly implicates loyalty to the first client and protection of that client's confidences. Similar considerations apply in nonlitigated matters. For

348

example, a lawyer negotiating a complex agreement on behalf of Seller could not withdraw and represent Buyer against the interests of Seller in the same transaction. Switching sides in a litigated matter can also risk confusing the trier of fact. Just as a lawyer may not represent both sides concurrently in the same case (see §§ 128–130), the lawyer also may not represent them consecutively.

d(ii). Attacking a lawyer's own former work. Beyond switching sides in the same matter, the concept of substantial relationship applies to later developments out of the original matter. A matter is substantially related if it involves the work the lawyer performed for the former client. For example, a lawyer may not on behalf of a later client attack the validity of a document that the lawyer drafted if doing so would materially and adversely affect the former client. Similarly, a lawyer may not represent a debtor in bankruptcy in seeking to set aside a security interest of a creditor that is embodied in a document that the lawyer previously drafted for the creditor.

Illustration:

> 1. Lawyer has represented Husband in a successful effort to have Wife removed as beneficiary of his life insurance policy. After Husband's death, Wife seeks to retain Lawyer to negotiate with the insurance company to set aside the change of beneficiary and obtain the proceeds of the policy for Wife. The subsequent representation would require that Lawyer attack the work Lawyer performed for Husband. Accordingly, Lawyer may not accept Wife as a client in the matter.

d(iii). The substantial-relationship test and the protection of confidential information of a former client. The substantial-relationship standard is employed most frequently to protect the confidential information of the former client obtained in the course of the representation. A subsequent matter is substantially related to an earlier matter within the meaning of Subsection (2) if there is a substantial risk that the subsequent representation will involve the use of confidential information of the former client obtained in the course of the representation in violation of § 60. "Confidential information" is defined in § 59. Substantial risk exists where it is reasonable to conclude that it would materially advance the client's position in the subsequent matter to use confidential information obtained in the prior representation.

A concern to protect a former client's confidential information would be self-defeating if, in order to obtain its protection, the former client were required to reveal in a public proceeding the particular communication or other confidential information that could be used in the subsequent representation. The interests of subsequent clients also militate against extensive inquiry into the precise nature of the lawyer's representation of the subsequent client and the nature of exchanges between them.

The substantial-relationship test avoids requiring disclosure of confidential information by focusing upon the general features of the matters involved and inferences as to the likelihood that confidences were imparted by the former client that could be used to adverse effect in the subsequent representation. The inquiry into the issues involved in the prior representation should be as specific as possible without thereby revealing the confidential client information itself or confidential information concerning the second client. When the prior matter involved litigation, it will be conclusively presumed that the lawyer obtained confidential information about the issues involved in the litigation. When the prior matter did not involve litigation, its scope is assessed by reference to the work that the lawyer undertook and the array of information that a lawyer ordinarily would have obtained to carry out that work. The information obtained by the lawyer might also be proved by inferences from redacted documents, for example. On the use of in camera procedures to disclose confidential material to the tribunal but not to an opposing party, see § 86, Comment *f*.

Illustrations:

    2. Lawyer represented Client A for a period of five years lobbying on environmental issues relating to uranium production. In the course of the representation in one matter, Lawyer learned the basis for Client A's uranium-production decisions. Lawyer now has been asked to represent Client B, a purchaser of uranium, in an antitrust action against A and others alleging a conspiracy to impose limits on production. It is likely that Client B's claims against A would include addressing the same production decisions about which Lawyer earlier learned. Use of confidential information concerning A's production decisions learned in the earlier representation would materially advance the position of Client B in the antitrust matter. The matters are substantially related, and Lawyer may not represent Client B without effective consent of both A and B (see § 122).

    3. Lawyer was general inside legal counsel to Company A for many years, dealing with all aspects of corporate affairs and management. Lawyer was dismissed from that position when

Company A hired a new president. Company B has asked Lawyer to represent it in an antitrust suit against Company A based on facts arising after Lawyer left Company A's employ but involving broad charges of anti-competitive practices of Company A that, if true, were occurring at the time that Lawyer represented Company A. Lawyer may not represent Company B in the antitrust action. Because of the breadth of confidential client information of Company A to which Lawyer is likely to have had access during the earlier representation and the breadth of issues open in the antitrust claim of Company B, a substantial risk exists that use of that information would materially advance Company B's position in the later representation.

4. Lawyer represented Client A, a home builder, at the closings of the sales of several homes Client A had built in Tract X. Lawyers performing such work normally might encounter issues relating to marketability of title. A is now represented by other counsel. Client B has asked Lawyer to represent him in a suit against A in connection with B's sale to A of Tract Y, a parcel of land owned by Client B on which A plans to build homes. The present suit involves the marketability of the title to Tract Y. Although both representations involve marketability of title, it is unlikely that Lawyer's knowledge of marketability of Tract X would be relevant to the litigation involving the marketability of title to Tract Y. Accordingly, the matters are not substantially related. Lawyer may represent Client B against A without informed consent of A.

As used in this Section, the term "matter" includes not only representation in a litigated case, but also any representation involving a contract, claim, charge, or other subject of legal advice (compare § 133, Comment e). The term "matter" ordinarily does not include a legal position taken on behalf of a former client unless the underlying facts are also related. For example, a lawyer who successfully argued that a statute is constitutional on behalf of a former client may later argue that the statute is unconstitutional on behalf of a present client in a case not involving the former client, even though the lawyer's success on behalf of the present client might adversely affect the former client (compare § 128, Comment f).

Information that is confidential for some purposes under § 59 (so that, for example, a lawyer would not be free to discuss it publicly (see § 60)) might nonetheless be so general, readily observable, or of little value in the subsequent representation that it should not by itself result in a substantial relationship. Thus, a lawyer may master a particular substantive area of the law while representing a client, but that does not preclude the lawyer from later representing another client adversely to the first in a matter involving the same legal issues, if the matters factually are not substantially related. A lawyer might also have learned a former client's preferred approach to bargaining in settlement discussions or negotiating business points in a transaction, willingness or unwillingness to be deposed by an adversary, and financial ability to withstand extended litigation or contract negotiations. Only when such information will be directly in issue or of unusual value in the subsequent matter will it be independently relevant in assessing a substantial relationship.

   e.   *A subsequent client with interests "materially adverse" to the interests of a former client.* A later representation is prohibited if the second client's interests are materially adverse to those of the former client (see § 121, Comments *c(i)* (adverseness) & *c(ii)* (materiality)). The scope of a client's interests is normally determined by the scope of work that the lawyer undertook in the former representation. Thus, a lawyer who undertakes to represent a corporation with respect to the defense of a personal-injury claim involving only issues of causation and damages does not represent the corporation with respect to other interests. The lawyer may limit the scope of representation specifically for the purpose of avoiding a future conflict (see § 16). Similarly, the lawyer may limit the scope of representation of a later client so as to avoid representation substantially related to that undertaken for a previous client.

Illustration:

   5.   Lawyer formerly represented Client A in obtaining FDA approval to market prescription drug X for treating diseases of the eye. Client B has now asked Lawyer for legal assistance to obtain FDA approval for sale of prescription drug Y for treating diseases of the skin. Client B is also interested in possibly later application for FDA approval to market a different form of drug Y to treat diseases of the eye, thus significantly reducing the profitability of Client A's drug X. Confidential information that Lawyer gained in representing Client A in the earlier matter would be substantially related to work that Lawyer would do with respect to any future application by Client B for use of drug Y for eye diseases (although the information would not relate to the use of drug Y for treating diseases of the skin). Client B and Lawyer agree that Lawyer's work will relate only to FDA approval for use of drug Y to treat diseases of the skin. Thus limited, Lawyer's

work for Client B does not involve representation adverse to former Client A on a substantially related matter.

f. A lawyer's subsequent use of confidential information. Even if a subsequent representation does not involve the same or a substantially related matter, a lawyer may not disclose or use confidential information of a former client in violation of § 60.

Illustration:

6. Lawyer, now a prosecutor, had formerly represented Client in defending against a felony charge. During the course of a confidential interview, Client related to Lawyer a willingness to commit perjury. Lawyer is now prosecuting another person, Defendant, for a matter not substantially related to the former prosecution. In the jurisdiction, a defendant is not required to serve notice of defense witnesses that will be called. During the defense case, Defendant's lawyer calls Client as an alibi witness. Lawyer could not reasonably have known previously that Client would be called. Because of the lack of substantial relationship between the matters, Lawyer was not prohibited from undertaking the prosecution. Because Lawyer's knowledge of Client's statement about willingness to lie is confidential client information under § 59, Lawyer may not use that information in cross-examining Client, but otherwise Lawyer may cross-examine Client vigorously.

g. A lawyer's duties of confidentiality other than to a former client. The principles in this Section presuppose that the lawyer in question has previously represented the person adversely affected by the present representation. Whether a client-lawyer relationship exists is considered in § 14 and § 121, Comment *d.* Two situations present analogous problems—communications with a prospective client and confidential information about a nonclient learned in representing a former client.

* * *

A lawyer who learns confidential information from a person represented by another lawyer pursuant to a common-interest sharing arrangement (see § 76) is precluded from a later representation adverse to the former sharing person when information actually shared by that person with the lawyer or the lawyer's client is material and relevant to the later matter (see Illustration 8, above). Such a threatened use of shared information is inconsistent with the undertaking of confidentiality that is part of such an arrangement.

h.   A lawyer with only a minor role in a prior representation. The specific tasks in which a lawyer was engaged might make the access to confidential client information insignificant. The lawyer bears the burden of persuasion as to that issue and as to the absence of opportunity to acquire confidential information. When such a burden has been met, the lawyer is not precluded from proceeding adversely to the former client (see § 124, Comment *d*, Illustration 3).

i.   Withdrawal from representing an "accommodation" client. With the informed consent of each client as provided in § 122, a lawyer might undertake representation of another client as an accommodation to the lawyer's regular client, typically for a limited purpose in order to avoid duplication of services and consequent higher fees. If adverse interests later develop between the clients, even if the adversity relates to the matter involved in the common representation, circumstances might warrant the inference that the "accommodation" client understood and impliedly consented to the lawyer's continuing to represent the regular client in the matter. Circumstances most likely to evidence such an understanding are that the lawyer has represented the regular client for a long period of time before undertaking representation of the other client, that the representation was to be of limited scope and duration, and that the lawyer was not expected to keep confidential from the regular client any information provided to the lawyer by the other client. On obtaining express consent in advance to later representation of the regular client in such circumstances, see § 122, Comment *d*. The lawyer bears the burden of showing that circumstances exist to warrant an inference of understanding and implied consent. On other situations of withdrawal, see § 121, Comment *e*.

* * *

j.   Cure of conflicts created by transactions of a client. A lawyer may withdraw in order to continue an adverse representation against a theretofore existing client when the matter giving rise to the conflict and requiring withdrawal comes about through initiative of the clients. An example is a client's acquisition of an interest in an enterprise against which the lawyer is proceeding on behalf of another client. However, if the client's acquisition of the other enterprise was reasonably foreseeable by the lawyer when the lawyer undertook representation of the client, withdrawal will not cure the conflict. In any event, continuing the representation must be otherwise consistent with the former-client conflict rules.

* * *

§ 133. A Former Government Lawyer or Officer

(1) A lawyer may not act on behalf of a client with respect to a matter in which the lawyer participated personally and substantially while acting as a government lawyer or officer unless both the government and the client consent to the representation under the limitations and conditions provided in § 122.

(2) A lawyer who acquires confidential information while acting as a government lawyer or officer may not:

(a) if the information concerns a person, represent a client whose interests are materially adverse to that person in a matter in which the information could be used to the material disadvantage of that person; or

(b) if the information concerns the governmental client or employer, represent another public or private client in circumstances described in § 132(2).

Comment:

* * *

b. Rationale. Prohibitions on the activities of former government lawyers are based on concerns similar to those protecting former private clients. Because those concerns apply somewhat differently to government clients, however, the rule of this Section is both broader and narrower than that of § 132.

First, the protection accorded government confidential information is parallel to that for confidential information of private clients. As discussed in § 74, however, statutes requiring openness in government operations might limit the government information that is given protection. Second, since government agencies have special powers to allocate public benefits and burdens, it is reasonable to prohibit a lawyer while in government from taking action designed to improve the lawyer's opportunities upon leaving government service.

On the other hand, government agencies must be able to recruit able lawyers. If the experience gained could not be used after lawyers left government service, recruiting lawyers would be more difficult. There is also a public interest in having lawyers in private practice who have served in government and understand both the substance and rationale of government policy. The experience of such lawyers might sometimes enable clients to achieve higher levels of compliance with law. Thus, this Section protects three government functions, those of client, recruiter of able employees, and law enforcer.

c. Personal and substantial involvement. This Section forbids former government lawyers or officers from taking on matters on which they worked personally and substantially while in government. Former government lawyers are not forbidden to work on matters solely because the matters were pending in the agency during the period of their employment.

The standard of "substantiality" is both formal and functional. A lawyer who signed a complaint on behalf of the government is substantially involved in the matter even if the lawyer knew few of the underlying facts. An action undertaken by a lawyer in the name of a superior is also within the rule.

Illustrations:

    1. While acting as special assistant to the Governor of a state, Lawyer participated in negotiation of the purchase of a new computer system for state government. Lawyer is now in the private practice of law. Lawyer may not represent the computer contractor in a dispute arising under the contract.

    2. While Lawyer was serving as general counsel of a government agency with many branch offices, a staff attorney in one branch office wrote a letter to X, a private citizen, initiating an official inquiry into a transaction involving X. The letter bore the stamped signature of Lawyer, but Lawyer had no personal involvement in the matter. After leaving government service, Lawyer is asked to represent X in resisting the inquiry. Lawyer may do so under this Section, unless an applicable statute or regulation prohibits the representation.

d. Adverse involvement is not required. The rule of this Section differs from § 132 in that prohibition applies even though the subsequent representation is not adverse to the interests of the former government client. There are three justifications for this distinction. First, prohibiting representation in a matter, even where consistent with the government's interest, diminishes the risk of subsequent misuse of information obtained by the government. If a former government lawyer could make use of confidential reports to an agency, for example, even in a cause that was consistent with the government position, it would go beyond the original purpose for making the reports and make it more difficult for the government to obtain voluntary disclosures from members of the public. Second, the rule removes an incentive to gain later advantages through methods of gathering information that are available only to the government, such

356

as a grand-jury investigation. Third, the rule removes an incentive to begin proceedings as a government agent with a view to obtaining a subsequent advantage in private practice, such as by filing a complementary action for a subsequent private client. Because the rationale for this rule is in part to prevent misconduct by government officials while still in government, in some circumstances the government should not be permitted to consent to the subsequent representation (see § 122(2)(c)).

* * *

e. Definition of a "matter." The term "matter," as applied to former government employees, is often defined as a judicial or other proceeding, application, request for a ruling or other determination, contract, claim, controversy, investigation, charge, accusation, arrest, or other particular matter involving a specific party or parties. Drafting of a statute or regulation of general applicability is not included under that definition, nor is work on a case of the same type (but not the same parties) as the one in which the lawyer seeks to be involved. The definition is narrower than that governing former-client conflicts of interest under § 132 (see id., Comment *d(iii)*).

* * *

g. Screening a former government lawyer. Screening of a former government lawyer will remove the imputed effects of the personally prohibited former government lawyer as provided in § 124(3) and Comment *e* thereto.

* * *

TOPIC 5. CONFLICTS OF INTEREST DUE TO A LAWYER'S OBLIGATION TO A THIRD PERSON

* * *

§ 134. Compensation or Direction of a Lawyer by a Third Person

(1) A lawyer may not represent a client if someone other than the client will wholly or partly compensate the lawyer for the representation, unless the client consents under the limitations and conditions provided in § 122 and knows of the circumstances and conditions of the payment.

(2) A lawyer's professional conduct on behalf of a client may be directed by someone other than the client if:

(a) the direction does not interfere with the lawyer's independence of professional judgment;

(b) the direction is reasonable in scope and character, such as by reflecting obligations borne by the person directing the lawyer; and

(c) the client consents to the direction under the limitations and conditions provided in § 122.

Comment:

* * *

f. Representing an insured. A lawyer might be designated by an insurer to represent the insured under a liability-insurance policy in which the insurer undertakes to indemnify the insured and to provide a defense. The law governing the relationship between the insured and the insurer is, as stated in Comment *a,* beyond the scope of the Restatement. Certain practices of designated insurance-defense counsel have become customary and, in any event, involve primarily standardized protection afforded by a regulated entity in recurring situations. Thus a particular practice permissible for counsel representing an insured may not be permissible under this Section for a lawyer in noninsurance arrangements with significantly different characteristics.

It is clear in an insurance situation that a lawyer designated to defend the insured has a client-lawyer relationship with the insured. The insurer is not, simply by the fact that it designates the lawyer, a client of the lawyer. Whether a client-lawyer relationship also exists between the lawyer and the insurer is determined under § 14. Whether or not such a relationship exists, communications between the lawyer and representatives of the insurer concerning such matters as progress reports, case evaluations, and settlement should be regarded as privileged and otherwise immune from discovery by the claimant or another party to the proceeding. Similarly, communications between counsel retained by an insurer to coordinate the efforts of multiple counsel for insureds in multiple suits and such coordinating counsel are subject to the privilege. Because and to the extent that the insurer is directly concerned in the matter financially, the insurer should be accorded standing to assert a claim for appropriate relief from the lawyer for financial loss proximately caused by professional negligence or other wrongful act of the lawyer. Compare § 51, Comment *g.*

The lawyer's acceptance of direction from the insurer is considered in Subsection (2) and Comment *d* hereto. With respect to client consent (see Comment *b* hereto) in insurance representations, when there appears to be no substantial risk that a claim against a client-insured will not be fully covered by an insurance policy pursuant to which the lawyer is appointed and is to be paid, consent in the form of the acquiescence of the client-insured to an informative letter to the client-insured at the outset of the representation should be all that is required. The lawyer should either withdraw or consult with the client-insured (see § 122) when a substantial risk that the client-insured will not be fully covered becomes apparent (see § 121, Comment *c(iii)*).

Illustration:

     5. Insurer, a liability-insurance company, has issued a policy to Policyholder under which Insurer is to provide a defense and otherwise insure Policyholder against claims covered under the insurance policy. A suit filed against Policyholder alleges that Policyholder is liable for a covered act and for an amount within the policy's monetary limits. Pursuant to the policy's terms, Insurer designates Lawyer to defend Policyholder. Lawyer believes that doubling the number of depositions taken, at a cost of $5,000, would somewhat increase Policyholder's chances of prevailing and Lawyer so informs Insurer and Policyholder. If the insurance contract confers authority on Insurer to make such decisions about expense of defense, and Lawyer reasonably believes that the additional depositions can be forgone without violating the duty of competent representation owed by Lawyer to Policyholder (see § 52), Lawyer may comply with Insurer's direction that taking depositions would not be worth the cost.

Material divergence of interest might exist between a liability insurer and an insured, for example, when a claim substantially in excess of policy limits is asserted against an insured. If the lawyer knows or should be aware of such an excess claim, the lawyer may not follow directions of the insurer if doing so would put the insured at significantly increased risk of liability in excess of the policy coverage. Such occasions for conflict may exist at the outset of the representation or may be created by events that occur thereafter. The lawyer must address a conflict whenever presented. To the extent that such a conflict is subject to client consent (see § 122(2)(c)), the lawyer may proceed after obtaining client consent under the limitations and conditions stated in § 122.

When there is a question whether a claim against the insured is within the coverage of the policy, a lawyer designated to defend the insured may not reveal adverse confidential client information of the insured to the insurer concerning that question (see § 60) without explicit informed consent of the insured (see § 62). That follows whether or not the lawyer also represents the insurer as co-client and whether or not the insurer has asserted a "reservation of rights" with respect to its defense of the insured (compare § 60, Comment *l* (confidentiality in representation of co-clients in general)).

With respect to events or information that create a conflict of interest between insured and insurer, the lawyer must proceed in the best interests of the insured, consistent with the lawyer's duty not to assist client fraud (see § 94) and, if applicable, consistent with the lawyer's duties to the insurer as co-client (see § 60, Comment *l*). If the designated lawyer finds it impossible so to proceed, the lawyer must withdraw from representation of both clients as provided in § 32 (see also § 60, Comment *l*). The designated lawyer may be precluded by duties to the insurer from providing advice and other legal services to the insured concerning such matters as coverage under the policy, claims against other persons insured by the same insurer, and the advisability of asserting other claims against the insurer. In such instances, the lawyer must inform the insured in an adequate and timely manner of the limitation on the scope of the lawyer's services and the importance of obtaining assistance of other counsel with respect to such matters. Liability of the insurer with respect to such matters is regulated under statutory and common-law rules such as those governing liability for bad-faith refusal to defend or settle. Those rules are beyond the scope of this Restatement (see Comment *a* hereto).

* * *

§ 135.   A Lawyer with a Fiduciary or Other Legal Obligation to a Nonclient

Unless the affected client consents to the representation under the limitations and conditions provided in § 122, a lawyer may not represent a client in any matter with respect to which the lawyer has a fiduciary or other legal obligation to another if there is a substantial risk that the lawyer's representation of the client would be materially and adversely affected by the lawyer's obligation.

Comment:

* * *

d. A lawyer as corporate director or officer. A lawyer's duties as counsel can conflict with the lawyer's duties arising from the lawyer's service as a director or officer of a corporate client. Simultaneous service as corporate lawyer and corporate director or officer is not forbidden by this Section. The requirement that a lawyer for an organization serve the interests of the entity (see § 96(1)(a)) is generally consistent with the duties of a director or officer. However, when the obligations or personal interests as director are materially adverse to those of the lawyer as corporate counsel, the lawyer may not continue to serve as corporate counsel without the informed consent of the corporate client. The lawyer may not participate as director or officer in the decision to grant consent (see 122, Comment *c(ii)*).

Illustration:

3. Lawyer serves on the board of directors of Company and is also employed by Company as corporate secretary and inside legal counsel. Company proposes to give bonuses to its five highest-paid officers, including Lawyer. Authority to pay such bonuses presents a close legal question. The directors have requested Lawyer to render an opinion as counsel concerning the legality of the payments. Lawyer's status as recipient of the bonus and role as a director to whom the opinion will be addressed create a substantial risk that Lawyer's opinion for Company will be materially and adversely affected. The conflict would not be cured by having the opinion prepared by a partner of Lawyer, because conflicts under this Section are imputed to affiliated lawyers. Both Lawyer's personal conflict and the imputed conflict are subject to effective consent by agents of Company authorized to do so (see § 122).

A second type of conflict that can be occasioned by a lawyer's service as director or officer of an organization occurs when a client asks the lawyer for representation in a matter adverse to the organization. Because of the lawyer's duties to the organization, a conflict of interest is present, requiring the consent of the clients under the limitations and conditions provided in § 122.

Illustration:

4. Lawyer has been asked to file a medical-malpractice action against Doctor and Hospital on behalf of Client. Hospital is operated by University, on whose Board of Trustees Lawyer serves. While Lawyer would not personally be liable for the

judgment if Client prevails (compare § 125, Comment *c*), the close relationship between Lawyer and University requires that Lawyer not undertake the representation unless Client's consent is obtained pursuant to § 122.

e. A lawyer as director of a legal-services organization. Service of a private-practice lawyer on the board of directors of a legal-services organization can usefully support the delivery of legal services to persons unable to pay for them. However, the agency's clients might from time to time have interests opposed to those of the lawyer's clients. Such service does not constitute an inherent conflict of interest with the lawyer's private clients, but the lawyer must be alert to the possibility of a conflict with respect to particular decisions. In general, if there is a risk that the lawyer-director's performance of functions as a director with respect to a particular decision would materially and adversely affect the lawyer's representation of private clients, the lawyer may not participate in that decision without the informed consent of affected clients.

* * *

f(i). A lawyer as public official—in general. Service by a lawyer as an official in local, state, or federal government carries fiduciary duties within the meaning of this Section. In many jurisdictions, private practice is permitted on the part of public officials in smaller communities and in certain offices, such as part-time judge and as legislator. Public duties can impair the lawyer's effective representation of private clients, requiring that the lawyer-official not represent the affected client, withdraw from the representation, or obtain effective consent (see § 122; cf. also § 122, Comment *g(ii)* (limits in minority of states on power of public agencies to consent to conflicted representation)).

* * *

Illustration:

6. Lawyer is a member of the city council of a town. The council is considering the mayor's proposal to raise the property tax rate by five percent. Some of Lawyer's private clients favor the proposal and some oppose it. Whether Lawyer may vote on the proposal is determined by public law. However, Company, one of Lawyer's private clients, seeks to retain Lawyer to persuade the city council to exempt Company's large and valuable tract of land from the tax increase. Lawyer may not accept the represen-

tation. Lawyer's responsibility as public official to vote on the merits of Company's planned exemption creates a risk that Lawyer's representation of Company would be materially and adversely affected. Public law would also likely prohibit Lawyer from participating in the matter of Client's exemption.

* * *

INDEX

References are to Sections, Comments

A

ABA CODES, ABA RULES
See Codes

ABUSE OF PROCESS
See Wrongful Use of Legal Process

ACCOMMODATION CLIENTS
Conflicts of interest, § **132 Com.** *i*

ADJUDICATIVE/NONADJUDICATIVE PROCEEDINGS
Legislative or administrative bodies, § **104 Com.** *d*

ADMINISTRATIVE AGENCIES
See Admission to Practice; Bar Examinations; Discipline

ADMINISTRATIVE PRACTICE
See Adjudicative/Nonadjudicative Proceedings; Legislative and Administrative Practice

ADMISSION TO PRACTICE
See also Bar Examinations; Jurisdiction; Legal Education; Multistate Practice; Pro Hac Vice
Generally, **Ch. 1, Top. 2, Tit. A Intro.;** § **2 Com.** *b*
Bar associations, mandatory, See Bar Associations
Admission on motion, § **2 Com.** *b*
Bar examination, § **2 Com.** *b*
Character
Generally, § **2 Com.** *d*
Citizenship, § **2 Com.** *f*
Federal court, § **2 Com.** *b*
Maintenance of status, § **3 Com.** *c*
Multistate practice, See Multistate Practice
Pro hac vice, See Multistate Practice
Residence, § **2 Com.** *f*

ADVANCING FUNDS
See Client-Lawyer Contracts

ADVERSARY SYSTEM
See also Advocacy; Evidence; Forensics; Opposing Lawyers; Prosecutors; Unpopular Clients; Wrongful Use of Legal Process

ADVERTISING
See Solicitation

ADVICE OF COUNSEL
Defense, § **29 Com.** *c*
Waiver of attorney-client privilege, § **80 Com.** *b*

INDEX

366

INDEX

367

INDEX

B

INDEX

BAR EXAMINATIONS
See Admission to Practice; Inherent Powers; Legal Education; Multistate Practice; Unauthorized Practice
Admission to practice, § **2 Com. *b***
Exceptions, admission on motion, § **2 Com. *b***

BILLING
See Client-Lawyer Contracts; Fee Disputes

BONDING
See Client Funds and Property

BUSINESS DEALINGS WITH CLIENTS
See Conflicts of Interest—Business Dealings with Clients

C

CHILD CLIENT
See Client-Lawyer Relationship; Conflicts of Interest—Third-Party Control; Diminished Capacity (Client)

CLASS ACTIONS
Anti-contact rule, § **99 Com. *l***
Conflicts of interest, § **125 Com. *f***

CLIENT DOCUMENTS
Delivery, § **46 Com. *d-e***
Right to inspect, § **46 Com. *c***
Safeguarding, § **46 Com. *b***

CLIENT FUNDS AND PROPERTY
See also Attorney Liens; Client Documents; Client-Lawyer Contracts; Client-Lawyer Relationship; Fee Disputes; Fees; Fiduciary; Nonlawyer Employees
Generally, § **44**
Accounting, and notifying of receipt, § **44 Com. *h***
Attorney liens, § **43**
Client files, § **43 Com. *b-c***
See also Law Firms, dissolution
Commingling, § **43 Com. *h***
Confidentiality, § **44 Com. *h***
Record keeping, § **44 Com. *a, d***
Retainer, § **34 Com. *e***
Safeguarding, § **44 Com. *e, g*;**
Surrendering possession, § **45**
Prompt delivery, § **45 Com. *b***
Stolen goods, § **45 Com. *f***

CLIENT-LAWYER CONTRACTS
See also Client-Lawyer Relationship; Discharge; Fee Disputes; Fees; Fees—Contingent; Fee Splitting; Publication—Rights Contracts; Withdrawal
Generally, § **18; § 18 Com. *e-h***
Advance payment, § **38 Com. *g*; § 44 Com. *f***
Advancing funds to clients, § **36 Com. *c***
Breach of contract, § **48 Com. *c*; § 55 Com. *c***
Construing, § **18 Com. *h* § 19 Com. *c*; § 31 Com. *h***
Discharge, § **32 Com. *b*; § 40 Com. *b-c***
Fees
Absence of contract, § **39**
Contingent, § **35; § 36 Com. *b*; § 38 Com. *b*; § 40 Com. *c***
Fair-value standard, § **39 Com. *c***

370

INDEX

INDEX

CO-PLAINTIFFS
Conflicts of interest, § **128 Com.** *d(i)*

CORPORATE PRACTICE
See Organizational Clients

COSTS
See Court Costs; Fees—Court Awarded

COUNSELING
     See also Advising Clients; Criminal Offenses; Disclosure; Negotiation
  Generally, § **94**
Law compliance, § **94 Com.** *c*
Law enforcement policy, § **94 Com.** *f*
Lawyer codes, § **94 Com.** *d*
Violating court orders, § **94(2)**; § **94 Com.** *d*

COURT-APPOINTED LAWYER
  See Access to Court; Pro Bono; Pro Se Representation; Public Defender; Right to
       Counsel; Unpopular Client

COURT COSTS
Payable by client, § **38 Com.** *e*

CRIMINAL OFFENSES
  See also Advising Clients; Counseling; Disclosure; Evidence; Negotiation; Perjury
Advising, § **8 Com.** *b*
Crime-fraud exception to attorney-client privilege, § **82**
Lawyers, during representation, § **8**

CROSS-EXAMINATION
See Harassment; Witnesses

D

DAMAGES
See Legal Malpractice

DEATH
Clients',
    Attorney-client privilege, § **77 Com.** *c*; § **81**
    Lawyer's authority, § **31 Com.** *e*
Lawyer,
    Vicarious liability, § **58 Com.** *i*

DECEPTION
See Criminal Offenses; Fraud; Misrepresentation; Negotiation

DELAY
See Harassment

DILIGENCE
See Competence; Legal Malpractice; Neglect

DIMINISHED CAPACITY (CLIENT)
Business dealings with client, § **24**
Client-lawyer relationship, § **24**

DISBARMENT
See Discipline

DISBURSEMENTS
See Client-Lawyer Contracts

INDEX

DISCHARGE
 See also Withdrawal
 Client discharge, § **32 Com.** *b*
 Fee recovery, § **40(1)-(2)**

DISCIPLINE
  See also Inherent Powers; Regulation
  Generally, § **5**; § **5 Com.** *b*
 Administrative agencies, generally
 Disability proceedings, **Ch. 1, Top. 2, Tit. C Intro.**
 Disclosure, § **5 Com.** *i*
 Grounds,
  Generally, § **5 Com.** *b*
  Acts as nonlawyer, § **5 Com.** *b*
  Appearance of impropriety, § **5 Com.** *c*
  Assisting or inducing illegal acts of another, § **94 Com.** *c*
  Attempts, § **5 Com.** *e*
  Catch-all provisions, § **5 Com.** *c*
  Failure to supervise employees, § **11**
  Fees, § **34 Com.** *f*
  Jury tampering, § **115 Com.** *e*
  Knowing conduct, § **5 Com.** *d*; § **56 Com.** *c*; § **94 Com.** *g*
  Lawyer codes, § **5**; § **5 Com.** *b-c, g-h*; § **11**
  Moral turpitude, § **5 Com.** *g*
 Judges, disciplined as lawyers, § **5 Com.** *i*
 Law firms, § **5 Com.** *b*; § **11**
 Proceedings,
  Generally, **Ch. 1, Top. 2, Tit. C Intro.**
 Regulation of discipline,
  Discipline agencies, **Ch. 1, Top. 2, Tit. C Intro.**
  Inherent powers of courts, § **1, Com.** *a & b*
 Reinstatement,
  Generally, **Ch. 1, Top. 2, Tit. C Intro.**
 Rehabilitation, **Ch. 1, Top. 2, Tit. C Intro.**
 Reporting misconduct, § **5 Com.** *i*
 Sanctions,
  Generally, **Ch. 1, Top. 2, Tit. C Intro.**
  Contempt, § **6 Com.** *g*
  Criteria, generally, **Ch. 1, Top. 2, Tit. C Intro.**
  Suspension, generally, **Ch. 1, Top. 2, Tit. C Intro.**

DISCLOSURE
  See also Advocacy; Attorney-Client Privilege; Confidentiality; Conflicts of
   Interest—Client Consent; Criminal Offenses; Misrepresentation; Or-
   ganizational Clients; Perjury; Witnesses
  Generally, § **20 Com.** *c-e*
 Ancillary business, § **10 Com.** *g*
 Business transactions with clients, § **126 Com.** *d*
 Ex parte and similar proceedings, generally, § **112**
 Lawyer self-interest, § **10 Com.** *g*
 Lawyer wrongdoing, generally,
  Confidentiality, § **5 Com.** *i*
  Lobbying, § **34 Com.** *g*
 Nonclients, § **98 Com.** *e*; § **103 Com.** *b*

DISQUALIFICATION
  See also Conflicts of Interest—Generally
 Remedy, § **6 Com.** *i*

DIVISION OF FEES
 See Fee Splitting

378

INDEX

INDEX

INDEX

FEES—GENERAL
See also Client-Lawyer Contracts; Legal Services

FIDUCIARY
See also Client Funds and Property; Conflicts of Interest—Business Dealings with Clients
Duty, in general, § **24 Com.** *c*
Breach of duty, § **49**

FILES
Confidentiality, § **6 Com.** *i*
Turnover on discharge or client request, § **46 Com.** *c*

FIRMS
See Law Firms

FOREIGN LEGAL CONSULTANTS
See Admission to Practice

FORENSICS
See also Adversary System; Advocacy; Contempt; Disclosure; Evidence; Extrajudicial Comment; Harassment; Juror-Lawyer Relationships; Prosecutors; Witnesses
Inadmissible evidence, § **107 Com.** *c*
Prohibited tactics, § **107**

FORWARDING FEE
See Fee Splitting

FRAUD
See also Advising Clients; Counseling; Criminal Offenses; Disclosure; Knowledge; Misrepresentation; Negotiation
Generally, § **56 Com.** *c*
Client counseling, § **94(2)**; § **94 Com.** *c, f*
Exception to attorney-client privilege, § **82**

FRIVOLOUS LITIGATION
See Advocacy; Harassment; Wrongful Use of Legal Process

FUNDS
See Client-Lawyer Contracts; Attorney Liens; Client Funds and Property

G

GIFTS
To lawyer, § **127**; § **127 Com.** *a, c, d-e, g*

GOVERNMENT PRACTICE
See also Admission to Practice; Attorney-Client Privilege; Conflicts of Interest—Government Practice; Federal Courts; Prosecutors; Public Defender
Generally, § **97**
Attorney-client privilege, § **74**
Invoking and waiver, § **74 Com.** *e*
Open-meeting law, § **74 Com.** *b*
Client-lawyer relationship, § **97 Com.** *a*
Constituents, § **97 Com.** *j*
Duties to client, § **97 Com.** *f*
Identity of client, § **97 Com.** *c*
Confidentiality, § **74 Com.** *b*; § **97 Com.** *d*
Conflicts of interest,
Imputed disqualification, § **123 Com.** *d(ii)*

INDEX

GOVERNMENT PRACTICE—Continued
Legal authority, § **97 Com. *b*, *h*;**
Mandamus, habeas corpus, agency proceedings, § **97 Com. *c***
Military proceedings, § **97 Com. *c***
Whistle-blowing, § **74 Com. *b***

GUARDIAN
Client with diminished capacity, § **24 Com. *c-f***

H

HARASSMENT
See also Advocacy; Intentional Wrongs; Threats; Wrongful Use of Legal Process
Discipline, § **106 Com. *c***
Frivolous litigation, § **110**
Litigation, § **106, Com. *c***
    Frivolous, § **110**

HOUSE COUNSEL
See Government Lawyers; Organizational Clients

I

IMPUTED DISQUALIFICATION
See Conflicts of Interest—Imputed Disqualification

IMPUTED KNOWLEDGE
See Authority; Knowledge

INCOMPETENT CLIENT
See Diminished Capacity (Client)

INFORMED CONSENT
See Conflicts of Interest—Client Consent

INHERENT POWERS
Generally, § **1, Com. *c***
Federal courts, § **1 Com. *c***

INTEGRATED BAR
See Bar Associations

INTENTIONAL WRONGS
See also Fraud; Harassment; Legal Malpractice; Misrepresentation; Vicarious
    Liability; Wrongful Use of Legal Process
Misrepresentation, § **98 Com. *b-c***

INTEREST ON LAWYERS' TRUST ACCOUNTS (IOLTA)
See Client-Lawyer Contracts; Client Funds and Property

INTERMEDIATION
See Mediation

IOLTA
See Interest on Lawyers' Trust Accounts

J

JAILHOUSE LAWYER
See Pro Se Representation; Right to Counsel

382

INDEX

JUDGE-LAWYER RELATIONSHIP
See also Advocacy; Contempt
Courtroom conduct, § **105 Com.** *e*
Criticism of judges, § **114**
Ex parte communications, § **113 Com.** *b*
Lawyer attempt to influence, § **113**

JUDGES
See also Judge-Lawyer Relationship
Discipline, as lawyer, § **5 Com.** *i*
    Reporting misconduct, § **5 Com.** *i*
Ex parte communications, § **113 Com.** *b*
Judicial misconduct, reporting, § **5 Com.** *i*

JURISDICTION
Generally, § **1 Com.** *b*; § **3**
Anti-contact rule, § **101 Com.** *b*
Controlling jurisdiction (definition), § **111 Com.** *d*
Expert witnesses, § **52 Com.** *g*
Extra-jurisdictional practice, § **3 Com.** *e*
Legal malpractice, § **48 Com.** *c*; § **50 Com.** *c*
Statutes of limitations, § **48 Com.** *c*

JUROR-LAWYER RELATIONSHIPS
Generally, § **115**
Posttrial contact, § **115 Com.** *d*
Pretrial contact, § **115 Com.** *b*
Tampering, § **115 Com.** *e*
Trial contact, § **115 Com.** *c*

K

KNOWLEDGE
See also Advising Clients; Counseling; Criminal Offenses; Evidence; Fraud;
    Misrepresentation; Perjury; Witness
Generally, § **94 Com.** *g*

L

LAW FIRMS
See also Associated Lawyers; Conflicts of Interest—Imputed Disqualification; Fee
    Splitting; Legal Services; Multistate Practice; Partnerships (Law Firms);
    Professional Corporations; Solo Practice; Subordinate and Supervising
    Lawyers
Ancillary business, § **10 Com.** *g*
Departure of lawyer, § **9 Com.** *i*
Dual practice, See Ancillary business
Fee splitting, § **10(3)**
Imputed disqualification, See Conflicts of Interest—Imputed Disqualification
Junior lawyers, § **12 Com.** *b*
Leaving with clients, § **9(3)**; § **9 Com.** *i*
Limited liability, § **58 Com.** *c*
Merger, See Conflicts of Interest—Imputed Disqualification
Nontraditional practice, § **10 Com.** *f*
Nonlawyers, limitations, § **10**
    Fee splitting, § **10(3)**
    Referrals, § **10 Com.** *d*
Organization and staffing, § **9 Com.** *b*
    Employee compensation, § **10 Com.** *e*

383

INDEX

M

NONLAWYER EMPLOYEES
See also Client Funds and Property; Competence; Confidentiality; Law Firms;
Fee Splitting; Legal Malpractice; Vicarious Liability
Confidential client information, § **123 Com.** *f*
Fee splitting, § **10(3)**; § **10 Com.** *b-d, g-h*

NONLAWYERS
See Bar Associations; Discipline; Law Firms; Legal Malpractice; Regulation; Right to
Counsel; Unauthorized Practice

NOTICE
See Authority of Lawyer; Client-Lawyer Relationship; Knowledge

O

OCCUPATIONAL LICENSING
See Regulation

OF COUNSEL
See also Law Firms
Generally, § **9 Com.** *f*
Imputed disqualification, § **123 Com.** *c(ii)*

OFFENSIVE PERSONALITIES
See Harassment; Opposing Lawyers

OFFERS
See Authority of Lawyer; Settlement

OPINION LETTERS
See Organizational Clients; Evaluation; Legal Malpractice

OPPOSING LAWYERS
Relationship, § **106 Com.** *d*

ORGANIZATIONAL CLIENTS
See also Advising Clients; Attorney-Client Privilege; Criminal Offenses; Conflicts
of Interest—Organizations
Constituents, § **96 Com.** *b, e-g*; § **103 Com.** *e*
Duties to client, § **96 Com.** *b, f-g*
Entity concept, § **96 Com.** *b*
Relationship, § **14 Com.** *f*; § **96 Com.** *b-d, g*
Types of organization, § **96 Com.** *c*
Withdrawal, § **96 Com.** *f*

OVERREACHING
Conflicts of interest, § **126 Com.** *b, e-f*
Governmental agency or officer, § **101 Com.** *b*

P

PARALEGALS
See also Law Firms; Nonlawyer Employees

PARTNERSHIPS (CLIENT)
See Conflicts of Interest—Corporate; Organizational Clients

PARTNERSHIPS (LAW FIRMS)
See also Associated Lawyers; Law Firms; Legal Malpractice; Professional
Corporations; Solo Practice; Vicarious Liability
Generally, § **9 Com.** *b*

Q

R

S

INDEX

SELF-REPRESENTATION
See Pro Se Representation

SETTLEMENT
See also Authority of Lawyer; Client-Lawyer Relationship; Represented Party
Offers, communicating to clients, § **20 Com. *c***

SHAM TRANSACTIONS
See Advising Clients; Counseling; Criminal Offenses; Fraud

SHAREHOLDER DERIVATIVE LITIGATION
See also Class Actions; Conflicts of Interest—Corporate; Fees—Court-Awarded
Attorney-client privilege, corporate, § **73**
Conflicts of interest, § **131 Com. *g***
Corporate fiduciary exception, § **85**

SOLICITATION
Generally, § **9 Com. *i***

SOLICITOR GENERAL
See Government Lawyer

SOLO PRACTICE
See also Associated Lawyers; Law Firms; Partnerships (Law Firm); Professional
Corporations
Generally, § **9 Intro.; § 9(1)**

SPECIALIZATION
See also Competence; Law Firms; Legal Malpractice
Competence, § **52 Com. *d***

SPOT AUDITS
See Client Funds and Property

STANDARD OF CARE
See Legal Malpractice

STATE OF MIND (MENS REA)
See Discipline

SUBORDINATE AND SUPERVISING LAWYERS
See Law Firms

SUBSTANTIAL-RELATIONSHIP TEST
Conflicts of interest—former client, § **132 Com. *d(iii)***

SUBSTITUTION
See also Discharge; Right to Counsel; Successor Lawyer; Withdrawal
Withdrawal, § **32 Com. *i*; § 33 Com. *b*; § 40 Com. *c***

SUCCESSOR LAWYER
See also Substitution

SUPERVISION
See Law Firms; Nonlawyer Employees; Subordinate and Supervising Lawyers

SUSPENSION
See Discipline

SWITCHING SIDES
Conflicts of interest, § **132 Com. *d(i)***

T

TAPE RECORDING
See Witnesses

392

INDEX

TESTIMONY
See Evidence; Witnesses

THIRD-PARTY FUNDS AND PROPERTY
See also Client Funds and Property
Duties, in general, § **44**; § **44 Com.** *d-e*
Surrendering possession, § **45**
Prompt delivery, § **45 Com.** *b*

THREATS
See also Criminal Offenses; Knowledge; Misrepresentation; Negotiations; Prosecutors

TORT LIABILITY
See Intentional Wrongs; Legal Malpractice; Wrongful Use of Legal Process

TRIAL PUBLICITY
See Extrajudicial Comment

TRIBUNAL
Disclosure duty, § **111 Com.** *c-d*
Lawyer appearance, § **25 Com.** *d*

TRUST ACCOUNTS
See Client Funds and Property

U

UNAUTHORIZED PRACTICE
See also Inherent Powers; Regulation
History, **Ch. 1, Tit. A Intro.**
Nonlawyers, § **4**
Definition, § **4 Com.** *c*
Permitted practice, § **4 Com.** *b-c*

UNDUE INFLUENCE
Gifts, § **127 Com.** *a*

UNFOUNDED LITIGATION
See Harassment; Wrongful Use of Judicial Process

UNIFIED BAR
See Bar Associations

UNINCORPORATED ASSOCIATIONS
See Conflicts of Interest—Corporate; Organizational Clients

UNPOPULAR CLIENTS
See also Repugnant Client Acts

UNREPRESENTED PARTIES
See also Nonclients—Represented; Nonclients—Unrepresented; Represented Parties

V

VICARIOUS LIABILITY
See also Associated Lawyers; Authority of Lawyers; Legal Malpractice; Nonlawyer Employees; Partnerships; Professional Corporations
Generally, § **58**; § **58 Com.** *b*
Independent agent, § **58 Com.** *e*
Independent contractor, § **58 Com.** *e*

393

INDEX